T0294760

Lee Harvey Oswald, Lyndon Johnson and the JFK Assassination

John Delane Williams, Ph.D.

Foreword by Gary Severson

Lee Harvey Oswald, Lyndon Johnson & the JFK Assassination

Published by:
Trine Day LLC
PO Box 577
Walterville, OR 97489
1-800-556-2012
www.TrineDay.com
trineday@icloud.com

Library of Congress Cataloging-in-Publication Data

Names: Williams, John Delane, 1938- author. | Baker, Judyth Vary, author of foreword.
Title: Lee Harvey Oswald, Lyndon Johnson and the JFK Assassination / John Delane Williams, Ph.D. ; foreword by Judyth Vary Baker.
Description: First edition. | Walterville, OR : TrineDay LLC, 2019. | Includes bibliographical references and index. | Summary: "Incorporating the work of Ernst Titovets, this book explores the life of Lee Harvey Oswald, painting him as a real person-not as the straw man concocted to match the image of a lone assassin in search of greatness or infamy. Among other facets of his life and personality, the text explores Lee Harvey Oswald's relationships with Jack Ruby, David Ferrie, and Judyth Baker"-- Provided by publisher.
Identifiers: LCCN 2019022653 (print) | LCCN 2019022654 (ebook) | ISBN 9781634242684 (trade paperback) | ISBN 9781634242691 (epub) | ISBN 9781634242707 (mobi)
Subjects: LCSH: Kennedy, John F. (John Fitzgerald), 1917-1963--Assassination. | Oswald, Lee Harvey. | Oswald, Lee Harvey--Friends and associates. | Assassins--United States--Biography. | Conspiracies--United States--History--20th century.
Classification: LCC E842.9.W4693 2019 (print) | LCC E842.9 (ebook) | DDC 364.152/4092 [B]--dc23
LC record available at https://lccn.loc.gov/2019022653
LC ebook record available at https://lccn.loc.gov/2019022654

First Edition
10 9 8 7 6 5 4 3 2 1

Printed in the USA
Distribution to the Trade by:
Independent Publishers Group (IPG)
814 North Franklin Street
Chicago, Illinois 60610
312.337.0747
www.ipgbook.com

Every accomplishment starts with the decision to try.

–John F. Kennedy

Foreword

From childhood's hour I have not been
As others were – I have not seen
As others saw.

– Edgar Alan Poe
– from Ernst Titovets' book *Oswald: Russian Episode*

The above quote seems apropos to begin a preface to Dr. John Delane Williams' new book, *Lee Harvey Oswald, Lyndon Johnson and the JFK Assassination*. The book is the latest to synthesize a view of Lee Harvey Oswald's short life from his childhood to his own assassination at the hands of Jack Ruby on November 24, 1963. The focus is mostly on Oswald's last five years of life. It is significant that Dr. Ernst Titovets chose Poe's quote to allude to his understanding of his three-year relationship with the young Oswald. Titovets' friendship with Lee Harvey Oswald is unique. It developed three years prior to the rest of the world's familiarity with Oswald because of his alleged murder of John F. Kennedy. Dr. Titovets' met Oswald in Minsk, Belarus where Oswald was in self-exile. Dr. Williams is able to draw on Dr. Titovets' account of this friendship to flesh out a fresh view of Lee Harvey Oswald.

Dr. Williams' book isn't just another summary of other authors' works but is a fresh approach to understanding the JFK assassination. This new synthesis is made possible because of the extensive interviews Professor Williams' conducted with Dr. Ernst Titovets, Judyth Vary Baker, Madeleine Brown and many others. I have done the same and can speak to the veracity of what we have found. This in-depth analysis of Lee Harvey Oswald's pre-November 22, 1963 life gives us a very unique view of Oswald that has not previously been available in one book.

It was an auspicious day when Dr. John Delane Williams and I met at a 1999 JFK assassination conference in Minneapolis

Professor Williams and Judyth Vary Baker

at the University of Minnesota. The meeting began a relationship spanning the next 20 years, both as friends and research associates investigating the JFK assassination. We had both been doing JFK assassination research from the 1960s to our first meeting in 1999, he in my hometown of Grand Forks, North Dakota at the University of North Dakota where he was a professor of "educational statistics." During that same time I was teaching history in Minnesota high schools including, coincidentally, at John F. Kennedy High School, in the Minneapolis area. There I taught the JFK assassination many times a year as a world historic event rather than just as a domestic crime.

My own interest began on September 25, 1963, two months before the death of JFK, when I was involved in an anomalous event as a sixteen-year old attending a JFK speech at what was to become my alma mater, the University of North Dakota. A seed was planted on that day because of the unusual nature of my presence at JFK's speech that day and his subsequent murder two months later. Ostensibly, my experience on September 25, 1963 was as a witness to either an aborted attempt on JFK's life or an assassination dry run. Richard Case Nagell robbed a bank on September 20, 1963. His purpose was to derail a late September plot to end JFK's presidency. This aborted assassination attempt was what I now believe I witnessed five days later in North Dakota.

During our first meeting at the 1999 Minneapolis JFK conference, I asked John if he had ever heard of the 1954 connection between Stanley, North Dakota and Lee Harvey Oswald. Even though he hadn't heard of this obscure event it immediately caught his attention. In 1998 I had become aware of research that placed Oswald in North Dakota and of course I was very interested because of my experience at Kennedy's speech years earlier. I then recounted my 35-year-old story to Dr. Williams. After that discussion, we decided to head to Stanley, North Dakota to investigate the theory. John, as a professional researcher, put together an impressive research protocol for interviews we planned to do in Stanley. With this trip, our twenty-year collaboration on the JFK assassination began.

What we discovered in North Dakota is still an ambiguous narrative that uncovered tangents that were unexpected but still inconclusive about Lee Harvey Oswald's possible time in Stanley. Oswald's actual time in Stanley became much more problematic but did open other possibilities for further exploration. I think for both John and I this was our first full-blown attempt at ferreting out something about Oswald that no one else had looked at as directly as we attempted to do. John Armstrong

Ernst Titovets, John Williams, Gary Severson, and Mark Newman at 2013 JFK Assassination Conference

(*Harvey and Lee*) had done the initial work on Oswald's supposed time in North Dakota, and he encouraged us to continue pursuing his research in more depth. Our research was published in the 2000 issue of the journal *The Fourth Decade*.

During the last 20 years we have continued to support each other at numerous conferences in New Orleans, Dallas, Minneapolis, and Grand Forks. Together we have interviewed many key witnesses of events leading up to the JFK assassination and its aftermath whose stories will now be available in one place in Professor William's new book.

Dr. Williams, being the scholar that he is, has been one of the most prolific researcher-writers that I know of. If one looks at his publishing history both in the area of educational research statistics and JFK assassination studies, you will see the amount of energy he has expended for both fields is truly impressive. Even when he embraces some of the more controversial narratives surrounding the assassination, his statistical analysis of the probability of certain events taking place has to be reckoned with.

It has been our privilege to meet many researchers on our journey to this point. They continue to motivate us to persevere in the search for truth. We agree that this tragedy is a most pivotal event in American history, and it needs to be resolved. Closure may never happen, but without it John F. Kennedy's assassination on November 22, 1963, will always leave a hole in the soul of the America we both love.

Gary Severson
Minneapolis
August 22, 2019

TABLE OF CONTENTS

INTRODUCTION

The assassination of John Fitzgerald Kennedy has fascinated readers from, as they say, Day One. In the reporting of the assassination and surrounding issues, initially, the traditional news sources reported what came into their hands. At a very early stage, there were anomalies. One such anomaly came from Christchurch, New Zealand. Within an hour of the taking of Oswald to the police station, the *Christchurch Star* published an article about Oswald's background, including his having lived in the Soviet Union (Russia). This story was out in a regular edition about four hours after Oswald was arrested. (*Christchurch Star*, November 23, 1963)

Sometimes ordinary citizens found themselves in circumstances that belied the official stories that came out of Dallas. One of these involved Junior Moore in Mobile Alabama on November 21, 1963. Junior was told to come down to the FBI office four blocks away. There, he was asked whether he knew anything about Lee Harvey Oswald. Perhaps the question came either because Oswald had given a lecture on Russia at Spring Hill College in Mobile the previous summer, or the interest could have been spurred by the telegram received at the New Orleans FBI on the previous Sunday about a possible assassination attempt in Dallas, November 22-23.[1] Were the FBI to have acknowledged that they had in fact interviewed someone regarding Lee Harvey Oswald just before the assassination, trying to maintain that they had little or no information on Oswald just *before* the assassination would be seen to be a lie.

A second anomaly relates to a neurophysiologist, Adele Edisen. She was re-entering the workforce and had obtained a post-doctoral fellowship at Tulane University. An administrator at the National Institute of Neurological Diseases and Blindness (NINDB) Dr. Jose Rivera, had conversed with Edisen at a national gathering. A number of quirky incidents occurred in their conversations. Rivera asked Edisen if she knew Lee Harvey Oswald. Rivera indicated that Oswald would be moving to New Orleans soon, and Edisen should meet Oswald and his Russian wife. He gave Edisen Oswald's telephone number when he got to New Orleans.

And Rivera told Edisen to tell Oswald to shoot the chief. The information seemed bewildering and nonsensical – until November 22, 1963.[2]

A third anomaly was that of Rose Cherami (nee Melba Christine Marcades), who, was with two unknown men on the early morning of November 20, 1963, near Eunice, Louisiana. As they were driving down the highway one of the men threw Rose out of the car. Rose was picked up and taken to a hospital, and then to a police station. Rose was said to have told those who would listen that President Kennedy would be killed in Dallas, two days later. No one seriously took what she said as being of any value.[3]

The Rose Cherami story is the only story of these three that surfaced any time near the assassination. It would be the 1990's before the first two would see the light of day.

One anomaly that did become a controversial issue is that of the "magic bullet." Initially, the Warren Commission had hypothesized three bullets, two hitting President Kennedy, and one hitting Governor Connally. Since one bullet missed the Presidential limousine entirely and hit a section of curbing that broke loose and hit James Tague as he was watching the motorcade, it became necessary to revise the scenario if the number of shots were to be limited to three.[4] It came to Arlen Specter, a lawyer serving on the investigative team, to come up with the magic bullet theory, wherein a bullet fired from the sixth floor of the Texas School Book Depository struck President Kennedy in the back of the head, exited his throat, made a 90 degree turn to the right and then entered Governor Connally, leaving several serious wounds and somehow ended up in a stretcher in the hospital, still in pristine condition. One more bit of magic was that the wound in President Kennedy's throat gave the appearance of an entrance wound and the wound in the back of his head gave the appearance of an exit wound![5]

Lee Harvey Oswald

Lee Harvey Oswald has been characterized, first by the Warren Commission, as a loner, a traitor, and a person who was unable to have sufficient income to support his family. Further he did not have any knowledge of Jack Ruby or David Ferrie. This is the "legend" that the CIA wanted to construct regarding Oswald. None of it was true.

Lee Harvey Oswald's life is a major part of this present writing. What is different here is that the entirety of his life is addressed. Two big chunks of his life that are omitted from most presentations are Oswald's time in the Soviet Union (Russia) and his time in New Orleans in 1963. Oswald's time in Russia was written about by his best friend there, Ernst Titovets.[6] At the time of Oswald's being in Russia, Titovets was a medical student. Titovets received his medical degree and subsequently two scientific doctorates; his career was as a medical researcher. Titovets was unaware of the characterizations of Oswald's life in Russia by American authors. For example, author John Armstrong made the statement that Oswald never spoke Russian in Russia, except possibly with Marina.[7] When I contacted Titovets about this, he said that, once Oswald learned to speak Russian, whenever Oswald and Titovets were with friends, they spoke Russian all the time.[8]

A second area that is most important is Oswald's time in New Orleans from April to September 1963. In April, 1963, Oswald met Judyth Vary (who shortly became Judyth Vary Baker upon her marriage to fellow University of Florida student Robert Baker). It is Judyth Baker's story that fills this gap in Oswald's life.[9] Not only is Oswald not a loner; two of his good friends were David Ferrie and Jack Ruby. Oswald met Ferrie when he was a cadet in the Civil Air Patrol, where Oswald was taught to be a pilot by Ferrie. In the Summer of 1963, Oswald was a currier for a secret medical research project in New Orleans funded by the CIA, under the direction of Anton Ochsner, M.D. [10] Oswald, Judyth Baker, and David Ferrie all worked closely with Mary Sherman, M.D. During the late spring and early Summer, Jack Ruby came to New Orleans and met with Oswald and Judyth Baker. It was during this time that, as a patron to the research project Ruby found out about the development of fast acting cancers, intended for use on Fidel Castro. This also gave Ruby the heads-up, after his murder conviction was overturned, that he was injected by a physician with, likely, cancer cells: that he also was being murdered.[11]

There is the issue of Oswald's financial circumstances. Oswald was directed by the CIA to give the appearance of being poor. As a son of a widow in his early life, there was little unique about Oswald. It was the depression at that time, and many were in frugal circumstances. Once he entered the military at age 17, though his take home pay was not high, he seemed to have extra resources. In Japan, Oswald was recruited to be a false defector. In that capacity, his needs were likely met. He seemed to be getting money from the CIA and the FBI on his return to the United States. His good friend George deMohrenschildt was given several thousand dollars to save for Oswald until some later point in time. He had also given Mrs. Ruth Paine money to buy a car for Marina. Oswald gave Judyth Baker $400 to help when they were able to reunite in Mexico. During his last two months of life, Oswald received $3665.89. according to a report by Richard Mosk, a staff lawyer for the Warren Commission, and Phillip Barson, an IRS Supervisor, which was turned over to the Warren Commission. This is not the financial information one would expect in 1963 for a poor man.[12]

It is a goal of this presentation to show that Oswald was not only a patsy for the persons planning the assassination of President Kennedy, but was in fact trying to intercede to stop it.

One other difference with most books about the assassination is the inclusion of the presidential terms of Lyndon Johnson. At a minimum, Johnson knew about the plan to assassinate President Kennedy, though he may not have known long before he went to the Murchison's home and went into a meeting taking place there. Most likely he made statements there about the assassination scheduled for the next day. He revealed as much to his longtime mistress, Madeleine Brown, directly after leaving the meeting.[13]

The reason to address Johnson's time in office is to compare it to what could be expected from a continued Kennedy presidency. In one sense, Johnson was very successful in getting Kennedy's initiatives passed much more quickly than JFK might have. Ironically, Johnson had cautioned President Kennedy to proceed slowly on civil rights and other social programs. Invoking Kennedy's name, Johnson used all the hand shaking and arm twisting to get the programs through. However, one could interpret Johnson's behavior as a prelude to getting his "Great Society" programs passed through congress. Put another way, President Kennedy's programs dovetailed perfectly with Johnson's Great Society. There were two differences. Johnson was perfectly willing to help the military with their Vietnam agenda. It was the undoing of the Johnson presidency. Additionally, there was the deliberate loss of the USS *Liberty* during the Six Day War in 1967, as a pretense to enter the war on Israel's side. The treatment of the survivors of the USS *Liberty* was inhumane. The deliberate attack on the USS *Liberty* was treasonous.[14]

An important issue to address is the legacy of President Kennedy, and what was lost forever with his assassination. One of the most important parts of his legacy was not known during his lifetime (and as of this writing, still not widely known). At the time of the Cuban Missile Crisis, between 95-100 of the 172 Soviet missiles were operational. The Joint Chiefs had every intention of bombing the missile sites; only the steadfastness of President Kennedy kept them from their goal.[15] Among the losses occurring from the assassination of President Kennedy, beyond the dynamic young president, was the carnage in Vietnam. It was President Kennedy's goal to remove all military, except for advisors, from Vietnam by the end of 1965. Instead, by the end of 1965, Vietnam had already become a bloodbath, and as President Kennedy foresaw, we did have men on the moon before the end of the decade.

Endnotes

1 Williams, J.D. (2004). Was the FBI Searching for Oswald the Day Before the Assassination? *The Dealey Plaza Echo*, 8, 2, 46-52.

2 Edisen's story was first published in the *Third Decade*, a JFK Assassination research journal, under the pseudonym K.S. Turner; Albarelli, H.P. (2013). *A Secret Order: Investigating the High Strangeness and Synchronicity of the JFK Assassination*. Walterville, OR: Trine Day, pp. 127-162.

3 Elliott, T.C. (2013). *A Rose by Many Other Names: Rose Cherami & the JFK Assassination.* Walterville, OR: Trine Day.

4 Tague, J.T. (2003). *Truth Withheld: A Survivor's Story*. Dallas: Excell Digital Press.

5 Groden, R.J. & Livingstone, H.E. (1989). *High Treason: The Assassination of President John F. Kennedy What Really Happened*. New York: The Conservatory Press, pp. 54-61.

6 Titovets, E. (2010). *Oswald's Russian Episode. Minsk Belerus*: MonLitera Publishing House.

7 Armstrong, J. (2003). *Harvey & Lee: How the CIA Framed Oswald*. Arlington TX: Quasar, pp. 339-340.

8 Williams, J.D. & Titovets, E. (November, 2013). *"Did Oswald Speak Russian in Russia?"* 50th Anniversary Conference, Arlington, TX. Also published in *JFK-E/Deep Politics Quarterly*, (2014). 1, 3, 21-34.

9 Baker, J.V. (2010). *Me & Lee: How I Came to Know, Love and Lose Lee Harvey Oswald*. Walterville OR: Trine Day.

10 Wilds, J. & Harkey, I. (1990). *Alton Ochsner: Surgeon of the South*. Baton Rouge LA: Louisiana State University Press.

11 Haslam, E. (2007). *Dr. Mary's Monkey: How the Unsolved Murder of a Doctor, a Secret Laboratory in New Orleans and Cancer-Causing Monkey Viruses are Linked to Lee Harvey Oswald, the JFK Assassination and Emerging Global Epidemics*. Walterville, OR: Trine Day, p. 337. See also, Haslam, E.T. (1997). *Mary, Ferrie & the Monkey Virus: The Story of an Underground Medical Laboratory*. Albuquerque NM: Wordsworth Communications,

12 Shenon, P. (2013). *A Cruel and Shocking Act: The Secret History of the Kennedy Assassination*. New York: Henry Holt & Co., p.452.

13 Brown, M.D. (1997). *Texas in the Morning: The Love Story of Madeleine Brown and President Lyndon Baines Johnson*. Baltimore: Conservatory Press,

14 Allen, R.J. (2012). *Beyond Treason*. Create Space. (Available Through Amazon.com).

15 Norris, R.S. & Kristensen, H.M. (2012). "The Cuban Missile Crisis: A Nuclear Order of Battle, October and November, 1962." *Bulletin of the Atomic Scientists*, 68, 6.

Chapter One

THE LEGACY OF JOHN FITZGERALD KENNEDY

In some ways, it seems strange to mention a legacy of an elected president who served only two years, 8 months and 2 days in office. Only four other presidents died in their first term after being elected. Among them William Henry Harrison, who caught pneumonia at his inauguration, expiring 31 days later; Zachary Taylor (who served 16 months); James Abram Garfield, who was shot less than 4 months into his presidency (dying 2 months later of the wounds); and Warren Gamaliel Harding. Only Harding (other than Kennedy) can be said to have left a legacy – and his was a negative one. He is best remembered for the Teapot Dome scandal, where his Secretary of the Interior, Albert Fall, was convicted of corruption for taking bribes in the leasing of government-owned oil reserves. More recently (2015) it was confirmed that Harding (a bachelor) had fathered the daughter of his long time mistress.[1]

Yet, in his 32 months in office, John F. Kennedy definitely left a legacy. His legacy can be described as those actions and activities, that were known during his lifetime, but their deeper and more personal importance only became known with the passing of time, and information about his activities became public knowledge after his assassination.

The Presidential Years

A first area of JFK's legacy is his speechmaking, his glibness, his humor, and his charismatic persona. First, it would be remiss not to acknowledge the brilliance of his speechwriter, Ted Sorensen. But Sorensen did not write the speeches totally on his own; through conversations with JFK and some of his other advisors, discussions would take place regarding not only the substance of the speech, but also what it would try to accomplish. Then Sorensen would set out to wordsmith a speech to meet these expectations.[2] One of the finest examples of this wordsmithing was JFK's inaugural address. While Sorensen was a master of the art, JFK in turn took the text (usually reworking it to fit his ideas) and masterfully delivered it, completely owning the speech. Phrases within the inaugural address resonate with us today:

"And so my fellow Americans: ask not what your country can do for you – ask what you can do for your country."

This was followed by:

> My fellow citizens of the world, ask not what Americans will do for you, but together what we can do for the freedom of man.
>
> Finally, whether you are citizens of America, or citizens of the world, ask of us here the same high standards of strength and sacrifice we ask of you. With a good conscience our only sure reward, with history the final judge of our deeds, let us go forth to lead the land we love, asking His blessing and His help, but that knowing that here on earth God's work must truly be our own.[3]

No one has ever topped it.

Putting a Man on the Moon

One of the more spectacular aspects of President Kennedy's legacy is his intent for America to land a man on the moon in the decade of the 1960's. Soviet Russia's success in space had, for the time being, relegated the United States to second place in the space race. The Soviets had the first orbiting satellite (Sputnik I) in October, 1957. They followed that with the first creature in space (a dog named Laika) in November, 1957. Only in January 1958 did the U.S. gets its first orbiting satellite. The Soviets sent a probe to the moon (Luna II) on September 12, 1959. This was followed by Luna III, which photographed the far side of the moon, October 4, 1959. And on April 12, 1961, Yuri Gagarin was the first human in space, making a 108-minute orbital flight in Vostik 1. Though Allen Shepard did make a sub-orbital flight into space on May 5, 1961, it was not the equivalent of Gagarin's earlier achievement. President Kennedy made a special presentation to a joint session of Congress on May 25, 1961, and asked for an additional 5 to 7 billion dollars over the next 5 years for the space program: The U.S. "should commit itself to achieving the goal before this decade is out, of landing a man on the moon and returning him safely to the earth."[4] While this did not occur in his lifetime, it was accomplished on July 16, 1969.[5]

Peace Corps

One of the enduring programs that was begun by President Kennedy was the Peace Corps. Though others had conceived ideas that involved citizens to help the needy in other countries, it would fall to the US Representative Jack Kennedy to propose in 1951 that "young college graduates would find a full life in bringing technical advice and assistance to the underprivileged and backward Middle East.... In that calling, these men would follow the constructive work done by the religious missionaries in these countries over the past 100 years."[6]

On the campaign trail in 1960, late at night on October 14, on the steps of the Union on the University of Michigan campus, John Kennedy announced that such an organization would be part of his presidency. On March 1, 1961, after being in office just over a month, Kennedy signed Executive Order 10924 creating the Peace Corps.[7] In 1963, President Kennedy proposed a Peace Corps for the underprivileged in the United States. That program, Volunteers in Service to America (VISTA), was enacted in 1965. Both programs continue to the present.

The Peace Corps program has sent over 220,000 volunteers in its history to 140 countries.[8] While the idea behind the Peace Corps was to have American volunteers go to other countries and attempt to help the people there with better farming techniques, or, perhaps teaching them English or teaching them in their own language. One unexpected outcome for the volunteers is that they were likely to learn something about themselves and about the United States. One Peace Corps volunteer observed, "One of the main things I learned is that the third world is not different; it is the United States that's different. We're the ones that are oddballs."[9]

The Bay of Pigs

Some might think it unusual to include the Bay of Pigs in a discussion of President Kennedy's legacy. Rather, its omission would miss an important aspect of his presidency. To understand the Bay of Pigs, necessarily includes the Eisenhower administration. The CIA had begun addressing Fidel Castro shortly after the revolution in Cuba. They had pleased President Eisenhower with a quick overthrow of President Jacobo Arbenz in Guatemala in 1954. Eisenhower approved a program to deal with Fidel Castro on March 17, 1960. Subsequently Eisenhower, tiring of the lack of progress to a developed plan, informed CIA Director Allen Dulles and CIA Deputy Director for Plans Richard Bissell that he didn't want to hear from them if they didn't intend to go through with the removal of Castro, that they should stop talking to him about it.[10] Vice President Nixon strongly supported the CIA's program, and hoped Castro could be successfully removed before the forthcoming presidential election. But life can become ever more complex. In the debates running up to the election, JFK hit two points hard: that if he were elected, he would move to close the missile gap with the Soviet Union, and that he thought that we should do more to help Cuba rid themselves of Castro by direct action. These points, which likely helped JFK's candidacy, were not successfully rebutted by Richard Nixon. As Vice-President, he knew the missile gap was false, (i.e., the Soviet Union was ahead of the United States in missiles) but being advanced by the CIA. Nixon also knew that the U.S. was planning an attack to remove Castro from Cuba, but secrecy kept him quiet. Instead, Nixon proposed a blockade of Cuba, which seemed weak compared to JFK's presented ideas. Shortly after the last debate, JFK was told that no missile gap existed. Perhaps he wasn't sure about the new information; the information he was given as a member of the Senate Foreign Relations Committee had emphasized this "missile gap." Given the amount of prior information, and the importance of this issue in his campaign, and the failure of Vice President Nixon to counter Kennedy's claim about a missile gap, and the possibility that this new information was misinformation, Kennedy continued to emphasize the gap in the final weeks before the election. In July 1961, satellite pictures from the Soviet Union showed that the CIA's estimate in Russia was greatly exaggerated. The Soviet missile strength was 3.5% of the CIA's claim.[11]

Bay of Pigs: The Decision to Not Allow a Second Air Raid

The Bay of Pigs has had several book-length treatments; one of the more definitive, in terms of JFK's involvement, is by Peter Wyden.[12] One critical point is the decision to call off the planned bombing of the remaining three Cuban aircraft. Fletcher Prouty stated, "But between the time of Kennedy's approval at 1:45 P.M. Sunday and the time for the release of the B-26's from the Hidden Valley Base at Puerto Cabezas, Nicaragua, the vital dawn air strike to destroy Castro's three remaining T-33 jets was called off by President Kennedy's special assistant for national security affairs, McGeorge Bundy, in a telephone call to General Cabell."[13]

If Bundy did in fact make such a call, it is inconceivable that he would have done so except on the explicit orders of President Kennedy. Shortly after a Presidential approval of a second bombing to eliminate the remaining three Cuban jets, McGeorge Bundy called General Cabell. "Bundy said no air strikes could be launched until after the Brigade had secured the Giron air strip, and strikes would ostensibly be launched from there. This was an order from the President."[14]

After Bundy's conversation with Cabell, Secretary Dean Rusk received General Cabell and Richard Bissell at his office. Earlier, Rusk had talked to President Kennedy, who told Rusk that the air strikes were to be called off unless there were "over-riding considerations."[15] Cabell and Bissell presented their case for the air strikes to Secretary Rusk. Rusk called the President and relayed their pleas for reinstating the air strikes. Rusk concluded in his presentation to JFK, that the air strikes were important, but there were no over-riding considerations. The president agreed with Rusk. Then Rusk asked Cabell if he wanted to speak to the President. Cabell, recognizing that the President was the Commander in Chief, said no. When the ultimate leader has said no twice, there is no reason to ask again.[16]

Not addressed by Wyden was the involvement after a call from the CIA commander at Puerto Cabezas urging Colonel L. Fletcher Prouty to call General Cabell at Operation Zapata to order the release of the planes to bomb the Cuban jets, using OSO/OSD authority. Prouty then attempted to call General Cabell. General Cabell wasn't in. "After that call, I reached the CIA's Zapata office and suggested they release the B-26's 'on Kennedy's orders' or the whole effort would fail."[17]

The person speaking to Prouty said that it was in the hands of McGeorge Bundy, Secretary Rusk, and General Cabell. Invoking JFK's name with no authority to do so would seem to demand serious consequences for Prouty. Fortunately for him, his ruse was rebuffed. It is remarkable that Prouty never addressed that his attempt to infuse the U.S. further into the Bay of Pigs fiasco would have been an act of war against Cuba. This attempt occurred at the very time that the actions of the United States vis-a-vis Cuba were being closely scrutinized at the United Nations meetings. The expectancy of the CIA and the military was that American air support could be called upon to insure the success of the mission. Prouty had never seemed to reconcile that the CIA had vastly underestimated the support the Cuban people had for Castro.

What went wrong? It seems to be a tragicomedy of errors and misconceived assumptions by many involved in this fiasco. The CIA, through Richard Bissell, Director of Covert Operations, the seeming heir-apparent to replace Director of the CIA, Allen Dulles, planned to overthrow Fidel Castro, with the Brigade of ex-patriot Cubans who fled to the United States. They would land in Cuba, and an uprising of dissatisfied Cubans would rise up and join them. This would be preceded by Cuban pilots, flying aging B-26 bombers taking out the Cuban Air Force. Kennedy tried to make it clear that no American military should participate beyond taking the ex-Cubans to their point of departure to invade Cuba. The plan B discussed by Bissell was that, if the invasion wasn't initially successful, they could go to the mountains and prepare for a Castro-like revolution on Castro. Most other persons involved knew that Plan B was totally impractical, but they (The Joint Chiefs of Staff) did not voice this concern. They apparently assumed that the U.S. military would assure success of the venture by whatever means necessary. President Kennedy opposed such actions, but apparently, it was thought that when push came to shove, President Kennedy would "turn the dogs loose." There was not only "A failure to communicate," participants seemed to reveal only information that would avoid cancelling the operation. Only Senator William Fulbright vociferously opposed the proposed action; he seemed to be alone in his opposition. President Kennedy seemingly made it explicitly clear to Bissell that no American military were to participate in the actual combat. Actually, six pilots flew B-26s and tried to help the Brigade establish a stronghold. Four of these pilots were killed in action. This information was not released until 1998.[18]

So, what happened? In a way, the immortal line from *Cool Hand Luke*, "What we got here is a failure to communicate" begins to explain what went on. Part of the Bay of Pigs planning process was a difference in the goals of the separate persons or groups involved. President Kennedy wanted US involvement limited to providing training for the Cuban "Freedom Fighters" and transportation to the point of drop-off with access to the Cuban beaches; any air support would be done by ex-Cubans flying B-26s. If the initial surge by the Freedom Fighters was unsuccessful, Kennedy understood that they would retreat to the mountains and prepare for a future attack, much like Fidel Castro accomplished in 1959. No American personnel would be involved either as pilots or on the ground. Kennedy "...had approved a quiet reinfiltration, plausibly Cuban in its essentials, not an invasion."[19] The President thought he was permitting the exiles to decide to risk their lives for Cuba without overt U.S. support."[20] For the CIA's Richard Bissell, a CIA planned assault would seemingly be successful, but American forces would surely help remove Castro because Kennedy would not want to leave the Freedom Fighters without the necessary support to win. The use of American forces was never communicated to President Kennedy, but Bissell presumed Kennedy would approve the involvement of American forces to avoid defeat. The Joint Chiefs of Staff, it appears, presumed the use of American forces; Bissell had scaled down the effort to get President Kennedy's approval to take the Freedom Fighters to Cuba, thus increasing the need for U.S. intervention. The Joint Chiefs of Staff were privately skeptical of Bissell's plan, but did not voice their skepticism to President Kennedy.[21] A further issue, that was less known to Bissell, was the disdain shown by the CIA trainers for the Cuban Freedom Fighters, who found themselves continually at loggerheads with their CIA handlers with providing adequate fire power. Initially, The LCVP's (Landing Craft Vehicle and Personnel) and LCU (Landing Craft Utility) were not equipped with guns for the crafts. The LCVP could carry 36 infantrymen. The Cuban Freedom Fighters were adamant that they would not go without guns on the crafts. Eventually, each LCU was equipped with two 50-caliber machine guns and each LCVP was equipped with a 30-caliber machine-gun.[22]

An interpretation of the process that led to the fiasco began with a woefully inadequate military plan by Bissell, which would begin by sending in the brigade, with the expectation of massive defections of the populace joining the Freedom Fighters to overthrow Castro. The success of the invasion would require a massive American force to overcome Castro's standing army of 200,000 men. The assumption was that Kennedy would not want to have a massive failure early in his presidency; it seems that this was the expectation that Nixon seemed willing to accept. The military kept their thoughts of the CIA plan to fail, and they also would expect Kennedy to send the military in to salvage the effort. Neither the CIA nor the Joint Chiefs of Staff wished to divulge the absolute need for a full American military involvement to insure success. If Kennedy was correctly apprised of the virtually zero chance of success following Bissell's plan, he would have been likely to cancel the invasion. The thought was that once Kennedy had approved a plan, he would continue the effort to success. Clearly, both the CIA and the Joint Chiefs of Staff were wrong about Kennedy's future actions.

How can the Bay of Pigs be considered part of JFK's legacy? Arguably, the Bay of Pigs was a turning point in JFK's presidency; this event can be seen as the beginning of the end of his being a cold-warrior. He was learning that neither the CIA nor the military brass were trustworthy.

Civil Rights

A fair assessment of President Kennedy's actions in the civil rights arena is mixed. JFK appointed un-sympathetic judges (to civil rights) in the South, he dragged his feet on civil rights legislation, particularly in school desegregation. It is not that JFK wasn't planning for these civil rights issues, it could be argued that when the issues were addressed that they might have a better chance of change, rather than running into a wall of opposition. The President's brother, Attorney General Bobby Kennedy, was choosing court cases to widen civil rights for school desegregation. Robert Kennedy successfully sued the Prince George County, Virginia school system, who had used federal money in construction, when the federal money was available because the children of personnel stationed or employed at a military installation were enrolled in the affected school. This occurred 11 days after President Kennedy proposed the Civil Rights Act of 1963.[23] As can happen in Washington, D.C., Congress can stall bills that they prefer not to enact. Though President Kennedy enjoyed a 64-36 edge in the Senate, Southern Dixiecrats began the "crawl' process on civil rights. The Civil Rights Act of 1963 would not be acted upon prior to November 22, 1963. One of Lyndon Johnson's most unselfish acts (some pundits would say his only unselfish act, and then spin it to be a selfish act) was to marshal John F. Kennedy's Civil Rights Act quickly through Congress, though it didn't seem quickly at the time. Opponents of the Civil Rights Act in the Senate filibustered for 57 days. Once the bill passed the Senate, the House quickly approved the bill which was signed into law on July 2, 1964.[24]

The passage of this bill was the spark that began the change for the former Confederate South from Dixiecrats to Republicons (Conservative Republicans). In the 1964 election, five Southern states and Arizona (Goldwater's home state) cast their electoral votes for Barry Goldwater, the Republican candidate. In Alabama, there was no Democratic candidate on the ballot. In contrast to the 1960 election, Kennedy beat Nixon in each Southern state; when in Mississippi, both lost to "Unpledged Democrat electors" who cast their electoral vote for Senator Harry F. Byrd of Virginia, who also got 6 (of 11) electoral votes in Alabama, and 1 in Oklahoma. This change from "Dixiecrats" to "Republicons" has been dubbed "The Southern Strategy," and was reportedly used by Nixon in the 1968 election. Nixon agreed to "go slow" on implementing various aspects of the civil rights act passed under President Johnson. One such example was the negation of withholding funds to schools that failed to meet integration in public schools. While the Southern Strategy was not totally successful, it was good enough to produce victories for Nixon in 1968 and 1972.[25]

The Cuban Missile Crisis

The Cuban Missile Crisis may well have been JFK's finest hour, though this would not be known except for a handful of persons.

When the Cuban missiles, installed by the Soviet Union, became known to President Kennedy, he implemented a calculated strategy that included back-channel communications with Nikita Khrushchev, the Soviet Premier. He chose to form a group later called ExCom, to deliberate with him as he addressed the grave issues then facing the United States. The members of ExCom were persons President Kennedy trusted, even if they disagreed with him.

A President for Peace

Perhaps one of President Kennedy's best speeches was the one given as a Commencement Address at American University in Washington D.C. on June 10, 1963. Ironically, while it was given front page coverage by *Izvestia* in the Soviet Union, it was virtually ignored by the press in the United States. Much of the speech related to the Soviet Union. President Kennedy defined the kind of peace he was seeking: "Not a Pax Americana enforced on the world by American weapons of war… I am talking about genuine peace, the kind of peace that makes life on earth worth living, the kind that enables men and nations to grow and to hope and to build a better life for their children, not merely peace for Americans but peace for all men and women- not merely peace in our time but peace for all time."

It was not just the Soviets who needed to change their ways of thinking, but Americans as well, particularly in regard to the Soviet Union. While Americans saw Communism as repugnant, the Soviet people can be commended for their many achievements, particularly in space. President Kennedy pointed out that if war broke out again, both the Soviets and Americans would be likely targets. The irony is that the two strongest countries would be the most likely to be slated for destruction. Both countries were spending vast amounts of money on war materials that could be better spent on other things that could be devoted to combatting ignorance, poverty, and disease. President Kennedy reasoned both sides have a vested interest in seeking a lasting peace and halting the arms race. "So, let us not be blind to our differences – but let us also direct attention to our common interests and the means by which those common differences can be resolved. And if we cannot now end our common differences, at least we can help make the world be safe for diversity. For in the final analysis our most basic common link is that we all inhabit this small planet. We all breathe the same air. We all cherish our children's futures. And we are all mortal."[26]

It could also be argued that this speech might have been the galvanizing moment for members of the military-industrial complex to begin serious planning for "Executive Action;" the assassination of the President of the United States.

Ich bin ein Berliner

On June 26, 1963, John F. Kennedy made a speech at the Rathaus Schoneberg, the building that held the governing mayor of West Berlin. In expressing his concern for those living in West Germany, he concluded a speech with, "All free men, wherever they may live, are citizens of Berlin, and, therefore, as a free man, I take pride in the words 'Ich bin ein Berliner.'"

In the speech he addressed the existence of the Berlin wall, which had been erected by the Soviets to keep Eastern Europeans under Soviet control from escaping to the West. This short speech (less than ten minutes) was a reassurance of continued support of Berlin from the United States, and by inference from Great Britain and France. The Berlin Wall would remain until the collapse of the Soviet Union, in 1989.[27]

An Important Part of John F. Kennedy's Legacy Not Widely Known During His Lifetime

The Cuban Missile Crisis was much closer to igniting a nuclear war than has been generally made available to the public. The Cubans, nuclear capacity had to some degree become operational at the time of the missile crisis. Of the 172 nuclear warheads, between 95-100 were operational. The United States did not think any of the Soviet nuclear warheads located in Cuba were operational. At the time of the Cuban Missile Crisis, the Joint Chiefs of Staff were arguing for bombing raids to take out the Soviet-Cuban missiles. Had bombings occurred at the sites of the missiles, nuclear warheads could have been used as a retaliation. President Kennedy's steadfast refusal to accommodate the attack suggested by the Joint Chiefs of Staff saved the world from being radically disrupted.[28]

Endnotes

1 DNA Test Reveals President Warren Harding's Affair and Love Child. cnn.com/2015/08/14/president-harding-affair-dna-revelation/

2 Sorensen, T. (2008). *Counselor*. New York: Harper.

3 John F. Kennedy's Inaugural Address, retrieved 1/20/2018.

4 Ibid.

5 Chronology of Manned Space Fights. Windows2Universe.org/space-missions-manual-table.html Retrieved, March 23, 2016.

6 Leamer, L. (2001). *The Kennedy Men.* (1901-1963). New York: Harper-Collins, pp. 331-338.

7 Exeutive Order 10924. Establishment of the Peace Corps (1961).

8 peacecorps.gov/about/fastfact/ Retrieved 3/23/2016.

9 David, R., Beard, M., Enger, C., Gershman, K., Vacek, J. Experiencing the Peace Corp: A Discussion,. in Williams, J.D., Waite, R.G., and Gordon, G.S. Eds. (2010). *John F. Kennedy, History, Memory, Legacy: An Interdisciplinary Inquiry*. Grand Forks: U. North Dakota. und.edu/JFKConference.

10 Wyden, P.(1979).*Bay of Pigs: The Untold Story*. New York: Schuster, p. 31.

11 Reeves, R. (1993). *President Kennedy: Profile of Power.* New York: Simon & Schuster, p.59fn.

12 Wyden.

13 Prouty, L.F. (2011). *The CIA, Vietnam, and the Plot to Assassinate John F. Kennedy.* Dover, DE: Skyhorse Publishing p. 130.

14 Wyden, p.197.

15 Ibid., p.199.

16 Ibid., p. 200.

17 Prouty, p. 131.

18 lasvegssun.com/news/1998/apr/23/nevada-focus-37-years-later-family-learn-how-father-died One of the four killed was Leo Francis Baker. Baker was shot down, and then executed on the battle field. His widow learned of his death several days later from her husband's friend, a member of the CIA. Unknown to her, his body was to lie in a Cuban morgue until at least 1979 before being buried in Cuba. The U.S. government steadfastly refused to acknowledge his or any other American involvement in the Bay of Pigs invasion. In 1982, the family received bronze and silver CIA medals secretly issued to Baker six years earlier. Only on March 13, 1998 were the Bay of Pigs documents declassified.

19 Wyden, p. 309.

20 Loc. cit.

21 Wyden, pp. 304-311.

22 Ibid., 82-84.

23 Landsberg, B.K. *The Kennedy' Justice Department's Enforcement of Civil Rights: A View from the Trenches.* (2010) In Williams et.al., 194-208.

24 Civil Rights Act of 1964. In nps.gov/subjects/civilrights/1964-civil-rights-act.htm Retrieved April 2, 2016.

25 Murphy, R. and Gulliver, H. (1971). *The Southern Strategy.* New York: Scribner's.

26 The actual speech can be viewed on U-Tube at youtube.com/watch?v=0fkKf4k40, retrieved 4/23/2018; the text can be found at presidency.ucsb.edu/ws/?pid=9266. retrieved 4/23/2018;

The text can also be found in Douglass, J.W. (2008). *JFK and the Unspeakable: Why He died and Why it matters.* Maryknoll NY: Orbis Books, pp. 382-388.

27 en/wikipedia/wiki/ich_bin_ein_Berliner retrieved 4/24/2018.

28 Norris, R.S. & Kristensen, H.M. (2012). "The Cuban Missile Crisis: A Nuclear Order of Battle, October and November, 1962." *Bulletin of the Atomic Scientists*, 68, 6.

CHEVROLETS

Chapter Two

TIMELINE TO DALLAS

There are several timelines for the assassination of John F. Kennedy, most notably the one done by Ira David Wood III. The following timeline varies in scope (longer) and detail (much less than Wood's). The most extensive timeline that I have seen is by Walt Brown, which covers a much longer time span, and extends beyond 3,000 pages. The timeline in this chapter extends from June 9, 1963 through November 22,1963 in Dallas. The second timeline goes from November 23, 1963 until January 1969.

June 9, 1963 to November 22, 1963

• June 9, 1963: President Kennedy flew from Hawaii to San Francisco where he had a conference with U.S. mayors, to get them to use their influence to get passage of the Civil Rights Act. Kennedy then flew back to D.C.; he and Ted Sorensen put the finishing touches on his Peace Speech.[1]

• June 9, 1963: Both Lee Harvey Oswald and Judyth Baker were separately interviewed for jobs with Reily Coffee in New Orleans. They separately interviewed with Dr. Alton Ochsner on the previous day. An arrangement was made to have Oswald and Baker involved with a secret research project during their employment. Baker was directly working on the research; Oswald served as a courier.[2]

• June 10, 1963: President Kennedy signed the Equal Pay Act, which had as its goal preventing salary discrimination against women.[3]

• June 10, 1963: President Kennedy delivered his Peace Speech at the graduation ceremony of George Washington University. Soviet Premier Khrushchev refused to meet with the Chinese delegation in Moscow; the Chinese were trying to get Khrushchev to take a harder line regarding the U.S. Governor George Wallace stood in the doorway at the University of Alabama, proclaiming, "Segregation now, segregation forever." On the following day, Wallace would be back to prevent black students from entering the University of Alabama.[4]

• June 11, 1963: Governor George Wallace was present at the University of Alabama, along with the Alabama National Guard, to prevent black students from entering the University. President Kennedy federalized the Alabama National Guard, with the order to escort Governor Wallace off campus. The black students then registered at the University. That evening, President Kennedy gave a televised speech where he stated that the enrollment of the black students was a moral issue. Later that evening, the jubilant field agent for the National Association for Colored People, Medgar Evans, was shot and killed in his front yard as his children watched him bleed to death.[5]

• June 11, 1963: Thich Quang Duc, a South Vietnamese Buddhist monk, immolated himself on the streets of Saigon. A photograph of this was seen around the world. *Izvestia*, the Soviet national newspaper, published the entirety of President Kennedy's Peace Speech.[6]

• June 16, 1963: The Soviet Union sent the first woman into space, Valentina Tereshkova.[7]

• June 19, 1963: President Kennedy sent his Civil Rights bill to Congress. They did not act on it in President Kennedy's lifetime.[8]

• June 19, 1963: A "hotline" was established between the Soviet Union and the United States.[9] A treaty was also signed between the U.S. and the Soviet Union limiting nuclear testing.[10]

• June 21, 1963: David Ferrie flew a plane from New Orleans to Toronto, Canada. At the last minute, he asked Lee Oswald to accompany him and possibly serve as a backup pilot.[11]

• June 24, 1963: Lee Oswald applied for a visa (passport) in New Orleans. It was processed and given to him the next day.[12]

• June 26, 1963: President Kennedy spoke in Berlin. Kennedy stated, "All free men, wherever they may live, are citizens of Berlin. And therefore, as a free man, I take pride in the words, 'Ich bin ein Berliner.'"[13]

• June 28, 1963: Continuing his European trip, President Kennedy addressed the Irish Parliament. He spoke these words, "You see things, and you say 'Why?' But I dream things that never were and I say 'Why not?'"[14]

• June, July 1963: Oswald spent a significant amount of time at the Adrian Garage, next door to Reily's Coffee, and across the street from Guy Banister's office. Several government agencies would park their cars at the garage. One such governmental agency was the CIA. On First Friday's Lee's visits with Adrian would be longer, since he had to wait for his CIA paymaster to show up and get his car. Then Lee would go outside on the sidewalk where his paymaster would pull his car to the curb and hand him an envelope. Adrian Alba reported seeing Lee do this: "Lee showed me one of the envelopes, which was full of crisp $20 dollar bills."[15]

• July 1,1963: Oswald's Fair Play for Cuba office, near the office of Guy Banister, was now closed. It operated during the month of June.[16]

• July 1, 1963: President Kennedy had his 12th Press Conference of 1963. He announced that the test ban treaty negotiations were back on track. He then urged that a prompt and substantial revision and reduction of the income tax was necessary to speed up economic growth.[17]

• July 19, 1963: Oswald was fired from Reily Coffee.[18]

• July 27, 2017: Oswald gave a presentation on Marxism at Spring Hill College, a Jesuit institution in Mobile, Alabama, where his cousin, Eugene Murret, was studying to become a priest.[19]

• July 31, 1963: The FBI raided an anti-Castro training camp in St. Tammany Parish North of Lake Ponchartrain near the town of Lacombe. Both Oswald and David Ferrie were associated with this camp, but neither were there the day of the raid.[20]

• August 7, 1963: Patrick Bouvier Kennedy was born to President John F. Kennedy and Jaqueline Bouvier Kennedy. Patrick would die 39 hours later. Though he was first buried in Boston, his final burial place would be in the Arlington Cemetery in Washington, D.C. next to his father and mother.[21]

• August 9, 1963: Oswald was passing out pro-Castro leaflets when confronted by Carlos Bringuier. Oswald was jailed. He was released on bail the following day. Oswald had to pay a fine of $10.[22]

• August 12, 1963: *U.S. News and World Report* featured a headline, "If Peace Does Come – What Happens to Business?"[23]

• August 16, 1963: Oswald passed out leaflets at the International Trade Mart, where Clay Shaw was the General Manager. WDSU-TV recorded this scene, and showed it that night on television.[24]

• August 17, 1963: Oswald appeared at WDSU-Radio on the program, "Latin Listening Post."[25]

• August 21, 1963:Oswald appeared on another WDSU-Radio Program, "Conversation Carte Blanche." This appearance was attended by Dr.

Alton Ochsner. The recording of this broadcast was turned into a 33 1/3 RPM vinyl record and put on sale in early 1964.[26]

• August 21, 1963: Diem declared martial law in Vietnam.[27]

• August 24-27, 1963: A meeting took place among Richard Case Nagell, Lee Harvey Oswald, "Angel," and an unidentified fourth person. Nagell had signed a contract with the CIA in 1962, but found himself, through the CIA, to be taking orders from the Soviet KGB. The KGB had ordered Nagell to "dispose" of Oswald. This meeting presumably took place in Mexico, and apparently was in regard to an assassination plot against President Kennedy.[28]

• August 28, 1963: Dr. Martin Luther King, Jr. gave his "I Have a Dream" speech in Washington D.C.[29]

• August 29, 1963: Oswald, together with Clay Shaw and David Ferrie, drove in a black Cadillac, owned by the International Trade-Mart, from New Orleans to Jackson State Hospital in Jackson, Louisiana. They stopped on the way in Clinton, Louisiana to pick up Estes Morgan, an orderly at Jackson State Hospital. After picking up Morgan, they stopped in Clinton where both Oswald and Morgan attempted to register to vote. Oswald was originally accepted as a voter until they discovered he was not a resident of Clinton. The group then proceeded to the Jackson State Hospital. Oswald carried the bio-weapon (virulent cancer) and observed it being inoculated into one of the volunteer prisoners.[30]

• August 31, 1963: Oswald returned to the Jackson State Hospital to check on the prison volunteer(s). He observed a volunteer, who was different from the one he saw inoculated.[31]

• September 2, 1963: In an interview with Walter Cronkite President Kennedy stated, regarding the government in South Vietnam, "In the final analysis it is their war. They are the ones who have to win it or to lose it. We can help them, we can give them equipment, we can send out men there as advisors. They have to win it, the people of Vietnam, against the Communists."[32]

• Mid- September 1963 to September 17, 1963: Nagell traveled to New Orleans to get Oswald to disassociate himself from the plans to assassinate President Kennedy. If Nagell couldn't persuade Oswald to quit that pursuit, then Nagell was to kill Oswald. Nagell had reached the conclusion that he (Nagell) had been conned by the CIA; and handed over to the KGB to do their bidding.[33] Perhaps Nagell saw that Oswald was working with a secret government-funded project that was trying to eliminate

Castro through injection of a poisonous material (cancer cells); the secret project was directed by Dr. Alton Ochsner. Nagell was going to try to help Oswald. (See September 19, 1963, this timeline.)[34]

• September 10, 1963: President Kennedy convened a meeting to determine whether to continue or terminate a "Commodity Import Program" in South Vietnam. He learned from David Bell, head of the AID Program that the program had already been terminated; in all probability, a decision made by the CIA. It was becoming increasingly apparent that the CIA considered themselves in charge of Vietnam.[35]

• September 15, 1963: Four black children were killed and 14 wounded by a bomb thrown into a church in Birmingham, Alabama.[36]

• September 19, 1963: Richard Case Nagell went to the Post Office and sent 3 letters: one was to Desmond Fitzgerald, CIA; A second letter was sent to another CIA agent, a "nastier note" than the one sent to Fitzgerald; the last one was sent to Lee Harvey Oswald. This letter contained $500 and an airplane ticket to Mexico City. It seems likely that Oswald never received this letter, due to possible government interception. (See November 1,1963, this timeline.)[37]

• September 20, 1963: President Kennedy spoke to the U.N. urging peace proposals and a joint US-Soviets peace flight to the moon.[38]

• September 20: Richard Case Nagell was arrested in El Paso, Texas for firing a gun in a bank.[39]

• September 24, 1963: The US Senate passed the Test-Ban Treaty, 80-19.[40]

• September 25, 1963: A Texas unemployment check for $33, made out to Lee Harvey Oswald, was cashed at a Winn-Dixie store in New Orleans. It was not endorsed by Oswald.[41]

• September 25, 1963: Oswald took a bus bound for Houston, scheduled to arrive there at 10:50 PM.[42]

• September 26,1963: 1:20 PM CDT. Oswald arrived in Laredo, TX, en route to Mexico City.[43]

• September 26, or 27, 1963: Sylvia Odio was introduced to Leon Oswald, by the two Spanish speaking persons who were with him.[44]

• September 27, 1963, 9:45 A.M. Mexican Time. Oswald was scheduled to arrive in Mexico City.[45]

• September or October, 1963: Aristotle Onassis invited Jacqueline Kennedy and her sister, Lee Radziwill, to stay on his yacht, following Patrick's death.[46]

• October 1, 1963: A person identifying himself as Lee Oswald at the Soviet embassy in Mexico City was confirmed from both voice and a picture to NOT be Lee Harvey Oswald.[47]

He was later identified as Ralph Geb, a classmate and football teammate of Mac Wallace, a known henchman of Lyndon Johnson.[48] However, according to Jay Harrison, the person was actually Frank Geb, a brother to Ralph Geb.[49]

• October 3, 1963: Oswald was back in Texas after his Mexico trip.[50]

• October 7, 1963: President Kennedy signed the Test-Ban Treaty.[51]

• October 7, 1963: Robert G. "Bobby" Baker, accused of financial collusion in the awarding of contracts, resigned his position as Secretary to the Democratic majority in the Senate.[52]

• October 10, 1963: The final letter in the Kennedy-Khrushchev correspondence was received by JFK.[53]

• Octoer11, 1963: NSAM 263 signed by President Kennedy; this presidential memorandum would have 1000 American troops out of Vietnam by the end of 1963, and ALL troops out by the end of 1965.[54]

• October 14, 15, or 16, 1963: The day Oswald began working at the Texas Schoolbook Depository, according to Marina Oswald.[55]

• October 19,1963: Oswald called Judyth Baker, telling her that he had become involved with a plot to assassinate President Kennedy; he felt the only way he could prevent the assassination was working on the inside with the plotters.[56]

• October 20, 1963: A second child, another daughter, was born to Lee and Marina Oswald.[57]

• October 23, 1963: The Senate Rules Committee planned to investigate the business affairs of Robert G. Baker, who had been the Senate Secretary under Senate Majority Leader, Lyndon Baines Johnson. Upon Johnson's election to the Vice-Presidency, Baker retained his position as the Senate Secretary.[58]

• October 24, 1963: Madam Ngo Dinh Nhu arrived in Dallas, publicly being very critical of the US in relation to Vietnam and the Diem regime.[59]

• October 24, 1963: Adlai Stevenson, US Ambassador to the United Nations, was spat on and hit with placards at the Adolphus Hotel in Dallas.[60]

• October 25, 1963: Lee Harvey Oswald and Michael Paine attended a meeting of the American Civil Liberties Union on the Campus of Southern Methodist University. At the meeting Oswald said to Paine, "President Kennedy was doing a good job in civil rights."[61]

• October 31, 1963: Secret Service SAC for Chicago, Maurice Martineau, ordered continued surveillance of four individuals who purportedly were planning the assassination of President Kennedy at the Army-Air Force football game on November 2, 1963. Kennedy's trip would be cancelled.[62]

• November 1, 1963: Oswald received his first paycheck from the Texas School Book Depository in the amount of $104.41: on November 15, he would receive his next and also last check in the same amount.[63]

• November 1, 1963: Oswald mailed a letter to Arnold Johnson of the Communist Party of the United States of America; Johnson did not receive the letter until December 27,1963, after Oswald was dead.[64]

• November 1-2, 1963: The overthrow and execution of Ngo Dinh Diem and his brother Ngo Dinh Nhu was accomplished by South Vietnamese generals in a U.S. sponsored coup.[65]

• November 2, 1963: Two men were arrested in Chicago, regarding the suspected attempt on the life of President Kennedy. Only one was identified by name, Thomas Arthur Vallee.[66]

• November 4, 1963: Richard Case Nagell stated "I had a motive for doing what I did. But my motive was not to hold up a bank. I do not intend to disclose my motive at this time."[67]

• November 9, 1963: In the early afternoon, someone who identified himself as "Lee Oswald" took a red Mercury for a test drive from Downtown Lincoln Mercury located just West of the Triple Overpass.[68]

• November 9, 1963: Lee Oswald is seen at the Sports Dome Rifle Range, located at 8000 West Davis, Dallas.[69]

• November 9, 1963: Miami police informant William Somersett had a conversation with Joseph Milteer; Milteer informed Somersett that President Kennedy was going to be assassinated.[70]

• November 17, 1963: Shortly after midnight, FBI Security Clerk William Walter received a teletype indication that President Kennedy would be assassinated on either November 21 or 22 in Dallas.[71]

• November 18, 1963: President Kennedy was in Tampa, Florida, where he addressed a large gathering about the U.S.'s future relations with Cuba. A planned assassination did not take place.[72]

• November 20, 1963: While there were several sightings of "Oswald" between 10 A.M. and 10:30 A.M., three apparently different sightings occurred. In one, Oswald was at work at the Texas School Book Depository; at 10:00 A.M. a second "Oswald" entered the Dobbs House Restaurant, located at 1221 N. Beckley, two blocks from 1026 N. Beckley, Oswald's Boarding house. This Oswald created a commotion after being served his breakfast. Oswald began cursing at the waitress, Mary Dowling; also present for this display were the owner, the chef, another patron, and a police officer, J.D. Tippit. Then at 10:30 A.M., Ralph Leon Bates, a refrigeration mechanic was driving on the R.L. Thornton Freeway where he spotted a hitchhiker, whom Bates stopped and gave a ride. The hitchiker had a package 4-4.5 feet long, wrapped in brown paper, which Bates said should be placed in the back of the truck. The hitchhiker preferred to keep the package close to him; the contents were said to be curtain rods. The hitchhiker asked several curious questions, including, did Yates think the president could be assassinated, by someone placed in a tall building with a high-powered rifle? Yates let the hitchhiker off at the corner of Houston and Elm Street. When Yates saw a photograph of Oswald after the assassination, he recognized the hitchhiker as Oswald, and surmised the "curtains" was a gun.[73]

• November 20, 1963: Wayne January reported to the FBI on November 27, 1963 that a young couple stopped in front of American Aviation at the Redbird Airport, South of Dallas, and they hoped to rent a Cessna 310 to fly to the Yucatan Peninsula on November 22. Sitting in the car alone was an individual who might have been Oswald.[74] Douglas added that part of January's refusal to rent a plane to the couple could have been a concern that the plane might be hijacked to Cuba.[75]

• November 20, 1963: The last telephone contact was made between Judyth Baker and Lee Harvey Oswald. Oswald related that an attempt would be made on President's Kennedy's life in Dallas. Oswald indicated that he had sent out information in an attempt to stop the assassination (perhaps this was the telegram that was sent to New Orleans just after midnight on November 17, received by FBI Security Clerk William Walter).[76]

• November 20, 1963: A formal attire reception was held at the White House for the U.S. Supreme Court. This was also Robert Kennedy's 38th birthday; he came to the White House as the reception for the Supreme Court was winding down.[77]

• November 20, 1963: In Eunice, Louisiana, a woman, Rose Cherami, was hit by a car after been thrown from another car. She talked about a plot to kill President Kennedy in Dallas, but she was ignored.[78]

• November 20, 1963:Secretary of State Dean Rusk, Secretary of Defense Robert McNamara, Chairman of the Joint Chiefs of Staff Maxwell Taylor, Ambassador Henry Cabot Lodge, and General Paul Harkins met for nine hours in Honolulu addressing a post-Diem coup position on South Vietnam. They were working on what would become NSAM-273, which they intended to present to President Kennedy on November 24.[79]

• November 21, 1963: According to CIA asset Marita Lorenz, shortly after 2 A.M. a meeting took place among Frank Forini Sturgis, E. Howard Hunt, Jack Ruby, and "Ozzie."[80]

• November 21, 1963: Several thousand handbills, accusing President Kennedy of "treasonous activities" were distributed in Dallas.[81]

• November 21, 1963: At 10:45 A.M. CST, President Kennedy boarded a helicopter to begin his flight to Texas.[82]

• November 21:1963: At 11:05 A.M., Air Force One was airborne.[83]

• November 21, 1963: At 1:30 CST, Air Force One landed in San Antonio, where President Kennedy was greeted by Vice President Lyndon Johnson and Texas Governor John Connally.[84]

• November 21, 1963: An aircraft carrying several cabinet members (Secretary of State Dean Rusk, Secretary of the Interior Stewart Udall, Secretary of the Treasury C. Douglas Dillon, Secretary of Agriculture Orville Freeman, and Secretary of Commerce Luther Hodges, together with Presidential Press Secretary Pierre Salinger) flew from California to Hawaii, where they prepared briefly in a pre-Asian "economic summit" and then, the next day, began a flight to Tokyo. In flight they were informed that the President had been wounded, at which time the plane was flown back to Hickman Field in Honolulu. On arrival at the Air Base, they were aware of President Kennedy's death. They then flew to Andrews Air Force Base in the D.C. area.[85]

• November 21, 1963: Wesley Frazier drove Lee Harvey Oswald to Irving Texas to the Paine residence after work.[86]

• November 21, 1963: The Presidential Party had finished dinner around 9:30 in Houston. Lyndon Johnson asked Jack Valenti to accompany him to Dallas.[87]

• November 21, 1963: At 11:03, the plane carrying the Vice-President and his entourage set down at Carswell Air Force Base, Fort Worth. Shortly thereafter Air Force One set down at the same location.: Johnson greeted the President on his arrival.[88]

• November 22, 1963: Sometime after midnight, Lyndon Johnson arrived at the Clint Murchison Party. He immediately went into a room with several of the attendees. When he came out, he told Madeleine Brown, *"After tomorrow, those goddamm Kennedy's will never embarrass me again. That's not a threat, that's a promise."*[89]

• November 22, 1963: After departing the Murchison party, Johnson went to an after-hours night club in Fort Worth. Coincidentally, several members of the Secret Service were also at the club, some staying until 4 A.M. According to David Wood, the last Secret Service agent left at 5 A.M. The next tour of duty began at 8 A.M.[90]

• November 22, 1963, 7:10 A.M.: Oswald left his wallet with $170 in a dresser drawer.[91]

• November 22, 1963, 7:15 A.M.: Oswald departed for work, wearing his Marine Corps ring, leaving his wedding ring behind. Oswald was taken to work by Buell Wesley Frazier with Oswald's "curtain rods" No one saw the package as Oswald entered the Texas School Book Depository.[92]

• November 22, 1963, 8:45 A.M.: Desmond Fitzgerald, senior CIA officer met in Paris with Rolando Cubela (AMLASH). Cubela is given a poison pen to assassinate Fidel Castro.[93]

• November 22, 1963, 9:00 A.M.: The final day of the deportation trial for Carlos Marcello began.[94]

• November 22, 1963, 10:30 A.M.: The 118th Military Intelligence Group was told to stand down rather than report to duty in Dallas.[95]

• November 22, 1963, 10;30 A.M.: Sheriff Bill Decker told his officers to stand outside the County Building during the motorcade but to take no part in presidential protection.[96]

• November 22, 1963, 11:17 A.M.: Air Force One took off in Fort Worth, arriving at Love Field in Dallas at 11:39 A.M.[97]

• November 22, 1963, 11:50 A.M.: Texas School Book Depository employee Charles Givens observed Oswald reading a newspaper in the domino room on the first floor while some employees ate their lunch. William Shelley also observed Oswald in the lunch room at that time.[98]

• November 22, 1963, 12:15 P.M.: Carolyn Arnold, Secretary to the Vice-President of the School Book Depository, saw Oswald in the second floor employee lunchroom. At 12:25, she saw Oswald on the first floor, near the front door.[99]

• November 22, 1963, 12:30 P.M.: Lyndon Johnson was in the Vice-Presidential automobile apparently listening to a walkie-talkie.[100]

• November 22, 1963, 12:30 P.M.: Abraham Zapruder is filming the motorcade.[101]

• November 22, 1963, 12:30 P.M.: Shots are fired at the motorcade. President Kennedy and John Connally are hit by bullets. Clint Hill jumps on the back of the Presidential limousine; his assignment was to protect Mrs. Kennedy. James T. Tague is hit by a piece of curbing jarred loose by an errant bullet. The most likely origin of that shot is from the second floor of the Dal-Tex Building, directly across the street from the TSBD. The "umbrella man" shown in the Zapruder film, opens and closes his umbrella almost simultaneous to the shots at the motorcade. The Presidential limousine apparently almost came to a stop during the shooting.[102]

• November 22, 1963, 12:30 P.M.: Several people filmed the motorcade on Elm Street: Abraham Zapruder was on the grassy knoll, Orville Nix on the South side of Elm Street, Beverly Oliver on the South Side of Elm Street, and Elsie Dorman filmed the motorcade from the 4th Floor window of the TSBD. Mary Moorman took a Polaroid picture that appeared to show a gunman behind the picket fence atop the grassy knoll.[103]

Ed Hoffman saw two men behind the picket fence, one with a rifle, who threw the rifle to the other man, who broke it down and put it in a box. After Oswald was taken into custody, Hoffman was told by an FBI agent to "Keep quiet or you might get killed." Only 22 years later did Hoffman tell his story.[104]

• 12:43 P.M.: The Presidential limousine arrived at Parkland Hospital.[105]

In Trauma room #1, Clint Hill was disoriented and walked around the room with a cocked .38 pistol in his hand. Doris Nelson, Supervisor of the

Emergency Room, turns to Hill and exclaims "Whoever shot the President is not in this room."[106]

• 12:44 p.m.: SS Agent Roy Kellerman returns from seeing the President, and confides to SS Agent Clint Hill. "The man is dead."[107]

• 12:49 p.m.: Captain Cecil Talbert was giving orders to seal off the TSBD.[108]

• 12:57 p.m. The last rites of the Catholic Church were administered to President Kennedy by Father Oscar Huber.[109]

• 12:58 p.m.: James Powell, special agent with the 112th Military Intelligence Group, took in Dealey Plaza. No inquiry was launched regarding why he was doing so.[110]

• 1:00 p.m.: Police officers were filmed by Ernest Charles Montesana removing a rifle from the roof of the TSBD. No official record was made regarding this rifle.[111]

• 1:00 p.m.: Dr. William Kemp Clark declared JFK to be dead.[112]

• 1:00 p.m.: J. Edgar Hoover called Bobby Kennedy and told him, "The President is dead."[113]

• 1:00 p.m.: A police car pulled up to Oswald's rooming house, honked and drove off.[114]

• 1:00 p.m.: Butch Burroughs, an employee of the Texas Theater, noticed a man, later identified as Oswald, enter the theater shortly after 1 p.m. Oswald came down from the balcony, purchased popcorn and went to the main floor at 1:15 p.m., where in short order, he sat next to 3 of the 6 other people on the main floor in the theater.[115]

• 1:03 p.m.: Oswald left the boarding house.[116]

• 1:04 p.m.: Helen Markham saw a police car driven by J.D. Tippit driving slowly on 10th Street.[117]

• 1:10 p.m.: Jack Tatum noticed a man walk towards Tippit's police car. Tatum heard shots, and noticed the police officer lying in the street. Tatum saw the gunman walk behind the car and then shoot Tippit in the head. Police found a set of fingerprints on the car; they do *not* belong to Oswald. The only witness that the Warren Commission called regarding the Tippit slaying was Helen Markham who initially failed to choose Oswald in a lineup as the shooter. Reportedly only on the fifth attempt at a lineup did she agree to pinpoint Oswald.[118]

• 1:06 P.M: Deputy Roger Craig, searching the TSBD, heard the police radio with the news that a police officer had been shot; he noted that his watch was at 1:06 P.M.[119]

• 1:10 P.M.: The cartridges found at the scene did not correspond to the .38 revolver taken from Oswald in the Texas Theater. Oswald's revolver had been rechambered to accept .38 Special bullets. When fired through a rechambered firearm, the cartridge is fatter than when fired through an unchambered revolver. The cartridges were of normal size, meaning they were not fired by Oswald's gun.[120]

• 1:10 P.M.: T.F. Bowley, driving West on 10th Street, noticed people around the fallen officer. Bowley got out of his car to help. He noticed that the time on his wristwatch was 1:10 P.M.[121]

• 1:16 P.M.: The time fixed by the Warren Commission for the shooting of Tippit as 1:16 P.M., which contradicted the 5 witnesses and the Dallas Police Report of the incident.[122]

• 1:20 P.M.: Police Officer W.R. Westbrook found a brown wallet next to where Tippit fell. The wallet had identification, including a driver's license belonging to Lee Harvey Oswald.[123]

A driver's license belonging to Lee Harvey Oswald turned up in the Department of Public Safety (DPS) the next week. Aletha Frair and 6 other DPS employees would handle the license. The file was then pulled for Oswald's driver's license in DPS.[124]

• 1:22 P.M.: The alleged murder rifle was found and identified as a 7.65 German Mauser. The CIA discounts the later finding of a Mannlicher-Carcano: "The weapon that appears to be employed in this criminal attack is a model 91 rifle, 7.35 caliber, 1938 modification...The description of a 'Mannlicher-Carcano' in the Italian and foreign press *is in error*."[125]

• 1:22 P.M.: No prints were found initially on the rifle. Lee Harvey Oswald's palm print would later be found on the rifle, though it was not new. Lt. Carl Day, indicated that the print was at least weeks old, if not months old.[126]

• 1:25 P.M.: "Texas law is breached and a critical link in the investigative process is violated. The President's body is taken illegally by force from the proper Texas state authorities by Secret Service agents. Technically, the Federal Government does not have any authority to take the body or to perform an autopsy."[127]

• 1:38 p.m.: Walter Cronkite announced that President Kennedy was dead in a CBS Special Report.[128]

• 1:43 p.m. A bullet was discovered on a Parkland Hospital stretcher. It became CE399, the "magic bullet."[129]

• 1:51 p.m.: Nick McDonald, one of 16 police officers to have entered the Texas Theater, approached Oswald and ordered him to stand. Oswald drew his revolver. A scuffle broke out between McDonald and Oswald. Oswald was subdued after the snap of Oswald's revolver was heard. It was determined that the firing pin was bent in Oswald's revolver. Oswald was escorted out of the front of the theater.[130]

• 1:51 p.m.: Bernard Haire, owner of Bernie's Hobby House, in the back alley, saw the police bring out a young white man dressed in a pullover shirt and slacks. Haire was certain that the man was being arrested. Haire saw the police put the young man in a squad car and watched them drive off. For over 25 years Haire was under the belief that he observed the arrest of Lee Harvey Oswald.[131]

Shortly after 1:51 p.m.: When Oswald would not identify himself, the police took his wallet (this was the 3rd wallet of Oswald in the day's proceedings). Oswald had in his wallet a selective service card in the name of Alek j. Hiddell and a social security card in the name of Lee Harvey Oswald. He also had a FPFC card in his own name, and a New Orleans FPFC card in his own name with the signature of A.J. Hiddell, Chapter President.[132]

• 2:00 p.m.: Lyndon Johnson made several calls, one to Abe Fortas, regarding the testimony of Don Reynolds before the Senate Rules Committee. Johnson wanted to know if Reynolds tried to link him with the Bobby Baker scandal.[133]

• 2:08 p.m.: A heated debate took place between Dallas officials and the Secret Service, who were intent on removing President Kennedy's body from Parkland Hospital. By law the body should have remained in Dallas for an autopsy. The Secret Service forcibly took the body to a hearse in order to fly back to Washington, D.C.[134]

• 2:14 p.m. The casket of President Kennedy was loaded on Air Force One.[135]

• 2:20 p.m.: At the Dallas press conference, Dr. Malcolm Perry said the throat wound was an entrance wound.[136]

• November 22,1963 2:20 P.M.: The Air Transport Wing at Andrews AFB was arranging for Air Force Chief of Staff Curtis LeMay to return to the United States.[137]

• 2:30 P.M. Judge Sarah Hughes arrived to swear in Lyndon Johnson as the new president. Only General Godfrey McHugh remained with the casket through the entire flight.[138]

• November 22, 1963, 2:46 P.M.: General LeMay's plane took off for Toronto. ETA 15:46.[139]

• November 22, 1963, 2:47 P.M: Air Force One airborne (Air Force One, refers to the plane the current president is in; in this case, it is also the same plane that President Kennedy flew to Dallas in. The plane that then Vice President Johnson flew in also returned to Washington, departing prior to Air Force One.)[140]

• November 22, 1963, 2:50 P.M. General LeMay left from Wairton, Ontario.[141]

• November 22, 1963, 2:50 P. M.:A plane with George H.W. Bush and his wife Barbara was allowed to land at Love Field in Dallas. They were delayed, circling the airport until Air Force One had taken off. The previous night Bush had spoken at a meeting of the American Association of Oil Drilling Contractors (AAODC) at the Sheraton Hotel in Dallas. Apparently, Bush was accompanied by Joe Zeppa, a friend and former president of AAODC. The next morning, they flew to Tyler, Texas, where Bush was to speak at a Kiwanis Club meeting, As he was speaking, he was informed that President Kennedy had been assassinated. At 1:45 P.M. Bush called the FBI in Houston to tell them he was calling from Tyler, Texas, and that a James Parrott, a young person who had been volunteering for the Republican party in Harris County Texas, where Bush was the County Chairman had made threats against Kennedy. Parrott was in Houston at the time of the assassination. Bush indicated to the FBI that he would be staying at the Sheraton Hotel in Dallas that evening, November 22, 1963. After getting off the plane (owned by Zeppa), the Bushes went back to their home in Houston by commercial plane service. [142]

• November 22, 1963: 2:50 P.M. A paraffin test was given to Lee Harvey Oswald. The test is positive for his hands and negative for his cheek. A positive outcome occurs because of the presence of nitrates. The handling of boxes, such as a person working in a book depository would often do, is likely to expose them to nitrites and nitrates, which are also likely to be generally present in the environment. Given the number of false positives and false negatives regarding the shooting of a gun, the test as it was performed in 1963 would have corroborative value only. But there was no reliable witness who saw Oswald shoot a gun of any sort from the 6th floor of the TSBD. Police Chief Jesse Curry would eventually state "We don't have any proof that Oswald fired the rifle, and never did. Nobody's yet been able to put him in that building with a gun in his hand."[143]

• November 22, 2:55 P.M.: A printed list of persons who were working at the TSBD showed that four had not returned to the building after the assassination.[144]

• November 22, 1963: 3:20 P.M.: Carlos Marcello was acquitted. He left the court room a free man. David Ferrie was attending at the trial. Later that night, he would drive to Houston.[145]

• November 22, 1963, 4:25 P.M. General LeMay departed Wairton1604 (4:04 P.M) ETA DCA (Washington National Airport) 1715.Secretarty of the Air Force Eugene Zuckert would meet Le May at Andrews AFB. Zuckert was changing the arrival to Andrews AFB so they could properly honor the fallen President.[146]

• November 22, 1963, 5:00 P.M.: LeMay sends the message, "Gen LeMay will land DCA not ADW."[147]

• November 22, 5:05 P.M. (6:05 P.M. EST) Air Force One set down at Andrews Air Force Base with LBJ; the casket was unloaded. A helicopter immediately took off from the other side of the aircraft; its function and destination were unknown. LBJ was flown to the White House in a helicopter.[148]

• November 22, 1963 5:12 P.M. LeMay landed at DCA, was driven directly to the Bethesda Base for the autopsy. In doing so he was disobeying his immediate Superior, Secretary of the Air Force Zuckert.[149]

• November 22, 1963, prior to Dr. James Humes going to perform the autopsy on President John F. Kennedy: Robert B. Livingston, M.D., Scientific Director of both the National Institute for Mental Health and the National Institute for Neurological Diseases and Blindness called Dr. Humes, the lead pathologist, before President Kennedy's autopsy was to begin. When Livingston heard the report of a small wound to the throat, he recognized a wound of entry. He therefore advised Humes that he [Humes] had to dissect this wound very carefully and that, if there was any evidence of shots from the rear, there must have been at least two assassins. At this point in his call, however, Humes told Dr. Livingston that the FBI insisted that they discontinue their conversation.

Not only was Dr. Livingston's suggestion not followed, the three physicians performing the autopsy claimed that they were unaware of a shot from the front, and testified to this at both the Warren Commission and the House Committee on Assassinations.[150]

• November 22, 1963, 6:35 P.M. EST The first delivery was made to the Bethesda morgue of the body of President John F. Kennedy, in a body bag inside a shipping casket. The team leader of this event was Dennis David. The deceased President's body was taken to the morgue where Dr. Humes performed surgery on the head. The body was then removed to a back area.[151]

• November 22, 1963, 7:17 P.M. EST The ceremonial casket was brought in at 7:17 P.M. EST. This empty casket was in the hearse, which was accompanied by Mrs. Jacqueline Kennedy. Mrs. Kennedy exited the hearse as they arrived at the morgue. The empty casket (that it was empty was unknown to the men carrying the casket) was taken into the morgue by FBI agents James Sibert and Francis O'Neil, and Secret Service Agents Kellerman and William Greer.[152]

• November 22, 1963 7:30 P.M. EST The body of John F. Kennedy was reintroduced into the ceremonial casket, which had just arrived. The casket was taken to the ambulance that had brought the President's body in a shipping casket. It was necessary for the Joint Service Casket Team to find the Presidents body so they could accompany it to the Bethesda morgue and not report that the chain of custody was lost. The Joint Service Team then took the casket into the morgue.[153]

• November 22, 1963, 8:15 P.M. EST: The autopsy began. When the coffin was opened, Dr. Humes exclaimed, "It is apparent that in addition to a tracheotomy, there has been surgery to the head area, namely, in the top of the skull."[154]

• November 22, 1963 9:00 P.M: David Ferrie and his young friends Alvin Beauboeuf and Melvin Coffee began a journey to Houston, getting to the Alamotel at 3 A.M. Their destination was the Winterland Ice Rink; David Ferrie was paid by G. Wray Gill, attorney for Carlos Marcello, for his work for Marcello. The money from Eastern Airlines as a settlement in his dismissal as a pilot, plus the money from Marcello amounted to approximately $8700. He was trying to cobble together enough money to start an ice rink in New Orleans; his two young companions had some money, but not enough to reach the necessary amount of $15,000. His spending time at the ice rink in Houston was to familiarize himself with ice rinks. The purchase did not materialize.[155]

- November 22,1963, 11:00 P.M.: Jack Ruby was back at the police station bringing about a dozen sandwiches for the various police present.[156]

- November 23, 1963: 12:01 A.M. Oswald was brought before a Press Conference in the basement assembly room. When Henry Wade mentioned Oswald was a member of the "Free Cuba Committee," Ruby corrected Wade, "Henry, that's the Fair Play for Cuba Committee."

Endnotes

1 Reeves, R.. (1993). *President Kennedy: Profile of Power*. New York: Simon & Schuster, pp. 507-516.

2 Baker, J.V. (2010). *Me & Lee: How I Came to Know, Love and Lose Lee Harvey Oswald*. Walterville, OR: Trine Day 261-277.

3 Brown, W. (2013). *The Chronology*. Hillsdale, NJ: Author, p. 2612.

4 Reeves, pp. 507-516.

5 Reeves, loc. cit., Brown, p. 2612.

6 Reeves, pp. 507-516., Brown, p. 2613.

7 Brown, p. 2613.

8 loc. cit.

9 loc. cit.

10 loc. cit.

11 Baker, pp. 347-348.

12 Ibid., pp. 352-354.

13 Brown, p. 2640.

14 Ibid., p. 2641.

15 Baker, p. 370.

16 Loc. cit.

17 Brown, p. 2668

18 Baker, p. 400.

19 Baker, p. 418.

20 Baker, p. 426; Brown, p. 2703.

21 en.wikipedia.org/wiki/patrick-bouvier-kennedy, retrieved 4/3/2018.

22 Baker, pp. 436-443.

23 The article in the *U.S. News and World Report* addressed the issues in moving to a "peace" economy, particularly on those industries that work with supplying the needs of a country at war. The U.S. had been, to some degree, on a war economy since at least 1942. Not only would those companies supplying the needs of the military be negatively affected, so also would their employees be negatively affected by a downturn by a major reduction in the needs of the military.

24 Baker, p.452.

25 Ibid., p. 454.

26 Baker, pp. 449-456.

27 Brown, p. 2772.

28 Russell, D. (2003) *The Man Who Knew Too Much*. New York: Carroll & Graf pp. 274-275.

29 Brown, p. 2786.

30 Baker, pp. 465-470.

31 Ibid., pp. 476-481.

32 Brown, p. 2814.

33 Russell, pp. 281-287.

34 Ibid., pp. 282-286.

35 Brown, p. 2823.

36 Ibid., p. 2830.

37 Russell, p. 290.

38 Address before the 18th General Assembly of the United Nations. Presidency. ucsb.edu./ retrieved 4/3/2018.

39 Russell, pp. 290-291.

40 Brown, p. 1857.

41 Armstrong, J.A. (2003). *Harvey and Lee: How the CIA Framed Oswald*. Arlington, TX: Quasar, p. 604.

42 Brown, p. 2870.

43 11 H 370-371.

44 WCR 732-733.

45 Brown, p. 2908.

46 Ibid., p. 2911.

47 Sample, G. & Collom, M. *The Men on the Sixth Floor*. Garden Grove, CA: Sample Graphics, 96-105.

48 Brown, p. 2915.

49 Ibid., p. 2919.

50 Ibid., p. 2941

51 Ibid., pp. 2942-2943.

52 Ibid., p. 2962.

53 Ibid, p. 2968. However, NSAM-263 was classified as Top Secret, and would not be declassified until the 1990's.

54 Baker, pp. 505-506.

55 Brown, p. 2989.

56 Ibid., p. 2991.

57 Ibid., p.3002; Williams, J..D. & Conway, D. (2001).*The Don Reynolds Testimony and LBJ. Assassination Chronicles*, 7, 1, 19-28.

58 Brown, p. 3006.

59 Baker, p. 504.

60 Brown, p. 3034.

61 Bolden, A. (2008). *The Echo from Dealey Plaza: The True Story of the First African American on the White House Secret Service Detail and His Quest for Justice after the Assassination of JFK*. New York: Crown.

62 Brown, pp. 3053-3054.

63 Ibid., pp. 3059-3061.

64 Ibid., pp.3063-3066.

65 Ibid., pp. 3067-3068.

66 Ibid., p. 3076; Russell, p. 13.

67 10 H 243-345.

68 10 H 356-357.

69 Groden, R.J. (1993). *The Killing of a President*. New York; Viking Studio Book pp. 155-157.

70 Williams, J.D. (2004). "Was the FBI Searching for Oswald the Day Before the Assassination?" *The Dealey Plaza Echo*, 8, 2, 46-52.

71 Waldron, D. & Hartmann, T. (2005). *Ultimate Sacrifice: John and Robert Kennedy, the Plan for a Coup in Cuba, and the Murder of JFK*. New York: Carroll & Graf, p. 574.

72 Brown, p. 3205.

73 Ibid., p. 3208. Armstrong, pp. 780-781.

74 Douglass, J.W. (2008). *JFK and the Unspeakable: Why He Died & Why It Matters*. Maryknoll NY: Orbis, pp. 242-243

75 Baker, pp. 519-524.

76 Brown, p. 3230.

77 Groden, R.J. & Livingstone, H.E, (1989). *High Treason: The Assassination of President Kennedy, What Really Happened*. New York: The Conservatory Press, p. 122. See also, Elliott, T.C. (2013). *A Rose by Many Other Names: Rose Cherami & the JFK Assassination*. Walterville OR.: Trine Day.

78 Reeves, p. 660.

79 Armstrong, p. 788

80 Brown, p. 3240

81 Ibid., p. 3250.

82 Ibid., p. 3253.

83 Ibid., p. 3256.

84 washingtonpost,com/politics/learning-of-kennedy's-death-while-in-flight/2013/11/21/ retrieved 4/5/2018.

85 Brown, p. 3264.

86 Ibid., p. 3287.

87 Ibid., p. 3290.

88 Brown, M. (1997). *Texas in the Morning: The Love Story of Madeleine Brown and President Lyndon Baines Johnson*. Baltimore: Conservatory Press, p. 166.

89 Wood, I.D. (2000). "22 November 1963: A Chronology," in Fetzer, J.H. (2000). *Assassination Science: Experts Speak Out on Death of JFK*. Chicago: Catfeet Press, p.18.

90 Loc. cit.

91 Ibid., pp. 18-19.

92 Ibid., p. 20.

93 Loc. cit.

94 Ibid., p. 22.

95 Ibid., p. 23.

96 Ibid., pp. 24-25.
97 Ibid., pp. 25-26.
98 Ibid., p. 28.
99 Ibid., p. 32.
100 Ibid., p.33.
101 Ibid., pp. 33-46
102 Loc. cit.; see also Ernst, B. (2012, 2013). *The Girl on the Stairs: The Search for a Missing Witness in the JFK Assassination*. Gretna, LA: Pelican Publication Company.
103 Wood, pp. 45-46.
104 Ibid., p. 59.
105 Ibid., p. 61.
106 Ibid., p. 62.
107 Ibid., p. 66.
108 Iibid., p. 68.
109 Loc. cit.
110 Loc. cit.
111 Loc. cit.
112 Ibid., p. 69.
113 Loc. cit.
114 Ibid., p.71.
115 Loc. cit.
116 Ibid., p. 71-72.
117 Ibid., p. 73.
118 Loc. cit.
119 Ibid., p. 74.
120 Ibid., p. 78
121 Loc. cit.
122 Ibid., p.79.
123 Loc. cit.
124 Ibid., pp. 80-81.
125 Ibid., p. 81.
126 Ibid., p. 83
127 CBS News Bulletin, November 22, 1963. I was standing in line at a bank when this unforgettable bulletin by Walter Cronkite was delivered.
128 Wood, p. 87.
129 Ibid., p. 88.
130 Ibid., p. 89.
131 Loc. cit.
132 Ibid., p. 92.
133 Ibid., p. 96
134 Loc. cit.
135 Ibid., p. 97.
136 Horne, D.P. (2009) *Inside the Records Review Board: The U.S Government's Final*

Attempt to Reconcile the Conflicting Medical Evidence in the Assassination of JFK. Author, Distributed by Amazon, p. 481

137 Wood, p. 98.

138 Horne, p. 481.

139 Wood, p. 100.

140 Horne, p. 481.

141 Baker, R. (2009). *Family of Secrets: The Bush Dynasty, the Powerful Forces that put it in the White House, and What Their Influence Means for America.* New York: Bloomsbury Press, pp. 49-63.

142 Wood, p. 101.

143 Ibid., p. 102.

144 Horne, p. 482.

145 Loc. cit.

146 Wood, pp. 103-104.

147 Horne, pp. 483-484.

148 Fetzer, J.H. (1998). *The Death of JFK, in Fetzer, J.H. Assassination Science: Experts Speak Out on the Death of JFK Chicago*: Catfeet Press, pp. 12-13.

149 Horne, p. 687.

150 Ibid., pp. 604-605, p. 687, p. xxxiii.

151 Ibid., p. 688.

152 Ibid., p.688.

153 loc. cit.

1534 Baker, J.V. (2014) *David Ferrie: Mafia Pilot, Participant in the Anti-Castro Bioweapon Plot, Friend of Lee Harvey Oswald and Key to the JFK Assassination*. Walterville, OR: Trine Day.

155 Wood, p. 115.

156 Ibid., p. 116.

157 Ibid., p. 117.

Chapter Three

TIMELINE NOVEMBER 23, 1963 THROUGH THE JOHNSON YEARS

• November 23, 1963: Shortly after midnight, the police searched for evidence at the Paine's house and garage. Most of the evidence found against Oswald failed the chain of custody test.[1] In this regard, when Gary Severson and I were interviewing Madeleine Brown, she made a statement that I've never heard reported before:

MB: See, through the years, I've met with Marina. Tell me what you want to know. She [Marina] couldn't speak English in those years. And she told [MB] that the police came out and picked up the rifle the next day *after* the shooting. I [MB] said, "Are you sure?" She said, "Yeah."[2]

• November 23, 1963: Around midnight, Lee Harvey Oswald was brought to the press in the basement assembly room at the Dallas Police Station. Henry Wade, Dallas District Attorney, mentioned that Oswald was a member of the "Free Cuba Committee." Jack Ruby who was in the group of the members of the press, shouted, "Henry, that's the Fair Play for Cuba Committee."[3]

• November 23, 1:30 A.M.:Oswald was formally charged with murdering President Kennedy.[4]

On Saturday, November 23, at 10:01 A.M. President Johnson spoke with FBI Director J. Edgar Hoover on the telephone. Hoover first informed Johnson that Oswald had been charged with the murder of the President. Hoover indicated that evidence they had at that time was not strong. It appeared there was someone impersonating Oswald in Mexico.[5]

President Johnson told Senator George Smathers (D-FL). We've got to carry on. We can't abandon this man's [President Kennedy's] program, he is a national hero and there is these people [who] want his program passed and we've got to keep this Kennedy aura with us through this election."[6]

• Saturday, November 23 and early Sunday November 24, 1963: Two versions of the Zapruder film were taken to the Kodak laboratory in Rochester, NY. They were developed by two different groups of employees. The second film was uncut, which implies that the first film was produced from a different uncut film.[7]

• Saturday, November 23, 1963: The autopsy of President Kennedy was replete with errors of omission and commission. It began with the fiasco of entry to the morgue. Kennedy's body was brought in twice, first in a body bag. Douglas Horne inferred that at least two separate brains were used. There appear to be alterations in the X-Ray films. Further, military brass (none of whom were pathologists) barked out directives through the examination.[8]

• November 24, 1963: Ruby received a telephone call at 10:19 A.M. from Karen Bennett Carlin, a stripper whose stage name was Little Lynn. Payday at the Carousel Club was Sunday, but the club would not be open and she needed some money to pay rent and buy groceries. Ruby indicated that he would send $25 by Western Union; he was going downtown anyway.[9]

• November 24, 1963: After sending $25 to Karen Carlin, Ruby went 55 feet beyond the ramp, and entered through the double door Main Street entrance. To get to the basement, Ruby saw two television cameramen having difficulty with their equipment. Ruby helped them and entered the basement with them. Then, the well-dressed Ruby joined the crowd. The policemen and reporters formed a human shield to protect Oswald. Ruby passed himself off as a reporter. Oswald then came into the basement handcuffed to James Lavelle.[10]

• November 24, 1963: Billy H. Combest, a detective from the vice section, saw Ruby lunge past Detective Blackie Harrison toward Oswald. A single shot from point blank range hit Oswald's stomach area.[11]

After the shot, Ruby was taken down by six detectives. Ruby said, "You know me. I'm Jack Ruby."[12]

• November 24, 1963: Oswald was rushed to the hospital. At the hospital, the doctors did all that could be done to save Oswald's life. Meanwhile, Lyndon Johnson, now President, asked that the physicians attending Oswald should try to get a confession out of the moribund patient.[13]

• November 24, 1963: Jack Ruby's reason for killing Oswald was that the mafia made him an offer he couldn't refuse: were he not to kill Oswald, not only would Ruby be targeted for elimination, so also would his brothers, sisters, their spouses and children be eliminated. This was revealed to Earl Warren.[14]

• November 25, 1963: The funeral and burial of President John F. Kennedy occurred with the world in mourning, many watching on television. A bevy of world leaders were in attendance. The burial was held at Arlington Cemetery. In contrast, the burial of Lee Harvey Oswald in Arlington, Texas, drew a few dozen observers, mainly reporters.[15]

• November 25, 1963: Upon taking office, President Johnson was opposed to having a Presidential Commission to investigate the assassination. But by November 29, 1963, he not only embraced the idea, he had appointed all members to the commission.[16]

• November 27, 1963: National Security Action Memorandum 273 was promulgated on November 27, 1963. The memorandum was written by persons who were part of President Kennedy's administration. Apparently, Johnson accepted the memorandum as written.[17]

• On November 27, 1963, President Johnson made a speech before a joint session of Congress, "Let us continue," that has been described as the finest speech he ever gave; coincidentally, Ted Sorensen, a speechwriter for President Kennedy, made major contributions to the speech. In the speech, Johnson heralded many of the points of unfinished business, particularly in the area of civil rights.[18]

• November 27, 1963: The Kennedy agenda may have been the precursor to Johnson's "Great Society" agenda.[19]

• December 6, 1963: Senator B. Everett Jordan, Chair of the Senate Rules Committee, conferred with President Johnson regarding the Don Reynolds testimony. Jordan would try to keep the issue from exploding.[20]

• December 9, 1963: The FBI released their version of the events that took place in Dallas.

Their report was completed 18 days after the assassination. It was 400 pages long in 5 volumes, which makes it sound weightier than it was. The essence of the report was that three shots were fired, two hitting President Kennedy, and one hitting Governor Connally.[21]

• January 8, 1964: This address, The State of the Union Message, covered many points as did the November 27, 1963 presentation to the joint session of Congress, though less eloquent, with the departure of Ted Sorensen. President Johnson continued to press for a civil rights act.[22]

• January 23, 1964: The 24th Amendment to the Constitution, the removal of poll taxes was ratified. It applied initially only to ballots that included federal elections (i.e., for President, Vice-President, U.S. Senators or Congressional Representatives.)[23] In 1966 the U.S. Supreme Court extended the elimination of poll taxes to all elections.

• February, 26, 1964: Originally proposed by President Kennedy in 1963, President Johnson pressed for a new program. Its final form was passed by the Senate and signed into law by President Johnson the same day. The law reduced taxation by roughly 20%. The goals of the act were to raise personal incomes, increase consumption and increase capital investments. It had the added effect of decreasing unemployment from 5.2% in 1964 to 4.5% in 1965 to 3.8% in 1966.[24]

• March, 1964: Johnson, seeming the consummate worrier, continued his concern that the Republicans would try to use the gift of the television-combo set and the advertising for Lady Bird's Texas TV station in the transactions with Don Reynolds, which would continue being a millstone around Lyndon's political future. Johnson continued his harangue regarding the Bobby Kennedy write-in campaign for Vice President.[25]

• March, 1964: Johnson, who entered no primaries in 1960, did not intend to campaign for any of the primaries as President. He wanted to be seen as being beyond partisan politics, a president for all, so to speak.[26]

• March 12, 1964: As an outcome of the write-in votes for Bobby Kennedy in New Hampshire, there was a continued effort to draft Kennedy to become Lyndon Johnson's running mate. There were at least two persons who opposed a Johnson-Kennedy ticket – Lyndon Johnson and Bobby Kennedy.[27]

• June 12, 1964: Senator Hubert Humphrey was shepherding the Civil Rights Bill through the Senate. When Humphrey was sure of the passage of the bill, the cloture vote was taken, the final vote was 71-29 in favor.[28]

• June 19, 1964: Passing the Civil Rights bill was a two-edged sword. Johnson saw that "we just delivered the South to the Republican Party for a long time to come." The signing party for the bill was set for July 2, 1964.[29]

• July 16, 1964: Barry Goldwater accepted the nomination for President by the Republican Party.[30]

• August 4, 1964: The bodies of Michael Schwerner, Andrew Goodman and James Cheyney were found six miles from where they were last seen alive, near Philadelphia, Mississippi. The civil rights workers had been missing since June 21, 1964.[31]

• August 7, 1964: The Gulf of Tonkin Resolution passed the House without a "No" vote. Only Adam Clayton Powell, a pacifist, voted "present." In the Senate, 88 voted for the bill and two Senators voted "No," Wayne Morse of Oregon and Ernest Gruening of Alaska. Curiously, there was no definitive proof that the North Vietnamese had actually been responsible for the actions giving rise to the Resolution.[32]

• August 8, 1964: The poverty bill passed the House on August 8; the Senate passed the House version on the same day. The title of the bill was The Economic Opportunity Act of 1964, with several different threads. It was signed into law by President Johnson on August 20. Included in the bill were Job Corps, Neighborhood Youth Corps, Work Study for lower income college students, Urban and Rural Community Action, and several other Great Society programs.[33]

• August 27, 1964: President Lyndon Johnson accepted the nomination of the Democratic Party for President.[34]

• September 24, 1964: The President's Commission on the Assassination of President Kennedy (the Warren Commission) completed their report; copies would be made available in Early October.[35]

• November 3, 1964: In the election, Johnson won 44 states in a landslide. Five of the six states that Goldwater won were part of the former Confederacy. Johnson was not even on the ballot in Alabama; there the Democrat candidate was "Unpledged Democratic Electors";. Mississippi gave Goldwater his largest victory, where Johnson received only 14.4% of the vote. Goldwater also won his home state of Arizona, but by less than 1%. In the overall results, Johnson received 61.1% of the vote.[36]

• December 1, 1964: A meeting with the Senate Rules Committee and Donald Reynolds took place; it would be the last such meeting of the committee with Reynolds. With a majority Democratic committee membership, and the President winning the election by landslide proportions, the political appetite for additional hearings had passed. The transcript of the committee's handling of Reynolds could still be interesting to researchers trying to gauge the political climate at this point in time.[37]

• January 1965: The building of Lyndon Johnson's Great Society was at full speed. The major components included civil rights, addressing poverty through a plethora of programs, programs in education from pre-Kindergarden to graduate school, the arts and cultural institutions, transportation, consumer protection, the environment, housing, and rural development. This development of the Great Society would continue through Johnson's tenure.[38]

• July 30, 1965: Two major programs were instituted that have become intrinsic to certain populations; these programs are Medicare and Medicaid. Medicare was initially applicable to persons 65 and over who had been covered in their working life in paying into social security (or a 65 year-old or older surviving spouse). Later it would include persons who became disabled, or persons who became disabled prior to age 21, whose parent was covered by social security. Medicaid is a medical program for those in poverty (or near poverty); qualifying for Medicaid has changed since its inception. These programs were signed into law on July 30, 1965. Former President Truman got the first Medicare card.[39]

The war in Vietnam vis-a-vis 1965: President Johnson agonized over the directions of the war in Vietnam, particularly in the months of May, June and July, 1965. Among other concerns, Johnson thought his "Great Society" was likely to be imperiled by the war, due to the greatly increasing demands for more men and more money to pay for the build-up. President Johnson reasoned that the war in Vietnam would end his presidency.[40] As a metric to changes in the conduct of the war during the Eisenhower years from1956-1960, the number of American war-related deaths was 9; during the Kennedy years 1961-1963, the American war deaths were 191; in 1964, the number of American war deaths was 216, and in 1965, the number was 1,928. This was but a prelude to the skyrocketing of death tolls in Vietnam for the final three years of President Johnson's full term.[41]

• June 21, 1966: France formally withdrew from NATO. They returned in 2009.[42]

• 1966: The War in Vietnam and the War on Poverty. The war in Vietnam was necessarily using funds that could not therefore be used on the war on poverty. It was not just the war in Vietnam that was causing funding for the war on poverty to reduce its impact. The perceived slowness of the impact of the programs did not keep pace with the expectancies for improvement.[43]

As to the war itself, it was hard to see any improvement, but it was getting easier to see hugely increasing costs. American deaths went up over threefold from the previous year, to 6350 in 1966.[44]

• May 25, 1967: The USS *Liberty* was ordered to proceed from the Ivory Coast to the Mediterranean Sea near Egypt and Israel. They arrived at this location June 8, 1967.The Six Day War had already begun. The Israelis were supposed to sink the *USS Liberty* (by order of Johnson). The Israeli's tried, but to no avail. Rescue attempts from the military were withdrawn due to Johnson's orders. The USS *Liberty* eventually returned to Malta; a news blackout was imposed. The crew was told never to reveal the events of the attack. With time, they did. This event is undoubtedly among the most heinous in Lyndon Johnson's administration.[45]

• July 23-July 29, 1967: In any given year, riots have occurred, but 1967 wasn't just any year; 159 riots took place. Of those, the Detroit riot was the worst. The city looked like a war zone; the number of police, state police, National Guard and troops from the 103rd Airborne numbered 17,000.[46] During the riot 43 non-police were killed. The one policeman who was killed was, by eyewitness account, the officer who apparently attempted to beat one of two men who were apprehended. The suspect and officer began scuffling, which ended in the death of the officer.[47]

• Vietnam 1967: The American death count for 1967 was 11,363 dead, more than had been killed in all previous years. The war continued as as guerilla war; the North Vietnamese /Viet Cong coalition proved to be not only difficult to defeat, but also difficult to count. Using General Westmoreland's estimate of enemy strength, their numbers were slowly going down, feeding Westmoreland's strategy to win by the enemy's attrition in combatants; however, the CIA's estimate was that their combatants were increasing.[48]

• January 22, 1968: For the first time in American military history an American ship was surrendered during peacetime to another country. The USS *Pueblo* had been stopped inside the 12-mile limit by the North Korean government. The ship and its crew were held hostage for 335 days.[49]

• January 30, 1968: The Tet Offensive was a major surprise to the South Vietnamese and the American military. Much of the territory in South Vietnam was lost to the North Vietnamese and the Viet-Cong, though the territory was mostly back in South Vietnamese control in two weeks. The larger issue was that the American populace became aware that any military victory seemed to be far in the future, if ever. Anti-war marches were occurring with increasing frequency in the United States.[50]

• March 12, 1968: In the New Hampshire primary, President Johnson was on the ballot, though he did not campaign there. One person opposed President Johnson in this primary, Senator Eugene McCarthy of Minnesota. McCarthy was not well known, but he represented an alternative to President Johnson. Johnson "won" the primary, 49% to 42%. McCarthy saw this as a win, and he was encouraged to continue.[51]

• March 16, 1968: Hundreds of unarmed Vietnamese were murdered by U.S. forces, led by 2nd Lieutenant William Calley. Calley was the only participant convicted in subsequent trials. He served 3½ years of house arrest until he was pardoned by President Nixon in 1974. Details about the atrocity were not known to the public for about a year after the massacre occurred.[52]

• March 16, 1968: Robert Kennedy entered the race for the Presidential nomination of the Democratic Party, opposing President Johnson.[53]

• March 31, 1968: President Johnson announced his decision not to seek re-election.[54]

In that same speech, President Johnson said that a request was made for 206,00 additional troops in Vietnam by the military; President Johnson denied the request. Also, President Johnson announced a partial bombing halt against North Vietnam.[55]

• April 4, 1968: The Reverend Martin Luther King, Jr., a winner of the Nobel Peace Prize, was assassinated on a balcony of the Lorraine Motel in Memphis, Tennessee.[56]

• April 4, 1968: At a meeting held in Indianapolis, Robert Kennedy addressed a crowd of mostly black persons, and announced the assassination of Martin Luther King. In his six-minute speech, Kennedy spoke from the heart, giving what has been called, "The Greatest Speech."[57]

• June 5, 1968: In a hotly-contested California Democratic primary, Robert Kennedy won over Eugene McCarthy 46% to 42%. After the California primary, the delegate total stood at Humphrey, 561, Robert Kennedy 393, and Eugene McCarthy, 258.[58]

• June 5, 1968: At the Ambassador Hotel in Los Angeles, Robert Kennedy and his wife were walking through the kitchen pantry on the way to a press conference, when a young man (Sirhan Sirhan) fired 8 shots from his .22 caliber gun. He was apprehended immediately. Robert Kennedy expired 26 hours later.[59]

• June 9, 1968: The coroner for Los Angeles, Thomas Noguchi M.D., performed the autopsy, after he called Cyril Wecht M.D., J.D., a well-known coroner in Alleghany County Pennsylvania. Dr. Wecht arrived and helped with forensic information. Sirhan was in front of Robert Kennedy and was never closer to Robert Kennedy than three feet. The three shots that hit Robert Kennedy were all fired from behind. The fatal shot was 1 ½ inches from Robert Kennedy's ear.[60]

• June 9, 1968: One person who was next to Kennedy, Thane Eugene Cesar, drew his pistol; he claimed he did not fire it. It was Thane Cesar's bow tie that was found next to the fallen Kennedy. The Los Angeles Police Department did not expend much effort investigating Cesar.[61]

• August 27, 1968: The day before the beginning of the Democratic Convention in Chicago, the streets were alive with protestors. Lyndon Johnson had harbored hope that the gathering would draft him to be the Presidential nominee; but the protestors in the streets brought him to conclude that it was too dangerous to go to the convention, and Johnson put out the word that he was declining to be drafted.[62]

• August 28-September 1, 1968: Perhaps the prevailing issue, for those watching the Democratic Convention on television, was the activities in the street. One such instance was a woman removed from a car and beaten by police. Demonstrators and bystanders were sprayed with mace and tear-gas. Many had broken no law, disobeyed no order, nor made any threat. This part of the action has been referred to as "The Chicago Police Riot."[63]

• August 29, 1968: Hubert H. Humphrey accepted the Democratic nomination for President.[64]

• Leading up to the 1968 elecion: Johnson wanted to give the appearance of being above the political fray. It could be argued that Johnson was upset by Humphrey's distancing himself from Johnson's policies, and preferred Nixon. An indication of this was a report that Greek military dictators had funneled more than half a million dollars into the Nixon campaign. Were this information to be made public, it could well have been very favorable to Hubert Humphrey. Johnson chose to not have this information disclosed.[65]

• The election of 1968: Three candidates received electoral votes (The third, George Wallace, Alabama governor, was running in the American Independent Party). Nixon, with 31.8 million popular votes and 301 electoral votes, won the election. Humphrey had 31.3 million popular votes and 191 electoral votes. Wallace had 9.9 million popular votes and 46 electoral votes. Nixon won the election with under 44% of the popular vote, beating Humphrey by less than one percent.[66]

• The last several months of the Johnson Presidency: A rash of bills related to the "Great Society" were brought up and several passed, including the vote for 18-year-olds, elimination of barriers for handicapped persons, a ten-fold increase in low and middle-income housing, protection from toxic, flammable and corrosives gasses, and food stamps.[67]

• Summer & Fall 1968: President Johnson tried to replace Supreme Court Justice Earl Warren with Associate Justice Abe Fortas. Though approved by the Senate Justice Committee, when the appointment went to the full Senate, the filibuster could not be broken; Johnson rescinded the appointment. In 1969, under the threat of impeachment, Fortas resigned from the Supreme Court.[68]

• Fall, 1968: President Johnson was trying to have secret negotiations with the North and South Vietnamese in Paris. Johnson looked to end the bombing in North Vietnam, providing the North Vietnamese government made an appropriate de-escalation. This attempt to make a bargain in Vietnam became known to Richard Nixon, who worried that a settlement in Vietnam prior to the election would bury his own attempt to win the Presidency. Nixon decided to have contact made with the Saigon government. Prior to the election, President Johnson became aware of Nixon interfering with the Paris Peace talks. The talks were being deliberately delayed until the day after the Humphrey-Nixon election. Johnson was also aware of an illegal $500,000 contribution to the Nixon campaign by the military dictatorship in Greece. This illegal contribution was said to have caused President Johnson to become livid. With what little time was left, Johnson made a few appearances supporting Vice President Humphrey.[69]

One situation, that occurred shortly before Lyndon Johnson's death (January 22, 1973) was that President Nixon was trying to short circuit a Senate investigation by asking Johnson to ask the Democratic Senators not go ahead with the investigation, to avoid Nixon releasing information about Johnson, who, according to Nixon, had his and Spiro Agnew's phones bugged during the 1972 election campaign. Nixon was told by Johnson that the FBI did not approve a wiretap; Johnson got only a list of telephone numbers contacting Nixon or Agnew. Nixon was also told that information regarding Nixon's interfering in the Peace talks with North and South Vietnam could be released, as well as the $500,000 illegally received by Nixon for the 1972 election from the Greek military Junta. Had this information been released, the impeachment-resignation process could have been greatly hastened.[70]

- By the end of 1968, Vietnam had cost President Johnson his presidency. More American military deaths (16,899) occurred in 1968 than any other year in Vietnam. The Tet Offensive showed the vulnerability of the American-South Vietnamese forces. The military sought ever-increasing forces, which President Johnson denied. Johnson had proposed reducing bombing in North Vietnam, which candidate Nixon undermined in his clandistine discussions with the South Vietnamese.

Endnotes

1 Wood, I.D. 22 November 1963. In Fetzer, J.H. (Ed) (2000). *Murder in Dealey Plaza: What We Know Now that We Didn't Know Then about the Death of JFK.* Chicago; Catfeet Press, p. 116.

2 Williams, J.D. and Severson, G. (2001). "Interview with Madeline Brown at the JFK Lancer Conference, November 17-18, 2001, Dallas." Available at johndelanewilliams.blogspot.com

3 This correction at the Press Conference can be seen on many different videos related to the assassination.

4 Wood, p. 117.

5 Beschloss, M.R. (1997). *Taking Charge: The Johnson White House Tapes, 1963-1964.* New York: Simon & Schuster, p. 22-23

6 Ibid, p. 25

7 Horne, D.P. (2009). *Inside the Records Review Board: The U.S. Government's Final Attempt to reconcile the Conflicting Medical Evidence in the Assassination of JFK.* Author, pp. 1185-1377

8 Ibid., pp. 389-588.

9 Kantor, S. (1978) *The Ruby Cover-Up.* New York: Zebra Books, Kensington Publishing Co., pp. 123, 131.

10 Ibid., pp. 147-149.

11 Ibid., p.149.

12 Loc. cit.

13 Armstrong, J.A. (2003). *Harvey & Lee. How the CIA Framed Oswald.* Arlington, TX: Quasar, p. 945.

14 Testimony of Mr. Jack Ruby. Taken by Earl Warren & Gerald R. Ford at the Dallas County Jail. mcadams.posc.mu.edu/russ/testimony/ruby/, accessed 8/13/2017.

15 *Four Days: The Historical Record of the Death of President Kennedy.* Denver: Rocky Mountain News, pp. 70-85.

16 Beschloss, pp. 32-61.

17 National Security Action Memorandum No. 273. [NSAM 273] Foreign Relations of the United States, 1961-63, Volume IV, Vietnam, August-December, 1963. history/state/gov/historical-documents/frus1961-63v4/d331, retrieved 8/30/2017

18 Barrett, A. Lyndon B. Johnson, "Let Us Continue" (27 November 1963). archive.vod.umb.edu/citizen/lbj1963int.htm retrieved 9/5/2017.

19 Ibid.

20 Beschloss, pp. 92-94.

21 The document given to the Warren Commission by the FBI can be seen at maryferrell.org.

22 Annual Message to the Congress and the State of the Union, President Lyndon B. Johnson, presidency.ucsb.edu/ws/?pid=26787, retrieved on 9/15/2017.

23 Twenty-fourth Amendment to the United States Constitution. wikipedia.org/wiki/twent-fourth_amendment_to_the_United-States_Constituition retrieved 9/17/2017.

24 Dolan, C., Frendreis, J., & Tatalovich, R. (2008). *The Presidency and Economic Policy.* Lanham, MD: Rowman & Littlefield, pp. 172-176.

25 Beschloss, (1997), pp.271-273.

26 Ibid., p. 309.

27 Dallek, R. (1998). *Flawed Giant: Lyndon Johnson and His Times 1961-1973.* New York: Oxford University Pres, pp. 135-139

28 Ibid., pp. 119-120.

29 Ibid., p. 120.

30 Barry Goldwater accepted the Republican nomination for President. The most quoted statement was, "Extremism in defense of liberty is no vice."

31 Beschloss (1997), pp. 501-502.

32 Dallek, pp. 143-146.

33 en.wikipedia.org/wiki/Economic_Opportunity_Act_of_1964, retrieved 11/28/2017.

34 President Johnson won the nomination on the first ballot; he named Hubert Humphrey as his running mate.

35 The Warren Report initially had a very positive reaction. With time, researchers found that the 26 Appendices had material that was potentially exculpatory regarding Lee Harvey Oswald.

36 Results of the 1964 election can be found in detail in the World Almanac publications, from 1965—1972; with summary data since that date. See also, White, T.H. (1965). *Making of the President 1964.* New York: Atheneum Publishers.

37 Hearings Before the Committee on Rules and Administration of the United States Senate (1964). Construction of the D.C. Stadium, and Matters Related Thereto. Part 1. Testimony of Don B. Reynolds, December 1, 1964. Washington: U.S. Government Printing Office.; Williams & Conway.

38 en.Wikipedia.org/wiki/Great-Society retrieved 1/13/2018.

39 CMS.gov./About_CMS/Agency_information/History/ retrieved 4/13/2018.

40 Beschloss, M. (2001). *Reaching for Glory: Lyndon Johnson's Secret White House Tapes, 1964-1965.* New York: Simon & Schuster, p. 178.

41 archives.gov/research/military/Vietnam_war/casualty_statistics, retrieved 2/15/2018. 41. archives.gov/research/military/Vietnam_war/casualty_statistics, retrieved 2/15/2018.

42 France ends Four-Decade NATO Rift. Newsbbc.co.uk.go/pr/fr/-/2/hi/Europe/7937666.stm, retrieved 12/28/2018.

43 Dallek, p. 350.

44 See [40].

45 Allen, R.J. (2012). *Beyond Treason.* Amazon: Create Space.

46 Sugrue, Introduction: John Hersey and the Tragedy of Race. In Hershey, J. (1968, 1996). *The Algiers Motel Incident.* Baltimore, The Johns Hopkins University Press. p. ix.

47 Hershey, p. 129.

48 McNamara, R.S. (1995). *In Retrospect: The Tragedy and Lessons of Vietnam.* New York: Random House, p. 240.

49 Lerner, M.B. (2002). *The Pueblo Incident: A Spy Ship and the Failure of American Foreign Policy.* Manhattan, KS: The University of Kansas Press.

50 Dallek, pp. 502-513.

51 Ibid., pp. 526-527.

52 Hersch, S.M. (1970). *My Lai 4: A Report of the Massacre and its Aftermath*. New York: Random House.

53 Dallek, p. 528.

54 Ibid., pp. 528-529.

55 Ibid., pp 528-529, 537

56 Pepper, W.F, (1995). *Orders to Kill: The Truth About the Murder of Martin Luther King*. New York: Carroll & Graf Publishers.

57 The Greatest Speech Ever.youtube.com/watch?v=GokzCff8Zbs. retrieved 2/23/2018

58 en.wikipedia.org/wiki/Democrativ_party_presidential_primaries_1968 retrieved 4/17/2018.

59 Wecht, C. (1993, 1994). *Cause of Death: The Shocking True Stories Behind the Headlines.* New York: Penguin Books, pp. 78-90.

60 Loc. cit.

61 Loc. cit.

62 Dallek, pp. 569-579.

63 en.wikipedia/wiki/1968_Democratic_National_Convention#The_Chicago_Police_Riot. retrieved 4/18/2018.

64 presidency.ucsb.edu/index.php?pid25964.

65 Dallek, pp. 577-588.

66 Ibid., p. 592.

67 Ibid., p. 552

68 Ibid., pp. 557-564.

69 Ibid., pp. 579-590.

70 Ibid., pp. 618-619.

Chapter Four

OSWALD'S EARLY YEARS

Lee Harvey Oswald was born October 18, 1939 to Robert Oswald (born in 1896) and Marguerite Clavier Pic Oswald (born in 1907). Lee was their second child. Both parents were in their second marriages. Robert Oswald had previously married Margaret Keating Oswald in 1920, with a divorce on January 3, 1933. Marguerite Clavier married Eddie Pic in 1929, had a son, John Pic on January 17, 1932. Marguerite separated from Pic when she was three months pregnant, in the summer of 1931. Helping her to move out was Robert Oswald. The Pic marriage was dissolved on June 28, 1933. Three weeks later, July 20, 1933, Robert Oswald and Marguerite Clavier Pic were married. Their first child, Robert Edward Lee Oswald, Jr. was born on April 11, 1934. On August 19, 1939, 43-year-old Robert Edward Lee Oswald, Sr. died of a coronary thrombosis, two months before his second son was born.

While Oswald Sr. had worked as an agent for the Metropolitan Life Insurance Company, he was well-paid, particularly during the Great Depression. At his death, his widow had the $5000 from her husband's life insurance policy, a house with a mortgage, two young sons and a third son born shortly after his father's death.[1] This life change for the young widow, during the Great Depression, at a time when there were almost no governmental supports for such circumstances, would likely be seen as catastrophic.

On January 3, 1942, John Pic and Robert Oswald were placed in the Evangelical Lutheran Orphan Asylum by their mother; Lee was too young to be placed there. Lee was at that time cared for by his aunt, Lillian Murret (Marguerite's sister). On December 26, 1942, Lee was also placed in the orphanage with his two brothers, after being tearfully removed from his aunt's house.[2] At the same time, Marguerite Oswald began working at Pittsburgh Paint & Glass, where she would meet Edwin Ekdahl, 20 years senior to Marguerite; they began dating. Marguerite would work at two hosiery shops, until being fired. On January 19, 1944, Marguerite took Lee out of the orphanage; she removed John & Robert from the orphanage in June 1944, and her family moved to Dallas to be near Ekdahl, who had an off-and-on relationship with Marguerite.[3]

On February 1, 1945, Marguerite wrote to the Evangelical Lutheran Orphan Asylum in New Orleans (the same orphanage that her children had been placed in), that upon her marriage to Edwin Ekdahl she would need to place her children back at the orphanage because she would be doing a lot of traveling with her new husband. Marguerite and Ekdahl were married on May 7, 1945. He seemed to enjoy the three boys and they looked forward to being with their stepfather. On July 7, 1945, Marguerite applied for admission to Chamberlain Hunt Military Academy for John and Robert, her two older sons. A month later, the boys were taken to the Academy in Ekdahl's 1938 Buick. On October 31, Lee was enrolled in Benbrook (Texas) Common School, with his birth date listed as July 19, 1939, making him six years old prior to the beginning of the school year; this school district required students to have reached their sixth birthday by September 1 to be enrolled in first grade.[4]

In May of 1946 Marguerite and Ekdahl separated. Shortly thereafter, Marguerite took her two older boys out of the Military Academy, and with Lee, moved to Covington, LA. After the Summer of 1946, John Pic and Robert Oswald were returned to Chamberlain Hunt Military Academy. On September 19th, Lee repeated first grade at Covington Grammar School; his two-month delay in enrollment in the previous year probably figured into the decision to retain him in first grade.

While Marguerite was living in Covington, Ekdahl moved out of the Worth Hotel in Ft. Worth, and moved into an apartment in Fort Worth, apparently with another woman. In early 1947, Ekdahl and Marguerite reunited in Fort Worth. Lee was then enrolled in first grade at Lily B. Clayton Elementary School in Fort Worth.

Marguerite began to get information about the other woman. Several confrontations took place between Ekdahl and Marguerite. In April, 1947, Ekdahl again moved out. At the end of the school year, John Pic and Robert Oswald returned to Marguerite in Fort Worth. The stormy Ekdahl marriage was nearing an end. Marguerite was accompanied by John Pic, and they found Ekdahl with another woman in his apartment in her nightgown. Another separation took place; a reunification was attempted in January, 1948; after the failure of their reunification, they proceeded to a divorce, which was granted on June 15, 1948.[5]

Both John Pic and Robert Oswald returned to Chamberlain Hunt Military Academy for the 1947-1948 school year. Lee initially enrolled in second grade at Lily B. Clayton Elementary School. On March 19, 1948, Lee

Oswald entered George Clark Elementary School (also in Fort Worth). During Lee's first two years of school his grades were As and Bs.[6]

Marguerite Clavier had gone through three marriages and had three children by the time she was 39. Through much of her early adult life, she lived through the depression. Her first husband separated from her shortly after she became pregnant, either because "they just couldn't get along" or "because of her infidelity, consorting with a local automobile salesman in New Orleans."[7] Robert Oswald, divorced from Margaret Keating Oswald, married Marguerite Pic three weeks after her divorce from Pic was finalized.[8] Robert Oswald and Marguerite Clavier Pic Oswald had two children, Robert (in 1934) and Lee Harvey (in October, 1939, two months after his father died). Marguerite was a 30-year-old widow with a 7-year-old son and a 5-year-old son when Lee Harvey Oswald was born, in the midst of a worldwide depression, at a time when there was little social welfare through the state or national policies. Other than family support, not much else was possible. Many able-bodied persons were unemployed. The decision for Marguerite to place her two older boys in an orphanage was not without precedent in these difficult times.[9] Beyond the older boys being in an orphanage, they had spent their school years going to military school away from their mother. This could suggest that coping with the demands of being a single mother without many resources was clearly difficult.

The 1948-49 school year was to be the first that all three brothers were living together and going to the local public schools in Fort Worth. Lee was in the third grade at Arlington Heights West Elementary School. Here Oswald received 5 A's 3 B's 3 C's and 1 D. One former classmate remembered Oswald as a tough guy. Robert Oswald was a ninth-grader at W.C. Stribling Junior High School, where one acquaintance would label Robert as a "very violent person" who was obsessed with the idea that he had to win every fight. John Pic was in the 11th grade. He wanted to join the Marine Corps Reserves, but was only 16. His mother signed an affidavit that John was 17, and John Pic enlisted in the Marine Reserves in October 1948. He then dropped out of high school and began working full time at Everybody's Department Store, where he gave his mother $15 of his $22.50 weekly take home income. He decided to go back to school so that he wouldn't always have a menial job. He re-entered high school in January 1949. He continued in school and attended summer school at Paschal High School. Marguerite began a job at Prudential Insurance in November 1948 that would last two months.[10]

In 1949, Lee attended a Summer camp sponsored by the YMCA. Lee enrolled at Ridglea West Elementary School in fourth grade. Ridglea was a new school and most students were unacquainted with one another. During the school year Oswald was administered an Intelligence test scoring 103, in the middle of the average range. On the Stanford Achievement Tests, Lee Oswald tended to be slightly below the norms. Robert completed the ninth grade and began working full time at the A&P Supermarket. John Pic entered the Coast Guard just three days before his high school graduation in January 1950. He made $80 a month. As John Pic also turned 18 at the same time, his father quit paying the $40 a month in child support. Marguerite began working at Lerner's Shop from Summer 1949 until the time she began working at Burt's Shoe Store in Fort Worth from September 10th to November 24, 1949. Marguerite then began working as a sales representative for the literary Guild at the Cox's Department Store. Marguerite was fired from this job on May 25, 1950, reportedly for creating friction with other employees. The pattern for Marguerite continued; she had no stability in her work life or her personal life. This obviously led to difficulties in her economic situation. She turned to her two older children to try to stay afloat. She began writing her oldest son (who made $80 a month in the Coast Guard) for money.[11]

One other event that took place in the Summer of 1950 is that the Murret's invited their nephew Lee Oswald to spend a couple of weeks with them, the first time they were able to see him in seven years. The 10-year-old Lee rode the train from Dallas-Ft. Worth to New Orleans (and back) by himself.[12]

The next school year found Lee Oswald still at Ridglea West Elementary School and in the fifth grade; at the time, he was one of the taller boys in class. He again took the Stanford Achievement Test, scoring somewhat below grade level. At the end of the school year, Lee had grades of 4 B's, 2 C's and 2 D's. He did seem to have acquired more friends than previously (as opposed to the Warren Commission's assessment that he had few friends).

Robert had dropped out of school and returned to his full-time job at the A&P Supermarket. Marguerite began a new job at the John Luker Insurance Agency. She would work there until March 6, 1952, when she voluntarily terminated this position. Her work was deemed satisfactory. This was perhaps her longest employment in a given job, to this point. During her employment at the insurance agency, Marguerite bought both Hospital insurance and life insurance for herself and her boys. She continued to seek extra money from John Pic. Despite not having any employment for the next six months, she was able to make house payments, buy food, pay utility bills, and take a trip to New York City in September. On August 18, 19-year-old John Pic married his 17-year-old girl friend, Margaret Dorothy Furhman.[13]

In the Fall of 1951, Robert returned to Arlington Heights High School as a junior, and continued to work at the A&P Supermarket afternoons and on Saturdays. Lee entered sixth grade, continuing at Ridglea West Elementary School. This school year seemed to be more productive for Lee. On the Stanford Achievement Test, Lee showed considerable improvement. He scored 7.4 in Reading Comprehension (almost a grade higher than his then current placement); 8.6 in Vocabulary (more than two grades above his placement), but 4.4 in Spelling (two years below his placement). His grades for the year were 2 A's, 4 B's, 4 C's and 3 D's. According to friends, neighbors and teachers, Lee Oswald was a normal boy. He was in good health, got along well with his classmates, very different from the way he was characterized by the Warren Commission.

A person who fed into the thought pattern accepted by the Warren Commission, was Lee's brother Robert, who wrote a book "Lee." In this book, Robert Oswald stated that Lee was living in a fantasy world at age 12. Among other observations, Robert stated that Lee overdosed on watching the television program, *I Led Three Lives,* including reruns. Robert had a falling out with his mother, and left home in June, 1952. On July 11, Robert enlisted in the Marine Corps. Robert stated that Lee watched the program every week without fail. Robert claimed that when he (Robert) joined the marines, Lee was still watching reruns.[14] In fact, *I Led Three Lives* was not first telecast until January 1, 1953. It was continued in production through 117 episodes for three years in the early 1950's. Re-runs began on a regular basis in 1956, showing that Robert Oswald's recollection of his brother's watching *I Led Three Lives* before Robert entered the Marines was without merit.[15]

The Move to New York

Marguerite and Lee drove to New York City in late August, 1952. While she informed her son John Pic of her coming, Pic did not communicate this information to his young bride Margaret; they now had an infant son. Margaret was surprised by the arrival of Marguerite and Lee. Marguerite looked into schools for Lee to attend. A nearby school seemed possible, but Lee demurred, in that negro children attended classes with white children. This circumstance was not part of his experience in the Southern United States. Pic agreed that the school did not seem to be desirable. Marguerite also indicated her intention was to live on a permanent basis with the young Pic family. Margaret Pic politely refused this request, as it would be entirely unsatisfactory. This situation reached a point that the young Mrs. Pic told Marguerite to either move out, or Mrs. Pic would have her brother come over and throw her out. Apparently, Marguerite attempted to enroll Lee in Trinity Evangelical Lutheran School. It appears this enrollment did not take place. Marguerite and Lee moved into a basement apartment in the Bronx. Lee was then enrolled September 30 at PS #117. Marguerite obtained a job at Lerner's in the Bronx and began work October 13. This employment ended on February 7, 1953. She began work again ten days later at Martin's Department store as a salesperson in the shoe department.[16]

Lee Oswald's attendance at PS #117 was erratic, and school officials were addressing what to do about the truant boy. His last day of attendance at PS #117 was January 16, 1953. Marguerite and Lee had moved to another apartment which was in rhe enrollment area of PS #44, but Oswald had failed to enroll or attend. Oswald's continual non-attendance led to Marguerite Oswald's appearing before the Domestic Relations Court on March 12, 1953 (Lee refused to appear with her). Oswald was said to have been ridiculed for his manner of dress and different accent. He refused his mother's attempts to have him go to school. Attendance Officer James Brennan filed a delinquency petition with the court against Oswald. Brennan's intent was to serve it to Oswald at the next court hearing seven days later; Lee failed to appear.[17]

Another Attendance Officer, Victor J. Connell, working in the area of the Bronx Zoo, noticed a clean, well-dressed boy, approximately 13 years old. Connell approached the boy. When Connell discovered his name was Lee Oswald, Connell apprehended him. Oswald referred to Connell as a "damned Yankee." Connell returned him to school; it is not known to which school Oswald was taken. On April 15, Lee appeared with Marguerite at the Bronx Children's Court. When Oswald admitted to being truant from school, the Judge deemed him a truant; he was remanded to the Youth House for psychiatric observation. On arrival at the Youth House, Oswald was first seen by a psychologist, Irving Sokolov, who administered a *Wechsler's Intelligence Scale for Children*; Oswald achieved a score of 118, significantly higher than the test administered in Texas. He was completely co-operative with authorities. He seemed to have made a good adjustment at the Youth House, though Oswald avoided contact with other young persons incarcerated at the Youth House.[18] Oswald was seen by at least two psychiatrists. The most renowned of the two was Dr. Milton Kurian, a former President of the American Psychiatric Association. Kurian interviewed Oswald toward the end of March 1953; in that the interview occurred on Kurian's last day working at the Domestic Relations Court, Kurian made no formal report. This interview took place prior to Oswald's having been placed in the Youth House. The second psychiatrist is the most readily remembered in relation to the JFK assassination; that was Dr. Renatus Hartogs. Hartogs is remembered more for his comments made post-assassination. On this account, the Warren Report is candidly accurate:

> Contrary to reports that appeared after the assassination, the psychiatric examination did not indicate that Lee Oswald was a potential assassin, potentially dangerous, that "his outlook on life had strong paranoid overtones" or that he should be institutionalized.[19] Dr. Hartogs did find Oswald to be a tense, withdrawn, and evasive boy who intensely disliked talking about himself and his feelings. He noted that Lee liked to give the impression that he did not care for other people but preferred to keep to himself, so that he was not bothered and did not have to make the effort of communicating.[20]

The Domestic Relations Court assigned Oswald to Joseph Carro, Probation Officer. Carro determined that Oswald was a small boy, a bright boy and a likable one. Oswald was extremely guarded in discussing certain areas in his life. Lee's problems seem to stem from his difficulty to adjust to his new environment, and his lowered economic status.[21]

An Interesting Encounter with a Border Agent

Probably in February or early March of 1953, on one of Oswald's "hookey" days, Oswald ventured all the way to Niagara Falls, on the Canada-US border. Apparently, the lad had hitchhiked his way there. He encountered a border agent (Customs), and Oswald said he wanted to go across the border so he could say he had been somewhere besides American soil. The border agent was Arthur Young. Young decided to allow the 13-year old boy to cross the border, but first he would need the boy's name and address. Oswald was concerned that he might be reported to the authorities and get into further trouble. Young reminded Oswald that he was an authority, in charge of the border station. After giving Young his information, Oswald was allowed to cross the border, and returned by dusk. Oswald told Young that his dream was to become a spy. Young gave him some names of persons in New York whom he might contact to further explore this ambition. Sometime later, Young contacted Oswald in New York, and they had lunch together. It was after this trip that Oswald was arrested and sent to Youth House. Oswald reported being brutalized in the Youth House. Young would later indicate that he helped Oswald get out of the Youth House. Shortly thereafter, Young moved to Florida. This incident might only be a sidebar, in isolation. But Young would run into Oswald again, on June 24, 1963; Young was the Customs agent who expedited Oswald's getting a passport, brought in from Miami for a day to accomplish this process.[22]

A Visit to North Dakota

During the Summer of 1953, the 13-year-old Oswald along with his mother, took a western trip. During this trip, they spent around two weeks in Stanley, North Dakota. Lee made an impression on several similar aged Stanley boys, and Marguerite Oswald made quite an impression on some of the Stanley women. Most of what we know about this episode stems from a letter sent by Mrs. Alma Cole, mother of William Timmer; after the assassination of President John F. Kennedy, Mrs. Cole sent a letter to President Johnson. Johnson turned it over to the FBI, on December 19, 1963.[23] On December 20, Mrs. Cole was interviewed at her home in Arizona. On December 21 & 22, the FBI conducted several interviews in Stanley, or where particular people moved away, in their new home. Among those interviewed was William Timmer, who was interviewed in Spokane, Washington. Timmer recalled that Oswald went by either Harv or Harvey. Timmer recalled that Oswald was a little older than him; Timmer was born May 14, 1941. Oswald was observed riding a bike with no chain guard, and he kept getting his pants caught in the chain. Oswald wore shabby clothes. Timmer met with Oswald perhaps half a dozen times. Lee showed Timmer a communist pamphlet, written by someone with a name like Marks (Marx?). Oswald was recalled as having been in a couple of fights. He was invited to his grandmother's property, where Timmer and his mother were staying in a trailer; Timmer showed Oswald his pet rabbits. Timmer wanted to introduce Lee to his mother, but Oswald rode off on his bicycle. At another meeting, Oswald told Timmer that he was going to kill the president.[24]

When the assassination occurred, hearing that Lee Harvey Oswald shot the president, the name didn't ring a bell with him, so Timmer dismissed it. Shortly thereafter, his mother (Mrs. Alma Cole) sent him clippings from Dallas, one of Oswald in jail, and the picture of him being shot. Timmer said that Oswald was the same boy he'd seen in Stanley.[25]

Regarding Marguerite Oswald, she had been seen in a restaurant by Cole's cousin, Francis Jeresed. Mrs. Oswald had been in Jeresed's restaurant, where Mrs. Oswald was loud, and wanted everyone to know she was from Texas. Cole also indicated that Oswald preferred being called "Lee Harvey" rather than "Lee'. Timmer was with Oswald when he stole the book by Marx from a small library in a room of the Memorial Building in Stanley.[26] Before returning to New York, the Oswalds continued West, perhaps seeing Yellowstone, but to Lee, the highlight was the Sawtooth Mountains in Idaho.[27]

Back to New York

Oswald and his mother returned to New York from their Western sojourn. Oswald returned to P.S. 44, and his attendance improved. According to his mother, Lee was elected President of his Eighth Grade class. In October, Oswald refused to salute the flag. For that offense, he was termed "unruly;" the incident was reported to his probation officer, and the behavior was noted in his record. Lee's time in New York would come to a close, with Lee and his mother exiting the state on January 10, 1954; a court date awaited him there. They were on their way back to New Orleans.[28]

New Orleans, January 1954 to August 1955

Lee Harvey Oswald and his mother returned to New Orleans and initially stayed at the Murret's residence for a short period of time. Oswald was enrolled at Beauregard Junior High School, in the attendance area for the Murret's home. When the Oswald's moved to 126 Exchange in the French Quarter, where his mother worked at a bar, Oswald was no longer in the Beauregard attendance area, but continued to attend there. His attendance was better than in New York. His grades continued to be somewhat below average; however, he spent considerable time reading, both at libraries and at home. On occasion, he was bullied at school. He still had no close friends, though one friend was Edward Voebel; their friendship began when Voebel assisted Oswald after a larger, older student accosted him on his way home from school. This skirmish left Oswald with a cut lip and a loose tooth. Voebel and Oswald threw darts and shot pool near Lee's apartment in the French Quarter. Oswald also became a member of the school Astronomy Club.[29]

His ninth grade year (1954-55) showed Oswald having a greatly improved attendance record compared to New York.[30] He obtained a job where his mother was working, at the Dolly Shoe Company. Oswald was hired on February 5, 1955 and worked there part-time until he was fired for poor performance on April 12.[31] More importantly, he began attending Civil Air Patrol meetings; the instructor at those meetings was Captain David Ferrie.[32]

Oswald Meets Captain David Ferrie

Before addressing the issue of his interactions with David Ferrie in the Civil Air Patrol (CAP) it would be remiss not to point out that the authors of the Warren Commission refused to acknowledge ANY interaction between Ferrie and Oswald, either in regard to the CAP in the 50's, or any relationship between the two in 1963. This early use of advocacy research[33] was seemingly felt necessary to avoid any interpretation of conspiracy in regard to the assassination of JFK. Were a conspiracy suggested by the Warren Commission, they might not have had a clean report to hand to President Lyndon Johnson prior to the 1964 Presidential election. Apologists for the Warren Report, particularly Gerald Posner[34] and Vincent Bugliosi,[35] denied any relationship between Ferrie and Oswald.

Lee Harvey Oswald became interested in the Civil Air Patrol and began attending sessions during late Fall 1954 and early Winter 1955 at the Lakefront Airport, New Orleans. His instructor was a Captain working for the Eastern Airlines, David Ferrie. Oswald attended several meetings, which sometimes may have involved an invitation to go to Ferrie's house.[36]

On one such occasion, Oswald went upstairs to see Ferrie's laboratory. After the other cadets left Ferrie's house, Ferrie went upstairs, and seeing Oswald alone in his laboratory, Ferrie came in and locked the door behind himself. As Oswald saw the door locked, he thought that he was in danger. Ferrie tried calming Oswald and telling him that he wished to discuss Oswald's lack of a father. Lee remembered what happened to him in New York when he was incarcerated there, and assumed that Ferrie might try to abuse him. He broke a window in order to get a shard of glass to use as a dagger against Ferrie. As Ferrie moved toward him, Oswald poked the shard of glass toward Ferrie. Ferrie, in telling the story, said he was furious at Oswald for disrespecting him and the aggression shown to him by one of his cadets. He decided to teach Oswald a lesson. A brutal fight ensued, in which Ferrie was delivering a serious beating, knocking Lee down several times, but each time, he got up. Finally, Ferrie hit Oswald in the mouth with a vicious blow, nearly knocking him out. Ferrie reluctantly admitted that, despite his intentions, he had an erection.

As Ferrie came to his senses, he remembered that Oswald's uncle was in the mob. Ferrie noticed a considerable amount of blood in Oswald's mouth. He apologized and begged Oswald not to tell on him. He then helped Lee up and noticed that he had a very loose tooth, which might fall out. He also noticed a cut in his gums, which were bleeding profusely. Ferrie explained that he would have to stitch the cut in Oswalds gums. Oswald took the stitch stoically. Ferris told him that if the tooth fell out, Oswald should soak the tooth in milk, and then go directly to the dentist, who could implant the tooth. Ferrie gave Oswald $20 for the cost of the dental services, and gave him an additional $10 for "ice cream." Once again, Ferrie begged Oswald not to tell on him. Oswald replied, "I'm no snitch." Then added, "But I never want to see your face again."[37]

Oswald stopped going to CAP meetings until he heard that Ferrie was no longer involved with CAP. Then he began attending CAP meetings at the Moisant Squadron (associated with the Moisant Airport in New Orleans). Oswald became resolute to meet the requirements for membership in the CAP; upon meeting the requirements he would be eligible to purchase a CAP uniform. To this end, he took a newspaper route to be able to afford the uniform; his aunt Lillian Murret also helped with the purchase of the uniform. Oswald was enrolled as a member in CAP July 27, 1955.[38]

But Oswald and Ferrie were destined to meet again in CAP. Lee attended a weekend bivouac of the CAP in early August, 1955, a session that was also attended by David Ferrie. It was at this bivouac that a photograph was taken, on August 7, 1955, that contains both Ferrie and Oswald. This picture has been shown on television, is available on the internet, and was published by Robert Groden[39] as well as several other places. A relationship between Oswald and Ferrie was denied by the Warren Commission; the need for this lack of relationship seemed to be a central tenet of the Commission's thinking. It is clear that a relationship between Ferrie and Oswald existed back in 1955. In a later chapter, it will be seen, that relationship was continued in 1963.

High School Dropout

In the Fall of 1955, Oswald took achievement tests as he entered Warren Easton High School in New Orleans. His scores in Reading (88) and Vocabulary (85) were better than average. His scores in Mathematics and Science were below average. His stay in high school did not last long. Oswald wanted to enter the Marines even though he had not reached his

16th birthday. He had Marguerite write a letter to the school that they were relocating to San Diego. Oswald tried to enlist, but they discovered he was under-age (It was necessary to be at least 17 years old). They remained in New Orleans for the next school year, though he never returned to Warren Easton High School. He spent much of his time at local libraries reading. He became very familiar with both the Marine Manual and the works of Karl Marx. Oswald also had attempts at employment. In November, 1955, he worked as a messenger for the Gerald F. Tujague Forwarding Company. Oswald quit this job in January 1956, when he took a job with the K.R. Michaels Company, and shortly thereafter, took a job as a runner for the Pfisterer Dental Laboratory.[40]

In August 1956, Oswald and his mother moved to Fort Worth. There, he enrolled in Arlington Heights High School. Oswald went out for football, trying out for the junior varsity team. After practice, the players would run "wind sprints," where the players would run at full speed for short distances (usually, 20-40 yards) and do it repeatedly, purportedly to help condition the players, but also to allow the coaches to evaluate the players speed in quick bursts. Oswald would have no part in this activity; he told the coach he didn't have to run if he didn't feel like it. This encounter ended with the coach telling Lee that he had to turn in his cleats; he was no longer on the team. When Oswald reached his 17th birthday on October 18, 1956, he dropped out of school. He entered the Marines several days later.[41]

Endnotes

1 J. Armstrong (2003). *Harvey and Lee: How the CIA Framed Oswald.* Arlington, TX: Quasar, pp. 13-17.

2 Baker, J.V. (2010). *Me & Lee: How I Came to Know, Love and Lose Lee Harvey Oswald.* Walterville OR: Trine Day, pp. 150-151.

3 Armstrong (2003). pp. 18-21.

4 Ibid., pp. 21-23.

5 Ibid., pp. 23-26.

6 Ibid., pp. 24-25.

7 Ibid., p. 14.

8 Ibid., pp. 14-15.

9 Iibid., p. 17. Orphanages were a common institution in the United States. In the depression and during World War Two, orphanages were a common place for children who had less than two parents. Single parents often lacked either the necessary economic means or the coping skills for the circumstances in which they found themselves. By the mid 1950's orphanages had started going into a steep decline, being replaced by foster care. Very few orphanages still remained by the 1960's. americanadoptions.com/adoptionarticle_view/article_id/4489, accessed 7/18/2017.

10 Armstrong (2003). p. 34-36.

11 Ibid., pp. 34-38.

12 Ibid., p. 38.

13 Ibid., pp. 38-41.

14 Ibid., pp.40-42.

15 en.wikipedia.org/wiki/I_Led_3_Lives accessed 7/17/2017.

16 Armstrong, pp. 50-52.

17 Ibid., pp. 50-52.

18 Ibid., pp. 52-54.

19 Oswald: Evolution of an Assassin. Life, 2/26/1964, p. 72.

20 The Warren Commission Report (WR). (1993). *The Official Report of the President's Commission on the assassination of President John F. Kennedy*. Stamford CN: Longmeadow Press, p. 379.

21 Armstrong, p. 55.

22 Baker J.V. (2010)., pp. 352-353, p.366.

23 Alma Cole letter to President Johnson. (12/11/1963). FBI File Minneapolis 105-2564.

24 Williams, J.D. & Severson, G. (2000a). "Oswald in North Dakota, Part 1." *The Fourth Decade: A Journal of Research on the John F. Kennedy Assassination*, 7 (2), 21-26; Williams, J.D. & Severson, G. (2010). Was Lee Harvey Oswald in North Dakota? In Williams, J.D., Waite, R.G. & Gordon, G.S. (Eds.) John F. Kennedy History, Memory, Legacy: An Interdisciplinary Inquiry. pp. 518-536. Grand Forks: The University of North Dakota. www.und.edu/JFKConference.

25 Williams & Severson (2010).

26 Ibid. See also Williams, J.D & Severson, G. (2000b). Oswald in North Dakota. Part II. The Fourth Decade: A Journal of Research on the John F. Kennedy Assassination, 7 (3). 19-22. Here we interviewed Lyle Aho, a tailor in Stanley, North Dakota, who as a youth met a Southerner named Lee, who was trying to recruit him and one other boy to go Central America and join Fidel Castro. When showed several pictures of Oswald, he identified several as being the person he saw in Stanley, probably the summer of 1955 or 1956. When we finished the interview, Aho asked, "Who is that guy, anyway?" When told "That's Lee Harvey Oswald." Aho still didn't know who that was, until we added, "You know, the person who was accused of assassinating President Kennedy." To which he replied, "Oh." This seemed unsettling to Aho.

27 Personal Communication from Judyth Baker, 12/1/2016.

28 Groden, R.J. (1995). *The Search for Lee Harvey Oswald.* New York: Penguin Books. p 16.

29 Ibid., p. 17.

30 Ibid., pp. 18-21; Baker, J.V. (2014). *David Ferrie: Mafia Pilot, Participant in Anti-Castro Bioweapon Plot, Friend of Lee Harvey Oswald and Key to the JFK Assassination*. Walterville, OR: Trine Day, pp. 67-72.

31 Baker, J.V. (2015, manuscript). *Harvey and Lee: A Discussion; Problem with Proffered Opinions*: The Dolly Shoe Company Opinion. Baker was disputing Oswald's employment as being only part-time. It is clear from the W-2 form, that from a wage of 75 cents an hour, a wage of $78.32 translate to 104 hours (or perhaps 104.5 hours). John Armstrong argued that this was fulltime employment, with a later start time than February 5. Armstrong was trying to establish a second Lee Harvey Oswald, a theory that he expounded in Harvey and Lee.

32 Baker, J.V. (2014)., pp. 67-72; Groden, pp. 18-21.

33 Williams, J.D. (2016). Advocacy Research: Revisiting the Warren Commission. *The Dealey Plaza Echo*, 19, 1, 14-19.

34 Posner, G. (1993). *Lee Harvey Oswald and the Assassination of JFK.* New York: Random House.

35 Bugliosi, V. (2007). *Reclaiming History: The Assassination of President John F. Kennedy.* New York: Norton.

36 Baker, J.V. (2010). p. 143.

37 Ibid., pp. 142-145.

38 Ibid., p.145.

39 Groden, pp.18-21.

40 Parnell, W.T. *Timeline of the Life of Lee Harvey Oswald*. jfkassassination.net/parnell/chrono.htm retrieved 12/15/2016.

41 Grodin, pp. 22-23.

Chapter Five

OSWALD'S MARINE YEARS

Lee Harvey Oswald's military years leave several question marks. The questions generally focus on, just what was he up to? Was he recruited by some U.S. intelligence agency, and if so, when?

How did Oswald go about learning Russian? Was he sent to a school such as the language school in Monterey California? If so, why? Did he study entirely on his own? Why would he want to learn Russian? Did he, at such an early date, think (or know) that he was going to Russia? Some of those questions are addressed in both this or the next chapter.

Oswald enrolled in the 10th Grade, he dropped out of Arlington Heights High School on September 28, 1956. He enlisted in the Marines on October 24, 1956, six days after his 17th birthday. Two days later, he reported for duty in San Diego, California. He was assigned to Platoon 2060 Second Training Battalion for boot camp. This ended in January 1957 when Oswald was assigned to Camp Pendleton for Advanced Infantry Training (AIT). At these camps Oswald appeared to be among the poorest shooters with a rifle. Upon finishing AIT, Oswald was assigned to the Naval Air Technical Center in Jacksonville, Florida, where he was taught radar theory and map reading. Upon completion of this course, Oswald was promoted to Private First Class; two days later, he reported to the Keesler Air Force Base in Biloxi, Mississippi, where he took the Aircraft Control and Warning Operator course. On June 25, Oswald was given the occupational specialty of aviation electronics operator. He reported to Marine Air Station in El Toro California, as a replacement trainee. The amount of training for Oswald appears to have been a bit unusual for a new recruit. He was being trained to be a specialist as a radar operator, a seeming coup for a 10th grade dropout.[1]

On August 27, 1957, Oswald left for Yokosuka, Japan aboard the USS *Behar*. He was assigned to a Marine Air Control Squadron 1 (MACS 1) in Atsugi, Japan. This command was the most sensitive intelligence unit of the United States in the Pacific. Atsugi had the largest CIA involvement in the area. They conducted chemical, biological and psychological experiments on unsuspecting American servicemen. More importantly, the U-2 flights would have been a major rationale for the heavy CIA involvement on Atsugi. Persons in Oswald's role would also track the high-flying U-2 planes routinely. Oswald had clearance for classified information likely up to the secret level.[2]

On October 27, 1957, Oswald "dropped a pistol and accidentally shot himself in the elbow." In April 1958 he was charged with unauthorized possession of a firearm, court-martialed, given a 20-day suspended sentence, fined, and reduced in rank. On June 20, 1958 Oswald again got into trouble – while drunk, Oswald poured beer over the head of a sergeant in the Bluebird Cafe in Yamoto. Oswald was court-martialed again, this time serving out both sentences at hard labor. He was released from confinement on August 13, 1958.[3] The length of time between his first offense and being charged would seem to call for an explanation. His treatment after the second court-martial would suggest a falling into disfavor with his superiors. In any event, after serving his time in confinement, Oswald would soon be released from his position at Atsugi.

From September 14 to October 5, 1958, Oswald and other MACS-1 personnel sailed to Taiwan. There, an incident occurred while he was on guard duty; he thought he saw intruders and shot in their direction 4 or 5 times. He admitted to Lieutenant Charles R. Rhodes "that he "just couldn't bear being on guard duty." Immediately after that Oswald was sent back to Atsugi, reportedly for medical treatment. At the hospital the only medical issue was discharge related to gonorrhea, a problem that he was being treated for prior to his deployment to Taiwan.[4] In the official language of the military, Oswald's obtaining this disease was "in the line of duty." Some have interpreted this to mean that the transaction in getting the disease was somehow "work related." Actually, this notation was to keep him eligible for benefits, such as receiving medical treatment at a Veteran's Administration Hospital. On the other hand, Oswald's gonorrhea may actually have been "in the line of duty."

The day after Lee returned from Atsugi (October 6, 1958) he was transferred out of MACS-1. Oswald was temporarily assigned to a Marine squadron at Iwakuni, a base 430 miles SW of Tokyo, which manned a Tactical Air Control Center for the Northern Pacific area. In case of an attack by the Communist Chinese, the Soviets or the North Koreans, it was the job of the Center to co-ordinate the American air defenses. Owen Dejonavich, a fellow Marine who had gone through radar training with Oswald, recognized him at Iwakuni; Dejanovich found that Oswald had become very bitter. He also noted that Lee spent a lot of time in the evenings with a beautiful Eurasian girl. Dejanovich wondered why such an attractive girl would spend time with a person well below her class. Another Marine in the unit, Dan Powers, reasoned that she was half Russian and was teaching Oswald Russian.[5]

He departed Japan on November 2, traveling to San Francisco, arriving November 15, 1958. Upon his arrival, he took a one-month leave. On December 22, he was transferred to MACS-9 in El Toro, California. Tested on his ability in Russian on February 25, 1959, he did very poorly on this test. Shortly after taking that test, Oswald tested for and passed a high school equivalency test, making him eligible to apply for college.[6]

On March 9, Oswald was promoted back to Private First Class. Shortly after this, he applied to the Albert Schweitzer College in Switzerland for the Spring 1960 Semester. On August 17, 1959, hes applied for a hardship disability discharge, presumably to help his mother, who had reportedly recently suffered an accident. On September 4, 1959, he applied for a passport; his discharge was granted and he was released on September 7, 1959. On September 16, 1959 he was en-route to the Soviet Union.[7]

What was his Relationship to other persons while in the military?

We don't have a diary of Oswald's military experience, so the information is mainly from persons who knew him in the service. And most of that comes from persons interviewed in relation to the Warren Commission investigation. This was, of course, after the assassination of President Kennedy, and Lee Harvey was the accused assassin. Oswald was also dead, having been murdered two days later. The persons interviewed would presumably see themselves as being questioned to establish a rationale for the assassination. They were not being interviewed as character witnesses for Oswald, but rather to mold an understanding of his motivation to commit the assassination. What the Warren Commission found was that Oswald was somewhat unusual, compared to the other Marines. One Marine, Allen Felde, who also enlisted as a 17-year-old who knew Oswald beginning with boot camp, commented that when a group of Marines had liberty, Oswald would go on the bus trip, but would go off by himself when arriving in Tijuana, Mexico and Los Angeles, California. Oswald was not well liked by other recruits. Felde was in the same units from boot camp to the Course in Aircraft Control and Warning Operator at Keesler Air Force Base. Felde said that Oswald would often start talking about some political issue, which was of little interest to his fellow Marines. Oswald tended to be polemic, wishing to debate various topics. It seemed that he didn't care which side of an argument he took, he just liked to argue. Felde described him as being a good talker with a large vocabulary. Felde thought Oswald was hard to understand. He didn't partake in the usual horsing around common to the other Marines. He would just sit on his bunk and read a book.[8]

Marine "Gator" Daniels met Oswald on the USS *Bexar* on the way to Japan. To Daniels, Oswald was just another country boy. Oswald admitted that he had never been with a woman; though it was probably true of several similarly aged men, few would come right out and admit it. He was just a good egg. Daniels and Oswald would become good friends at Atsugi. And Oswald enjoyed camaraderie with other men, something that he had never experienced before. The time in Atsugi was the first (and perhaps only) time that Oswald consumed alcohol, at the behest of his new friends.[9]

Paul Edward Murphy was a Marine who was stationed in Atsugi, Japan and also in Santa Ana California at the same time as Oswald. Murphy was in the barracks in Atsugi on October 27, 1957 when he heard a shot in the next cubicle. He found Oswald sitting on a foot locker. When asked what happened, Oswald replied, "I believe I shot myself." One difference in Oswald's behavior in the two settings is that he was quite socially involved in Japan but reclusive in California. Murphy opined that Oswald was very proficient at his job and kept his area very neat, but lacking in discipline and military courtesy.[10]

First Lieutenant John E. Donovan first met Oswald at the Cubi Point Base in the Philippines, while he was part of the MACS-1 group in Atsugi, then deployed to Cubi Point. Donovan clearly remembered discussing U-2 radar blips with him. Donovan was in charge of the radar crew at El Toro Marine Base in California, where Oswald was assigned when he left Atsugi.[11]

Donovan was a recent graduate of Georgetown University, majoring in foreign service. Donovan's view was that Oswald was not the usual 18-year-old. His interests did not include drinking beer and dating young women; he preferred reading and talking about international affairs. Donovan had heard that Oswald subscribed to some Communist newspapers, though he never observed Oswald reading Communist newspapers. Oswald explained that getting another perspective beyond U.S. newspapers was useful in receiving balanced information about international issues. Oswald would discuss issues with other officers and found them lacking in understanding of those issues. Oswald wondered why they were the leaders. Donovan tried to explain that they were to be proficient in their area of expertise, not in international affairs. Donovan opined that Oswald had an interest in

Castro and Cuba, thinking that Castro could help Cuba in getting a new direction from Batista's dictatorship. Noting that these conversations took place shortly after Castro took power, Oswald's views were not particularly different from other Americans.[12]

Nelson Delgado was a fellow Marine who bunked near Oswald for almost a year, until Lee was discharged, and transferred to Delgado's hut after an issue in another hut; apparently Oswald refused to participate in clean-up. He spoke to Delgado in Spanish, though Oswald's command of Spanish was rudimentary. He thought there was something not quite right about our government. Oswald thought Castro might have good ideas for Cuba, and never said anything subversive. He was mostly a reader and a thinker. Delgado could get Oswald to cooperate in tasks that others failed to gain Oswald's cooperation.[13]

Oswald's Touch of Success

Oswald's marine experience early on was barely satisfactory, particularly with his poor shooting skills. When he started taking his Marine courses in aviation electronics things started to change for the better for Oswald. His next course, in radar operation, saw Lee beginning to shine. At the end of the class, he, after taking the battery of tests, finished 7th in his class of 30. He was then designated an Aviation Electronics Operator. Oswald was then assigned to Atsugi, after a detour to El Toro Marine Base in California, as a replacement trainee.

If we look at Oswald's probable state of mind, one could imagine that he was feeling better about himself than he had previously experienced. When he got to Atsugi, his job had him at a base with significant CIA involvement; he was a radar operator, among other things, monitoring U-2 flights, and apparently doing a good job; his supervisor, Captain Francis J. Gajewski, noted in Oswald's record, six months after he came to Atsugi, "As a matter of fact [Oswald] has done a good work for me. I would desire to have him work for me at any time...he minds his business and he does his job well."[14]

The Queen Bee

The Queen Bee was a bar in Tokyo. It catered to patrons who had significant money to spend. It was one of the three most expensive nightclubs in Tokyo. It catered to elite clients, pilots (including U-2 pilots) and other upper-grade officers and the few junior officers who had significant income beyond their military pay. To take a girl out included not only her fee but also payment to the bar for using her time. There were several (over 100) very attractive hostesses, who typically cost between $60 and $100 for a "date." Oswald's monthly income was around $85. It would seem unlikely that he would have much success with the hostesses.

Oswald told fellow Marine David Bucknell that he had been in the bar alone when he was approached by a hostess who asked about his "top secret" work. Lee reported the incident to his superior officer, who arranged a meeting between him and a civilian (The "civilians" nearby were mainly personnel from the CIA). The civilian told Oswald that the woman was a known KGB agent. Lee was given money and told that he could do a service for his country by giving the woman false information about the U-2 spy plane. Using these instructions, he returned to the Queen Bee and began what was to be his first love affair; he fell head-over-heels in love with this beautiful Eurasian woman.[15]

Oswald began pursuing his new-found love, even bringing her back to the base at Atsugi to show his girl to his Marine buddies. To a man, this relationship amazed them. Oswald, who had little money and little else to offer, with such a beautiful girl? Oswald seemed far out of his league.[16]

This point in Oswald's life may have been when he was perhaps almost ecstatically happy; he was after all living out his dream to be a spy, and he was very definitely doing work that would count as espionage, but he also did quite well in his classes to get there. He was seen as being a valued member of the Atsugi Marine community. And very importantly, he was in love with a beautiful girl, and he hadn't even reached his 18th birthday.

But this was to change. Right around his birthday, he found that his beautiful girlfriend had befriended another American serviceman, a 'buck" sergeant.[17] He also heard that his unit was scheduled to ship out to the South China Sea and the Philippines. A possible Marine landing in Borneo might have been in the offing. This prospect seemed disheartening, perhaps because he might be unable to get his girlfriend back. In any event, on October 27, 1957, just after his 18th birthday, a gunshot was heard, in the barracks at Oswald's bunk. It appeared that a shot grazed his arm, and he admitted that he had shot himself. Perhaps he thought such action might send him to the hospital, and he would be able to avoid being shipped out, and then he could go back to the Queen Bee to win back the love of his beautiful girlfriend.

Still, Lee was seemingly in good stead regarding the Marines. He did ship out with the other Marines in his unit. Oswald seemed to be interested in advancing his career. He was studying to try to pass the test to be promoted to being a Corporal. He did in fact pass that test on January 15, 1958, while they were stationed at Cubi Point, in the Phillipines, their place of deployment. Also on that day, Private Martin Schrand was shot to death while on guard duty. An investigation showed that Schrand was shot by his own gun. It was not possible for Schrand to have purposely shot himself because the gun was too long for this to occur. It was surmised that Schrand accidentally dropped the gun and it discharged.[18] Persons wishing to involve Oswald as a shooter in the assassination of President Kennedy, to bolster the idea somehow Oswald had a propensity to violence, to justify claiming him as the assassin, tried to implicate him in this shooting of Private Schrand. No evidence for Oswald to be involved in Private Schrand's death was found.

Back at Atsugi, Oswald's shooting of himself in October 1957 wasn't going away. Had the gun been a military issue, the incident could have simply been an accident. In fact, Oswald reported that he shot himself with a military issue .45 caliber automatic pistol. The bullet that wounded him was a .22 caliber pistol, a gun that he was not authorized to have. Having an unauthorized firearm on base was a court-martial offense. Oswald was court-martialed. On April 11, 1958, he was convicted of having an unauthorized weapon. Oswald was reduced in rank to private, fined $50 and sentenced to 20 days at hard labor. The 20 days were suspended for six months provided that Oswald kept out of further trouble. Being reduced in rank nullified his having passed the test to move to corporal. Further, his officer in charge, Technical Sergeant Miguel Rodriguez, put him on mess duty, taking him away from working with radar. Oswald was not allowed back to radar duty, even though his officers had requested that he be returned.[19] It was that same Sergeant Rodriguez who Oswald poured the beer on that got him court-martialed and sent to the brig.[20]

A Changed Man

After getting out of the brig, Oswald, according to his fellow Marines, was a changed man. He again became cold, withdrawn and bitter, spending more time with his Japanese friends and less with Marines. Oswald apparently found a new girlfriend, one who had been a housekeeper for a naval officer. Again, she was seemingly out of Lee's class. She was a Russian-Eurasian. Purportedly, Oswald asked her to help him with his Russian.[21]

Recruiting Oswald to Go to the Soviet Union

It was revealed at the House Select Committee on Assassination (1976) that LHO had been recruited by the CIA when he was stationed at Atsugi to be a double-agent in the Soviet Union. This was testified to by James A. Wilcott, a CIA finance officer. Wilcott testified that he had personally handled the funding for Oswald's mission. Other CIA employees denied all knowledge of such a mission.[22] That the other CIA officers would testify that they had no knowledge of such a mission could have been true, but there still could have been such a mission. If they did have knowledge of such a plan, they could still be expected to testify otherwise, to protect the agency.[23]

Endnotes

1 Benson, M. (2002). Encyclopedia of the JFK Assassination. New York: Checkmark, p. 196; Groden, R.J. (1995). The Search for Lee Harvey Oswald. New York: Penguin Books, pp. 25-26.

2 Groden, p. 29.

3 Benson, M. pp. 196-197.

4 Epstrein, E.J. (1975 Legend: The Secret World of Lee Harvey Oswald. New York: McGraw-Hill, pp. 81-82

5 Ibid., pp. 82-83.

6 Benson, p. 197.

7 Ibid., pp. 196-197.

8 XXIII, pp. 797-798. (When Roman Numerals are used as a reference, they refer to the Appendices of the Warren Commission Report).

9 Epstein, p.70

10 XIII, 288-289.

11 Epstein, E.J., cited in Benson, p. 197.

12 VIII. p.105, p. 291, p. 293.

13 VIII pp. 232-233, p. 237.

14 Gajewski, cited in Epstein, p.68.

15 Benson, p. 199.

16 Epstein, p. 12.

17 Ibid., p. 72.

18 Ibid., pp. 75-76.

19 Ibid., p.73-78.

20 Ibid., p. 78.

21 Ibid., pp. 82-83.

22 Benson, p. 199.

23 Weisberg, H. (1974). Whitewash IV: JFK Assassination Transcript. Frederick, MD: Author., p. 62

CHAPTER SIX

OSWALD'S RUSSIAN EXPERIENCE

Getting to the Soviet Union

Oswald planned his trip to Russia no later than March 1959 when he applied to Albert Switzer College in Switzerland. The following summer, he applied for a hardship discharge, stating that his mother suffered an injury, and he would be needed to help her. Marguerite fully backed Oswald's request with a statement agreeing with the earlier statements. After signing a non-disclosure statement regarding classified information that he had access to in the Marines, on September 11 he traveled to Fort Worth to see his mother and brother prior to going to New Orleans where on September 17, 1959, he booked passage on a freighter *Marion Lykes,* which he boarded the next day with passage to La Havre, France. There were three other passengers, a retired Lieutenant Colonel George B. Church (U.S. Army) and his wife, and the 17-year-old Billy Joe Lord, who planned to study at the Institute of French Studies in Tours, France. Oswald and Lord were roommates for the 16-day voyage. Oswald essentially avoided meaningful interactions with his three passage mates. He would answer questions with vague responses or something out of his Marxist thinking (There is no God; the depression was due to the failures of Capitalism). They arrived at Le Havre on October 6.[1]

It is not entirely clear how Oswald proceeded from there. He flew from Heathrow Airport in to Helsinki. There he visited the Soviet Embassy and obtained a six-day visitor visa for the Soviet Union. There is also evidence that Oswald may have traveled to Stockholm to visit the Soviet Embassy there. On October 15, he boarded a train in Helsinki, bound for Moscow: two days later, he arrived in Moscow, and stayed at the Metropole Hotel during his time in Moscow (October 17, 1959 to January 5. 1960).[2]

Two weeks later, he went to the United States Embassy. Oswald was directed to the office of Richard E. Snyder, a CIA intelligence operative. Snyder asked how he could help him. Oswald replied that he wished to renounce his American citizenship, and handed Snyder a handwritten note indicating he wished to renounce his citizenship and swear his allegiance to the Union of Soviet Socialist Republics. Snyder asked Oswald for his reasons. Oswald replied that he was a Marxist. When Snyder realized that he did not seem likely to dissuade Oswald of renouncing his citizenship, he asked questions that might have intelligence use. Among the findings in this discussion was that Oswald intended to turn over classified information from his working as a radar operator in Japan. Oswald's answers suggested to Snyder and another CIA operative that Oswald had been tutored in the process of renouncing citizenship. Snyder told Oswald that he had to come back on Monday of the following week. Oswald did not return, leaving his renunciation not acted upon. The embassy made further attempts to have Oswald to come in, all of which were refused.[3]

Oswald continued to stay at the Metropole Hotel. His main visitors were two In-tourist guides, Rimma Shirokova and Rosa Agafonova. He did have at least two other visitors, Aline Mosby and Priscilla Johnson. The interviews with Aline Mosby, a UPI reporter, resulted in a story that was published in the local Fort Worth paper, *Fort Worth Defector Confirms Red Beliefs.*[4] This story caused a massive investigation by United States intelligence agencies, trying to discern how much classified information had been compromised. A number of codes were changed to avert that. However, whatever information Oswald reported on the U-2 spy plane could be used by the Soviets. Pricilla Johnson's interviews would form the basis on her book about Oswald and Marina Prusakova Oswald, *Marina and Lee.*[5]

Oswald was awaiting his decision to remain in Russia and to become a Soviet citizen. He heard his answer on October 21, 1959: his request for citizenship was denied. Around noon, a police official informed him that he needed to be out of the country in two hours (Oswald had a different timeline in his tome, *Historic Diary*). Both In-tourist guides (Rimma Shirokova and Rosa Agofonova) were trying to arrange for a car and to take Oswald to a meeting at 3 P.M. to attempt to change the decision for his removal from the Soviet Union. When Rimma Shirokova arrived at his hotel room about 2 P.M., she found Oswald unconscious and, in the bathtub, with the water turned red from his cut wrist. He was rushed to the hospital, had five stitches in his wrist, and placed into a psychiatric ward. When he awoke the next day, he complained about his placement in the psychiatric ward. Upon release from the hospital, he was returned to his room in the Metropole Hotel.[6]

The summer prior to Oswald's going to Russia, he was considered a Russophile by his fellow Marines. One date was arranged for Oswald by his aunt with an attractive airline stewardess from New Orleans; she was studying Russian in preparation to take the State Department's Russian examination. She had been studying with a Berlitz tutor for over a year. She found Oswald to have a much deeper understanding of Russian than she. One could imagine that Oswald had some degree of confidence that he might be conversant in Russian when he arrived there.[7] He was in for a surprise. While he spoke Russian very well with another American student, the student-to-student experience is entirely different from student to a native Russian speaker. It appears that Oswald became aware of the distance between his Russian and the native Russians. Oswald spent the next two months studying Russian and practicing with his two In-tourist aids, rarely leaving the Metropole Hotel.[8]

The only important thing Oswald did, other than study Russian, was that, a week after his release from the hospital, he was taken by Rimma to a meeting with four Soviet officials at the Passport and Registration Office. Oswald handed his discharge papers from the Marines to the officials, and was told that he'd have to wait for their decision. Shortly thereafter, Oswald took a taxi to the American Embassy and turned in his passport; he suspected that the Soviets had bugged the Embassy and were able to hear the conversation.[9]

Oswald is Allowed to Stay in Russia

On January 4, 1960, Lee was called to the Soviet Passport and Registration Office and told he had a residency document to live in the Soviet Union; citizenship was not currently being offered to him. He was told that he would be going to Minsk, in Bylorussia, one of the Soviet Republics. Oswald received 5000 Rubles from the Red Cross, and received a 700 Rubles subsidy each month from the Red Cross, and another 700 Rubles from the radio plant where he would be employed. Oswald would later find out that his 1400 Rubles a month put him at the same income level as the manager at the Radio plant. On January 7, 1960, Oswald arrived in Minsk where he was met by two Red Cross officials, who pointed out important places on their way from the train station to the Hotel Minsk, where a single suite room had been booked for him. He also met two new In-tourist aides, Rosa Kuznetsova, a pretty girl, perhaps a year or two older than Oswald, and Stellina, a woman perhaps in her early forties. On the day after his arrival in Minsk, Oswald had a meeting with the mayor, who was greeting him to his new home.[10]

Working at the Radio Factory

Oswald began working on January 13, 1960 at the New Developments Shop at the Radio Factory. Though his first name was Lee, this seemed like a Chinese name to the other workers, so he was called Alik Oswald. There were communication problems initially. None of the workers spoke English, and Oswald's attempts at Russian seemed to be not understandable. But through smiles and body language, the other workers were friendly to Oswald. The Radio Factory produced both radios and television sets for the general marketplace. The Factory also worked for the Soviet military, as a developer and producer of radar instrumentation. This required clearance to work on the classified work. The stream of classified work and non-classified work took place in the same setting. A casual observer would not be able to differentiate the separate work flows. The conjecture could be made that, given Oswald was exposed to this work, it might expose him, were he a spy.[11]

On breaks, the younger workers would gather in the "smokers nook." Though a non-smoker, Oswald would join in with the similar-aged workers. They, of course, had curiosities about this American in their midst. Oswald was still hampered by a lack of expressive abilities in spoken Russian, and he was reticent to speak before a group of his fellow workers, which they had asked him to do. It would be a couple of months before Oswald was more conversive in Russian. Oswald was introduced to an engineer, Stanislav Shushkevich, to teach him Russian. As the assignment came from the Communist Party secretary, Shushkevich took the job seriously, but his skills were lacking in teaching Russian to a non-Russian speaker.[12]

Oswald's interactions with his fellow workers was somewhat unusual. Generally, his fellow workers tried to be accepting of this American who was clearly different from the Russian workers. Oswald tended to be lacking in talking about himself; being an American working in Russia was clearly a novelty. He had no interest in attending compulsory meetings that addressed politics. He preferred to attend opera, or going to other cultural offerings. He would try some of the activities shared by his co-workers. He would go to the area where the other men would play volleyball. When he did get chance to play, he seemed to exhibit very little interest. He went to the firing range once, but he missed the target on all five shots. One observer thought the problem was with the gun, until an observer took the gun and hit the bullseye with 4 of 5 shots. Still, Oswald would go with his fellow workers on hikes and hunting forays on which he seemed to enjoy himself and the company of the other men.[13]

The Apartment

After barely nine weeks, Oswald was given an apartment at no cost to him. It took him some time to find out just how well he was being treated. The apartment he was given, comparatively speaking, was among the very best available in Minsk. Oswald did not know that most Soviet persons would first have to qualify, and then wait years to move to the new apartment. And the requirement to be on the list was severe; where a family currently lived had to have less than six square meters per person (64.8 square feet). If it was found that they had as much or more than this meager amount, they would be removed from the list. Oswald originally thought his apartment was small. It had an anteroom, a living room, a kitchen, a separate bathroom, and a long balcony. The apartment overlooked a green park area, with a river flowing through the park. Within five minutes' walk, there was a large grocery store with a cafe attached to it. The radio factory was an eight-minute walk. There was also a laundry and barbershop within easy walking distance. The opera house was just a few minutes' walk from his apartment. The opera house also had ballets, and special concerts. There was a movie theater nearby.

Oswald would soon find out that his apartment was a 10-minute walk to the Foreign Language Institute, which had a dormitory with many same aged English-speaking females. His flat would have been very attractive to a marriage-oriented Russian girl. Just across the street was a well preserved wooden house, turned into a museum, which was the site of the meeting place of the Russian Social Democratic-Workers Party, first used in 1878, which became the Communist Party. Clearly, the Communist leaders in Minsk had been inclined to go out of their way for this young American, a proclaimed Marxist.[14]

If Oswald had an interest in spying on the Soviet Military, he could have accomplished it from his apartment, as the Byelorussian Regional Military Region Headquarters was also visible. He could have observed the various comings and goings, write down license plates, see the various officers or other interesting occurrences. The down point on this was that someone else with binoculars could have observed Oswald.[15] And of course, the KGB had bugged his apartment.[16]

The U-2 Incident and the Subsequent Trial.

A mission for the U-2 spy plane was carried out on May 1, 1960 over Russia. This was *the* holiday when Russia would display its military might, an important holiday in Soviet Russia. One might wonder what the thinking of the planners were. Were they trying to sabotage the flight and subsequently scuttle the upcoming talks between Premier Khrushchev and President Eisenhower? The U-2 program was under the control of the CIA. The flight was arguably the most dangerous planned by the CIA. It was over 2000 miles, from Peshawar, Pakistan to Bodo, Norway, crossing the Soviet Union when few if any military flights were airborne, other than those in relation to the May Day celebration in Moscow. Gary Francis Powers was flying at an altitude Of 70,000-74,000 feet, far below the typical altitude of 90,000 feet. The higher altitude would probably have put the U-2 out of the range of the Soviet missiles. The plane that Powers was flying had been in a crash barely nine months previously.

The plane was shot down and crashed 1,200-1,300 miles inside the Soviet border, directly East of Moscow near Sverdlovsk.[17] This event occurred just two weeks prior to a meeting in Paris between President Eisenhower and Premier Khrushchev, scuttling the meeting. That this act was deliberate on the part of the CIA has been entertained.[18]

In the aftermath of the hitting of the aircraft, Powers was able to parachute and survive, landing on the ground and soon apprehended by Soviet authorities. Powers chose not to take the poison in the hollow coin supplied to him by the CIA. This non-act got him labeled as a traitor or a coward by some.[19]

The trial of Gary Francis Powers had some interesting moments and one intriguing sidebar. The trial took place July 17-19, 1960. An interesting aspect of the trial is that Powers' behavior was remarkable. The Soviets were in total control of what Power knew. In his imprisonment after the crash of his plane he never had any contact except for Soviets who gave him no useful information, except that his crime could easily get the death penalty. In the presentation of evidence against him, they began with a map, which was claimed to be Powers' flight map. He asked to see the map and inspected it closely. When finished, Powers stated, 'Yes, this is my flight map."

Then, the Commission presented a pistol, which they had determined was Powers,' and he would have used it to kill Soviet citizens. The judge turned to Powers and asked, "Is that your pistol?" To which Powers explained, "Yes, that is my .22 caliber pistol." If Powers had crashed, and was alone in the woods, he could use the gun to shoot birds, rabbits or squirrels for survival. The Commission then surmised that the coin/poison pen would be used to poison Soviet citizens so they wouldn't even know they'd been poisoned. The judge turned to Powers and asked his comments. Powers explained that this poison was also part of his accident gear. In case he was in agony, or attacked by wild beasts, he could end his life quickly and painlessly. (Or to end his life under questioning.)[20]

Powers was found guilty of Criminality Responsibility for States Crimes. He received a sentence of 10 years; three years of prison, and seven years of prison camp. Powers was exchanged with student Frederick Pryor, in exchange for Colonel Vilyam Fisher.[21] This exchange was depicted in the 2015 movie, *Bridge of Spies*.

The sidebar involves Oswald. Oswald claimed to have been in Moscow for a May Day celebration, which would have to have been in 1960, the day Powers was shot down. A more interesting bit of information, which is rarely addressed, is that Oswald had remarked seeing Gary Powers' U-2 in Moscow, which could only have been at Powers' trial.[22] Why would Oswald have been in Moscow for both the May Day celebration and the trial? It was most likely because the Russians wanted him to be there. Their motivation could have been a test for Oswald to allow him to stay in the Soviet Union.

Oswald Meets Ernst Titovets

Ernst Titovets was a medical student in Minsk when he met Oswald. Titovets had heard as early as January that an American was living in Minsk. This was important to Titovets, because his hobby was learning the English language as well as he could. There was only one native English speaker in Minsk prior to Oswald's arrival. She was Mrs. Mary Mintz, a native of the United States, who was on the faculty of the Institute of Foreign languages, where she taught English. Most of the other teachers of English were Russians who learned English as a second language; Titovets noted that, when someone spoke to them in English, there would be a delay while they translated the speaker's English into Russian. They would come up with a reply in Russian, and then had to translate it into English. He noted that Oswald had a similar trait, translating a speaker's utterance into English, thinking up a reply in English, and then translating into Russian to reply to the other person.

Ziger was an engineer and supervisor of the transistor radio department at the same factory where Oswald was employed. Ziger took a liking to Oswald, perhaps because he was a lonely English speaker in Russia. Ziger, who was from Argentina, had Spanish as his native language. He was also fluent in English and Russian; he had invited Oswald to the Ziger apartment numerous times. As it happened, Ziger had two daughters, Eleanora and Anita, whose given name was Anna, but since her mother's name was Anna, her youngest daughter was called Anita, that is, Little Anna. At the Zigers', Oswald spoke Russian when other younger persons present, other than just Titovets.

Titovets, who was called Erick by his friends, was somewhat apprehensive in speaking English to his newly found American friend. They were walking together after leaving the Zigers. Titovets was trying to think of an appropriate statement as they were parting for the night and thanking Oswald for his patience in listening to Titovets. But what Titovets blurted out was, 'I'm going to expose you..." Oswald went ballistic. But as Lee cooled down, he invited Titovets to come to his apartment the following week, on Wednesday September 28, 1960.[23]

Oswald and Titovets Become Good Friends.

The meeting at Oswald's went well, and he invited Titovets to attend "The Queen of Hearts" by Pyotr Tchaikovsky at the Opera House on Saturday night.[24] Again Titovets was impressed by his American friend. He had secured two tickets to the opening night at the Opera House, which would have been more expensive, and a festive occasion. Such events attracted the city's cultural and intellectual elite. At such occasions, the production company would seek the best singers and portray the best works. While Titovets wore his best suit, he imagined Oswald would wear a tuxedo and certainly a bow tie. Instead, Oswald wore a gray jacket, dark trousers, and a full length red tie. Titovets still imagined that Oswald was well versed in classical music, and familiar with the details of performing music. Titovets asked Oswald who was his favorite composer and what was his favorite type of music. Oswald gave a vague answer, and Titovets concluded that it was too early for such questions. As they entered the theater, Titovets saw that Oswald had acquired tickets in the first row just behind the orchestra pit; such tickets were more expensive and prestigious. Titovets was used to being further back, particularly in the elevated (balcony) sections.

As Titovets asked Oswald about his musical interests and experience, Titovets learned that Oswald didn't have any appreciable background in different types of music, or any experience with playing an instrument. However, Oswald seemed to enjoy the evening. Titovets thought this showed that Oswald, whether or not he had been musically educated, thoroughly enjoyed good music.[25]

Oswald and Titovets began spending more time together. One of their favorite haunts was to go to one or another of the dormitories for young women who were attending the Language Institute. Oswald had in fact been doing this prior to meeting Titovets. One of the dormitories was close by his apartment, and he had made acquaintances with the young ladies there. Many of the students (mostly female) were studying British English. They seemed to delight in Oswald's visits, and Oswald enjoyed going to see them. Oswald's Russian was often faltering, but in English he was the only native speaker, even if they were speaking British English. And presumably he could improve his spoken Russian when the conversations moved in that direction. In that Titovits had also been going to the women's dormitories on his own, the pair found another avenue of shared experience. Titovets first interest was speaking to others in English, though the possibility of romance did not escape him. Oswald apparently was more interested in the experience. As a native speaker of American English, his presence was sought. But his Western ways and mannerisms were much more interesting to them than a typical native Russian speaker, even if they also spoke English. In these circumstances, Oswald was the "cock of the walk."[26]

For many of the dormitories this welcome would eventually wear off, but his mystique at the dormitory nearest him seemed to hold. On one occasion, as he entered the dormitory the Commandant (Dormitory Supervisor) asked for his ID. Oswald had forgotten to bring it, and argued that the Commandant knew him, and knew he was no stranger; because the Commandant spoke no English, the conversation had to be in Russian. When she was unrelenting in her demands for his ID, Oswald increasingly became exasperated as his Russian became less coherent. Finally, a compromise was agreed upon; if one of the girls would accept full responsibility for Oswald's behavior, Oswald could remain.

One of the young women came and collected Oswald and Titovets. The group would discuss any number of topics. Then the topic became "true love." How would one recognize it, and did it have to mutual? Could one supply most of the love? When it became Oswald's turn to address this question, he took the view that, if he completely loved a woman, he would not expect the woman to reciprocate. If he could show his love, then perhaps she could accept it, and that might be good enough. Among the four young women and Titovets, there were none that accepted his position as appropriate.[27]

Recording Oswald's American English

Titovet's initial interest in Oswald was to study his American English. Other than Mrs. Mintz, Titovets had never spoken to a native American. British English came from listening to broadcasts on the British Broadcasting Corporation (BBC).

Russian students believed that the English were a very polite and reserved people. This led them to conclude that English did not allow the full breadth of language and freedom of expression experienced by Russian speakers. Were they to have heard Cockney English, it could easily be seen as another language, not only for the accent but for the colloquialisms and local phrases and words. And as Henry Higgins said in *My Fair Lady,* "There even are places where English completely disappears. In America, they haven't spoken it for years!"[28]

In December, 1960, Titovets took Oswald to the Foreign Language Institute with the specific intention of recording his voice so that Titovets could study it. Getting the librarian to co-operate with their efforts was relatively easy. The entered a room where they had the necessary equipment. Titovets gave Oswald some textual materials to read from. Oswald misread and/or mispronounced several words in his Southern US dialect. Upon hearing the recording, Titovets was immediately disappointed with his Russian accented British English speech; Oswald seemed pleased with his performance. As they were relaxing afterward, they began chatting about the girls at the Foreign Language Institute. Oswald remarked, "They are OK, but some of them are goddamn fucking idiots."[29] This degradation into profanity was a cause of excitement for Titovets, in that he was unfamiliar with this type of speech in English, but he realized that it moved into an area of full breadth of language with freedom of expression, which he had never experienced in English before.

Next, Titovets wanted to introduce Oswald to Mrs. Mary Mintz, a native speaker of American English. When Titovets broached the topic with her, Titovets was surprized by her emotional outburst in denying such an introduction. Mrs. Mintz said that he was an uneducated and uncultured man. Oswald turned out to be the only native English-speaking person that Mrs. Mintz refused to meet.[30]

Ella German

Ella German was also a worker at the same radio factory where Oswald was employed. She was Jewish and just over a year older than Oswald. They did not meet until April 1960, when she came to the radio factory on her day off to meet with two of her young women friends who worked there. Oswald happened to be walking by. The young women wished to introduce Ella to the American named Alik. Shortly after they were introduced, Oswald was called back to work. Soon, Oswald began persistently trying to gain her attention. He would wait outside the factory until Ella came out, and walk her home. Then he began taking her on walks through the streets or to a park. He would also take her to a movie or to the theater. Then one day, he invited Ella to his bachelor's flat. They listened to classical music. Ella was impressed with his interest in classical music, but also that he did not attempt to make any advances toward her. During summertime, they would go to a secluded park where they would sit side-by-side by a bay and absorb the beauty of the natural setting. Very few words were spoken; Oswald would gently kiss her lips, musing, this must be the reason he came to Russia, to meet this wonderful woman. To Oswald's way of thinking, this slow-moving romance seemed to be going well. Still, although he walked Ella home regularly, he had never met her parents.

On New Year's Eve 1960, Lee met Ella in the afternoon in a park and informed her they would not be going to a party at a friend's place that they had planned to attend. An argument ensued, and Ella walked off, telling Lee that he was free to do whatever he pleased. Lee arrived at Ella's home several hours later with gifts for Ella and to apologize for his behavior.

Oswald told Ella that he would give her the gifts and go back to his apartment, perhaps hoping that he might be invited in. Ella asked her family if they might invite Oswald to their party. His ruse worked. Oswald met Ella's family for the first time. The evening was all that Oswald could have wished. When he walked to his apartment, full of great food and drink, he decided to propose to Ella. On January 2, the two of them went to the cinema. When arriving at Ella's doorstep, Oswald proposed. Ella, hesitated and then said "No." She explained, "Someday, you may be arrested simply because you are an American." As Oswald turned to go, he noticeds Ella snicker as he awkwardly left.[31] Oswald later wrote in his diary, "I am miserable about Ella. I love her but what can I do."[32]

Oswald was taking stock of his future, and his future was coming fast. January 4, 1961 would be his first anniversary of getting a residency permit. And he would have to decide, just two days after his proposal to Ella German was turned down, whether to apply for Soviet citizenship, or to get a one-year extension on his present residency permit. He considered that if he chose the latter, the first option may not be offered again. If he chose Soviet citizenship, getting back to the United States could become complicated.

This all goes back to his original intent when coming to the Soviet Union. Was he offered a return to the United States as was suggested to him back at Atsugi, Japan by the CIA? Was he irrevocably preferring to remain in the

Soviet Union? We can address these questions by his behavior in the Soviet Union. He decided not to formally go through the process of renouncing his American citizenship when he first arrived. There are other aspects of his lack of interest in remaining permanently in the Soviet Union. In the daily routine of working in the Radio Factory, he disliked the 10 minutes of exercise that was mandatory for all workers. It wasn't the exercise that he quarreled with, it was that the exercise was mandatory. He saw this as an imposition. He also fervently disliked the mandatory sessions held on the political structures of the Soviet Union, again, because they were mandatory. The Russian youths were accepting of them, because they could read a book or other sedentary activity such as studying for a class. Oswald had to do these two mandatory requirements, but as a non-citizen he was excused from the mandatory weekend work effort at the State Collective farms that other workers were obliged to. Further, though he was paid well, there were few interesting things that he could spend the money on. There were no bowling alleys, or many other activities that were readily accessible in the United States.

And he was particularly tired of being the novelty American, who people would come and stare at, or ask him endless questions. And yes, he longed to see and speak to Americans again. As he reflected on his options his choice was clear, particularly since perhaps the only person who could keep him in the Soviet Union had rejected his offer of marriage. If Oswald came to Russia as a starry-eyed believer in the Soviet system, the everyday reality of life there was stultifying. Oswald chose to get a one-year extension on his residency. The die was cast. On February 1, 1961, Oswald wrote the U.S. Embassy in Moscow that he wished to return to the United States. Oswald was told that he needed to come to Moscow to start the process. But to go to Moscow, he would need state permission to go there.[33]

Socialism vs. Capitalism and Who's Army is Better?

Titovets and Oswald became involved in discussion about the difference in the lives of persons in the two systems, Russian Socialism and American Capitalism. Titovets got in licks on the issue of slavery, on the plight of blacks in America, given that there were no segregation issues in the Soviet Union. Oswald conceded on this point, but with the caveat that Titovets had too little information about the topic to form a qualified opinion. As Titovets kept expounding on the superiority of the Soviet system, Oswald countered with, "You can't say it surely because you're influenced with your breeding and education. You don't know some of the negative features of the socialist system! You can't go abroad! You live like those slaves!"[34]

This 'debate' occurred on January 8, 1960. Oswald's remarks gave flesh to his decision to no longer seek Russian citizenship. It could be conjectured that only the possible relationship with Ella German could keep him in Russia; barring that, Oswald's 14-month sojourn in Russia convinced him that the Soviet system had more problems than he had imagined; he wished to return to the United States. Titovets concluded that Oswald's thinking was firmly based in the West, which was more suited to him than Soviet Russia. Titovets mused that Oswald was better prepared in their debate in that he was more conciliatory to good points about the Soviet system, something that Titovets had not even considered about American society.[35]

Five days later, the two got together and played army games, using drills from their own experiences. Both thought they proved to the other, the superiority of their own systems.[36]

On Sunday, March 12, 1961, Oswald and Titovets went to see the University of Michigan Philharmonic Wind Band. Oswald had obtained the tickets from his Minsk In-tourist guides, Rosa and Stellina. This appearance by any American group in Minsk was highly unusual; Oswald was very happy to get to see some Americans – it had been a year and a-half since he had any interaction with one. Upon the conclusion of the concert, Oswald quickly went to the stage where the band was standing, and immediately tried to connect to the band members. Oswald seemed contrite. He began by saying he was an American living in Minsk. The Americans were caught by surprise by Oswald's revelations. Nobody came forward to embrace the newly found countryman. Their smiles turned to masks and they turned to go away. The eagerly anticipated meeting with his countrymen had to have been disappointing.[37]

Oswald Meets Marina Prussakova

Oswald and Titovets went to a lecture on March 17, 1961 by Professor Lydia Cherkasova, who had accompanied the Soviet delegation to the 15th anniversary of the United Nations. To Americans this was best known for Premier Khrushchev taking off his shoe and pounding it on his desk. While this incident was widely reported in the West, no mention of it was made in the Soviet Union. While Oswald was very interested in the lecture, as he was looking for any information about his homeland, Titovets was not interested in another lecture by a Communist Party member; Titovets' main interest was in attending the dance, and perhaps meeting girls.

The generic version of the events of that evening was that Oswald, after attending the lecture, went to the dance hall where he saw a very attractive girl in a red dress and white shoes with at least four young men vying for her attention, went up to her and asked her to dance and proceeded to keep her away from her other suitors. At one point, he sought out Titovets to come and translate for him. Oswald asked her to repeat her telephone number, something he could clearly have done on his own. More likely, Oswald wanted Titovets to get a glimpse at the attractive young woman he had found. Later, Oswald, Marina, and her several suitors went to Professor Cherkasova's apartment to talk with her and partake in the after-lecture party. Then either Oswald and Sasha Peshkarev, or Oswald by himself walked Marina home. A slightly amended report would include Oswald somehow finding his way through a labyrinth and joining Yuri Merezhinsk, the son of Lydia Cherkasova in the orchestra pit and helping him with the slides for the lectures.[38]

Titovets mused about what he knew, and what he had learned when he tried to find the entrance to the orchestra pit – virtually no one could have found the right door that eventually opened up to the orchestra pit, particularly on their first try. Also, the coincidences seemed to be too improbable. Then putting together observations he had, including that many people known to Oswald were either reporting to the Communist Party, or were party regulars themselves. Oswald's apartment and many of the other places he frequented were bugged, including the radio factory, since Oswald declined to seek Soviet citizenship, and had begun contacting the American Embassy in Moscow (which was also bugged), what may have seemed coincidental could have been well planned. By listening to Oswald's casual conversations, the KGB would know his preference for flashy girls. As for Marina, she lived with her uncle, who was a Party member, and knowing more about Marina was useful. At 18, Marina had completed training as a pharmacy assistant, had lived in Leningrad for a short period until she was expelled to Minsk for prostitution, and had been quite sexually active in Minsk. Perhaps they could rid themselves of both Oswald and Marina if they would marry and go back to the United States. As for the young men vying for Marina's attention, this was to draw Oswald's attention to Marina. Most of the young men vying for her attention had already experienced sex with Marina. And Cherkasova, her husband and her son were all Party members. Oswald's supervisor at work was a party member. Oswald was the target at the dance.[39]

Endnotes

1 Epstein, E.J. (1978). *Legend: The Secret World of Lee Harvey Oswald.* New York: McGraw-Hill, pp. 89-93.

2 Ibid., 94-104.

3 Ibid., p. 97.

4 Ibid., pp. 98-101.

5 Johnson, P. (1977). *Marina and Lee. New York*: HarperCollins.

6 Wronski, P. (1991-2004). *Lee Harvey Oswald in Russia: Part Two*. Author: russianbooks.org.

7 Epstein, p. 87.

8 Ibid., p. 107.

9 Loc. cit.

10 Ibid., pp. 107-108. Titovets, E. (2010). *Oswald Russian Episode.* Minsk, Belarus: Mon Litera Publishing House, pp. 36-38. Ernst Titovets was a young man, close in age to Oswald, and a medical student, and who was Oswald's best friend in Russia. Titovets would gain his medical degree, and would eventually also gather two more doctorates, a Ph.D. in biochemistry and a D.Sc. in medical research. He wrote several books regarding his medical research, as well as many scientific articles. He began writing his book on Oswald in the 1990's. It was published in 2010 in Russian and English versions.

11 Titovets, pp. 46-48.

12 Ibid., pp. 48-49. Shushkovetch would, in 1991, become the first Premier of the newly established independent nation, Belarus. email from E.P. Titovets, 7/11/2019.

13 Ibid., pp. 48-55.

14 Ibid., pp. 56-60.

15 Ibid., p. 60.

16 Ibid., p. 61.

17 The U-2 Incident. mtholyoke.edu/acad/intrel/U2.htm

18 Marrs, J. (1989). *Crossfire: The Plot that Killed Kennedy.* New York: Carroll & Graf, p. 114.

19 Sibilla, C. (2013). Moments in U.S. Diplomatic History: The Show Trial of U-2 Pilot Gary Francis Powers. adst.org/2013/01/the-show-trial-of-Gary-Francis-Powers. accessed 1/27/2017.

20 Ibid.

21 Ibid.

22 Epstein, pp. 121-122.

23 Titovets, pp. 87-100.

24 Ibid., pp. 101-104.

25 Ibid., pp. 105-113.

26 Ibid., pp. 114-134.

27 Ibid., pp. 134-137.

28 *My Fair Lady*, Motion picture (1964).

29 Titovets, p. 152.

30 Ibid., pp. 146-155

31 Ibid., pp. 63-66, 156-158.

32 Oswald's Historic Diary, WCE XXIV, p. 101.

33 Titovets, pp. 166-174.

34 Ibid., pp. 178-179.

35 Ibid., pp. 179-180.

36 Ibid., pp. 182-187.

37 Ibid., pp. 210-216.

38 Ibid., pp. 246-247.

39 Ibid., pp. 250-260. The city of St. Petersburg had been renamed Leningrad during the Soviet era; it has since reverted back to St. Petersburg.

Chapter Seven

OSWALD RETURNS TO THE USA

The SS *Maasdam* arrived in port at Hoboken, New Jersey on June 13, 1962.[1] Waiting was Spas T. Raikin. According to the Warren Commission, Raikin worked for the Travelers Aid Society, and had been asked by the State Department to meet with the Oswalds.[2] Raikin was more than an assistant to travelers; he was born in Bulgaria and became involved in anti-communist activities both in Bulgaria and the United States. At the time of Oswald's arrival, Raikin was the Secretary-General of the American Friends of Anti-Bolshevik Nations, a private anti-communist organization with considerable intelligence relationships.[3] In 1966, Raikin started teaching at East Stroudsburg State University, where he taught for 25 years and had 20 books published on Bulgarian history and politics.[4]

Oswald tried to avoid meeting with Raikin and was uninterested in giving him any information. Raikin did get Oswald to give an explanation of his activities in Russia. Oswald claimed that he was stationed as a Marine at the US Embassy, renounced his citizenship, worked in Minsk, and had married a Russian woman; Oswald also claimed that he had waited for over two years to get an exit visa, and that he paid all of his travel expenses himself. Oswald originally refused to take money from his brother Robert to get him and his family to Texas, though he eventually accepted it. Raikin arranged for the New York Department of Welfare to get the Oswalds a room in a Times Square Hotel before they took a flight to Love Field in Dallas.[5]

Meeting them at the Love Field Airport was Robert and his family. Lee and his family were taken to his brother's home in Fort Worth, where they stayed for a month. Oswald's mother then moved to Fort Worth specifically to allow Lee and his family to have more space; Lee, Marina and June moved into his mother's newly acquired home.[6]

In the third week in July, Lee obtained work as a sheet metal worker with the Louv-R-Pak Division of the Leslie Welding Company; he had been referred to this job by the Texas Employment Commission. Around the middle of August, the Oswalds moved into a one-room finished apartment, as Lee preferred having his own apartment to continuing to live with his mother. Oswald quit his job at the Leslie Welding Company. He worked on October 8, 1962, but did not appear to work the next day, when he went again to the Texas Employment Commission.[7] The second job they sent him to interview for was at the Jaggers-Stiles-Stovall Company, described by the Warren Commission Report as a graphic arts Company.[8] While they did do graphic arts work, they also did classified work for the government, and worked with maps for them. Shortly before Oswald arrived, they began getting more work involving Cuba.[9] [10] This was, of course, was just before the Cuban Missile Crisis occurred.[11]

In early September 1962, Oswald made the acquaintance of George deMohrenschildt, a Russian born geologist who befriended him and his family.[12]

George deMohrenschildt

By any standard, George deMohenschildt had an unusual background. deMohrenschildt was born April 17, 1911 in Mozyr, Russia (now part of Belarus, near Minsk) of mixed Russian descent. His father was arrested in 1920 for anti-communist activity. The family was able to escape to Poland. He received a doctor of science degree in international commerce from the University of Leige in Belgium in 1938. He immigrated to New York shortly after receiving his degree. First suspected of being pro-German, he later worked with a French national against the Germans. He became friends with the Bouvier family, and Jacqueline called him Uncle George.[13]

In 1945, deMohrenschildt received a Masters Degree in petroleum geology from the University of Texas. He worked in Venezuela for a company owned by William Buckley. Later he moved to Dallas and worked as a petroleum geologist for Clint Murchison. DeMohrenschildt became involved with several civic and business groups in Dallas.[14]

In the late Summer, deMohrenschildt and Colonel Lawrence Orloff drove to Fort Worth from Dallas to meet the Oswald family. The deMohrenschildts' first impression of Oswald was of a sincere and forward man. Oswald showed in his conversation all of the elements: concentration, thought and toughness. He had the courage of his convictions, and he did not hesitate to express them. Lee spoke Russian very well when the conversation switched to the Russian language. DeMohrenschildt had some misgivings about Lee Oswald and thought to check on him with a local FBI agent that deMohrenschildt met when he got back to Dallas after a government mission to Yugoslavia. He asked agent J. Walton Moore point blank, "I met this young ex-Marine, Lee Harvey Oswald, is it safe to associate with him?" Agent Moore's response was, "He is OK. He is just a harmless lunatic." The Oswalds went over to the deMohrenschildts' home several nights later. That meeting solidified a friendship between the two families. The deMohrenschildt's two dogs, Nero and Poppaea, took an immediate liking to Lee, sitting on either side, and being very attentive to him. Jeanne said that was good because the dogs were good judges of character.[15]

The Russian émigré community in Dallas was very kind to Marina, providing her and June with clothing and other goods. Marina was given over 100 dresses. Lee appeared to see this as attacking his ability to be a provider and he became furious. Marina seemed to want, at least in Lee's eyes, all of the creature comforts that were available in the United States, but seldom available in the USSR. Marina also discussed with Jeanne deMohrenschildt aspects of her personal life. Marina claimed that Lee would only engage in sex about once a month, and even that was abrupt. She recalled that she had an active pre-marriage sex life. She thought the Cubans were interesting; she also enjoyed encounters when the sons of wealthy oligarchs would have an apartment for a weekend with the parents on vacation, and orgies would occur. It also incensed Oswald that Marina kept writing to one of her former lovers in Russia. One of the letters he intercepted expressed Marina's interest in returning to Russia without her husband Lee.[16]

Then there were the fights. Marina would have bruises on her face, and Lee would have scratches on his face and arms. Marina had infected teeth, which Jeanne thought would require removal. Lee did not approve of Marina smoking; on one occasion, he took a lit cigarette out of her mouth and put it out on her skin.[17]

Marina complained to Jeanne deMohrenschildt about, "That idiot Lee who does not make enough money."[18]

Jeanne asked, "Why don't you try to make something out of yourself...I came penniless to America, worked hard and became a successful designer. Go to school, learn English, revalidate your degree."[19]

Marina was uninterested in the prospect of finding a job.[20]

The deMohrenschildt's attempted a separation-intervention with the Oswalds. They found a couple in the Russian émigré community that was willing to take Marina and baby June in on a temporary basis. Oswald became livid at the idea that he could not have access to his wife or baby girl. He told (shouted) at George deMohrenschildt that he would tear up Marina's clothes and break June's toys. He did respond positively to George's reasoning, and asked for the telephone number where his wife and daughter could be reached. A few weeks later, the family was reunited.[21]

"I remember that Lee did not like any political parties, anywhere. He was just a native-born nonconformist. But he told me that he used to teach his co-workers English in Minsk, he tried to present [the] United States in the most favorable light and wasn't too popular with the authorities because of that.... And so, Lee tried to create good feeling in two opposing countries, in two opposing systems of government."[22]

Lee and Marina were reluctantly invited, at deMohrenschildt's insistence, to a Christmas party held by Declan Ford, a geologist, and his Russian émigré wife. The Oswalds arrived in unexpectedly smart attire for the event. Lee was the life of the party. One of the Russian émigrés commented that she had spent 30 years in the U.S., and her English wasn't as good as Oswald's Russian. A young female Japanese musician became engaged in conversation with Lee; Marina would later find the girl's address in Lee's pocket, and became furious at him.[23]

Shortly after that Christmas 1962 party, a party was held at the home of Edward Glover, a scientist working for an oil company. A tall, dark-haired woman in her 20's asked if Marina spoke any English, then starting speaking Russian with her. The woman was Ruth Paine. The two women would become friends.[24]

The Last Meeting Between The Demohrenschildts And The Oswalds

On Easter evening, April 14, 1963, the deMohrenschildts decided to see the Oswalds for one last time before the deMohrenschildts left to go to New York, on their way to Port-Au-Prince, Haiti, where George would try to wrap up his project there. The Oswalds had recently moved into a newer, and nicer apartment on Neeley Street, much nicer the one they lived in on Elsbeth Street. The deMohrenschildts had brought with them a giant toy rabbit for June. They found that the Oswalds would soon be moving again to New Orleans. Lee said that he enjoyed his job at Jaggers-Stiles-Stovall. Marina was showing her company the rooms in the new apartment. In the closet a rifle was found. George deMohrenschildt jokingly said to Lee, "Is that the gun you shot at General Walker with?" Lee was stoic without a response. (After the assassination, Oswald was accused of having shot at General Edwin Walker.) Shortly thereafter, Lee was on his way to New Orleans, with Marina to join him later.[25]

The DeMohrenschildt's Actions after the Assassination Regarding Oswald

As the deMohrenschildts moved to Port-Au-Prince, Haiti, George resumed work on his project. After the assassination, deMohrenschildt mentioned both at the American Embassy and among friends that an FBI Agent in Dallas had told him that "He is OK. He is just a harmless lunatic," regarding Oswald. However, after the assassination, this statement was greatly distressing to the FBI. Relating it to others brought another FBI agent to Haiti, Agent W. James Wood, asking George deMohrenschildt to deny his statement. Asked for clarification, the agent replied that the statement deMohrenschildt made was false.

DeMohrenschildt responded, 'False statement! Man, you must be out of your mind!'

And so the agent told deMohrenschildt, "Unless you change your statement, life will be tough for you in the states."

DeMohrenschildt had initially accepted that Oswald was the assassin of President Kennedy. After his interaction with Agent Wood, deMorhenschildt began to have doubts about Oswald's guilt. He told the agent that either the FBI or CIA was implicated in the assassination.[26]

The Warren Commission wanted George and Jeanne deMohrenschildt to testify before them, providing airfare and all expenses associated with coming to Washington. Jeanne said they would come only if they could bring their two dogs. The government accepted these conditions.

George deMohrenschildt was the first to be deposed, before Albert Jenner. George remembers saying some unkind things about Lee at the deposition. Jenner also tried to get George to deny his statement about Oswald being harmless.

Then, Jeanne deMohrenschildt was deposed by Jenner. She brought her dog Nero with her. For the most part, Jenner asked her innocuous personal questions that seemed to have no relation to any issue at hand. The more interesting point in her deposition was that Jenner shied away from Nero (the dog). Jeanne said Nero would not bite; he never bit Lee Oswald, because Lee was a good human being – to which Nero would be willing to swear.[27]

Near the end of his manuscript, George deMohrenschildt summed up Lee Harvey Oswald's life: "Lee hoped that the two powerful countries [the United States and Russia] would become friends, and [his attempt] to achieve it may be naive and maybe foolish but sincere.... It is clear now that war between these two countries would be a holocaust. And so, Lee Harvey Oswald had dreamed and hoped for detente and for friendship, not so bad for a high school dropout from a New Orleans slum."[28]

Endnotes

1 CE 279, p. 630-631.

2 WCR, p. 713.

3 Summers, A. (1981). *Conspiracy*. New York: McGraw-Hill, p. 217.

4 hoover.org/news/oswalds-bulgarian-connection-spas-raikin-papers.

5 WCR, p. 713.

6 WCR, pp. 714-715.

7 WCR, p. 715.

8 Loc. cit.

9 Epstein, E.J. (1978). *Legend: The Secret World of Lee Harvey Oswald*. New York: McGraw-Hill, pp. 191-196.

10 A personal note: In December 1961, I. and about 30 other graduate students in mathematics and physics at the University of Oregon, were invited to a presentation regarding "government employment." I agreed to fill out an application, which as I recall was something like 54 pages long. In about February, a retired woman who was my next-door neighbor was interviewed by someone from the government. They showed her a list of names of 21 subversive groups and asked her if I were a member of any of them. She said to me that she told them that "I refused to tell them anything, telling them that whatever groups you might belong to was a private matter, and none of their business." I surmised that this probably was in regard to the application that I had filled out the previous December. Frankly, I was pleased by her response to them. I guessed that my job possibilities were, however, struck down. Then at 5 A.M. Pacific Standard Time on July 5, 1962, I got a telephone call from a woman at the CIA in Langley, Virginia offering me a position at the CIA. I asked, " What was the work involved in the position?" She replied that aerial photographs were being taken in Cuba. My job would be to take the photographs and digitize them for computer usage. I thought for a few seconds, reviewing that a few months earlier that I had a job possibility at a bombing range in Nevada. At that time, I thought I didn't learn mathematics so that my skills would be used in war efforts. I wanted to work in areas where I could make positive efforts for society. I also thought the work would become boring quickly. Without any further hesitation, I told the woman: "I wasn't interested."

11 Sorensen, T. (2008). *Counselor: A Life on the Edge of History*. New York: Harper-Collins Publishers, pp. 285-309. The Cuban missile Crisis began on October 16, 1962 with President Kennedy reporting to his close advisors that U-2 surveillance photographs taken over the previous weekend showed the beginnings of Soviet intermediate range missiles in Cuba. The missiles would be capable of delivering nuclear payloads to the United States. As would be found out much later, the missiles were in fact operational.

12 WCR, p. 717.

13 en.wikipedia.org/George-de-Mohrenschildt. (retrieved 3/5/2017).

14 Ibid.

15 DeMohrenschildt, G. archive.org/details/ImAPatsyImAPatsy (retrieved 3/5/2017). This manuscript, originally completed in 1976, was donated to the House Committee on Assassinations by deMohrenschildt's widow in 1978.

16 Ibid.

17 Ibid.

18 Ibid.

19 Ibid.

20 Ibid.

21 Ibid.

22 Ibid.

23 Ibid.

24 Ibid. Marina would go to live with Ruth Paine when Lee departed for New Orleans. Marina would live with Ruth up to the assassination, except when Marina joined Lee in New Orleans for about two months..

25 Ibid.

26 Ibid.

27 Ibid.

28 Ibid.

Chapter Eight

THE SUMMER OF '63: OSWALD'S RETURN TO NEW ORLEANS

On April 23, 1963, Oswald purchased bus tickets for his wife and child to go to New Orleans on the following day. Prior to their leaving, Ruth Paine invited Marina and Junie to stay with her until Lee had secured an apartment and got a job. Oswald got a refund on Marina's ticket, and left for New Orleans on April 24. He arrived later that night.[1]

Oswald rented a room at the YMCA in New Orleans. On April 26, he went to the post office. There he was in line behind a young brunette woman. She dropped her newspaper, and Oswald picked it up for her. She thanked him, speaking in Russian; she would often do that as an ice breaker at parties. He responded by saying "You're welcome," in Russian. This nuance in language would become an early bond; Oswald told her, in Russian, "It's dangerous to speak Russian in New Orleans."[2]

They spent some time talking on a park bench, learning about each other; they learned that neither of them was available. Oswald was married with a young daughter, and the young woman, Judyth Vary, was to be married within the week. Judyth Vary was a 19-year-old university student who had been conducting research on cancer, beginning when she was in high school, where she induced lung cancer in mice, using cigarette products, in record time. Oswald was 23 and had spent 2 1/2 years in the Soviet Union. Judyth was in New Orleans to work with Dr. Mary Sherman, having been invited by Dr. Alton Ochsner, a noted physician; Ochsner was among the earliest physicians who drew a connection between smoking and lung cancer. Dr. Ochsner was founder and Director of the Ochsner Medical Foundation. Oswald interjected that Judyth should meet Dr. David Ferrie, a cancer researcher who was working on a cancer project with Dr. Mary Sherman. That meeting took place on the next day.[3]

The next morning Oswald went to the fast food restaurant, Royal Castle, where Judyth Vary was temporarily working until she was to begin her position with Dr. Sherman. Oswald said that he had called Dr. Ferrie that morning, and that the three of them were to meet for lunch. He also suggested that they both get better part-time work until their "real" jobs started. Oswald mentioned that he had some work to do for his uncle, Charles "Dutz" Murret, but that Oswald did not want to get tangled up with Marcello's people. As Judyth Vary would soon learn, Marcello was the top Mafioso in his district, which included Dallas. Oswald also started filling Judyth in on information about Dr. Ferrie, so that she wouldn't be shocked when she saw him. First, there was Ferrie's physical appearance. He suffered from alopecia, which left him with virtually no body hair. Wearing wigs (ill-fitting) and other attempts to disguise his appearance were ineffectual. Ferrie had wanted to be a priest, but his homosexuality (he was particularly interested in teenaged males) kept him from being ordained. Oswald felt that Ferrie was brilliant and had many talents, including being an airline pilot.[4]

Prior to seeing Dr. Ferrie, Oswald and Judyth Vary went first to his Uncle "Dutz" Murret's home though (since Lee was married) Judyth was told to wait a couple of homes away so she wouldn't be seen by the Murrets. Emerging from the house, Oswald said they needed to go to the Town and Country Motel, a long bus ride away. Oswald had to do a favor for his uncle. When they arrived at the motel they sat in the restaurant. When the waiter came to the table, Lee said that he only wished to see "Mr. T." When Mr. T. came to the table, he and Oswald spoke briefly. Judyth Vary noticed that Mr. T. passed a wad of bills under the table to Oswald. They returned to the Murrets' home (with Judyth Vary again stationed a few doors away). Murret gave Oswald an additional $200. Finally, they were on their way to meet with Dr. Ferrie at a local restaurant.[5]

David Ferrie

Ferrie explained to Judyth that he and Dr. Sherman were engaged in confidential work; they were investigating cancer with drugs not available in the United States. Ferrie explained that they were getting results faster than typical science research projects, because they did not have to do all the paperwork; this project was under the direction of Dr. Alton Ochsner. Dr. Ochsner served as a physician to many wealthy and influential South Americans, who made big donations to his clinic, which allowed his clinic to conduct creative cancer research with no outside oversight. They were looking at fast-acting cancers, an area where Judyth had also conducted research, even at her young age.[6]

Later that evening, Judyth and Oswald met Ferrie at Ferrie's apartment. There, Ferrie had some of his laboratory materials and part of his mouse colony.[7] He had the larger mouse colony in a nearby apartment.[8]

Ferrie's laboratory was unlike any laboratory Judyth had ever seen. Ferrie's apartment seemed to be in shambles.

The following night, April 28, 1963, Judyth and Oswald were invited to a party at Ferrie's apartment. Dr. Sherman was to be there and Judyth looked forward to meeting her. The party was a big disappointment for Judyth. Dr. Sherman would not even speak to her. Dr. Sherman spoke with some Cubans, then took some biological materials out of Ferrie's refrigerator and departed the party.[9]

Ferrie was trying to recruit Judyth to work with him on a secret CIA project. It appeared to be a project to get rid of Fidel Castro, but would require Judyth's background in working with fast-acting cancers. Judyth demurred, saying she would need to talk to Dr. Ochsner first. Ferrie responded that that would be fine; after all, Dr. Ochsner was the head of the project.[10]

Guy Banister

Judyth had misgivings about the project described by David Ferrie and wanted to know if this was actually authorized by the United States government. Oswald took her to see Guy Banister at his office at 600 Camp Street. Guy Banister was a former FBI agent, who came to New Orleans, hired by the New Orleans Police Department to root out corruption. In Banister's view, corruption won, and he was fired. Banister elected to stay in New Orleans and work as a private detective and try to find the corruption on his own time. Banister did in fact acknowledge that the project was a U.S. government program, whose intent was to get Castro. Banister also said that Ferrie and he were involved in identifying subversives, i.e. Communists or communist supporters.[11]

Banister displayed on his walls a plethora of certificates and citations from his many years in the FBI. Banister also told Judyth that Oswald was working with him and was being groomed for his part in saving Cuba from communism. Banister also told Judyth that she was needed for her expertise to help in the project.[12]

Dr. Alton Ochsner

Alton Ochsner was born in South Dakota in 1896 (making him 67 in 1963). He attended the University of South Dakota, gaining a bachelor's degree in 1918. He completed the first two years of medical school in his junior and senior year. He spent the next summers at a Chicago Hospital under the tutelage of his uncle A. J. Ochsner, a surgeon. Alton Oschner received his medical degree from the University of Washington in St. Louis.

Upon graduation, he went to Germany to widen his knowledge and experience. Two years later, he returned from Europe and accepted a position at the Columbia Hospital in Chicago. A son, Alton Jr., was born on the trip to the United States aboard a passenger ship. An issue for Ochsner at the hospital was that he wasn't getting any experience in surgery. He was teaching a class at Northwestern University, which Ochsner found quite rewarding. He found one approach to teaching that became his forte; Oschner avoided textbooks as the main focus of a course. Ochsner preferred using up-to-date articles, which gave students state of the art experience. The drawback was continual change in the articles to be included. Ochsner then accepted a position at the University of Wisconsin, as an assistant professor. Ochsner there performed thoracic surgeries; his research writing continued.[13]

Background on Ochsner's Feud with Huey Long

An offer to be the Chair of Surgery at the Medical School in Tulane University came to Ochsner, which he accepted. It came with one drawback; Ochsner was to be a full-time professor and Chair, precluding additional income for surgeries. This restriction would eventually be removed. Ochsner was also appointed chief visiting surgeon at the Charity Hospital in New Orleans. In one sense Tulane informally used Charity Hospital as a teaching hospital.

Shortly after Ochsner arrived in New Orleans, Huey Long became Governor of Louisiana. Long had a tendency to expect fealty from those he considered within his realm. In particular, Long seized control of the Charity Hospital Board of Administrators, which would put Ochsner in the path of Long's wrath. Arthur Vidrine became Superintendent of Charity Hospital after Huey Long fired the current superintendent. Vidrine was the son of one of Long's supporters. Vidrine chose which Tulane faculty members who would be appointed as physicians at Charity Hospital; previously, these appointments were made by the Dean of Medicine at Tulane. Vidrine then asked to be appointed as chair of otolaryngology at Tulane, even though that was not his specialty. Tulane denied an appointment to Vidrine. (Vidrine had announced that, under his direction, they would reduce the mortality rate at Charity Hospital. The change Vidrine made was the scheduling of many more tonsillectomies, which were only rarely fatal. This change by Vidrine artificially reduced the overall mortality rate.)

Ochsner was brought into the path of Long, when Ochsner refused to recommend Vidrine to be a Professor of Surgery. Ochsner reasoned that, since Vidrine was a political appointee as superintendent, both he and Vidrine would be criticized by others for such an appointment. When in 1930, Ochsner was offered a position at the University of Virginia, he wrote to a friend asking about the advisability of such a move. In his letter he wrote about the politics interfering with surgeon training at Tulane. A carbon copy was given to Ochsner, who put the copy in his coat pocket and hung it up while he was performing surgery. When he returned to retrieve his coat, the carbon copy was missing. It would end up in the possession of Huey Long.

Long dismissed Ochsner from his position, and barred Ochsner from practicing at Charity Hospital. Shortly thereafter, Long instituted a Medical School at Louisiana State University, in New Orleans, with Vidrine as Dean. Vidrine promptly went about hiring several members of the faculty at the Tulane Medical School. Though Ochsner was oriented to accept a position at the University of Illinois, Jeff Miller, a physician and faculty member at Tulane, convinced Ochsner not to leave under fire. Tulane asked the American Medical Association Council on Medical Education to investigate regarding the reported harassment by Long and Vidrine. The AMA Council on Medical Education hinged LSU's Medical School accreditation on addressing this issue. The new circumstances that faced Ochsner were improved even beyond his original arrangement. Tulane opened a clinic adjacent to Charity Hospital. Dr. Ochsner would now be able to receive payments from patients. Many of the more influential locals rallied to Ochsner; they were buoyed by Ochsner's surviving Long's wrath. And many of them tended to be of a more conservative frame of mind. Ochsner also opened the Ochsner Clinic and Foundation Hospital in 1942.[14]

INCA

Ochsner advanced anti-communist views and he helped organize the Information Council of the Americas (INCA). The other organizers were Edward Scannell Butler, a young former intelligence officer in the army, and A.E. Papele, Dean of the Law School at Loyola University in New Orleans. INCA's purpose was to prevent "Communist Revolutions" in Latin America by distributing information about the evils of communism to the Latin American masses. Ochsner was the President and Chairman of INCA. INCA personnel would interview Cuban politicians and refugees and produced at least 120 "Truth Tapes" from the interviews and sent copies to radio stations in Latin America (175 stations, according to biographers Wilds and Harkey). INCA also produced a movie, *Hitler in Cuba*; the *New York Times* reviewed the film, calling it "the crudest form of propaganda," and a "tasteless affront to minimum journalistic standards."[15]

Dr. Ochsner was a prolific scholar. He had 584 published articles, many of them with co-authors. In these articles, there were 135 different co-authors. The person most often a co-author was Ochsner's best student, Michael DeBakey, who co-authored 71 of the articles. DeBakey is remembered for developing several medical devices and procedures. He co-developed with Robert Jarvik the first artificial heart.[16]

The Cutter Incident

With the development of the Salk polio vaccine, a controversy arose when bacteriologist Bernice Eddy, a researcher at the National Institute of Health (NIH), used a batch of the vaccine on her monkeys; they fell paralyzed in their cages. Eddy realized that the virus in the vaccine was not dead. Eddy sent pictures of the monkeys to NIH's management and warned of an impending tragedy. A handful of prominent physicians stepped into the controversy on the side of the Salk vaccine. Among those physicians was Alton Ochsner, who had invested in Cutter Laboratories, one of the vaccine's producers; he inoculated two of his own grandchildren. His grandson died after seven days; his granddaughter was infected by polio but survived. This was a devastating experience for Dr. Ochsner; 1955 was not kind to him. And 1956 brought the end of Alton Ochsner's Chairmanship in Surgery; the claim was made that he was spending so much time at his clinic, he was not properly addressing his chair duties. Ochsner fought this decision bitterly, but to no avail. In 1961, Ochsner was subject to mandatory retirement at the Tulane Medical School; though Ochsner fought the process, he was unable to get around this obstacle.[17]

Ochsner was, in 1963, an even more complex man. Ochsner had become an adamant anti-communist; like many of his wealthy Southern patients, his politics could be described as ultra-right-wing. While he had earlier been involved with the FBI in classified research activities, they allowed Ochsner to conclude his relationship with them (in 1959) in order to work with another government entity (most likely the Central Intelligence Agency).[18]

The Project

The year 1959 (On January 1) was the beginning of the Fidel Castro regime in Cuba. It was also the same year that Alton Ochsner began a relationship with an agency more clandestine than the FBI, and legally able to do covert work outside the United States, as for example, the CIA does. As Castro moved closer to the Soviet orb, various government agencies were working on means to remove Castro from power. Presumably that was the rationale behind Ochsner's secret project. As we now know several other groups were working toward the same objective, albeit with different means of accomplishing that outcome. The rationale behind enlisting Dr. Ochsner and his team of medical scientists would clearly be in the medical arena. It would seem likely that they would be enlisted in developing a biological weapon to incapacitate Castro. Perhaps considered were either poisoning or infecting him with a disease that would quickly disable him. As it happened, Dr. Ochsner and his associates were proficient working with cancer and its cure. Perhaps they could change their direction to developing a fast-acting cancer, and coincidentally, also learn how to stop it. It's just that, in Castro's case, the last part wouldn't be necessary.

It is known through the testimony of CIA Director Stansfield Turner that the CIA funded 159 medical research centers to do classified medical research. It is highly likely that one of these centers was Alton Ochsner's facility. [19]It was shown by Ed Haslam that Ochsner's team had access to a particle accelerator.[20] In most cases, the information on the particle accelerator had to be meticulously documented, but apparently not for secret research being conducted through the CIA.[21] In fact, Haslam has gone to great lengths to show the existence of a particle accelerator in New Orleans, and the likelihood that the accelerator was involved in the mysterious death of Ochsner close associate, Dr. Mary Sherman. Prior to Haslam's research, the existence of a particle accelerator (LINAC) was covered up.[22] It is most likely that the accelerator was already installed prior to the beginning of the project. Dr. Ochsner received millions of dollars in donations from right-wing oil millionaires who despised both John F. Kennedy and Fidel Castro.

The project, (The New Orleans Project) was brought into existence within a week after Attorney General Robert Kennedy approved removal of Fidel Castro from Cuba, likely with extreme prejudice (assassination). This approval came in March 1962. With this came the approval of using the already functional linear accelerator. Undoubtedly several such projects were approved to such an end. The major planners were Dr. Ochsner and Dr. Sherman, with some inclusion of David Ferrie. As they developed the plan, numerous colonies of mice were to be raised, with little or no knowledge of the plan by the mice's caretakers. A group of mice would be injected with cancerous materials, which originated from monkeys that had the SV40 virus, a virus that infected some of Jonas Salk's monkeys in developing his polio vaccine. The viruses (there may have been other viruses beyond SV40 in the monkeys) were then subjected to the LINAC, then injected into mice and then placed in the care of another set of handlers until the mice were deemed harvestable. Those mice with the largest tumors were then sacrificed, their most aggressive tumors removed, and then the tumors were put into a blender to create a material from which the virus mix and selected cancer strains could be identified and cultivated. This product would be injected into a new set of mice. This process would continue for several iterations. At a point in 1963, marmosets replaced the mice. The marmosets were then replaced by green monkeys. Eventually, the developed biological weapon would be injected into a "volunteer," to test the efficacy of the weapon. Given Fidel Castro's well known habit of smoking cigars, it would seem plausible that Castro's cancer was due to his smoking.[23] A more complete description of this process is given in Baker's book, *Me & Lee*.[24]

Jack Ruby

On May 6, 1963, Lee Oswald and David Ferrie saw a beat-up brown and green Chevy drive up to Dave's apartment; they went outside and came back with a man they introduced as Sparky Rubenstein.[25] Judyth was told that Mr. Rubenstein's "connections" had helped finance Ochsner's cancer project. Rubenstein asked Dave whether he was using the blender that Rubenstein gave to him. Judyth chirped, "He's using it to liquefy tumors." In the conversation, Judyth learned that Mr. Rubenstein and Oswald had known each other for several years, probably through the Mafia connections of Oswald's uncle, Dutz Murret. (Judyth never knew that Sparky Rubenstein was better known as Jack Ruby, until well after the assassination.)

When Ruby was first getting set up to be Marcello's helper in Dallas, he attended several of Marcello's parties; in attendance at several of them were Oswald's mother, and Dutz and Lillian Murret. When Lee and his mother moved to Fort Worth, Dutz Murret asked Ruby to "Watch over my boy Lee." Ruby/Rubenstein also had suggested to Lee Oswald that he could secure lucrative employment with Marcello. Lee had declined, saying he'd rather be in the Marines, like his brothers. David Ferrie commented that Sparky (Ruby) loved Oswald like a son.[26]

Arriving several minutes later were three men who were associates of Jack Ruby. One, identified by Oswald, was a Mr. Gaudet, which could refer to William George Gaudet, a CIA employee who allegedly obtained a tourist card at the same time as Oswald, from the Mexican Consulate in New Orleans in September 1963. Oswald's card and Gaudet's card were sequentially numbered. Gaudet both admitted, and then denied, traveling to Mexico on a bus with Oswald. Gaudet also wrote for an anti-communist magazine for Dr. Ochsner for distribution in Latin America.[27] The second man was Sergio Arcacia Smith, who had come from Houston. A close friend of Ferrie's, Smith. had formerly been active in anti-Castro activities in New Orleans. He helped start the Cuban Democratic Liberation Front. He was expelled from this group for mishandling their money. He moved to Texas, where he became friends with General Edwin Walker and H.L. Hunt.[28] The third man was a heavyset Latino, who was unknown to Oswald. The Latino was around 6'2" and 250 lbs.[29]

The Application Process for Jobs at Reily Coffee

Judyth Baker said that she and Lee Oswald were to reply to ads carried in the *New Orleans Times Picayune*. The ads ran from April 27, 1963 to May 10, 1963. They were supposed to apply for these jobs (Baker as a Clerk-Typist, Oswald as a Maintenance Mechanic Helper) near the end of the time the ads were running in the paper.[30] On May 9, 1963, Oswald had already been interviewed and hired by Al Prechter; on the same day, Judyth Vary Baker was also interviewed and hired by Prechter. It was decided that Baker was to take the place of two advertised clerk-typist positions, as the finance and security secretary to the Vice-President, former FBI Officer William I. Monaghan. Prechter was concerned that Baker could only type 15 words a minute (Judyth claimed that she was then up to 19 words per minute). In any event Baker and Oswald were hired at Standard Coffee, then a small subsidiary of W. B. Reily Company; Monaghan personally ran Standard Coffee. The two new hires would be switched to Reily Coffee the following week, "after their records were laundered."

The jobs at Reily were cover jobs for both Oswald and Baker. She would have to punch the time clock for Oswald at or before 8 A.M. and clock him out at the end of the day as well, if he were unable to do so himself. Her supervisor, William I. Monaghan, was in concert with the project, so her absences would be accepted. There would also be some specific duties she'd need to perform for him.[31]

Only top-level, key people would know that both new employees would spend much of their time working on the cancer project. In Lee's case, there would be other job responsibilities.[32]

Interview by Dr. Ochsner

The interview with Dr. Ochsner actually occurred the day before the interview by Al Prechter, at Charity Hospital. Oswald was interviewed by Dr. Ochsner first, for about 45 minutes. Fifteen minutes later, Judyth Baker was led to Dr. Ochsner's office.

Ochsner explained that Judyth would be handling most of the duties in David Ferrie's primitive lab set-up. The original intent was that Judyth not be involved beyond her laboratory duties as Dr. Sherman's assistant, so that she would see it simply as cancer research; but it was too late for that. She was told too much, through a series of assumptions that were made because Ochsner and Sherman had been out of town when Judyth arrived in New Orleans. Her involvement in Ferrie's lab, principally, was because the cancers would be getting increasingly virulent, and extreme care was needed in their handling. But also, Ferrie would need to be doing other duties. Ochsner also stated that she was an unconventional thinker, and they needed her input. They had reached an impasse, and her serendipity was needed. She would also be required to devour, on a daily basis, the considerable research that was being reported, some of which were raw studies. When Judyth asked about her internship with Dr. Sherman, Ochsner replied that she would be working closely with Dr. Sherman on the present project. The specimens would be couriered from Ferrie's lab (by Oswald). But also, she could receive tutelage from Dr. Sherman when she began attending Medical School at Tulane in the Fall.[33]

Was Their Getting Jobs at Reily a Chance Event?

Some researchers have opined that Judyth Baker embellished the story of her employment at Reily Coffee and also opined that Judyth's and Oswald's working at Reily at the same time was a chance event. I was asked by Baker to look at the process of getting their jobs as to whether or not it was a chance event. Judyth Baker supplied me with copies of the want ads from the *New Orleans Times Picayune* for the duration of the advertisements. Judyth had received the copies of the want ads from Kelly Thomas, then a graduate student at Louisiana State University-Lafayette. I chose to focus on the dates from Saturday, May 4 through Thursday, May 9. A simple probabilistic approach was used with the positions that they might have applied for separately, and using the positions as the unit of analysis. For May 4, there were 195 jobs for which Oswald was qualified and possibly might be interested in. For Baker, there were 137 such jobs. Then, under the assumption that their hiring was unrelated, chances of them applying at the same time for these specific positions (and only these positions; Reily Coffee had two ads during this time period: one for a male, and one for a female) on the same day would be (1/195)(1/137)= .0000374, or slightly less than 4 in 100,000. For most persons, this outcome is sufficient to conclude that their applications to those positions was NOT a chance outcome, or in other words, there was a relationship to their being interviewed for these positions on the same day. On each subsequent day, the number of jobs might vary. This process was repeated for each of the other 5 days; the result for May 9 was p=.0000314. If we ask, what is the probability that they will both be hired, we have to take into account Reily's hiring rate; during that time period, there were 50 applicants and 10 hires, or a 20% hire rate for each applicant interviewed. The probability of both being hired at Reily would then be, for May 9, be .0000314(.2)(.2) or p=.0000012, or slightly over 1 in a million chances. If a Bayesian approach were taken, with the assumption that they were working in consort, the outcome would be very close to certainty for them applying at the same employer. Even then, the chance for both to be hired would be p=(.2)(.2)=.04.[34]

Dr. Mary Sherman

Dr Mary Sherman received her medical degree from the University of Chicago, and became a faculty member there. She was trained as an orthopedic surgeon. Eventually, she became the Chairperson of the Pathology Committee of the American Academy of Othopedic Surgeons. While at Chicago, she was close to physicist Enrico Fermi and she became an expert in the field of the medical uses of radiation. In 1953, she moved to New Orleans where she was an associate professor at the Tulane Medical School and a partner in the Ochsner Clinic.[35]

The Get-Together at Dr. Sherman's Apartment

Dr. Mary Sherman invited Judyth Baker for lunch at her upscale apartment at 3101 Charles on May 11, 1963. Unknown to Baker, Dr. Sherman had also invited David Ferrie. Dr. Sherman was sharing her opinion on unfairness to the public, about the cancer-causing virus in the original polio vaccines with the SV40 contamination, which was still being distributed in both the United States and across the world. This was eight years after the discovery of the tainted vaccines. The corporate interests were giving Dr. Sherman threatening phone calls about her continued comments on the use of the contaminated vaccines. Dr. Sherman explained to Baker that she was working on altering the simian cancer-causing virus with radiation. They had developed rare and very potent cancer strains. They had not yet developed an antidote to the virus. However, the altered simian viruses might themselves be useful; they might be used, particularly if the virus could be improved, to eliminate Fidel Castro and make it appear that it was due to natural causes.

Then, without mentioning him by name, Ferrie related how the enemies of President John F. Kennedy were plotting against him, for not going to war (with Cuba) and for possibly forcing the retirement of FBI Director J. Edgar Hoover, and for increasing taxes on "Big Oil." Ferrie stated, "They'll execute him, reminding future Presidents who really controls this country … those who rise to the top will gain everything they ever hoped for, and look the other way."[36]

Ferrie continued, "If Castro dies first, we think the man's (President Kennedy) life can be spared.… If Castro dies, they'll start jockeying for power over Cuba.… It will divide the coalition that is forming."[37]

Judyth asked, " Where … did you get this information?"[38]

Dr. Sherman replied, "You are very young, but you will have to trust us, and we will have to trust you. If we really were with them, you wouldn't be privy to this information. These people have the motive, the means, and the opportunity. They will seem as innocent as doves. But they're as deadly as vipers."[39]

When asked about the stance of Dr. Ochsner, Dr. Sherman continued, "I don't know. I can't tell."[40]

Ferrie broke in, "But we know he is friends with the moneybags. He thinks Mary and I hate 'the man,' just as he does."[41]

Dr. Sherman thought Ochsner might unknowingly aid some of the plotters. "His interest originally was to bring down Castro, because he is anti-Communist to the core. But he's remarkably naive."[42]

Dr. Sherman continued, "We believe we have something, but we want to see what you make of it.… You induced lung cancer in mice faster than had ever been done before, under miserable lab conditions."[43]

Ferrie chimed in, 'You're untraceable. With no degree, nobody will suspect you, because you are working at Reily's, and you're practically a kid."[44]

"We have only until October," said Dr. Sherman.[45]

When the conversation turned to Judyth's involvement, both Dr. Ochsner and Dr. Sherman told her she still had a choice, to work only with Dr. Sherman on an internship or work with Dr. Sherman on the project for the summer, and then attend Tulane Medical School in the Fall. Dr. Sherman then told her that before she made a choice, there was something she would like Judyth to see. There were two sets of slides that Dr. Sherman wished her to look at under the microscope. The first slide set were typical cancer cells. They were in order and were shown by age, in hours and minutes. Judyth confirmed that they appeared as she had previously experienced them. Then Dr. Sherman gave her access to the second set of slides, again in sequence, by age, in hours and minutes. The difference was dramatic: these cells were rapidly dividing. Judyth exclaimed, "These are monsters!"[46]

They had an aggressive growth rate, the fastest growth rate for cancer cells she had ever experienced. She was hooked. Her own interest was fast-growing cancers. Her choice was made.[47]

Getting into Their Jobs

Judyth had two distinct jobs. One was at Reily's. As she learned more about Mr. Monaghan, her supervisor, Judyth found that he too had some other activities beyond Reily's. He was out of the office to a considerable extent. He had some sort of intelligence background. Most of Judyth's afternoons (Wednesday through Friday) were spent at the laboratory in David Ferrie's apartment.

Lee's assignment, outside of Reily's, was more varied and not completely known to Judyth. First, he was to be a courier within the project taking specimens from Ferrie's apartment to Dr. Sherman's apartment. Oswald was also working with Guy Banister, and would shortly have an office in Banister's building for the faux Fair Play for Cuba Committee (FPFC) Oswald organized. Oswald would hand out leaflets, ostensibly to attract new members. The real reason was to find persons who were oriented to this "Communist" state and put them on a list of communist sympathizers, a big interest of Banister's. They would also go to Tulane and other local college campuses for the same reason. Oswald was to go to gatherings of Cubans and sort them into Castro sympathizers and persons who opposed Castro. There would also be a film to be made later in the summer at a camp where Cubans were being trained for a future invasion of Cuba.[48]

Lee Harvey Oswald's Driver License

At the time of the Warren Commission's Proceedings, it was thought that Oswald did not drive, as he had no driver's license. Actually, Oswald held a Texas driver's license. Oswald said that he had to stash it away. He had been warned that the Texas Highway Patrol had tagged his license as "belonging to a known communist." If he were involved in a traffic stop, when they called in his license, and they determined he was a "known communist," he was subject to arrest on some trumped-up reason. Shortly after his murder, workers in the Texas driver's license bureau found evidence of his license, which was then expunged from the record, or otherwise removed from public access. Oswald drove on several occasions in New Orleans, either his Uncle Dutz Murret's car, or one owned by Carlos Marcello.[49]

The Library Card

On June 4, 1963, after a meeting at Banister's office regarding importing guns to New Orleans (to be used by the anti-Castro Cubans who would be training near New Orleans), Ferrie loaned to Lee Oswald his Tulane University Medical School library card. It could also be used by Judyth to check out materials from the library. Since Judyth would probably be in Medical School in September, she could get her own card then.[50] By the end of summer both Ferrie and Baker forgot that she still had the card. Not knowing where his card was caused Ferrie consternation after the assassination, until Baker told him she still had it. Ferrie then told the FBI that the card was probably among the goods that the FBI had confiscated from his apartment.

The 500 Club

Ferrie informed Judyth that she was to be at the 500 Club for a special evening. The man she met in May, Sparky Rubenstein (Jack Ruby) would be footing the bill.[51] When Ruby came in, he sat with Lee and Judyth. At their table was David and Anna Lewis (The Lewis's would double date with Oswald and Baker from time to time). Ruby conversed with the group until Carlos Marcello showed up, with two bodyguards; Ruby immediately went to be with Marcello. Among others at the dinner were Clay Shaw, and Marcello's two brothers. Oswald and Judyth were invited because Marcello needed to talk to Oswald about the shipment of guns. It was important that the shipment be both concealed and protected. When Ruby invited Oswald to come to Marcello's table, Oswald sat between Clay Shaw and Marcello. One outcome of the evening was that Oswald and Judyth were given carte blanche to the Marcello-connected restaurants in New Orleans; they could eat out free whenever they wished.[52]

June 16, 1963: Passing out FPFC leaflets to Sailors and Stevedores

Lee Oswald was handing out FPFC leaflets to sailors and stevedores who were on the ship USS *Wasp*. Stevedores who showed interest in the leaflets were removed from the dock to protect the upcoming arms shipment. Ostensibly this was an assignment given to him by Banister.[53] In retrospect, it could be argued that this exercise could be interpreted as a sheep-dipping process, in case Oswald might need to be used as a patsy in a future plan, perhaps even unknown to Banister.

An Unexpected Flight to Toronto for Oswald

On June 21, David Ferrie had become aware of the affair between Lee Oswald and Judyth Baker. When Judyth arrived at the Lakefront Airport she saw Oswald talking with David Ferrie, Clay Shaw, and a large Cuban man; Ferrie was getting ready to fly the two men to Toronto. Just before takeoff, as the plane taxied down the runway, Ferrie brought the plane to a stop, jumped from the plane and ran toward Oswald and Judyth. Ferrie pleaded with Oswald to come aboard as his co-pilot. Ferrie was so tired, he thought he might go to sleep. Oswald accompanied Ferrie, returning the following afternoon.[54]

The Passport

On June 24, 1963, Lee Oswald was at the Custom House in New Orleans. Judyth was invited to meet Arthur Young.[55] Young was processing Oswald's application to get a passport. Oswald's passport was completed within 24 hours. All other applicants on that day were also given expedited processing, though they probably weren't including Cuba and the Soviet Union in their proposed itineraries. Young was there for only one day and was returning to Miami. The cab that Judyth arrived in would also take Young to the airport. Young spoke seemingly flawless Spanish with the Latino cab driver; however, he spoke English with a German accent. Judyth did learn that Young wasn't his actual name.[56] His actual name was Charles Thomas. Oswald and Young had previously met when Oswald was a young boy and seeking to cross over into Canada; Young was on border control that day, and decided to accommodate the boy, given several strictures, which Oswald dutifully obeyed.[57]

To get the passport, Oswald needed to have an updated vaccination record on a health card, that was not stamped in the Soviet Union. He got the vaccinations from Dr. Ochsner. Apparently, it was decided that it was better to not have the health card show Dr. Ochsner's name. Instead, a fake card was made, with the doctor listed as Dr. A.J. HIDEEL, a variant of A. J. Hidell, which Oswald had used for his FPCC leaflets. Oswald explained that the name was a 'project' name, used on fake ID's to access certain funds. Oswald also said that he wasn't the only person using that name; Richard Case Nagell had on occasion also used this alias.[58]

The Gun Shipment from Venezuela

On June 28, Ferrie picked up Judyth to go to the Trade Mart area. Ferrie was ecstatic about receiving the shipment of guns, sent to the U.S. with the camouflage suggested by Judyth. Accompanying Ferrie was a young man, Layton Martens, who, like Lee, had been in Ferrie's Civil Air Patrol group in New Orleans. Oswald was already at the Trade Mart, processing the guns and helping to hide them among banana boxes.[59] Several days later, Clay Shaw handed Oswald $1000 (in hundred dollar bills) for his part in the gun shipment.[60]

June 29, 1963; The Marriage Proposal

On June 29, 1963, Lee Harvey Oswald, a married father of a baby girl, and with a pregnant wife, proposed to Judyth Vary Baker, twenty-year-old wife of a University of Florida senior, Robert Baker. Clearly, they had several impediments to overcome. Both seemed amenable to this situation, with both their marriages headed toward divorces. "We both said our vows and declared ourselves married to whatever God was in heaven."[61]

The Crescent City Garage

The Crescent City Garage was next door to Reily's Coffee Co. It was important to Oswald for a couple of reasons. One was to slip out of Reily's to go to Guy Banister's office across the street and around the corner or to one of Oswald's other destinations. A second reason was that a government car would pull up periodically to deliver a cash payment to Oswald. But he liked to spend time there reading magazines, sometimes eating his lunch and sometimes talking to one of the workers there.[62] Unlike most workers, Oswald had freedom of movement and rarely had people looking over his shoulder at work.

Lee and Judyth's Handlers

One of Oswald's handlers was George deMorenschildt. "George was in charge of Lee's stowed away money, and could help us, making sure that a large sum would be given to Marina and the children after we disappeared. Some of it was Company pay, accrued while Lee was a spy in the USSR. George was one of Lee's immediate handlers."[63]

In a later conversation, Judyth asked Oswald would he now be able to confide to her his clandestine adventures. Lee responded, "If I won't tell you, then God himself is not allowed to know."[64]

Judyth followed with, "Alright, what Agency do you work for, and who is your most important handler?"[65]

Oswald responded, "You little spy! Here's the answer: I'm loaned to the CIA, and sometimes must help the FBI, but who my main handler is, not even God knows the answer to that. Certainly, I don't. I call him Mr. B."[66]

Mr. B had been an elusive character in American intelligence lore. His actual pseudonym was "Maurice Bishop." He was unmasked by the important work of Gaeton Fonzi.[67] Fonzi eventually settled on a conclusion that Maurice Bishop and David Atlee Phillips were one and the same person.[68]

On November 20, 1963, when he called Judyth for the last time, Oswald mused, "Know how we wondered who my handler was? Mr. B? Benson, Benton or Bishop? Well he's from Fort Worth, so it has to be Phillips. He is a traitor. Phillips is behind this (the assassination of President Kennedy). I need you to remember that name – David Atlee Phillips."[69]

Back in July, Judyth wondered if she had a handler. Oswald replied, "Of course you do. It's me."[70]

On July 19, 1963, after taking a glass out of a box of tea, and giving it to Judyth, Oswald was fired from Reily Coffee; this was simply the act that allowed Oswald's supervisor to get rid of him.[71]

The Anti-Castro Training Camp

In the following week, Oswald went to the training camp in St. Tammany Parish North of Lake Pontchartrain where anti-Castro Cubans were being trained.[72] He appeared in various scenes of a training film being made there, and also helped David Ferrie process the film.[73] On July 31, 1963, the camp was raided and closed down.[74] One of the persons who was training the anti-Castro Cubans was Gerry Patrick Hemming.[75]

Oswald's First Trip to Mexico City

Sometime in July, 1963, Oswald took a short trip to Mexico City.[76] That may have been July 25 to perhaps the morning of July 27. Oswald took a plane from New Orleans to get materials for "The Project" in another city. He would be back in time for his seminar at Spring Hill College in Mobile, Alabama.[77] In Mexico City, he met Richard Case Nagell at the Luma Hotel. He reportedly also visited the Cuban Embassy, and an attempt was made to visit the Soviet Embassy. Apparently, pictures were taken of Oswald at the Cuban Embassy. While the reason for this trip was not stated by Nagell, the two went to an area where they could shoot guns at a cactus. Nagell's assessment was that "Oswald couldn't hit the side of a barn."[78]

Spring Hill College

On Saturday, July 27, 1963, Oswald was driven by Dutz Murret to Spring Hill College, where the Murret's son was studying to become a priest, and delivered a lecture on Marxism to the Catholic College. One aspect of the college's interest was the emergence of "liberation theology" in the Central American and South American Catholic Church, an issue that needed to be addressed within the American church. The experience seemed to sit well with Oswald.[79]

Premonitions of Being a Patsy

On Monday, July 29, 1963, Lee Oswald seemed depressed to Judyth. She asked him what was wrong, and he replied, "I think they're going to kill me."[80]

Oswald continued, "I know too much ... I was supposed to spy on the project for the CIA, just to keep everybody honest. And then all the other little things they had me do, such as those pro-Castro stunts ... as if they still want me to enter Cuba! What a joke! Both sides would prefer to see me dead first."[81]

When Judyth asked, "Why?" Oswald continued, "Because I'm not important enough for either side to take a chance on, knowing what I know. If I can't find a way to avoid being expendable soon, then it's over. Now that's the truth. They'll kill me just to get rid of me."[82]

Lee then reasoned about what he learned regarding the various people and groups he'd interacted with in New Orleans, and the comments he'd heard about significant others, including politicians, Texas Big Oil, the military, and the CIA, many of whom were from Texas. From the perspective of these power brokers, we had a President who was holding the country hostage because he was unwilling to allow a war to bring Communism to its knees. To them all, insofar as they even knew about Oswald, he was just a pawn to use or discard as they saw fit.[83]

Lee continued, "My concern is this. They want to kill the chief. And as the only "insider" with a publicly provable motive to shoot him – since I'll look like Castro's agent – they could set me up so easily. I can see it coming."[84]

Aftermath of the FBI Raid on the Anti-Castro Training Camp and the Leaflet Campaign

Oswald admitted to Judyth that he gave information to the FBI on the location of the Anti-Castro training camp near the Lake Pontchartrain. He didn't want the anti-Castro Cubans to find out, so he concocted a story to put the blame on an actual pro-Castro spy who had penetrated Banister's group. His name was Fernando Fernandez, from Miami. Fernandez turned out to be a spy for the FBI, and it was the FBI who conducted the raid. Word was spread around that Fernandez was the actual person who betrayed the camp. Because Fernandez had fled back to Miami on August 8, Oswald's passing out of leaflets for the Fair Play for Cuba Committee on August 9 was not expected to attract many anti-Castro Cubans to try to harm him.[85]

Lee Oswald had befriended Carlos Bringuier, an anti-Castro Cuban living in New Orleans, and had arranged with Bringuier to interfere with the leafleting with a staged fight; the intent was to get Oswald arrested in order to have the pro-Castro base see him as a supporter of Castro.[86] This would be important in order for Oswald to be able to take a bio-weapon (the one being prepared in Dr. Ochsner's and Dr. Mary Sherman's project) to Mexico City without suspicion. The bio-weapon would be handed off to a contact to be transported to Cuba and injected into Castro, which should give Castro a fast-acting lung cancer, killing him within three to five weeks. Since Fidel Castro had been a long-term cigar smoker, it would seem plausible that he might be susceptible to lung cancer.

The staged fight took place; Oswald was arrested. He stayed in jail overnight. Emile Bruneau, a lawyer and business partner of Dutz Murret, posted bail. On the following Monday, Oswald was convicted of disturbing the peace and fined $10.[87]

Dutz Murret Came to Oswald's Apartment

On Sunday night August 11, 1963, Dutz Murret came over to the Oswald apartment, and gave him a tongue-lashing, castigating Lee for getting arrested, and the subsequent fight. He then told Oswald to straighten out his life, get a job, and start taking care of his family. In tears, he walked his uncle to the car. Oswald tried to explain his situation, saying, "Things aren't the way they seem. "

Murret placed his hand on Oswald's shoulder and stated, "I know, son."

Lee asked him, "Do you know what I'm really about?"

Murret responded, "Do you know how long Marcello and I have been friends?" Murret then put his arms around Oswald and hugged him.

Then Murret continued, "I don't know what she knows ... I felt that if you trusted me enough – sometime, somehow – you would confide in me, and you finally did. So I'm telling you son, and don't forget. I've known since you arrived in town what you are about. And I am proud of you."[88]

Later, Lee told Judyth, "He's the father I never had."[89]

Passing Leaflets at the Trade-Mart

Things were starting to move fast for Oswald. He had just been through the leafleting, the fight, jail, and convicted in court of disturbing the peace, and now, a leafleting at Clay Shaw's Trade-Mart was planned. This appearance was tightly staged. Arrangements were made, through an anonymous tip to WDSU-TV, that Oswald would be handing out leaflets at the Trade-Mart on Friday, August 16 at a given time. (The tipster was Lee himself). The entire episode was captured on film; as soon as the filming stopped, so did the passing out of leaflets. This was to avoid another arrest.[90] One intriguing aspect is that an almost unknown person, Rafaelo Cruz, was filmed at this event. Cruz did not hand out any leaflets. He was there to "watch Oswald's back," i.e. make sure no one started any trouble. Cruz was working for both the FBI and the CIA. This became important in the 2016 Republican primaries, when candidate Donald Trump accused Rafaelo Cruz of somehow being implicated in the assassination. Rafaelo Cruz was the father of Ted Cruz, a Senator from Texas and a prominent candidate for the Republican nomination for President in 2016.[91] This accusation would only matter to those who still believe the Warren Commission's findings, including many Republicans.

Conversation Carte Blanche, featuring Lee Harvey Oswald

Shortly after the Trade Mart incident, Oswald was invited to speak on a radio program hosted by Bill Stuckey. This was his second appearance on WDSU radio; he had briefly appeared on August 17, 1963. A full program occurred on Wednesday, August 21. Stuckey also invited Carlos Bringuier, and Ed Butler, one of INCAs founders and its Executive Director at that time. Backing up Stuckey was Bill Slatter, an experienced WDSU reporter. Also present was Dr. Alton Ochsner. A recording of this program was made and distributed after the assassination. The title was *Oswald: Portrait in Red.*[92]

August 23-27, 1963; Richard Case Nagell

On August 23-27, or fewer days within those dates, Lee Harvey Oswald met with three other people in a place described as Houston, though according to one participant, Richard Case Nagell, was neither in Houston or Texas. Earlier in late July, 1963 (or possibly early August), Nagell met with Oswald in Mexico City. A third person was "Miguel" and the fourth person was not identified.[93]

Before going into the substance of the meeting, it is helpful to know more about a most remarkable man, Richard Case Nagell. Nagell was born August 5, 1930 in Greenwich New York. Nagell never knew his father. He was placed into foster care at 4, and at 11 into an orphanage. On his 18th birthday, he enlisted in the army and was assigned to paratrooper school. While in training, he spent his free time reading. On September 2, 1949, Nagell completed Enlisted Intelligence Specialist's School at Fort Riley. Next he finished a Russian language course at the 525th Military Intelligence Group at Fort Bragg, April 3, 1950. Next a Leadership School at Fort Jackson was completed in September 1950. Finally, Nagell completed Officers Candidate School at Fort Benning, with commissioning as a 2nd lieutenant, occurring on August 1, 1951. At age 21, he became an instructor at Leadership School of the 5th infantry division in Pennsylvania. He had also taken an extension course in Mandarin Chinese from the University of California.

In the Fall of 1951, he was shipped off to the Korean War. On Christmas Day 1951, he was promoted to 1st Lieutenant the same day that he received his first battle wound. Nagell proved to be a fearless fighter. A second wound took place on December 6, 1952, when hand-grenade fragments struck him in the legs and in the face. On June 11, 1953 he sustained his most serious wound when fragments from a mortar or artillery shell struck him in the buttocks and face, and he received a concussion. Just as hostilities in the Korean War were coming to a conclusion, General Wilbur Dunkelberg had Nagell's promotion to Captain backdated to July 15, 1953, making Nagell the youngest person ever to get a battlefield promotion to Captain. While in Korea, Nagell was the only survivor of a plane crash, by quickly deploying his parachute from a low-flying plane.[94]

Immediately after coming back to the United States, Nagell was assigned to the Army Language School in Monterey, California, to study Japanese. Nagell was then assigned to the Army's Counter-intelligence Course (CIC). In mid-course, Nagell took a Thanksgiving leave to visit a girl in San Francisco. On November 28, 1954, he was returning to Fort Holobird in a B-25 Bomber, the only Army person among five Air Force personnel; the plane was approaching Andrews Air Force Base, when, because of driving rain, they chose to turn the plane to Friendship Airport near Baltimore; the plane went down with Nagell the only survivor. This crash resulted in months of rehabilitation. He reported back to duty at the CIC training center in May 1955. In August 1955, he was designated a Counter-Intelligence Officer. In this role he would become a plain-clothes man, where he would interview civilians suspected of some transgression against the military. Unfortunately, the disfigurement in his face scared many of the persons whom he was to interview. He had a wide scar on the left side of his face and paralysis of an eyelid. His disfigurement was treated with some plastic surgery, and he was redeployed to the Far East.[95]

In the Far East, Nagell was working within Field Operations Intelligence (FOI) a unit that was very secretive and funded by the CIA. The FOI operated as special agents under the direction of the CIA.[96] It was in the Far East where Nagell first met Lee Harvey Oswald,[97] at a German Beer Hall in Tokyo, as well as at the Queen Bee. Russell suggested that Oswald and Nagell likely entered into a plan that involved developing a "cover" to do intelligence work against the Soviet Union. They both seemed to harbor interests in Marxism. This process might have led to Oswald's "defection" to the USSR.[98]

This information on Nagell and Nagell's relationship to Oswald in Japan paints a different picture regarding the meeting that took place between August 23-27, 1963, in "Houston." . The subject of conversation in the "Houston" meeting was the assassination of President Kennedy. The beginning of the meeting transpired in Spanish; Nagell translated for Oswald. Later the conversation proceeded in English. The name of Sergio Arcacha-Smith, a Cuban exile. came up. The name Raul came up as well ("Raul" was a cover name for David Atlee Phillips.) Nagell surreptitiously tape recorded the meeting.[99]

As a final note on this incident, it should be pointed out that neither John Armstrong nor Judyth Baker have any indication of the whereabouts of Lee Harvey Oswald ("Harvey" to Armstrong) for the dates in question (August 23-27, 1963).[100]

Jackson

Most authors who have written about the trip to the Jackson State Hospital (East Louisiana State Mental Hospital) write about the portion of the trip that included Clinton, Louisiana. As an example, the book by Henry Hurt, *Reasonable Doubt* is used.[101] It is not that what is reported is in any way inaccurate, it is that there seems to be no sensible reason for the trip. A threesome was driving to Clinton on August 29, 1963, including David Ferrie, Lee Harvey Oswald and either Clay Shaw or Guy Banister. (The third person was Clay Shaw, who was driving the black Cadillac limousine owned by the Trade Mart.) It is addressed in Hurt that the effort might have been an attempt to smear the Congress of Racial Equality (CORE) which was in Clinton trying to get black citizens registered to vote. If CORE could be construed to be related to Oswald, that could hurt CORE, with Oswald's supposedly Communist leanings. That was not the reason they were in Clinton. They were parked adjacent to a pay phone, waiting for it to ring, to inform them that the prisoner volunteer was on the way. This delay unexpectedly lasted for hours, forcing the car and its occupants to remain under the gaze of curious onlookers.

When they finally got the call, they proceeded to Jackson, where medical personnel injected at least one prisoner, and perhaps more, with the fast-acting cancer. This of course was the final test of all of the research to get a vaccine that would be able to kill Fidel Castro in a short period of time. Each of the persons there had a part to play. Ferrie had been involved with producing the material to be injected, instructed clinicians on how to keep the material alive and where it was to be injected. Oswald was memorizing what Ferrie told the technicians, since there could be no paper trail. Oswald would be entrusted to take the live material to Mexico City to hand off to a Cuban medical person for transport back to Cuba and have it injected into Castro on a ruse that it would help him with medical issues.[102]

Judyth had been told that the volunteer already had cancer and was terminally ill. Since she needed to know what type of cancer the volunteer had, so she could differentiate between the two cancers, she asked David Ferrie about the other cancer. Ferrie replied, "He doesn't have cancer. He's a Cuban about the same age and weight as Castro, and he's healthy."[103]

Judyth's reaction was to view the experiment as murder. She was reminded of the holocaust. How could the great man do this? This was unethical and violated the Hippocratic Oath. Judyth sent a note to Dr. Ochsner stating: *Injecting disease causing-materials into an unwitting subject who does not have a disease is unethical.* J.A.[104]

When Ochsner was informed of the contents of the note, over the clinic's intercom, he went through the roof. Judyth would no longer have a place at the Tulane medical school. Her future as a medical researcher was over. She did have to go to do blood tests on the patient at the Jackson State Hospital on Saturday, August 31, which she agreed to because she was the only person in the project with the experience to conduct time-sensitive tests. Then she was done with the project and it's personnel. Her future had indeed been shattered in regard to medicine.[105] Judyth explained, "I hope that the product didn't "take," or if it did, I could recommend ways to help reduce the pain the victim would suffer."[106]

On Friday August 30, Judyth and Lee were planning their future together, and Lee gave her an envelope with twenty $20 bills ($400). That would give her enough to join him in Mexico when the time came.[107]

On Saturday, August 31, Judyth and Lee were getting ready to go to Jackson to test the progress of the cancer in the Cuban prisoner. Lee was driving an old Kaiser-Frazier, which presumably had no major mechanical problems. By the end of the day, it would overheat three times. At the Jackson State hospital, the medical personnel would not let Judyth actually go into the room with the prisoner volunteer; she was given the blood samples to test in a nearby room. The number of samples suggested that there was more than one volunteer. It appeared that the cancer cells were present and multiplying. As this was Judyth's last effort, someone else would have to do the subsequent visits to the state hospital.[108]

On Tuesday, September 3, Judyth and Lee would see each other for the last time. Judyth was on her way back to Florida to continue at the University of Florida with her husband Robert. Still, she and Lee Oswald had their plans.[109]

Note: The book, *Me & Lee,* is very much a love story; that love story has been only briefly represented here. Readers are encouraged to read her original writings.

Endnotes

1 Armstrong, J. (2003). *Harvey and Lee*. Arlington TX: Quasar, p.528.

2 Baker, J.V. (2010). *Me and Lee*. Walterville, OR: Trine Day, pp.112-113.

3 Ibid., pp. 113-116. "Dr." Ferrie's degree was awarded by an Italian diploma mill.

4 Ibid., pp. 121-125.

5 Ibid., pp. 131-137.

6 Ibid., pp.138-141

7 Ibid., pp. 138-145.

8 Haslam, E.T. (1995). *Mary, Ferrie & the Monkey Virus: The Story of an Underground Medical Laboratory*. Albuquerque NM: Wordsworth Communications, pp. 54-64.

9 Baker (2010). pp. 163-164.

10 Ibid., pp. 165-166.

11 Ibid., pp. 171-173

12 Ibid., pp. 173-177.

13 Wilds, J. & Harkey, I. (1990). *Alton Ochsner: Surgeon of the South*. Baton Rouge: Louisiana State University Press, pp. 1-47.

14 Ibid., pp. 61-81.

15 Haslam, pp. 102-104; Wilds & Harkey, p. 201.

16 Haslam, pp. 128-132;

17 biography.com/people/michael-debakey-929009, retrieved 4/3/2017.

18 Haslam, p. 102.

19 Haslam, E.T. *Dr. Mary's Monkey: How the Unsolved Murder of a Doctor, a Secret Laboratory in New Orleans and Cancer-Causing Monkey Viruses are Linked to Lee Harvey Oswald, the JFK Assassination and Emerging Global Epidemics*. Walterville, OR: Trine Day, p. 161.

20 Ibid., pp. 243-271.

21 Loc. cit.

22 Ibid., pp. 227-241, 352-356.

23 Baker, J.V. (2014). *Ferrie: Mafia Pilot, Participant in the Anti-Castro Bioweapon Plot, Friend of Lee Harvey Oswald and Key to the JFK Assassination*. Walterville, OR: Trine-Day, pp. 185-199.

24 Baker (2010). pp. 207-211.

25 On May 2, 1963 Judyth Vary and Robert Baker were married in Alabama, after failing to be married in Louisiana; there was a three-day waiting period in Louisiana, and Robert had to be back at work on May 3. No one was invited to their wedding; in particular, Robert did not want his parents to find out, in fear that they would refuse to pay his schooling expenses for his last semester at the University of Florida. Baker (2010). pp. 189-205.

26 Ibid., pp. 233-236.

27 Ibid., pp. 235-237; Duffy, J.P.& Ricci, V.L. (1992). *A Complete Book of Facts: The Assassination of John F. Kennedy*. New York: Thunder Mouth Press, p. 195; archive.org/GaudetWilliamGeorgeCIA/ accessed 4/8/2017.

28 spatacus-educational.com/sergio-arcacha-smith, accessed 4/8/2017.

29 Baker (2010) p. 237.

30 Williams, J.D. & Thomas Cousins, K. (2005). "Judyth and Lee: Was Their Employment at Reily Coffee a Chance Event?" *Dealey Plaza Echo*, 9, 2, 37-43.

31 Baker (2010). pp. 222-223, pp. 261-264.

32 Ibid., p. 253, pp. 267-270.

33 Ibid., pp. 252-255.

34 Williams & Thomas Cousins.

35 Baker (2010). p. 280.

36 Ibid., pp. 279-283.

37 Ibid., p. 283.

38 Loc. cit.

39 Loc. cit.

40 Loc. cit.

41 Loc. cit.

42 Loc. cit.

43 Loc. cit.

44 Ibid., p. 284.

45 Loc. cit.

46 Ibid., pp. 284-285.

47 Ibid., pp. 285-286.

48 Ibid., pp. 303-321.

49 Ibid., p. 149.

50 Ibid., p. 330.

51 Ibid., pp. 333-334.

52 Ibid., pp. 335-336.

53 Ibid., p. 341.

54 Ibid., pp. 347-348.

55 This Arthur Young, was the same Arthur Young who allowed Oswald to cross the border into Canada as a 13-year-old (See the section "An Interesting Encounter with a Border Agent" in Chapter 4).

56 Baker (2010)., pp. 353-354. Oswald, and presumably the other passport applicants, received their passport on the following day.

57 Ibid., p. 366. The co-author to the reference [30], this chapter, is Kelley Thomas Cousins, a grand-daughter of Charles Thomas.

58 Baker (2010). p. 338.

59 Ibid., pp. 356-360. Leyton Martens was living with Ferrie at the time of the assassination and was a person of interest at the time of the trial of Clay Shaw.

60 Ibid., p. 380.

61 Ibid., pp. 360-364. Judyth's book, *Me & Lee*, is the story of her love affair with Lee Harvey Oswald. She told the story as only she could. That is but one more reason to read her story in the original. Judyth's statement about her and Oswald's marriage was communicated in an email on July 11, 2017.

62 Ibid., pp. 361-362.

63 Ibid., p. 371.

64 Ibid., p. 389.

65 Loc. cit.

66 Loc. cit.

67 Fonzi, G. (1993). *The Last Investigation*. New York: Thunder's Mouth Press, pp. 125-126, pp. 128-133, pp. 138-139, p. 145.

68 Ibid., pp. 271-277.

69 Baker (2010). p. 521.

70 Ibid., p.389.

71 Ibid., pp. 397-404;

72 Ibid., p. 385.

73 Ibid., pp. 414-416.

74 Ibid., pp. 423-432.

75 Ibid., pp. 408-409.

76 Russell, D. (2003). *The Man Who Knew Too Much*. New York: Carroll & Graf pp. 237-241. Judyth Baker wrote in an e-mail (July 11, 2017) that she thought this trip to Mexico might have occurred during August 5-9.

77 Baker (2010) p. 414.

78 Russell, pp. 237-241.

79 Baker (2010) pp. 415-416.

80 Ibid., p. 418.

81 Loc. cit.

82 Loc. cit.

83 Ibid., pp. 418-419.

84 Ibid., p. 419.

85 Ibid., pp. 433-435.

86 Ibid., p.432.

87 Ibid., p 443.

88 The original source for this incident was John Quigly, then an FBI agent in New Orleans; reported in Baker (2010). p. 443.

89 Baker (2010). p. 443.

90 Ibid., pp. 452-453.

91 e-mail from Judyth Baker, December 5, 2016.

92 Baker (2010). pp. 454-456.

93 Russell, p. 275.

94 Ibid., pp. 42-45.

95 Ibid., pp. 46-51.

96 Victor Marchetti telephone conversation with Dick Russell, January 28, 1977, in Russell, p. 51.

97 Russell, pp. 71-72.

98 Ibid., pp. 81-82.

99 Ibid., p.275.

100 Armstrong; Baker (2010).

101 Hurt, H. (1985). *Reasonable Doubt: An Investigation into the Assassination of John F. Kennedy*. New York: Holt Rinehart & Winston, pp. 280-283, 285, 295-296.

102 Baker (2010). pp. 465-469. Armstrong (p. 517) stated that, on August 27, 1963, Oswald signed an unemployment claim form in New Orleans. Russell (p. 275) reports that the FBI could not authenticate that the signature was done by Oswald.

103 Ibid., p. 470.

104 Loc. cit.

105 Ibid., pp. 471-473.

106 e-mail from Judyth Baker, August 11, 2017.

107 Baker (2010). pp. 474-475.

108 Ibid., pp. 478-481.

109 Ibid., p. 489.

Chapter Nine

THREE WEEKS IN SEPTEMBER

These are the three weeks between Judyth's leaving New Orleans and Oswald beginning his trip to Mexico, with an emphasis on the actions of Richard Case Nagell.

The Plan

The plan that Lee Oswald and Judyth Baker had for the future was for Lee to get ready for the delivery of the bioweapon in Mexico City. After the successful delivery, an arrangement had been made with Alex Rorke to fly Judyth Baker from Eglin Air Force Base in Florida to Yucatan Province in Mexico where she would meet up with Lee Oswald, and they could start their lives together. They might go to Mexico City by commercial air. They might chose to continue their educations at a university in Mexico City.

There were particular details that needed to be ironed out, but the overlying structure was as soon as the bioweapon proved to be successful, it would be prepared for travel to Mexico City; Oswald would also get prepared for the trip.[1]

Waiting for the Cancer

One of the important jobs, perhaps the most important job for Oswald, was to prepare for his role in carrying the bioweapon to Mexico City. This would involve being available when the bioweapon, confirmed in its effectiveness, was ready to go. He actually spent much of this time staying at home, and reading, often on the front porch. Meanwhile, he was to avoid any more pro-Castro activities.[2]

A Meeting in Dallas with Mr. B

A first (and perhaps only) meeting between Mr. B. and Oswald occurred in late August (perhaps also in the interval between August 23-27, when Oswald met with Richard Case Nagell and two other individuals). A description of that meeting, taken from Russell is as follows: The description comes from Antonio Veciana, a Cuban expatriate who was one of the founders of Alpha 66. Veciana met Maurice Bishop (David Atlee Phillips, also called Mr. B.) in the company of a young man. They met at either a bank or insurance company, then walked to a cafeteria. The young man was with Veciana and Mr. B. only 10 or 15 minutes. He was told that Mr. B. would meet him in 2 or 3 hours. No names were exchanged.[3]

Compare this meeting which occurred in late August, to a meeting described by Lee Oswald to David Ferrie, who related the description to Judyth Baker; the conversation took place around September 10th.

Oswald arrived in Dallas around noontime to prepare for his trip to Mexico City. He went to a large building downtown, where he met two men. One was his handler. Mr. B accidentally told Oswald that his name was Benton (Previously he said his name was Benson. Oswald was told that he would meet his handler and the contact who would make sure that the bioweapon got to Cuba. The second person, a Latino, referred to Mr. B as "Bishop," suggesting to Oswald that Mr. B could use any surname starting with a B. No names were exchanged, it was an eyes-only affair, and then the meeting was abruptly ended. Oswald was not even invited to lunch, being sent back to New Orleans with an empty stomach. Oswald was given as little information as possible. Mr. B.'s treatment left Lee Oswald with a nagging feeling about the future.[4]

The similarity of these two descriptions suggest that they may be descriptions of the same event.

Oswald's Meeting with Richard Case Nagell in New Orleans

"In September 1963, "Laredo" (a code name unknown to Oswald) met with Oswald in Jackson Square in New Orleans where both were photographed."[5] "Laredo" was a code name for Richard Case Nagell. This probably occurred shortly before September 17, as Nagell departed New Orleans that day.[6] This meeting was at the discretion of Nagell. Presumably, Nagell wanted to know more about Oswald's future motives. Nagell had been given the job of killing Oswald at the request of the KGB; the CIA had "loaned" Nagell to the KGB. This involved murdering an American citizen at the request of a foreign government, though probably to take place in Mexico when Oswald went there later in the month.[7]

Nagell was not the most forthright person in relaying pertinent information; Dick Russell was able to pick out the codename "Laredo" as being a codename for Nagell himself in the previous paragraph. Thus, we do not know what Nagell and Oswald spoke about in New Orleans. What we do know is that Oswald was directed to get a 15-day visa to Mexico, which he applied for on September 17.[8] By inference we know the decisions Nagell made in relation to their meeting. His decision was to not only *not* kill Oswald, but Nagell also would deliberately commit a crime a few days later, guaranteeing that he would be in jail/prison when Oswald was in Mexico, and/or if President Kennedy was assassinated. Also, Nagel would send Oswald $500 and plane tickets to get to Mexico.[9]

This would suggest that Nagell supported Oswald's assignment in Mexico. One might consider that Oswald gave some information to Nagell about his efforts in New Orleans, and his role in delivering the bioweapon for the elimination of Fidel Castro, hopefully thereby ending plans for the assassination of President John F. Kennedy.

Another Oswald Impersonator

An interesting detail was later revealed, probably emanating from Nagel:

> "Leon Oswald, Male, Caucasian, American, 24-26, 150 lbs., 5' 9" . Alive on September 14 or 15, 1963. Not alive after September 19, 1963."[10] This information was not elaborated on, but one of the Lee/Leon Oswald impersonators apparently was eliminated. Russell was unable to determine just how it related to Nagell, but it does add to the number of Oswald impersonators.

Nagell in El Paso, September 20, 1963

On September 20, 1963, Nagell drove around the streets of El Paso, perhaps trying to decide exactly what he would do. Nagell parked his Ford Fairlane in an alley near the post office, by a "No Parking" sign. He had written three letters, one to Desmond Fitzgerald, then Chief of the CIA Cuban Task Force, and previously, from 1957-1962, Chief of the CIA Far East Division.

A second, and nastier letter went to an unnamed CIA official at the Langley Headquarters; the third letter was to Lee Harvey Oswald, which contained five $100 bills, and an airline ticket to Mexico City. Later, Nagell indicated that the FBI was aware of this letter.[11] In a letter to lawyer Bernard Fensterwald, Jr., in reply to Fensterwald's question, "Why did Oswald take the bus to Mexico City, instead of using the plane ticket?" Nagell responded, that he had "cause to believe that he (Oswald) was never given, or did not receive, the five hundred dollars."[12]

Nagell mailed the three letters at the downtown post office. Nagell then walked across the street to the State National Bank and shot two bullets into the wall. In that Nagell had threatened no one and did not attempt to rob the bank, he presumed that he would be charged with only a misdemeanor. He then casually left the bank, went to his car, and waited to be arrested. Finally, a young policeman. James Bundren arrived and asked, "Why did you try to rob a bank?" Nagell replied, "I didn't know there had been a robbery." Nagell left several clues about what he was doing; he said his actions would... " keep anyone from following me." Nagell also stated, "All my problems have been solved for a long time, and now I won't have to go back to Cuba."[13]

Nagell would be right about his last statement. Instead of being charged with a misdemeanor, Nagell found that firing a gun in a bank was a felony. He was to spend several years in prison. Finally, he was released from Leavenworth April 29, 1968.[14]

Success at the Jackson State Hospital

Oswald was on watch regarding the prisoner(s) who were injected with cancer cells. With the death of the prisoner(s) Oswald was on a quick countdown to get the bioweapon to the Cuban medical person to take to Cuba. Once the bioweapon was successfully delivered Oswald would have sufficient money to start his new life, Judyth Baker would be given the word, and she was to go to Elgin Air Base in Florida, where Alex Rorke would fly in, and take Judyth to a drop-off place in Mexico. This process could start on a minute's notice. It would appear that starting a new life was imminent. The call for Oswald to take the bioweapon to Mexico came on September 23; the prisoner(s) had died.[15]

Endnotes

1 Baker, J.V. (2010). *Me & Lee: How I Came to Know, Love and Lose Lee Harvey Oswald.* OR: Trine Day, p. 492.

2 Ibid., p. 491.

3 Russell, D. (2003), *The Man Who Knew Too Much.* New York: Carroll & Graf, p. 268.

4 Baker, J.V. pp. 490-491.

5 Russell, p. 282.

6 Ibid., p. 289.

7 Ibid., p. 282.

8 Ibid., p. 286. Oswald went to the Mexican Consulate in New Orleans sometime before noon on September 17, 1963 to obtain a tourist permit. He used his birth certificate, rather than his passport to obtain the tourist permit. He was directly behind William George Gaudet in line. Gaudet was a New Orleans based CIA agent.

9 Loc. cit.

10 Ibid., p. 288. Russell obtained this from New Orleans District Attorney James Garrison's files on Richard Case Nagell.

11 Ibid., p. 290.

12 Letter from Richard Case Nagell to Bernard Festerwald, Jr., August 26, 1974, quoted in Russell, D., p. 290.

13 Russell, D. pp. 291-292.

14 Ibid., p. 418.

15 Baker, J.V. p. 492

Chapter Ten

MEXICO: LATE SEPTEMBER–EARLY OCTOBER 1963

Oswald's trip to Mexico City is the first documented evidence of Oswald's being impersonated by another person. What is not clear is, were there more than one? For some of these activities that have been attributed to Oswald, we can definitely label the person involved as an impersonator; for some of the others, we know it was definitely Oswald. And yet other sightings are less definite.

The Trip from the Mexican Border to Mexico City

Oswald was aboard a bus from Houston to Laredo, Texas, according to a British couple.[1]

At mid-afternoon August 26, he boarded a different bus going to Mexico City. No passenger list for this bus has ever been found; the manager of the bus company said the passenger list was taken by investigators of the Mexican government, after the assassination.[2] Two Australian girls on that bus said the man talked about living in Japan and Russia.[3] On the morning of September 27, Oswald allegedly checked into the Hotel Comercio.[4] Early that afternoon, either he or an impersonator appeared at the Cuban Embassy.[5]

The Problem of Impersonators

There is no question whatsoever that Oswald was impersonated in Mexico City. The question is how many, and what was the motivation? First, the Bardwell Odum photograph, published in the Warren Commission exhibits was a picture of a man other than Oswald, but identified as Oswald.[6] Apparently at least 12 (and perhaps 20) pictures of this man (or of two men) were taken by the CIA in Mexico City in late September-early October, 1963, leaving or entering the Cuban or Soviet Embassies. The man (or men) bear little resemblance to Lee Harvey Oswald. The person(s) appear to be older (around 35) much heavier (perhaps over 200 lbs), and taller, around 6'. A person named Gene Nesbit recognized the pictured person as being an old high school friend, Ralph Geb. As it happens, Ralph Geb[7] was a high school football teammate of Mac Wallace, well known as a hitman for Lyndon Baines Johnson.[8] As yet another twist in this scenario, Jay Harrison concluded that the man is actually Frank Geb, a brother to Ralph Geb.[9] In looking at 12 of apparently the same or similar pictures, Richard Case Nagell indicated there were at least two different men in the pictures. Lee Oswald was not.[10] The phone call that the CIA finally admitted to monitoring was made to the Russian Embassy, supposedly by Oswald, was actually an American "with very poor Russian" – obviously not Oswald.[11]

A flight was made from Mexico City on the night of November 22, 1963, with photographs of a certain person, together with tape recordings of the voice of that certain person, and sent to Gordon Shanklin's FBI office in Dallas. In looking at the pictures and listening to the voice, the FBI agents present quickly assessed that the pictures and voice were not Lee Harvey Oswald. Later, both Shanklin and the CIA would deny that any voice recordings were sent.[12]

The next morning, November 23, 1963, J. Edgar Hoover spoke to the new president, Lyndon Johnson on the phone. In response to LBJ's question about Oswald being at the Soviet Embassy in September, 1963, Hoover replied:

> No. That's one angle that's very confusing, for this reason – we have up here the tape and photograph of the man who was at the Embassy using Oswald's name. That picture and the tape do not correspond to this man's voice, nor to his appearance. In other words, it appears that there is a second person who was at the Embassy down there.[13]

The CIA and FBI both denied that the tapes existed post-assassination, having been reputedly "routinely erased." Yet some Warren Commission staffers recalled listening to them in April, 1964.[14]

The Project

The bio-weapon was to be handed over to the Cuban medical technician on the night of September 27, 1963. Oswald went to the designated drop-off spot, a souvenir shop. The technician failed to show. Oswald then attempted to contact Mr. B; he was told that Mr. B. had flown to Washington, D.C. To Lee, it appeared that he had been abandoned in Mexico City. Oswald contacted a "cutout" who said he would try to help. The person was a young blond-haired man, who had friends at a local university medical school. He met the young blond man at a bullfight. The two decided to go together to the Cuban Consulate, as Oswald would try to take the bio-weapon by himself, with all the difficulties that might involve. Either Oswald or his young blond friend handed in the application for a transit permit to Cuba. The person accepting the application was Sylvia Duran. Duran explained that the process would take at least several weeks (The application was actually approved on Oswald's birthday, October 18).[15]

Oswald became cognizant that his efforts had likely come to naught. The future looked much darker than the plans that he had made with Judyth Baker. The news of Alex Rorke being missing, together with the lack of a liaison with the Cuban medical technician and Mr. B's having left Mexico City, leaving Oswald no path to complete his task for the project, and salvage his plan for his and Judyth's future life.

Without a transit visa, and a bio-weapon that would soon expire, Oswald contacted the CIA station in Mexico City as to what should be done. Oswald had earlier been told that after he delivered the bio-weapon, he could remain in Mexico and start a new career as a CIA asset. At the CIA station, Oswald was told that life in Mexico would come later, but at this point he was to return to Dallas for a "de-briefing." Oswald was not to be overly concerned about the failure of the bio-weapon mission, particularly with the impending likelihood of a major hurricane. Perhaps he was set up for failure, even in that circumstance; perhaps he could somehow pull victory out of the jaws of defeat. And he was invited to a party by Sylvia Duran.[16]

Sylvia Duran

Sylvia Duran invited Lee to a party where several of the people there thought they heard his name as Harvey Lee Oswald.[17] During the remaining time he was in Mexico, he and Sylvia Duran were sexually intimate at least once. Oswald did relate this information to Judyth Baker; he said that after the party, he slept with Sylvia Duran. He explained to Judyth that he wanted to get her cooperation (perhaps getting a tourist visa "under the table" and to get vital information and help from Duran). Judyth's response was that, by this point, the two of them were not hiding things of that nature from each other.[18]

Robert Clayton Buick

Undoubtedly one of the more intriguing characters who came in contact with Lee Harvey Oswald was Robert Clayton Buick. Buick met

Oswald, who went by the name Alek Hiddell, in either the Summer of 1962 or Summer of 1963. It appears that he saw him on two separate occasions, in August 1963, in the presence of Richard Case Nagell and in September-October 1963, at a time that Nagell was incarcerated due to the events on September 20, 1963 in a bank in El Paso.

Buick was born Bogdan Buich from Serbian immigrant parents. Later, Bogdan had his name changed to Robert Clayton Buick, though through a clerical error, his last name was changed, which was not his intention. He became a matador in Mexico. As such he became known as "El Ciclon Del Norte" (The Cyclone of the North). He clearly was as flamboyant as he was a successful torero. He was a well-known bullfighter at the time he met "Alik Hidell." Buick was not much bigger than some jockeys. He stated that his greatest weight was 138 pounds. He seemed to always have an expensive convertible as his means of transportation.

His meeting with Hidell came about because Buick had agreed to become an informant for two government employees working out of the U.S. Embassy in Mexico City, known to Buick only by their first names, Ben and Jack. Apparently, Buick's beat was to be aware of any unusual goings-on at the Hotel Luma. Buick remembers Nagell in the company of Hidell/Oswald in July 1963. The dates might be somewhat off, in that he only had a name for him at the time of Hidell's last appearance in Mexico, late September to early October, 1963.[19] Because of the relationship between Nagell and Oswald, these sightings by Buick were most likely Oswald rather than an impersonator.

Hidell/Oswald gave the appearance of someone knowledgeable about a possible upcoming assassination of President Kennedy.[20] At the time, Oswald was also seen with Franz Waehauf, who seemed to have some control over him. Waehauf was a bartender at the Luma Hotel, but also seemed to have intelligence connections. Buick also saw Waehauf as being well above a bartender in importance.[21]

Buick became involved in robbing banks in the United States at the same time he was a matador. The FBI put him on the Most Wanted List in March 1966 and he was apprehended five days later. He spent 5 years in Federal prison. A few years after his release, he became involved, in a small way, as a thoroughbred horse owner, which he was reasonably successful at. Later, he became the author of several books, 3 of which addressed the assassination of President Kennedy.[22]

Return to Dallas

With nothing further to try to accomplish, Oswald took a bus to Dallas. On October 3, 1963, David Ferrie called Judyth and informed him that "Hector" was in Dallas, ("Hector" was a codename for Oswald.)[23]

Judyth was also told that she needed to get a new birth certificate, because if anyone inquired as to where she lived at the time she ordered her most recent certificate, it would say New Orleans. That was unacceptable to her former colleagues in New Orleans.[24]

Endnotes

1 Russell, D. (2003). *The Man Who Knew Too Much*. New York; Carroll & Graf, p. 311.

2 Ibid., pp. 311-312.

3 WC XL 15-17. See also Russell, p. 312.

4 Russell, p. 312.

5 Loc. cit.

6 CE 237. Though the photograph in CE237 was not taken by Bardwell Odom, Odom was responsible for getting it to the Warren Commission; it was then referred to as the Odom Exhibit.

7 Sample, G. & Collom, M. (1997). *The Men on the Sixth Floor*. Garden Grove, CA: Sample Graphics, pp. 96-105.

8 Ibid., pp. 87-95.

9 Brown, W. (2013). Chronology.

10 Russell, p. 321.

11 Summers, A. (1980). *Conspiracy*. New York: McGraw-Hill, p. 385.

12 Ibid., p. 361.

13 Mary Ferrell Foundation: maryferrell.org/pages/The_Mexico_City_Tapes.html. Retrieved 6/11/2017.

14 Ibid.,

15 Baker, pp. 499-500.

16 Ibid., p. 501.

17 Scott, P.D. (2013). *Oswald, Mexico, and Deep Politics: Revelations of CIA Records on the Assassination of JFK*. New York: Skyhorse Publishing, p. 119.

18 Baker, p. 501.

19 Buick, R.C. (2010). *Tiger in the Rain*.: Xlibris Corporation. www.Xlibris.com.

20 Ibid. p. 189.

21 Russell, pp. 245-247.

22 Buick, pp. 499-505.

23 Baker, p. 503.

24 Loc. cit.

Chapter Eleven

OCTOBER 1963

Another Imposter

On September 28, when Oswald was in Mexico, Malcolm H. Price had adjusted a scope on a rifle that Price would later identify as being in the possession of Lee Harvey Oswald, after the assassination.[1] Price also saw the same person on the rifle range on four or five occasions. On each occasion he wore a bulldogger shirt, Texas-style hat and was chewing bubble gum or chewing tobacco.[2] Another witness, Garland Slack, said that the man he later identified as Oswald had shot at Slack's target, which resulted in an altercation between the two men. A father and son, Dr. Homer Wood and Sterling Wood, talked to the man who they identified as Oswald, about Oswald's gun.[3]

Returning to Dallas

When Oswald returned to Dallas on October 3, 1963, he stayed at the YMCA. The following day, Oswald applied for a job as a typesetting trainee at the Padgett Printing Company: this job fell through when the plant superintendent at Padgett checked with Oswald's former employer, Jagger-Chiles-Stovall. Oswald then hitchhiked to Mrs. Paine's home where he stayed through Sunday.[4]

Alex Rorke

On Sunday, October 6, Oswald called Judyth and informed her that Alex Rorke, the pilot who was supposed to fly Judyth to Mexico to re-unite her with Oswald in Mexico, was missing and presumed dead, probably shot down over Cuba. This seemed to be a beginning of the unraveling of Oswald's and Judyth's future plans, though Dave Ferrie promised to get another pilot to fly Judyth to Mexico.[5]

Events Surrounding President Kennedy

On October 7, 1963, President Kennedy signed the Test-Ban Treaty, after it was passed by the Senate. This affirmed the the tri-lateral agreement made by the United States, Great Britain (United Kingdom) and the

Soviet Union (Russia) on August 5, 1963.[6] Also on October 7, 1963 Robert G. "Bobby" Baker was accused of financial collusion in the awarding of contracts; he resigned his position as Secretary to the Democratic majority in the Senate.[7] October 10, 1963, the final letter in the Kennedy-Khrushchev correspondence was received by President Kennedy.[8]

National Security Action Memorandum 263 (NSAM-263)

President Kennedy was trying to get some sensible solutions to the seemingly endless war that became increasingly hard to justify. The favored idea, getting the South Vietnamese to conduct the war on their own, seemed the only humane solution. Yet the Joint Chiefs of Staff were having none of Kennedy's reasoning. President Kennedy wished to begin the process of withdrawal in the immediate future, with total withdrawal on an acceptable schedule. Only Secretary of Defense Robert McNamara was onboard with his proposal. Around May, 1962, Kennedy began pursuing an exit strategy from the Vietnamese conflict. He increasingly saw that this conflict/war was unwinnable by the Saigon forces, even with extensive help from the United States. The Joint Chiefs of Staff were slow to come up with an exit plan. By May 1963 the Joint Chiefs finally presented a plan to Secretary McNamara, which he rejected because it was at least a year too slow. McNamara ordered that an expedited plan be constructed. On August 20, 1963, the Joint Chiefs responded that given the religious and political issues surrounding the government in Saigon, that no units should be withdrawn from Vietnam. The Joints Chiefs thought any changes should wait until at least October.[9]

Secretary of Defense Robert McNamara and General Maxwell Taylor, President Kennedy's representative with the Joint Chiefs of Staff, went to Vietnam on a fact-finding mission, and cabled their information back to General Victor Krulak's Pentagon office. Krulak's team worked continuously putting together a report. Krulak met with President Kennedy and Attorney General Robert Kennedy. The two brothers dictated to Krulak the recommendations of the McNamara-Taylor Report. A final report was typed and bound in a leather cover, sent to Hawaii and presented to Secretary McNamara and General Taylor on their way back from Vietnam. They read the report on their flight back to Washington. The report was presented to President Kennedy on the morning of October 2, 1963. Kennedy accepted the report (after all, he had a hand in writing it).[10]

When NSAM-263 was issued, it was classified as "Top Secret" and was only made public when the Pentagon Papers were released surreptitiously by Daniel Ellsberg in 1971. There was one rather strange point in NSAM-263: "The objectives of the United States with respect to the withdrawal of U.S. military personnel remain as stated in the White House statement of October 2, 1963." NSAM-273 contains precisely the same language. The textual differences between the two memoranda are that NSAM-263 does not deviate from the concept that the war was, in the final analysis, the South Vietnam's government to win or lose. NSAM-273 changed this now, the United States was there to help the South Vietnamese win the war. The change paved the way to a total commitment for the United States. The important point is, where was the White House statement of October 2, 1963, regarding the withdrawal of American troops?[11]

The McNamara-Taylor Report on Vietnam

The McNamara-Taylor Report was written, as indicated earlier, by General Krulak and John & Robert Kennedy, put into a leather cover and sent to Honolulu for Secretary McNamara and General Taylor to read on their flight back to Washington; it is true that the data for the report came from Secretary McNamara and General Taylor's gathering of information in Vietnam. The relevant parts of the McNamara-Taylor Report addressing the withdrawal of American troops follow:

> The military program in South Vietnam has made progress and is sound in principle, though improvements are being energetically sought. Major U.S. Assistance in support of this military effort is needed only until the insurgency has been suppressed or until the national security forces of the Government of South Vietnam are capable of suppressing it.

Secretary McNamara and General Taylor reported their judgment that the major part of the U.S. military task can be completed by the end of 1965, although there may be a requirement for a limited number of U.S. training personnel. They reported that by the "end of this year, the U.S. program for training Vietnamese should have progressed to the point where 1,000 US military personnel assigned to South Vietnam can be withdrawn."[12]

The reason for referring to the withdrawal of troops to an earlier report, rather than include the relevant information directly in the NSAM, could be due to using some degree of obfuscation to mask this information from inquiring eyes. It would surely had been easier to know what was being recommended.

What Were President Kennedy's Views on Withdrawing American Military Personnel in Vietnam, Both Public and Private?

President Kennedy's public view was expressed in an interview with Walter Cronkite: "I don't think that unless a greater effort is made by the government [of South Vietnam] to win popular support that the war can be won out there ... in the final analysis it is the people and the government itself who have to win or lose this struggle. All we can do is help, and we are making it very clear, but I don't agree with those who say we should withdraw. That would be a great mistake."[13]

His private view is more candid. President Kennedy told Hyannis Port neighbor Larry Newman on October 20, 1963, "I'm going to get those guys out, because we're not going to find ourselves in a war that is impossible to win."[14]

Why was there such a difference between the two views? One explanation is that President Kennedy's perception that to come out on his own in 1963 with the withdrawal plan described in the McNamara-Taylor Report (that President Kennedy had a major hand in writing), could cost him the Presidential election in 1964. Thus, there was to be no public announcement about the withdrawal which was planned to occur prior to the end of 1963. Note also that the McNamara-Taylor report was crafted by, among others, President Kennedy and his brother Robert. NSAM-263 was itself made TOP SECRET, and not declassified until three decades later. Even with a copy of both NSAM-263 and NSAM-273 in hand, without the McNamara-Taylor Report and the reference to it in both NSAMs, the planned withdrawal in Vietnam would not be known. The persons interested in the workings of the Kennedy administration have argued about whether President Kennedy remained a "true Cold Warrior," or if he became dis-enthralled with that position and its tenets, including the "Domino Theory," that countries near communist countries would "fall like dominos" to Communism. The first withdrawal, at the end of 1963, may have been planned to be announced either as it was taking place, or after it had been accomplished.

Oswald Starts Work at the Texas Schoolbook Depository; His Second Child is born.

Oswald found a rooming house that looked acceptable at 1026 North Beckley, however he was told that there wasn't a current vacancy. Oswald chose a room at 621 Marsalis Street, $7 for a week's rent. He told his landlord that he would pay the $7 when he returned. He was told he would have to find another place to live. The following week, he returned to 1026 Beckley, where a vacancy had occurred. The cost was $8 a week. Oswald moved in immediately, using the name O. H. Lee.[15]

Oswald had been helped in finding a job by Ruth Paine. Reportedly, Mrs. Paine was told that jobs were available at the Texas School Book Depository (TSBD). Paine called Superintendent Roy Truly, who confirmed the opening.[16] When Oswald called Ruth Paine that evening, she told him about the job. Oswald was interviewed by Truly the next day, and began work the following day, Wednesday October 16. His job was to fill book orders; his hours were 8 A.M. to 4:45 P.M.[17]

The weekend was celebratory. Friday the 18th was Oswald's 24th birthday. His second daughter, Rachel, was born late Sunday/early Monday morning.[18]

Just previous to the weekend, Oswald spoke to Judyth Baker. On October 16th they were upbeat, both had begun new jobs that day. Oswald felt that he was going back to Mexico before long, perhaps trying to rekindle their plan.[19] A call three nights later took on a very different tone. He finally told Judyth that he had been recruited to an actual assassination planning group. He reasoned the only purpose he provided was to be the patsy. Lee said that he would send on any information to someone who could help stop the assassination. Oswald thought it likely that he could be snuffed out.[20]

Walker, Stevenson, and the ACLU

On the evening of October 23, Oswald attended the USA Day Rally, whose major speaker was General Walker; Ruth Paine attended as well. On October 24, at the UN Day Celebration in Dallas, Oswald demonstrated against the UN with 100 others. At this event, Adlai Stevenson was spat on and hit with placards. Oswald saw this event as an insurance that tighter security would be given when President Kennedy came to Dallas in less than a month. Michael Paine was a witness on this occasion. On October 25, they attended a John Birch Society meeting. And on October 26, Oswald and Michael Paine attended a meeting of the American Civil Liberties Union, at which Oswald made some remarks. This sort of activity would have been unusual for a "loner."[21]

A Car for Marina

Oswald had arranged with the Paines to have them "give" a car to Marina. This gesture gives considerable information: the Paines knew that Oswald had other sources of income; but it kept Marina and the others around them with the view that Oswald was "dirt poor."

This was probably the view that Oswald's handler, David Atlee Phillips wanted Oswald to show to the public.[22]

The Bobby Baker Situation

On October 23, the Senate Rules Committee planned to investigate the financial affairs of Bobby Baker. This investigation would ultimately involve Donald Reynolds, an insurance salesman, who through Bobby Baker, sold an insurance policy to Lyndon Johnson. While this was only one of the areas where the Senate was investigating Bobby Baker, it was an area of particular concern to Lyndon Johnson.[23]

Endnotes

1 WC, XXVI, CE 3077, p. 680. See also Twyman, N. (1997). *Bloody Treason: The Assassination of John F. Kennedy*. Rancho Santa Fe, CA: Laurel Publishing, pp. 314-315.

2 WCR, XXVI CE 2910, P. 366

3 WCR, pp. 318-319.

4 WCR, p. 337.

5 Baker, J.V. (2010). *Me & Lee: How I Came to Know, Love, and Lose Lee Harvey Oswald*. Waltersville OR: Trine Day, p. 503.

6 Brown, W, (2013). *The Chronology*. Hillsdale, NJ: Author, p. 2941.

7 Ibid., pp. 2942-2943.

8 Ibid., p. 2968.

9 Douglass, J.W. (2008). *JFK and the Unspeakable: Why He Died and Why it Matters*. Maryknoll, NY: Orbis, p. 187.

10 Ibid., pp. 187-190.

11 Appendix B: Copies of NSAMs 263 and 273, and Some Primary Supporting Documents. ratical.org/ratville/JFK/USO/appB.html, retrieved 3/27/2018.

12 Ibid., p. 15.

13 Cited in Douglass, p. 189.

14 Loc. cit.

15 6 H 407.

16 3 H 34.

17 2 H 214-216.

18 3 H 39-40.

19 Baker, p. 504.

20 Ibid., p. 505.

21 Ibid., p. 512.

22 Ibid., pp. 506-507.

23 Williams, J.D. & Conway, D, (2001). "The Don Reynolds Testimony and LBJ." *Assassination Chronicles*, 7, 1, 19-28

Chapter Twelve

ASSASSINATION ATTEMPTS PLANNED PRIOR TO DALLAS

Chicago, November 2, 1963

An assassination attempt on President Kennedy was planned for Saturday November 2, 1963, during the Presidential motorcade on the route to Soldier Field, where the President was expected to attend the Army-Air Force football game. For this attempt, there was a group of four men who were to be the actual shooters; a lone person, Thomas Arthur Vallee, could serve as the scapegoat/patsy. Vallee's background would seem reminiscent of Lee Harvey Oswald. Vallee had served in the Marines from 1949-1952, and from 1955-1957, when he was honorably discharged with a diagnosis of schizophrenic reaction, paranoid type, with manifestations of homosexuality and femininity. Vallee had some involvement with the John Birch Society. Vallee had trained Cuban exiles to assassinate Fidel Castro for the CIA. Vallee was heavily armed and a person who had publicly voiced his contempt for President Kennedy. On Thursday, October 30, the Chicago Secret Service had a pretext interview with Vallee. At the time, he had two M-1 rifles, a .22 caliber revolver, and an estimated 1,000 rounds of ammunition in his possession. Vallee was not involved with the four-man team allegedly planning the assassination attempt. His place of employment overlooked the Jackson Street exit ramp on the motorcade route. One might surmise that, in the event of an actual assassination on November 2, Vallee might have served as an excellent patsy.[1]

On October 30, 1963, The Chicago FBI informed the Chicago Secret Service about a suspected assassination attempt by the four-man team related to President Kennedy's scheduled appearance at the Army-Air Force football game. The information came from a woman who owned a rooming house in Chicago's North Side. She had gone to a room to do some housekeeping where she discovered two rifles equipped with telescopic lenses. She had rented the room to two men she deemed to be Hispanic and noticed two white men going in and out of the room. Knowing that President Kennedy would be in Chicago soon, she called the authorities.

With this information, Acting Secret Service Chief for Chicago, Maurice Martineau, who was having a meeting with the other agents, called James Rowley, Chief of the Secret Service. Rowley told Martineau to investigate. Rowley also ordered that there were to be no written reports, no file number was to be associated with the assassination planned in Chicago, and Martineau was to report orally by phone to Rowley.

Three agents interviewed the owner of the rooming house. They then began following two of the men in their car. One of the agents had neglected to turn off his two-way radio, which made a loud squawk as they passed by the suspects. The suspects quickly bolted, and initially lost the agents in traffic. They were eventually apprehended, but the other two men couldn't be accounted for. With this information, President Kennedy's trip to Chicago was cancelled on the morning of November 2, 1963.[2]

November 18, 1963: Tampa

Less is known about the aborted Tampa attempt to assassinate President Kennedy. A brief article appeared in the *Tampa Tribune* on November 23, 1963. It appeared in only one edition of the paper. Two persons were of interest (perhaps as potential patsies): Gilberto Lopez and Miguel Casas Saez. Lopez had a brother who was then studying in Russia; Saez had learned Russian in Cuba from Russian instructors. The CIA had received two reports on Saez between the aborted Chicago attempt and the planned Tampa attempt. Lopez was actually a member of the Tampa chapter of the Fair Play for Cuba Committee (FPFC) and attended meetings. Unlike the supposed chapter in New Orleans that Lee Harvey Oswald formed, the Tampa chapter was a real group. There was a reported meeting among Oswald, Lopez and a key member of the Tampa FPFC.[3] If there was such a meeting, it involved an Oswald impostor. Oswald was reported to be at his rooming house throughout the weekend by the owner, Earlene Roberts.[4]

Apparently, the rationale for such a meeting was to link Oswald and Lopez. Both Lopez and Saez crossed into Mexico shortly after the assassination, returning to Cuba. Supposedly, Oswald was to have left for Cuba at the same time. Both Lopez and Saez were reportedly in Dallas on November 22, 1963. Lopez's wife remained in the United States and had not heard from him since November 1963; as of 2005, they were not divorced.[5]

Abraham Bolden's Proposed Testimony to the Warren Commission

Abraham Bolden was the first African American to serve on the White House detail in the Secret Service. His stay was short-lived, only three months. He became disillusioned with the White House detail for their apparent racist ways of acting, their playboy approach to their jobs, and their excessive consumption of alcohol. He was reassigned to the Chicago Secret Service group. After the assassination, Bolden thought he would like to testify before the Warren Commission about several issues. First there was the attitude in the White House detail that accepted drinking and carousing even when on assignment such as happened in Dallas, where they were in a strip club until the early hours into the morning of November 22, 1963. It is possible that one of the agents lost his commission book identifying him as a Secret Service agent. This would account for the man on the grassy knoll in Dealey Plaza who, upon being asked by a Dallas Police Officer, reportedly presented a leather-bound commission book identifying him as an agent of the U.S. Secret Service.

It is probably not happenstance that in January 1964, acting Chief Martineau announced to the Chicago agents that the Secret Service intended to update the identification books throughout the Agency. All agents were asked to turn their current books in immediately. The new books were received from Washington about 30 days later. The only apparent change, other than a new photograph, was the addition of the Word "The" in the title, replacing " Treasury Department" with "The Treasury Department." It seemed to Bolden that this change was made to cover up the apparent loss of the ID book in Dallas.[6]

Bolden intended to testify to these deficiencies in Secret Service procedures, but also to the aborted attempts on President Kennedy's life in both Chicago and Tampa. This would have made the eventual decision by the Warren Commission, that there was no conspiracy involved in President Kennedy's assassination, probably untenable. It would have also put the Secret Service on the hot seat in being involved with presidential protection.

On May 17, 1964 Bolden, along with other agents, were in Washington, D.C. for a workshop for agents, which was to begin the next day. Bolden tried to call the counsel for the Warren Commission, J. Lee Rankin, but he didn't know how to accomplish this. He called the White House switchboard; Bolden wished to let some member of the Commission know that he was interested in giving his observations and complaints about past Secret Service agent conduct.[7]

The Ordeals in Abraham Bolden's Life

The ordeal would begin on the day following his attempted call to the Warren Commission. Shortly after lunch at the Secret Service training session, Howard Anderson, Personnel Director for the Secret Service, poked his head into the classroom and motioned to Bolden, and Gary McLeod, also a Chicago Secret Service agent to come to him. Bolden was told that Acting Director Martineau had called and wanted both of them to return to Chicago immediately. Anderson took the two agents directly to the Airport; other agents would pick up their luggage and deliver it to the airport separately. The two agents were told the reason for the return was a particular case. Anderson said it should be finished in time to return to the Secret Service training. Inspector Gerard McCann had picked up the luggage after hastily shoving their belongings into their respective luggage. Bolden, seeing that the contents of his luggage seemed jammed in, wished to straighten it out. He was told there wasn't enough time for that by Anderson, that the airplane was waiting for them on the runway. When they got to the airplane, McLeod was assigned the aisle seat with Bolden in the middle seat, and McCann in the window seat. When Bolden hesitated for a minute, McCann offered to change seats with him.

Bolden suddenly realized that the two men weren't his traveling companions, they were his escort.[8]

When back in Chicago. Bolden was taken directly to the Secret Service offices. He was not allowed to call his wife or have any food, and was not told what was going on, other than there was no new counterfeit investigation.

Bolden was informed a warrant had been issued for his arrest, but his request to have his attorney present was ignored. The questions that were asked addressed his attempt to contact the White House switchboard. Inspector Gerard stated, "Listen Abe, Kennedy is dead. We did our best to protect him, and it didn't work out. We are not going to stand by and let you bury our careers and destroy the Secret Service."[9]

The Two Trials

The first trial began on July 6, 1964. The judge was J. Sam Perry. Perry kept a tight rein on Bolden's lawyer, but gave considerable latitude to the prosecution. Bolden was charged with trying to sell a Secret Service file to Joseph Spagnoli. Spagnoli was a suspect in a counterfeit operation. The file in question regarding Spagnoli was read by Bolden, as instructed by Agent John Russell, Bolden wrote his comments on the report and handed the report to Agent Conrad Cross. Spagnoli was in the office area that same afternoon; Agent Cross then noticed the file was missing. It was concluded that Bolden re-entered Cross's office and took the file, and that Bolden proceeded to try to sell the file to Spagnoli for $50,000; no thought was given to the possibility that Spagnoli might have stolen the file himself. The justice system in the US seems to be most effective when the defendant is not a minority; it seems to affect whether the government feels obligated to treat the defendant fairly. Also, the wealth of the defendant seems to affect their treatment. Bolden lost on both counts.

Throughout the trial, one might gauge that Bolden faced difficult odds. For example, several items were placed in evidence; a fingerprint expert testified on several specimens. The expert admitted that none of the exhibits were tested for Bolden's fingerprints. This did not detract from the exhibits being used by the prosecution. Bolden was also implicated by Frank Jones, a two-time convict, with a third charge waiting for him. From Bolden's point of view, the government was manufacturing evidence (and testimony) against him. It is worthwhile to remember that the Warren Commission was still taking testimony at the time of the trial; perhaps they didn't want to hear from Bolden either. In any event, he would never be allowed to testify before the Warren Commission.

During the trial, Bolden wanted to show that the Secret Service was manufacturing evidence so that the service itself was not threatened. Bolden wanted to show that the Secret Service had failed in its mission with regard to John F. Kennedy. His attorney responded: "You have a chance to win this case as it stands now, and I don't want you to complicate things more than necessary. Judge Perry isn't going to admit anything about Kennedy or what happened at Dallas in to your trial. The only thing you will accomplish by bringing Kennedy into this is going to put your life and the lives of your wife and children in jeopardy. You're dealing with people who killed the president in the street in the broad daylight."[10]

The case appeared to be headed for a hung jury. Perry included an opinion to the jury with, "I will express to you my comment on the evidence. In my opinion, the evidence sustains a verdict of guilty on counts one, two, and three of the indictment." As prejudicial as this statement was, the jury remained unable to reach a verdict. The judge set a new trial date for August 3, 1964.[11]

Before the second trial, Bolden went to a real estate company that he and Agent Cross visited on May 11, 1964, but Cross denied under oath that he had ever gone there. An office worker at the real estate agent found a record of the two of them being there but had to ask her employer to make a copy. Both the record of the visit and the employee would be unavailable for the second trial. The trial was even more unevenly handed than the first, but with a bizarre twist. The judge ordered everyone out of the courtroom while the jury was deliberating, except himself, the Secret Service agent, and the government attorneys. Whatever transpired in the building that night, the jury rendered a verdict of guilty the next day.[12] Bolden was sentenced to six years in prison (He was convicted on two other charges, each with a sentence of five years, with the sentences to run concurrently).[13]

Spagnoli's Trial

In a subsequent trial for Joseph Spagnoli's case, Spagnoli acknowledged that he lied in court when he testified about Bolden; J. Sam Perry was also the judge in this trial. Spagnoli asserted that one of the government lawyers, Richard Sikes, had told Spagnoli to lie. Conceivably, this revelation would cause a re-investigation of Bolden's conviction. Ray Smith, Bolden's appeal lawyer, was able to get a copy of an exhibit that was in Sikes and Spagnoli's handwriting regarding the alleged perjured testimony. Spagnoli had stolen it from Sikes desk. In an appeal of Bolden's case, Judge John Hastings directly asked Sikes, ..."did you solicit perjured testimony in any of the Bolden trials before the court of District Court Judge J. Sam Perry?" Sikes response was, "Your honor I refuse to answer that question on the grounds that my answer might tend to incriminate me."[14]

Eventually, the Court of Appeals would affirm Bolden's conviction. Bolden's thought in this regard was, "My conviction had to stand undisturbed in order to silence the echo from Dealey Plaza."[15]

The Ordeal Continued

Bolden was first taken to county jail, until he was sent to prison. His first prison was in Terre Haute, Indiana. He was moved around to several prisons, serving all but four months of his six-year sentence. To be sure, prison is particularly difficult for a former enforcement officer, as they are often targeted by other inmates. Though Bolden did encounter some difficulties, the reasons were seemingly the mental instability of some of the other inmates rather than a revenge motive. In a sense Bolden was somewhat of a minor celebrity due to his relationship to President Kennedy and to being a person with evidence of government misfeasance and malfeasance regarding President Kennedy's assassination; several inmates that he came into contact with were quite familiar with his story. One had collected articles about Bolden, even before meeting him. The occasional visitors from the Jim Garrison investigation made inmates aware of his continued importance in regard to the assassination.[16]

Upon his release from prison (September 25, 1969) he returned to Chicago to his wife and family. He returned to work with Ingersol Products, a firm he had worked for after his career with the Secret Service ended, and prior to his being imprisoned. When Ingersol Products indicated they were relocating out of Chicago, he became employed in management positions in quality control at other manufacturing firms in the Chicago area.[17]

Bolden continued the pursuit of justice regarding his wrongful conviction and imprisonment. Two petitions were submitted to the United States Attorney general, in 1974 and 1976.[18] It is not surprising that the petitions were denied; in 1976, Gerald Ford was the President of the United States, following Richard Nixon's resignation in disgrace. Ford had also served as a commissioner on the Warren Commission. Addressing Bolden's circumstances was a can of worms that the appointed president was not going to open. Ford's personal legacy would be situated on being on the Warren Commission, and *Portrait of an Assassin,*[19] a book that presents Oswald as a madman.

Bolden attempted to purchase transcripts of all his trials. In August 1973, the clerk of the district court phoned Bolden and informed him that none of those transcripts could be located. They had been ordered by the court of Judge J. Sam Perry, but the clerk never received them back.[20]

In January 1978, Bolden was interviewed by investigators from the House Committee on Assassinations. His interview, along with several other Secret Service agents, as well as their other sources of information, allowed them to make several conclusions including: " The Committee believes, on the basis of the evidence, that President Kennedy was probably assassinated as a result of a conspiracy."[21] "The Secret Service was deficient in the performance of their duties. The assassination of President Kennedy was the first and only such crime since the Secret Service was assigned responsibility for full time protection of the President in 1902"[22] "The Secret Service possessed information that was not properly analyzed, investigated, or used by the Secret Service in connection with the president's trip to Dallas; in addition Secret Service agents in the motorcade were inadequately prepared to protect the President from a sniper"[23] Another point of interest in the report is that an assassination attempt was planned on November 18, 1963, but in Miami. This attempt was averted by moving President Kennedy to his destination by helicopter instead of motorcade.[24] The report makes no mention of the planned Tampa assassination attempt. The Report of the House Committee on Assassinations vindicated, to a considerable degree, many of Bolden's concerns about the Secret Service. Yet the clearing of his record still eludes Abraham Bolden.

The Proposed C- Day Coup, Planned for December 1, 1963

The known published reference to the C-Day Coup was made by Lamar Waldron and Thom Hartman.[25] In fact, the only references to this event refer back to Waldron and Hartman. To their knowledge, no other name than C-Day is associated with this plot. C-Day was only one of several plots to remove Fidel Castro from power in Cuba. Waldron & Hartmann claim that both John and Robert Kennedy were on board with this plan; in John Kennedy's case, being on board with *any* plan to remove Castro from power seems questionable. His movements as president were towards peace, particularly with Soviet Russia, and by extension, with Cuba. The Bay of Pigs and the Cuban missile crisis seemingly taught President Kennedy that any plan directed toward violently removing Castro was bizarre. Somewhere there was a disconnect among the Kennedy's, the anti-Castro Cubans, the CIA, and any CIA operatives (which includes some Mafia members as did some of the other anti-Castro plots).

A close reading of JFK's intentions would show that, were any US involvement to take place, Castro would first have to be removed from power. In JFK's speech in Tampa on November 18, 1963 addressing the Cuban situation, which according to Waldron & Hartmann, had a special message for the C-Day coup leader (they did not reveal the coup leader's name in *Ultimate Sacrifice*, but later revealed him to be Juan Almeida, Commander of the Cuban Army, in *Legacy of Secrecy*.[26] The C-Day plan became known (to Waldron & Hartmann) as the JFK-Almeida plan. That message was to show the solidarity of JFK to the C-Day plan. The scheduled date for the plan was December 1, 1963.[27]

The text of the Tampa speech, allegedly directed at Commander Almeida was:

> ...The goals proclaimed in the Sierra Maestra were betrayed in Havana. It is important to restate what divides Cuba from my country and from the other countries in our hemisphere. It is the fact that a small band of conspirators has stripped the Cuban people of their freedom and handed over the independence and sovereignty of the Cuban nation to forces beyond the hemisphere. They have made Cuba the victim of foreign imperialism, an instrument of the policy of others, a weapon in an effort dictated by external powers to subvert the other American republics.
>
> This, and this alone divides us. As long as this is true, nothing is possible. Without it, everything is possible. Once this barrier is removed, we will be ready and anxious to work with the Cuban

> people in pursuit of those progressive goals which a few short years ago stirred the hopes and the sympathy of many people throughout this hemisphere ... [28]

Given the experience of the Bay of Pigs, the peace talks with Premier Nikita Khrushchev, and Kennedy's peace speech at Washington University, it would seem abundantly clear that JFK's understanding of the so-called JFK-Almeida plan would only involve Cubans then living in Cuba until Commander Almeida had successfully removed Castro from power. It would not seem to involve another tragic landing as occurred in the Bay of Pigs. There were camps of Cuban exiles who were training for such an endeavor, but when their existence became known the FBI would close them down. One such training camp was raided in late July, 1963, near Lake Pontchartrain in Louisiana. In one part of the raid, eleven men were briefly detained and their munitions taken from them. The other part of the raid was at the training camp led by Gerry Patrick Hemming[29] and Frank Sturgis,[30] who were training anti-Castro Cubans. No arrests were made in these raids.[31]

What Ever Happened to C-Day/JFK-Almeida?

Those who search their memories for an answer to this question might reply: "To my knowledge such an event never happened." So, what did happen? A simple response might be: Well, President Kennedy was assassinated on November 22, 1963. Maybe that ended it. But that event wouldn't seem to satisfy the objective of the removal of Fidel Castro, who would hold office another 45 years before turning it over to his brother.

According to Waldron & Hartman, after the assassination, Bobby Kennedy put the JFK-Almeida plan on hold. When Bobby Kennedy told the newly functioning President Lyndon Johnson about it (Johnson was totally unaware of the plan) Johnson did not signal a go-ahead for the plan's continuance, so that to Bobby Kennedy, the plan was on hold. The continued efforts through January 1964 failed to garner Johnson's support; LBJ made it clear that no such plan was appropriate at that time; Johnson suggested any of the Cubans preparing for the plan be allowed to assimilate into the US military or seek employment in the US, ending the JFK-Almeida plan.[32]

In trying to interpret the ending of the plan, a conjecture can be made as to what might have happened. When President Johnson first heard of the plan, it would seem likely that he would seek out FBI Director J. Edgar

Hoover regarding what Johnson might do. In that scenario, Hoover would seemingly have said something like, "Lyndon, why would your presidency be stymied the same way JFK was, in a plan that seems very much like the Bay of Pigs?" Hoover would inform LBJ, if LBJ didn't already know, that the FBI had been closing down groups of Cubans who were being trained to go back to Cuba, much as prior to the Bay of Pigs. The difference here was that the Cubans were alerted to plans in the US to depose Castro. Castro had been planning for a second invasion, and now had the backing of Soviet Russia.

Hoover would have pointed out that such a scenario would in effect preclude LBJ from ever winning the presidency on his own. Of course, LBJ might possibly figure this out, but Hoover would have seemed to be part of LBJ's informational base.

Yet another interpretation is just as possible. The JFK-Almeida plan might have been a ruse to hide the actual reason for what happened. The original reason for the plan might have been a coup-d'état to eliminate Present Kennedy, and the ruse would keep many of the participants out of the loop as to the actual reason for the plan.

Looking at the career of Commander Juan Almeida might lend credence to this alternative interpretation. Almeida was studying law at the University Havana when he and Castro met in 1952. At the time, Castro was a candidate for the Cuban congress. Fulgencia Batista then overthrew the Cuban government and cancelled the elections. Almeida joined forces with other followers of Castro (123 men and women) and in 1953, they attacked an army barracks in Moncada. This action was unsuccessful. Castro and Almeida were sent to prison but were released in 1955. Castro and his men went to Mexico, where they planned to return to Cuba and attempt an overthrow of the Batista dictatorship. In late 1958, they were able to cause Batista to flee from Cuba. On January 1, 1959, Castro took the reins of power. By this time Almeida had been named head of the Santiago Column of the Revolutionary Army.

From this point forward, it appears Castro and Almeida remained friends and allies.[33] Almeida's wife and two children were taken out of harm's way prior to December 1, 1963.[34] If Almeida was the alleged coup leader, the only visible evidence would seem to be the exodus from Cuba of his family. Apparently, Castro determined that the C-Day (JFK-Almeida) plot was just another CIA plot. There is no indication that Almeida was willing to become a traitor to Cuba. In 1966, Almeida became a member of the Central Committee and Political Bureau. In 1976, he was elected to the National

Assembly of People's power. In 1998, he was granted the title "Hero of the Republic of Cuba." For many years he was the third-ranking member of the Council of State for Cuba. Upon Almeida's death on November 11, 2009 the retired former head of State, Fidel Castro, issued the statement, "I don't know, neither did any of us, know just how much pain news of his passing would bring. I was privileged of his exemplary conduct during more than half a century of heroic and victorious resistance."[35] Perhaps the reason that the C-Day/JFK-Almeida plan stopped on the assassination of John F. Kennedy is that the real goal had been met in Dallas.

Endnotes

1 Waldron, L. & Hartmann, T. (2005). *Ultimate Sacrifice: John and Robert Kennedy, the Plan for a Coup in Cuba, and the Murder of JFK*. New York: Carroll & Graf, p. 627. See also Williams, J.D. (2006). "Ultimate Sacrifice-The Whole is Less than the Sum of its Parts." *JFK Deep Politics Quarterly*, 11, 3, 15-21.

2 Bolden, A. (2008). *The Echo from Dealey Plaza*. New York: Harmony Books, pp. 55-56. See also Williams, J.D. (2008). "Echo from Dealey Plaza-Abraham Bolden." *The Dealey Plaza Echo*, 12, 3, 51-54.

3 Waldron & Hartman, (2005), p. 754.

4 Armstrong, J. (2003). *Harvey & Lee: How the CIA Framed Oswald*. Arlington, TX: Quasar Ltd. p. 773.

5 Waldron & Hartmann, (2005), p. 762.

6 Bolden, p. 54-55.

7 Ibid., p. 72.

8 Ibid., p. 62.

9 Ibid., p.74.

10 Ibid., pp.145-146.

11 Ibid., p.161.

12 Ibid., pp. 165-189.

13 Ibid., p. 188.

14 Ibid., pp. 213-215.

15 Ibid., p. 221.

16 Ibid., pp. 226-228.

17 Ibid., pp. 277-278.

18 Ibid., pp. 279.

19 Ford, G.R. (1965). *Portrait of an Assassin*. New York: Simon & Schuster.

20 Bolden, pp. 279-280.

21 HSCA Final Assassinations Report (1979).history_matters.com/archive/jfk/hsca/report/html/, p. 95.

22 Ibid., p. 227.

23 Ibid., p. 228.

24 Ibid., p. 230.

25 Waldron & Hartman (2005).

26 Waldron, L. & Hartmann, T. (2008). *Legacy of Secrecy; The Long Shadow of the JFK Assassination*. New York: Counterpoint.

27 Waldron & Hartmann (2008). p. 1.

28 Ibid., p. 693. According to Waldron and Hartmann, this speech became classified by the CIA, and later declassified. What rational thinking person classifies a public speech by an American President delivered to several thousand people?

29 Gerald Patrick Hemming was an ex-Marine soldier of fortune who had been a person of interest in many writings about the JFK assassination. Hemming was an imposing figure at 6'6" and 230 lbs. Hemming had been part of Castro's revolutionaries, who uprooted Fulgencio Batista in late 1959. He became an asset for the CIA. Hemming admitted meeting Lee Harvey Oswald on a few occasions. See Twyman, N. (1997). *Bloody Treason: The Assassination of John F. Kennedy*. Rancho Santa Fe, CA: Laurel, pp. 647-748.

30 Frank Sturgis, aka Frank Fiorini, is best known for his participation in the Watergate break-in.

31 Hinkle, W. & Turner, W. (1992). *Deadly Secrets: The CIA-MAFIA War against Castro and the Assassination of JFK*. New York: Thunder's Mouth Press, pp. 223-229.

32 Waldron & Hartmann (2008). pp. 270-288.

33 wikipedia.org/wiki/Juan_Almeida_Bosque, retrieved 7/10/2016.

34 Smith, L, (2006). *New York Post*, 22nd September 2006. Also cited in ref. 33, this chapter.

35 wikipedia. org/wiki/Juan_Almeida_Bosque

CHAPTER THIRTEEN

EARLY NOVEMBER TO NOVEMBER 21, 1963

As the calendar turned to November, the outlook for both President Kennedy and Lee Oswald was ominous. The coup in South Vietnam was successfully carried out by the work of a group of Vietnamese generals and the hegemonies of several Americans including Ambassador Henry Cabot Lodge, Jr. and Ambassador at Large Averell Harriman. Though President Kennedy supported a coup of the Diem regime, he instructed that it be a bloodless coup. It is said that Kennedy was at first shocked and then became profoundly irritated when he found out that both Diem & Nhu were assassinated.[1]

And Vietnam was not his only concern; on that very same day, an assassination plot was directed at him in Chicago. Fortunately, Abraham Bolden was able to get the information to the White House in time to cancel President Kennedy's scheduled trip to see the Army-Air Force game at Soldier Field. Officially, President Kennedy cancelled his trip to Chicago because they had to deal with the coup in South Vietnam that left Diem and his brother Nhu dead.[2] But there was a movement in the United States that was willing to assassinate the young President. Would this continue through his presidency, perhaps ending it? By hindsight we know the terrible answer to that question.

As to Vietnam, on November 8, President Kennedy recognized the new regime in South Vietnam. Would NSAM 263 stand? Or would President Kennedy move even more quickly to withdraw forces from South Vietnam? For those who opposed the Kennedy presidency, how would they see his stance affecting their interests? Surely the contents of NSAM 263 would have been known to the Joint Chiefs of Staff, who were among Kennedy's strongest detractors. They may well have taken issue with having 1,000 service members home before Christmas 1963, and withdrawing all service personnel by 1965.[3] Would they advocate an assassination of the president here at home?

Oswald's Concerns

Oswald had begun working at the Texas School Book Depository on October 16, 1963. On weekdays he stayed at the boarding house at 1026 North Beckley and spent his weekends at the Paine household with Marina and his two daughters. On weekday evenings, some of his time was with the assassination planning group at the behest of David Atlee Phillips (Mr. B.). From Oswald's point of view, he was infiltrating this group. Because Oswald was a paid FBI informant,[4] he knew that he could convey information to the FBI about the assassination plans. The group continued to meet on a regular basis, but the membership seemed to always have some changes.[5] A person introduced himself to Oswald as a Secret Service agent, and spent time going over possible places that might be used by shooters. It may seem more likely that this person was a CIA agent gathering information on Oswald's own knowledge of goings on regarding the plot. If the person was working with the CIA, they most likely were investigating Oswald at the behest of David Atlee Phillips. Presumably Oswald was wary of Phillips being the person at the center probably trying to make Oswald the patsy.

The FBI person working with Oswald might have been authentic. There is evidence that the source of the information regarding the planned assassination was a person referred to only as "Lee."[6] Dr. Mary Sherman gave Oswald several contacts in Chicago, where Dr. Sherman previously practiced medicine. It appears Oswald did in fact call a person or persons in Chicago in regard to the planned assassination attempt in Chicago. Most likely Oswald would have made the contact by pay telephone leaving his name as "Lee."[7] Also, Oswald likely gave a Dallas area FBI agent information on the scheduled attempt in Dallas. A telegram was sent to the FBI office in Washington, and probably several other FBI offices in the United States, including New Orleans.

A telegram was received by William Walter and his wife Josey early Sunday morning, November 17, 1963, at the FBI office in New Orleans. After processing the telegram Walter asked his wife to type a copy of it. Walter made notes of it, and reconstructed the telegram from them.[8]

William Walter was called to testify before the House Subcommittee on Assassinations (HSCA). Walter related that FBI Agent John Lester Quigley requested that he check the New Orleans FBI files to see if there was a file for Lee Harvey Oswald. Walter found the file, which had an informant classification. Walter also recalled that Special Agent Warren deBrueys' name was on the jacket of the file. Walter also addressed the telegram that was received at the New Orleans FBI office regarding a possible assassination attempt in Dallas by a militant revolutionary group. However, no other FBI employee could (or would) corroborate Walters testimony; the HSCA chose to ignore his testimony. Walter, who had left the FBI to begin a career in banking, summed up his former colleagues' reticence to testify, "I had gotten the [gut] feeling from everybody I talked to that 'we know it is true, but we are not going to talk about it.'"[9]

Oswald met with an FBI agent and gave him the information that Oswald had learned from the assassination planning group. The agent apparently sent the information to FBI headquarters in Washington, D.C. Subsequently, headquarters sent a telegram with Oswald's information to at least three other stations, including New Orleans.[10]

Joseph Adams Milteer

On November 9, 1963, Joseph Adams Milteer was involved in a conversation with Miami police informant William Somersett. Milteer was a wealthy right-wing extremist and a founder of the National States Rights Party. He was also a member of the Congress of Freedom and the White Citizen's Council of Atlanta. Somersett had infiltrated the National States Rights Party and became acquainted with Milteer.[11] In retrospect, Milteer seemed prescient regarding the assassination. Milteer indicated that it would be easy to hit Kennedy from a multi-story building. The plan was "There ain't any countdown to it, we've just got to be sitting on go. Countdown, they can move in on you, and on go, they can't. Countdown is alright for a slow, prepared operation. But in an emergency operation, you've got to be sitting on go."[12]

Milteer indicated that someone would be picked up within an hour of the shooting, but that was to satisfy the public. Somersett undoubtedly passed the information on to the FBI; when President Kennedy visited Miami in the ensuing week, he was flown by helicopter from the airport to his venue, bypassing a motorcade, thus avoiding tall office buildings. The following week Milteer called Somersett from Dallas, saying he was waiting for President Kennedy's motorcade to come by. When Milteer was questioned on November 27, 1963, he denied any conversations with Somersett (despite tape recordings of their respective voices).[13]

Several questions come to mind regarding Milteer. Why would he even know about the means of effecting the assassination of President Kennedy? Who would have entrusted him with that information? Is it possible that members of his right-wing groups could accurately posit the ensuing assassination without having contact with the plotters?

November 20, 1963: Three Oswalds

November 20, 1963: While there had been several multiple sightings of "Oswald," between 10 A.M. and 10:30 A.M., three apparently different sightings occurred. One Oswald was at work at the Texas School Book Depository; at 10:00 A.M. a second "Oswald" entered the Dobbs House Restaurant, located at 1221 N. Beckley, two blocks from 1026 N. Beckley, Oswald's Boarding house. This Oswald created a commotion after being served his breakfast. Oswald began cursing at the waitress, Mary Dowling; also present for this display were the owner, the chef, another patron, and a police officer, J.D. Tippit. Then at 10:30 A.M., Ralph Leon Yates, a refrigeration mechanic was driving on the R.L. Thornton Freeway where he spotted a hitchhiker. Yates stopped and gave the hitchhiker, a young man, a ride. The young man had a package 4-4.5-foot-long, wrapped in brown paper, which Yates said should be placed in the back of the truck. The hitchhiker preferred to keep the package close to him; the contents were said to be curtain rods. The hitchhiker asked several curious questions, including, did Yates think the president could be assassinated, by someone placed in a tall building with a high-powered rifle? Yates let the hitchhiker off at the corner of Houston and Elm Street. When Yates saw a photograph of Oswald after the assassination, he recognized the hitchhiker as Oswald, and surmised the "curtains" was a gun.[14] It is quite interesting that we have simultaneously Oswald and persons posing as Oswald in Dallas. Information like this would have to be suppressed once the future Commission decided that Oswald was a loner and there was no conspiracy. Prior to the assassination, such decisions obviously hadn't been made. But *two* Oswald impersonators in Dallas at the same time? Perhaps the various plotters either were not aware of one another, or some other mistake was made by the plotters.

Rose Cherami

Rose Cherami is one of the dozens of names for Melba Christine Marcades, born in Houston, Texas on October 23, 1923. Melba was somewhat of a "wild child," who began her documented life of crime with stealing a car at 17. When she died at 41, she had been arrested over 50 times. The charges included larceny, auto theft, possession of narcotics, driving under the influence of narcotics, driving while intoxicated, prostitution, arson, vagrancy, and, drunk and disorderly behavior, among others.[15]

She was more than the record on her police blotter. Perhaps the outpouring of names was related to new and changing periods in her life. She variously tried more routine vocations, at least for short periods of time. As late as 1957, she was working as a telephone operator, and referred to herself as a wife, in a picture (though there does not seem to be a record of a marriage; still, one of her aliases was Mrs. Albert Rodman). She had a son, born in 1953, who was named Michael Marcades. She also ran narcotics for the Marcello organization, and worked as a strip tease dancer for Jack Ruby. But generally, she enjoyed the thrill of the road, usually with male companions.

In 1963, she was stationed out of Thibodaux, Louisiana. In mid to late November, she was traveling from Florida with two Italian-looking men. They were near Eunice, Louisiana, having just left either Kilroy's or the Silver Slipper, or both (both were "cathouses"; Rose had plied her wares at the Silver Slipper). Early in the morning on November 20, 1963, Rose Cherami was found near Highway 190. Though the racier version of the story is that she was thrown out of the car to be abandoned by her two companions, the more likely story is that her companions abandoned her at the Silver Slipper after she became too high from drugs. One of her companions slapped her around. She then tried to hitchhike and was grazed by a car, causing her to fall to the ground. Lt. Francis Fruge picked her up at roadside. She was taken to the Moosa Hospital in Eunice. Rose Cherami presented as having been thrown out of a car. Louis Pavur, a radiologic technologist, saw no evidence of this having occurred.

Cherami revealed to Lt. Fruge and perhaps to the police at the jail she was transferred to, that she and her two companions began in Florida and were continuing to Dallas where they would assassinate President Kennedy on Friday, November 22, 1963. With the money that she would get, she would go to Houston and pick up her 10 year-old son at her parents' house. One would guess that she was considered to be in a state of psychotic hallucination or something similar, and Lt. Fruge next transported her to the Louisiana State Hospital in Jackson, the same hospital that Lee Harvey Oswald had applied to for a job less than three months previously. As it happened, this was Rose Cherami's second trip to the State Hospital in Jackson. Her claims about the assassination of President Kennedy were passed off as the ramblings of a woman best placed in a state hospital – until the events of November 22 had occurred. Then, all records regarding Rose Cherami, by both hospitals, the Eunice jail, and the notes made by Lt. Fruge were seized by government agents. Only Louis Pavur made a copy of the page in the Moosa Hospital where Rose Cherami signed her name upon admission.[16]

Rose Cherami's life was destined to end on the highway. She was found beside Highway 155, about one and one-half miles east of Big Sandy, Texas on September 4, 1965. Jerry Don Moore was driving by an area that seemed strange. He was driving back on the same stretch of highway that he had driven only 15 minutes before, but the scene was quite different. This time, there were three or four suitcases laid along the line in the middle of the road. Cherami appeared to be sleeping, with her elbows out. She was just off the road. Moore swerved to avoid hitting Cherami. Moore found that Cherami was still breathing. Moore noticed tread marks on her arms. It appeared that the suitcase was positioned so that an unsuspecting driver would run over Cherami. Moore tried to assist. He picked up Cherami and placed her lying in the back seat, trying to seek medical attention. He stopped briefly in Hawkins, Texas where a policeman told him that the nearest hospital was in Gladewater, but the policeman said there was a local doctor that could see her. The policeman escorted Moore to the doctor's home. After examining Cherami, the doctor called the Gladewater Hospital, who dispatched an ambulance.

Moore left Cherami with the doctor, and first went to the bizarre scene. The luggage was still in the road. Moore collected the luggage, and went through it, looking for any identification. He did find a "douche bag" in one of the cases, which suggested to him she might be a prostitute.[17]

On the way to the hospital in the ambulance, Cherami said that "I Worked for Jack Ruby."[18] Moore returned to his home in Tyler, Texas, but couldn't sleep. He proceeded to the Gladewater Hospital, arriving between 9:30 and 10:00 A.M.; he was informed that the lady had died. But the mystery didn't end there. She was listed as D.O.A., but her listed time of death was 11:00 A.M.[19]

The Last Telephone Contact Between Lee Oswald and Judyth Baker

At 11:00 P.M. on November 20, Lee Harvey Oswald called Judyth Baker, pay phone to pay phone. They spoke for 90 minutes. Oswald mentioned that he had two more telephone calls later that night. And he mentioned that he was able to send out information that may be able to save President Kennedy (probably a reference to the telegram sent to the Headquarters of the FBI in Washington, D.C.). Oswald said that he was no longer alone and that an abort team was sent to Dallas. Oswald proclaimed that if he had to give his life to save President Kennedy, this would make his life meaningful. Judyth suggested that he take a sick day, something like playing hooky at school. Oswald reasoned that if he didn't show up for work, the plotters would come for his family and look for Oswald until they found him. They would come for Judyth, too. Oswald said that there wouldn't be another call from him unless he reached Laredo. They reviewed their plans if Oswald reached Mexico (which possibly could be in the next several days).[20]

Oswald said, "You'll get on the plane.... I'll make sure you'll be okay. I'll be there if ... if I don't make it out, then you'll have to go on without me."[21]

Judyth replied, "How? Who could ever replace you in my heart?"[22]

Oswald continued, saying that Judyth could make babies. The conversation had become very depressing. Judyth asked, what would Lee do tomorrow? Lee replied that he would say goodbye to Marina and his two daughters. Oswald ended with, "Know who my handler was ... Mr. B., Benson, Benton or Bishop? Well he's from Fort Worth, so it has to be Phillips. He is a traitor. Phillips is behind this. I need you to remember that name, David Atlee Phillips."[23]

They would never have a chance to communicate again.

November 21, 1963

After conversing with Mike Forrestal, the new assistant to McGeorge Bundy, about all options in Vietnam, President Kennedy was preparing to leave for his Texas trip. Jacqueline Kennedy was traveling with him on a political trip for the first time since the election campaign of 1960. First, they boarded a helicopter at 10:45 A.M. CST. Twenty minutes later, Air Force One was in the air. Their first stop was San Antonio, where President Kennedy dedicated the Aerospace Medical Center. Then they went to Houston, for a testimonial dinner for Representative Albert Thomas. The Presidential party finished their dinners. Vice President Johnson left in his airplane (Some called it Air Force Two) with Jack Valenti, so that they would be at the Carswell Air Force Base in Fort Worth to greet the President when he arrived. Kennedy's airplane arrived minutes after Johnson's. JFK and Jackie stayed at the Texas Hotel in Fort Worth. In their room, the hosts had assembled a world-class group of paintings which included a Monet, a Picasso, and a Van Gogh, among others, assembled from several different local museums for that one night.[24]

In Dallas, Wesley Buell Frazier gave Lee Harvey Oswald a ride to the Paine residence after work. Oswald almost never went to the Paine residence during weekdays, but the night of Thursday, November 21, 1963 was "special." In his mind, Oswald knew that the events that were to transpire would make this evening the last time he could see his two girls and Marina, perhaps for a long time, perhaps forever.[25]

Endnotes

1 Reeves, R. (1993). *President Kennedy: Profiles in Power.* New York: Simon & Schuster, pp. 635-652.

2 Douglass, J.W. (2008). *JFK and the Unspeakable: Why He Died and Why it Matters.* Maryknoll, NY: Orbis, p. 213.

3 National Security Action Memorandum No. 263, October 11, 1963 (1991). Foreign Relations of the United States, 1961-1963, Volume IV: Vietnam: August-December1963. Washington: U.S. Printing Office, p. 396.

4 Douglass, p. 64.

5 Baker, J.V. (2010). *Me & Lee: How I Came to Know, Love and Lose Lee Harvey Oswald.* Walterville, OR: Trine Day, pp. 515-516.

6 Douglass. p. 200, p. 217, pp. 363-364.

7 Baker, pp. 516-517.

8 Williams, J.D. (2004). "Was the FBI Searching for Oswald the Day Before the Assassination?" *The Dealey Plaza Echo* 9, 2, 46-52; Junior Moore sent to this writer a homemade video of himself and William Walter discussing their respective roles as witnesses regarding Oswald.

9 From William Walter's Executive Session testimony to the HSCA, March 23, 1978, HSCA document #014029. See also Williams, J.D. (2016). "Why is Oswald Still Considered the Assassin?" *The Dealey Plaza Echo*, 19, 2, 14-22.

10 La Fontaine, R., & La Fontaine, M. (1996). *Oswald Talked: The New Evidence in the JFK Assassination*. Gretna, LA: Pelican Publishing Company, pp. 299-300.

11 Marrs, J. (1989). *Crossfire: The Plot That Killed Kennedy.* New York: Carroll & Graff, pp. 265-267.

12 Groden, R.J. (1993). *The Killing of a President.* New York: Penguin, pp. 153-155.

13 Marrs, pp. 265-267.

14 Brown, W. (2013). *The Chronology.* Hillsdale, NJ: Author, p. 3205.

15 Reitzes, D. (2012). *The JFK 100: The Prediction of Rose Cherami.* jfk-online.com/jfk100cher.html, retrieved 7/8/2017.

16 Elliot, T.C. (2013). *A Rose by Many Other Names: Rose Cherami and the JFK Assassination.* Walterville, OR: Trine-Day. Rose Cherami's son received a doctorate and taught music at Columbia State University in Georgia. He wrote a book about his mother, Rose Cherami; *Gathering Fallen Petals*, published by JFK Lancer in 2016.

17 Ibid., pp. 61-66.

18 Ibid., p. 65.

19 Ibid., p. 66.

20 Baker, J.V. pp. 519-520.

21 Ibid., p. 520.

22 Loc. cit.

23 Ibid., p. 521.

24 Reeves, pp. 660-661. Brown, W. p. 3250, p. 3253, p. 3256, p. 3287, p. 3290.

25 Roffman, H. (1976). *Presumed Guilty: A Factual Account Based on the Commission's Public and Private Documents.* New York: A.S. Barnes & Co., p. 56.

Chapter Fourteen

NOVEMBER 22, 1963

Sometime after midnight, Vice-President Lyndon Baines Johnson arrived at the Clint Murchison estate in Dallas and hurriedly went into the meeting that had been going on for some time and apparently was about to break up. The meeting was about honoring J. Edgar Hoover, who in just over a month would turn 68 and presumably be subject to mandatory retirement. The guest list included John McCloy, who had an illustrious career in government, entrusted with responsibilities by Presidents from President Franklin Roosevelt to President Ronald Regan. McCloy had been President of the World Bank, and significantly, he would become one of the seven members of the Warren Commission; other guests included Richard Nixon; George Brown of Brown & Root; R.L. Thornton, businessman, philanthropist, and former mayor of Dallas; H.L. Hunt, billionaire oil tycoon, and a host of other Texans, many involved in oil.[1]

Madeleine Brown was surprised to see her former lover and father of her 12-year-old son, Lyndon Johnson, show up at the party. He had been in a whirlwind of activity, first with the Pepsi convention where Richard Nixon had spoken on Tuesday. Then he was involved with President Kennedy's Texas trip. Yet there he was. After going into the party only briefly Johnson re-emerged and came up to Madeleine. He squeezed her hand, so hard that she felt it was being crushed, and whispered into her ear, *"After tomorrow, those goddamn Kennedy's will never embarrass me again – that's no threat – that's a promise."*[2]

Then Johnson went like a flash to Pat Kirkwood's "Cellar Door," an after-hours night club. At this same club were at least a few Secret Service men who stayed until 4 A.M.[3]

Buell Wesley Frazier

Having brought Oswald to the Paine's residence on Thursday night, Frazier stopped at the Paine residence to pick him up Friday morning. Oswald was carrying a package he described as being curtain rods. Only two witnesses recall seeing Oswald with the package, Frazier, and a neighbor, Linnie Mae Russell. Both described the package to be less than

28 inches long. However, the wooden stock of the barrel of the Mannlicher-Carcano rifle was 34.8 inches long; if the witnesses testimony were accurate (and there were no more witnesses), the package could not have contained the rifle. No one at the Texas School Book Depository, other than Buell Wesley Frazier, reported seeing the package.[4] Prior to going to work with Frazier, Oswald left his wedding ring on the dresser in their bedroom; he had never left his ring before. He also left a wallet holding $170 in the dresser door.[5]

Vice President Johnson Calls Madeleine Brown from Fort Worth

Lyndon Johnson called Madeleine Brown on the morning of November 22, 1963, from the lobby of the Texas Hotel. The only words Madeleine got in were "About last night."[6]

Still aflame with his fury, Johnson blurted out, "That son-of-a-bitch crazy Yarborough and that goddamn fucking Irish mafia bastard."[7]

Madeleine replied, "I'm looking forward to tonight."[8]

Johnson replied, 'I've got a minute to get to the parking lot to hear that bastard!," and then slammed down the telephone.[9]

The Morning in Fort Worth

At 8:45 A.M. President Kennedy left his hotel and walked across the street to address a group of people waiting in a parking lot. After speaking there, he returned to the hotel to speak at the Chamber of Commerce breakfast. He was in a jovial mood, joking about how both his wife and Lyndon's wife would be asked about the outfits they were wearing, whereas no one cared what he and Lyndon were wearing. President Kennedy was also given a Western hat. President Kennedy eschewed the wearing of hats. When asked when he might wear the hat, President Kennedy indicated that if a person were interested they could come to his office next week and he would put it on. After breakfast, President Kennedy and his entourage were taken to the airport for the short flight to Love Field in Dallas.[10]

Arriving in Dallas

Minutes after takeoff in Fort Worth, Air Force One landed in Dallas at Love Field. A large and enthusiastic crowd was there, awaiting President Kennedy's arrival. To the dismay of the Secret Service, President Kennedy became engaged with several of the well-wishers, to their delight. Jacqueline Kennedy was given a large bouquet of red roses.[11]

The Whereabouts of Richard Nixon

Richard Nixon had some difficulty recalling where he was on November 22, 1963, but tended to give a general version that he flew out of Dallas in the morning and arrived in New York at 12:56 p.m., Dallas time. He claims he first heard of Kennedy being shot after entering a cab, and someone yelled that President Kennedy had been shot; a variation of this is that a reporter revealed that President Kennedy had been shot.

Another version (not due to Nixon) was that Nixon was in Dallas at the time President Kennedy was shot. A young man was listening to a talk at his school on April 2, 1975 regarding Nixon's whereabouts. The speaker had iterated one of the Nixon stories. The young man was the son of Mr. Harvey Russel of the Pepsi Cola Company. He had been told by his father that Richard Nixon was still at the Pepsi Convention in Dallas when the announcement that President Kennedy had been killed was made. Nixon boarded a plane later that afternoon. Mr. Russel confirmed the information that his son had conveyed. Why was the truth so hard for Nixon to bear?[12]

Security Stripping the Motorcade

The concept of "security stripping" regarding the trip to Dallas has been articulated by Vincent Palamara.[13] There were several aspects to security stripping in Dallas. First, the planning of the Presidential motorcade would have been predicated to some degree on the choice of the venue for the luncheon. Two venues were considered; The Trade-Mart (which was the site chosen) or the Women's Building. Different routes would be needed for these two sites. The Trade-Mart, the much smaller (but newer) venue seemed to be preferred by those who wanted the luncheon to be more of an elite affair, whereas the Women's Building was much larger and could accommodate a bigger (and less elite) crowd. Taking the route that was eventually chosen violated the rules of the Secret Service regarding parade routes; the turn at Houston Street to Elm Street in front of the Texas School Book Depository called for a left-hand turn of 120 degrees, obviously greater than 90 degrees. The motorcycle placement in Dallas was uniquely different in that no motorcycles were astride the Presidential limousine. A Dallas Police Department squad car containing homicide detectives was removed by the Secret Service.[14]

The man wearing a raincoat and apparently signaling by opening his umbrella should have been intercepted by theSecret Service.[15] There was/were a person or persons posing as Secret Service agents who were encountered by four police officers and at least three spectators. Apparently, Lee Harvey Oswald was also encountered by this agent in front of the Texas School Book Depository.[16]

The police detail on the parade route ended just before the 120-degree turn onto Elm Street on the way to the Stemmons Freeway.[17] Dallas Sheriff Bill Decker told his men in no way to participate in the security of the motorcade. Decker had given this order after previously having offered to have his men incorporated as additional personnel for the security of President Kennedy. The change was made after Decker was told by someone in Washington to withhold security in Dallas.[18]

The Order of the Vehicles in the Parade

The listing of the vehicles in the parade was as follows:

1. Advance Car
2. Pilot Car
3. Lead Car
4. Presidential Limousine
5. Presidential Secret Service Follow Up Car
6. Vice-Presidential Car
7. Vice-Presidential Secret Service Follow Up Car
8. Mayor's Car
9. National press Pool Car
10. Camera Car #1
11. Camera Car #2
12. Camera Car #3
13. Congressman's Car #1
14. Congressman's Car #2
15. Congressman's Car #3
16. VIP Car
17. White House Press Bus #1
18. Local Press Pool Car
19. White House Press Bus #2
20. Extra Car #1
21. Western Union Car

22. White House Signal Corps Car
23. Extra Car #2
24. Official Party Bus
25. Rear Police Car[19]

It is not clear what the logic was for placing the vehicles in this order, but one point is clear; presidential safety was not the first criterion. Looking at the order it is not clear why Admiral George Burkley, President Kennedy's personal physician is located in the official party bus, the last vehicle other than the final police car! In an emergency, he was as far removed from the president as it was possible to place him. I would have preferred he be in the presidential Limousine, or possibly the follow up Secret service car. Why wasn't a video car just preceding the president? And perhaps one of the White House Press Busses could have been placed between the president's Secret Service car and the Vice-President's car. But putting the president's personal physician at the back of the parade was absurd.

The Motorcade

The motorcade was to follow a circuitous 11-mile route from the Love Airport to the Trade-Mart. The plastic bubble-top was removed, and the bullet-proof side windows were rolled down. The motorcade began to roll at 11:50 A.M. All went quite well; the crowd seemed enthralled by the Kennedys, right up to that 120 degree turn onto Elm Street en route to the Stemmons Freeway on the way to the Trade-Mart. Shortly after turning onto Elm Street several shots rang out. It appeared that both President Kennedy and Governor Connally had been hit by one or more shots. Between 3 and 10 shots were variously posited as having been fired. The President and the Governor were rushed to Parkland Hospital. President Kennedy's injuries appeared to be grave. Nearby onlookers viewed the president's head exploding with blood, and matter from his brain being blown out the back of his head; one of the motorcycle policemen was splattered by the spraying blood and matter.[20]

The security stripping not only left the President wide open to snipers, but also the lack of video equipment failed to more accurately pinpoint the direction and explosiveness of the shots. Given the number of potential assassination attempts in November, and the explicit warning sent to FBI headquarters about an assassination attempt in Dallas (by Oswald through an FBI agent), the stripping of security was empowering to any assassination attempt. Arguably, security arrangements in Dallas were at a particularly low level.[21]

LBJ's Behavior in the Motorcade.

LBJ was reportedly not particularly sociable as he rode in the motorcade. Although he may have been disappointed to be forced to ride with Senator Ralph Yarborough, some writers attribute his mood to the investigation going on in the Senate Rules Committee, a hearing that had Donald B. Reynolds, who was being interviewed regarding LBJ's ethical violations – specifically, the sale of an insurance policy to Johnson, but only after Reynolds was forced to pay a bribe to Johnson. This investigation, had it continued, could have led to getting Johnson removed from the office of Vice President, thereby freeing JFK to name a new running mate for the 1964 election.

Others might attribute Johnson's mood to a foreknowledge of possible gunfire in the motorcade; if so, Johnson may have been concerned for his own safety. One reported story is that Secret Service Agent Rufus Youngblood, sitting in the front seat, leaped in the back seat, covering Lyndon Johnson. This description may have come from statements to that effect from Johnson, and Youngblood did not wish to contradict the new President. Penn Jones commented on Johnson's behavior that he was "the only one who ducked." Perhaps this represented foreknowledge, and Johnson wished to insure his own safety. Johnson may have been listening to Agent Youngblood's walkie-talkie. One photo, taken by Al Volkland on Stemmons Freeway, does show Youngblood covering Johnson with his body.[22]

As to the meeting in the Senate Rules Committee, the committee had adjourned for the day prior to hearing that President Kennedy had been shot. No record of that day's deliberation was entered into the Congressional Record as their work was not complete. The hearings would continue on January 8, 1964, but did not address ethical violations of the new President. Several more days of hearings were held, spaced in time. It was not until the December 1, 1964 hearings that the events of November 22, 1963 were readdressed. Reynolds testified that the questioning on November 22, 1963 was with hostile intent toward him, much like they were questioning him on December 1, 1964. The Democrats held a 6-3 majority on the Rules Committee,and it was not likely to have provided the impetus to get Johnson removed from office.[23]

A Chance Spectator at the Motorcade

James T. Tague was rushing to get to an appointment for which he was already a half-hour late. He had been driving under the triple underpass when the car in front of him stopped. Tague got out to see what was going on.

He walked three or four steps to the narrow divider between Commerce and Main Streets at the east edge of the triple underpass. Shortly thereafter, he noticed a limousine headed down Elm Street moving toward where Tague was standing. Tague at that moment remembered that President Kennedy was in town and this might be his motorcade. He thought it would be nice to see the President as he drove by. Then he heard popping sounds and wondered what kind of nut would set off firecrackers when the President came by? Then he recognized they were rifle shots and they were shooting in Tague's direction. Tague jumped back over the curbing. Later, when talking to Deputy Sheriff Buddy Walthers, Tague recalled that something stung him during the shooting. Walthers noticed blood on Tague's cheek. The two of them went back to where Tague had been standing. Walthers found a mark where a bullet dislodged some cement. Tague was apparently hit by a piece of the dislodged cement. This errant shot would play a large role in the subsequent investigation by the Warren Commission.[24] Since there were only three cartridges found on the sixth floor of the TSBD, to maintain a single assassin shooting from the TSBD sixth floor, the construction of the magic bullet hypothesis was necessary for the purposes of the Warren Commission.

Inside the Texas School Book Depository

Before we address any other detail, the planned time for President Kennedy's limousine to pass by the TSBD was 12:15 P.M. so that he would arrive at the Trade-Mart at 12:30 P.M. First, it is useful to track Lee Harvey Oswald from 11:45 A.M. until he left the TSBD. At 11:45 A.M., Oswald was on the sixth floor, the area where he had been working with other workers that day. When fellow employee Charles Gibbons was first asked by police, Gibbons said that he saw Oswald at 11:50 in the domino room (on the first floor), reading a newspaper.[25] Bill Shelly saw Oswald shortly before noon (perhaps 10-15 minutes) near a telephone on the first floor.[26] Another employee, Eddie Piper, talked to Oswald at 12 Noon on the first floor.[27]

Oswald apparently then went to the second-floor lunchroom, purchased a soda, and returned to the 1st floor where he sat and ate his lunch at the same time as another employee, Harold Newman, who also sat in the same room eating his lunch. Carolyn Arnold, a secretary at the TSBD, said that she went to the domino room at 12:15 and saw Oswald sitting there. She was familiar with Oswald, as he often came to her office seeking change.[28] Carolyn Arnold stayed in the lunchroom until 12:25. Oswald was still there.[29]

The next report of the whereabouts of Oswald was within 90 seconds of the shooting; motorcycle Officer Marion Baker and Building Superintendent Roy Truly encountered Oswald on the second-floor lunchroom with a soda in his hand. Superintendent Truly indicated that Oswald was an employee, and the two proceeded to walk the stairs from the second floor to the fifth floor, then took the elevator to the seventh floor.[30]

It might be instructive to address Oswald's state of mind during these critical minutes. Perhaps as late as 12:25 P.M., the anxiety that Oswald likely experienced might have begun to lessen. Oswald, through the FBI agent, had sent a message to the FBI central office that an assassination attempt was planned for Dallas. Because the President was expected to pass through Dealey Plaza at 12:15, perhaps Oswald's notice about the planned assassination was heeded, and the President passed through Dealey Plaza without incident, if Oswald had been successful. The appearance of Officer Baker seemed to be an indication that something had happened. Were that so, Oswald should then begin the plan to escape from the scene; his cover for being a CIA asset might be in jeopardy; there was also the possibility that he might have been used as a patsy if in fact President Kennedy had been hit.

To address Oswald's whereabouts near the time of the assassination, it is instructive to note four women at the TSBD who worked on the fourth floor: Mrs. Dorothy Garner, Sandra Styles, Victoria Adams, and Elsie Dorman. Mrs. Garner was the supervisor of the other three women. Prior to the motorcade, the four women gathered by a window facing the route of the motorcade. Elsie Dorman was recording the motorcade with a camera. As the shots rang out, their view was obscured by the leaves on the trees. Sandra Styles and Victoria Adams left immediately to go down the stairs; Mrs. Garner stationed herself between the stairs and the elevator. Neither Styles nor Adams heard anyone on the stairs either in front of them nor behind them. They went out the back door to find out what had happened. Mrs. Garner saw no one either go up or down the stairs, until Roy Truly and Officer Marion Baker came up the stairs after they had encountered Oswald on the first floor. It seems most likely that Oswald was downstairs during the crucial period of the shooting. But it appears that no one else, other than a policeman and other investigators, went up or down stairs during the time that Mrs. Garner was sitting between the elevator and stairs, from 12:30 P.M. and 2:30 P.M. It seems unlikely that anyone was shooting from the sixth floor between 12:30 P.M. to 12:31 P.M.[31]

Oswald's Whereabouts Between 12:33 P.M. and 1:00 P.M.

It appears that Oswald left the TSBD around 12:33 P.M. At about 12:40 P.M. Oswald entered a bus driven by Cecil McWatters. Oswald paid the

23-cent fare and took a seat. After going two blocks in four minutes and then the bus being unable to move, Oswald asked for a transfer and left the bus.[32] Oswald then walked until he could find a cab. He came to a cab being driven by William Whaley. Oswald asked if he could have the cab. Whaley agreed. As Oswald was entering the cab, a woman asked if she could have a cab Oswald said, "You can have this one." The woman said that the driver could call another one for her.[33] Oswald was in the cab approximately five minutes, entering at 12:47. Oswald exited the cab in the 700 block of North Beckley, though he desired to be left off at the 500 block of North Beckley. Oswald walked the remainder of the way to his room, getting there shortly before 1 P.M.[34] He changed his clothes. A policeman drove by the rooming house, stopping briefly, honked twice and continued driving. Earlene Roberts, the owner of the rooming house, noticed Oswald standing at the curb by the house a few minutes after 1 PM.[35]

George Bush in Dallas

One of the more unusual episodes in Dallas in those fateful days in November involves George Bush. Bush was in Dallas on November 21, 1963 to address the American Association of Oil Well Drilling Contractors. Bush stayed overnight in Dallas, (perhaps being one of the several persons at the Murchison party that Lyndon Johnson joined after midnight), but upon hearing of the assassination, Bush drove to Tyler, Texas at breakneck speeds. Bush then called the FBI to report a possible person who might have been involved in the assassination, a James Parrott. Parrott was a young student at the University of Houston, a right-wing member of the campus Young Republicans. It was speculated that Bush was trying to give both himself and Parrott (who was in Houston) alibis for the time of the assassination. It should be noted that Parrott would in 1992 be involved with Bush's presidential re-election bid. More troubling is that FBI reports on Parrott and his right-wing associates were removed from FBI files, perhaps at the time that Bush was the Director of the CIA.[36]

J.D. Tippit

J.D. Tippit was born in 1924 in East Texas in the Red River Valley into a farming family. Growing up in the depression, his life as a youth was "hard times." He attended school through his sophomore year in high school, quitting because it was a struggle for him to make passing grades. He served as a paratrooper in the U.S. Army towards the end of World War II. Upon returning to Texas in 1946, he met and married, on the day after Christmas, a local girl, 18-year-old Marie Gasaway, four years junior to her husband. Tippit worked in three different jobs in Dallas. Upon being laid off, he returned to his home in East Texas, working the land next to his father's. That too was a struggle. A brother-in-law and a friend were policemen. After several conversations with these two men, J.D. applied to the Dallas Police Department. He became an apprentice policeman in July, 1952, and was promoted to being a patrolman in October, 1953, the last promotion that he would receive. He would be described as an average cop. Tippit was always very quiet and seldom engaged in conversations beyond a perfunctory level.[37]

It appears that J.D. had at least one affair during his marriage. He worked part-time on weekends in security at Austin's Barbeque, where he met Johnnie Maxie Thompson, a waitress there. They presumably became involved, with Johnnie leaving her husband and filing for divorce in April, 1963. The divorce was granted in August of that year. Johnnie claimed that the father of her fifth child was her former and future husband, Steve Thompson. Thompson claimed Tippit was the actual father of his wife's child.[38] Thompson was seen by some researchers as being the one person with an actual motive to kill Tippit. This line of reasoning was not pursued by the Warren Commission. Instead, the Commission was trying to establish Oswald as the killer of Tippit, as a means of showing a violent side to Oswald, thereby inferring that, ipso *facto*, Oswald killed the President. The Tippit killing was the linchpin for this line of reasoning. David Belin, an assistant counsel for the Warren Commission, called the Tippit killing "the Rosetta Stone" of the JFK assassination.[39] That Tippit's killing was the "Rosetta Stone" could be another key; if Oswald did not kill Tippit, it makes it more unlikely that he killed the President.

The last hour-and-a-half of Tippit's life is filled with numerous anomalies. His widow specified that they had lunch together – yet it is difficult to pinpoint when he had time to do this. Coupled with only 5 ounces of food in his stomach at autopsy, after supposedly being served breakfast by his wife, more than one meal that day might seem unlikely; he might have skipped lunch altogether.[40] But why the lie by the family? And if he DID have lunch at home, that would tend to suggest something suspicious about his 1:11 call from Top Ten Records, as it was unlikely he was calling home. Who else would he call? The mistress? A conspirator?

The reports of the various witnesses to the Tippit's shooting and the aftermath appear to be irreconcilable. The descriptions of the assailant(s) do not mesh; some describe a single person, some suggest two assailants, and one witness describes a third person waiting for them in a car. What is more generally agreed on is that several of the shots (probably 3) were at a short distance, and one shot, probably after Tippit had expired, was delivered at close range into the side of his head as he was lying on the pavement, a sort of gangland slaying, a *coup de grace*.

The final shot was not what might be expected from someone who wished to hurry away from the scene.

Perhaps the reason Oswald was immediately suspected was a black wallet found at the scene and taken into possession by Captain W.R. Westbrook. The wallet had in it identification for Lee Oswald and Alek J. Hidell. The wallet was shown to FBI agent Robert Barrett and then became unaccounted-for. It can be recalled that Oswald left a wallet at home for Marina so that this is wallet number two.[41]

Timing is a major problem in tying Oswald to Tippit. Oswald was said to have entered the Texas Theater between 1:00 PM and 1:07 P.M. by Warren H. Burroughs, a theater employee. The Warren Commission had Tippit's shooting occurring near 1:15 P.M. Dale Meyers, who wrote the most comprehensive study regarding Tippit's murder, timed the shooting at 1:14:30 P.M.[42] Even if the shooting occurred somewhat earlier than indicated by the Warren Commission, Oswald would have already been in or near the theater if Burroughs is correct.

Events at the theatre seem to be different from police reports. One huge discrepancy is that it appears two different persons were removed from the theatre by the police. Oswald was taken out the front door, while another person was taken out the back door. This "arrest" was viewed by Bernie Haire, the proprietor of Bernie's Hobby Shop, who saw several police cars at the rear of the theater take a man into custody. Haire thought he had witnessed the arrest of Oswald. It was 28 years later, when viewing the movie *JFK* that he finally realized he saw someone else taken by the police. Another apparent discrepancy is the unusual report of Officer Maurice McDonald, who claimed that he had pulled a gun on Oswald. McDonald then claimed Oswald struck him, pulled out his gun and attempted to shoot McDonald, all while McDonald held a gun on Oswald. McDonald claimed that Oswald's gun had a primer that caused it to misfire, a statement which was disproven by FBI firearms expert Courtland Cunningham, who testified that, "We found nothing to indicate that this weapon's firing pin had struck the primer on any of these cartridges."[43] Sgt. Gerry Hill, present at the time of the theatre fracas, told researcher Walt Brown that the photos of McDonald, showing facial bruises, were the result of Dallas cops hitting McDonald when they were aiming for Oswald.

After Oswald was taken into custody and taken to the Dallas Police Department Headquarters, a THIRD wallet was taken from Oswald. It was a brown wallet. Officer C.T. Walker removed the wallet from Oswald's rear pocket. The contents of the wallet were recorded; the wallet and its contents were turned over to J.B. Hicks of the Dallas Police Department Identification Bureau at 4:30 P.M. on November 23. Four days later, Captain Will Fritz turned over the wallet and its contents to FBI agent James Hosty.[44] It does seem unlikely that Oswald would be carrying two wallets after he left his rooming house. The disappearance of the second wallet occurred after they used it to tie the murder to Oswald. It seems much more likely that the wallet at the Tippit murder scene was planted to get the suspicion to center on Oswald.

Parkland Hospital

On arrival at the Parkland Hospital, the President's condition was grave. Because he was the President, Herculean efforts were made to attempt to revive him; simultaneously, a Catholic priest was summoned. Father Oscar Huber and one other priest came to President Kennedy's side and administered the last rites. Shortly thereafter, the president was declared dead, though this information was not then communicated as being official. Press Secretary Pierre Salinger, Secretary of State Dean Rusk, Treasury Secretary Douglas Dillon, Interior Secretary Stewart Udall, Secretary of Labor W.W. Wirtz, Secretary of Commerce Luther Hodges, and Secretary of Agriculture Orville Freeman were aboard an airplane headed to Japan, which was instructed to turn around and fly directly to Washington. For many Americans (including this writer) the announcement was made by Walter Cronkite at 1:38 C.S.T., "From Dallas, Texas, this flash, apparently official; President Kennedy died at 1:00 P.M. Central Standard Time, two o'clock Eastern Standard Time – some thirty-eight minutes ago."[45] (I was standing in line at a bank at the time. There was a murmur – Oh, no!, then deafening silence – the world had changed.)

When the knowledge of President Kennedy's death was known, the yet unsworn-in President Johnson was told by Kenneth O'Donnell to go to Air Force One and prepare to return to Washington, D.C. Johnson departed for Air Force One at 1:30 P.M.[46]

The Charged Atmosphere at Parkland Hospital

Because President Kennedy had been declared dead, the Parkland Hospital physicians were at the point of turning his body over to the pathologists to perform an autopsy. When a person died in Texas, if an autopsy was to be performed it was to be performed in Texas, in accordance with state law. Because President Kennedy was killed by a gunshot wound, by necessity, an autopsy needed to be performed. Dr. Earl Rose refused to listen to the pleading of the Secret Service and others from the presidential party. Dr. Kemp Clark agreed with the presidential party that Kennedy could be taken back to Washington D.C. Dr. Rose was adamant that the autopsy should be held in Texas, according to state law. Also, at the time, the killing of a president was not covered by federal law. The only law violated was Texas state law.

Dr. Rose saw the Secret Service agents wheeling the casket containing President Kennedy's body out of the trauma room. Dr. Rose blocked their way, with his own body, stating, "No, that's not the way things are. When there's a homocide, we must have an autopsy."[47]

Special Agent Roy Kellerman responded, "He's the President. He goes with us."[48]

Equally adamant, Dr. Rose, clearly stated, " The body stays."[49]

Special Agent Roy Kellerman became fully erect and brought his firearm to ready position. The other men undraped their coats exposing their holstered firearms. Kellerman then stated, "My friend, I am Roy Kellerman. I am Special Agent in charge of the White House detail of the Secret Service. We are taking President Kennedy back to the Capitol."[50]

Dr. Rose responded, "You are not going to take the body anywhere. There's a law here. We are going to enforce it."[51]

Admiral George Burkley, White House Medical Officer said, "Mrs. Kennedy is going to stay exactly where she is until the body is moved. We can't have that ... he's the President of the United States."[52]

"That doesn't matter. You can't lose the chain of evidence" explained Dr. Rose.[53]

"Goddammit get your ass out of the way before you get hurt," shouted another man with the president's group.[54]

Yet another man yelled, "We're taking the body, now."[55]

Though they would never be charged, they broke a plethora of laws in forcibly removing the body of President Kennedy. In retrospect, they were doing this so that the experienced and well-trained pathologists in Texas would not be allowed to perform the autopsy, breaking the chain of evidence and leaving the autopsy to military pathologists with little experience in this kind of homicide, under the control of mostly non-medical military brass, who would command them as to what they could and couldn't do. Perhaps that was the precise reason for the actions that took place in Parkland Hospital by the dead president's "bodyguards."

Taking President Kennedy's Remains to Air Force One

As it happened, Aubrey Rike, with his assistant Dennis McGuire, had brought Jerry B. Belknap to Parkland Hospital; Belknap had suffered an epileptic seizure in Dealey Plaza. They were asked to remain, in the event that President Kennedy might need to be taken to another hospital. They remained there until they were asked to get a coffin and take the President's body to Air Force One. A coffin was supplied by the O'Neal Funeral Home. When the casket arrived, President Kennedy's body was placed in it. The casket was removed and placed into the hearse that had also been brought to the hospital by the O'Neal Funeral Home.[56] President Kennedy's coffin was accompanied by several Secret Servicemen to Air Force One. In trying to remove the coffin from the ambulance, the Secret Servicemen were unaware that Aubrey Rike had locked the coffin in so that it would not move. They pulled on the handles to try to dislodge it, cracking one of the handles. They were eventually able to get the coffin to the door, but felt they had to remove two handles to get it in, which they eventually did.[57]

Though President Johnson was preparing to take off, he decided he should be sworn in before leaving Dallas; he had a friend, Judge Sarah Hughes, that he wished to do the swearing-in, and she was called. Johnson asked Mrs. Kennedy to be present for the swearing-in. Shortly after Judge Hughes and other Dallas persons who'd watched the oath of office being administered departed Air Force One. At 2:47 p.m. CST, Air Force One took off for Andrews Air Force Base,[58] and arrived at 6:05 p.m. Simultaneously, a helicopter took off on the other side of the Air Base.[59]

Oswald at the Dallas Police Station

Interrogation began with Oswald shortly after his arrival at the Dallas Police Department (DPD).

Oswald had remarkably good self-control. He seemed to cooperate reasonably well. No notes or tapes were used by the DPD,[60] though at least FBI Agent James Hosty did take some notes. At 2:55 p.m., The Texas School Book Depository reported that four other employees were still out of the TSBD building: L.R. Viles, Mrs. William Parker, Dolores Koonas, and Virgie Rackley.[61] At 4:35 p.m. CST, Oswald was taken to his first of several lineups. Jack Ruby was observed at the DPD. At 7:00 p.m., Oswald was formally charged with the murder of Officer J.D. Tippit.[62] At 8:55, Detectives J.B. Hicks and Robert Studebaker took Oswald to the homicide office for fingerprinting. They were joined then by Detective

Pete Barnes to perform a paraffin test for Oswald's hands and cheeks. The test on the hands show that Oswald might have fired a gun (or handled cardboard boxes) but a negative outcome on his cheeks would preclude him having fired a rifle.[63] At 11:00 P.M., Jack Ruby returned to the DPD with 12 sandwiches to give to policemen at the station.[64]

Update from New Orleans

Robert Kennedy was trying to get Carlos Marcello deported. However, Marcello won the case, and was allowed to remain in the United States. David Ferrie had attended the trial, having done some investigative work for Marcello. Ferrie then began a 360-mile trip and ended up at an ice rink in Houston. It was never clarified why this trip was taken.[65]

The Dallas Press Conference

Less than an hour after the Secret Service forcibly removed President Kennedy's body from Parkland Hospital, a press conference was held regarding President Kennedy's wounds. Two of the physicians participated in the press conference: Dr. Malcolm Perry, who performed a tracheotomy, and Dr. Kemp Clark, Chief of Neurosurgery at Parkland Hospital. One wound was just below the Adam's Apple, and appeared to be an entry wound. Another wound was at the back of the head. Dr. Perry also indicated that President Kennedy was moribund. Dr. Clark, a neurologist, observed that President Kennedy's wounds were lethal.[66]

A Telephone Call from Dr. Robert B. Livingston to Dr. Humes

Dr. Livingston was the Scientific Director of both the National Institute for Mental Health and the National Institute for Neurological Diseases and Blindness, positions he had held in both the Eisenhower and Kennedy Administrations. After the assassination, and after he had become aware that Dr. Humes would be performing the autopsy, Dr. Livingston placed a call to Dr Humes: "I [Dr. Livingston] told him [Dr. Humes] about reports describing the small wound in the President's neck. I stressed that, in my experience, that would have been a wound of entrance. He emphasized the importance of carefully tracing the path of the projectile and of establishing the location of the bullet or any fragments. I said carefully, if that wound were confirmed to be a wound of entrance, that would prove beyond peradventure of doubt that a bullet had been fired in front of the President – hence if there were shots from behind, there had to more than one gunman. At just that moment, there had been an interruption in our conversation.

Dr. Humes returned after a pause to say, 'Dr. Livingston, I'm sorry, but I can't talk with you any longer. The FBI won't let me.'"[67]

A conundrum

As will be seen at Bethesda, two different coffins arrived at the site of the autopsy. President Kennedy's body initially arrived at 6:35 in a shipping container with his body in it. Later, a second empty casket arrived. Apparently, President Kennedy's body, which had preliminary work done on it by Dr. Humes, was then placed into the ornate coffin. Where did the first exchange take place? There are three possibilities, either at the Parkland Hospital, at Love Field or at Andrews Air Base. But we know there was an exchange somewhere, because President Kennedy's body was in the shipping casket, which arrived several minutes before the ornamental casket without President Kennedy's body in it.

General Curtis LeMay's Change in Plans

Four-Star General Curtis LeMay was Chief of Staff of the Air Force in 1963. He had been a very successful member of the Army Air Force (which became the Air Force), leading US. forces in the defeat of Japan. On the Joint Chiefs of Staff (1961-1965) General LeMay clashed with President Kennedy on a continuing basis. President Kennedy learned LeMay's philosophy of warfare; LeMay espoused the use of nuclear warfare and favored the Single Integrated Operational Plan for the Fiscal Year 1962 (SIOP-62). The SIOP-62 plan supported a continuing and massive destruction of the entire Communist bloc. The enormity of that plan would potentially be the largest destruction ever of humanity. When President Kennedy heard of these plans, he walked out of the meeting of the Joint Chief of staff commenting, "And they call themselves humans."[68]

General LeMay was the consummate hawk. LeMay and President Kennedy quickly developed a strong dislike for one another. Two events that happened in the Kennedy Presidency cemented this mutual contempt, the Bay of Pigs, and the Cuban Missile Crisis. LeMay saw these situations as potentially escalating hostilities, particularly the Cuban Missile Crisis. That nuclear war was averted seemed to be a bitter pill to LeMay.[69]

After the Cuban Missile Crisis, President Kennedy stated, 'Gentlemen we've won. I don't want you ever to say it, but you know that we won, and I know that we won."[70]

LeMay pounded on the table in the cabinet room and blurted out, "Won, hell, we lost! We should go in and wipe them out today." Then, Le-

May called the resolution of the missile crisis, "the greatest defeat in our history.... Mr. President, we should invade today!"[71]

So vast was the chasm between their world-views that agreeing to disagree wasn't even on the table.

On November 22, 1963, General LeMay was in or near Wairton, Canada. Upon hearing of the assassination of President Kennedy, LeMay contacted the Air Transport Wing at Andrews Air Force Base to send a plane to pick him up and take him back to Washington. Initially, he asked the plane to be flown to Toronto. Once the plane took off (2:46 P.M.), LeMay asked that he be picked up at Wairton. (2:50P.M.) General LeMay departed from Waitron at 4:04 P.M. LeMay stated that he was to be taken to Washington National Airport (DCA). Secretary of the Air Force Eugene M. Zuckert had a message sent to LeMay saying that Zuckert would meet LeMay at Andrews Air Base. Zuckert was LeMay's immediate superior. It could be reasoned that Zuckert wished LeMay to be there to meet Air Force One, due to arrive at 6:00 P.M. At 5:00 P.M. LeMay sent the message that he would land at DCA. This action represented LeMay's disobeying the order of his superior. LeMay's plane landed at DCA at 5:12 P.M. By landing at DCA rather than Andrews Air Base, LeMay was avoiding the formality of being there for the fallen Commander in Chief, and it put him closer to Bethesda to attend the autopsy there.[72]

The Delivery of the President's Body to the Autopsy in Bethesda

Three separate entrances were made to the Bethesda morgue. The first occurred at 6:35 P.M., led by Dennis David, E6, Petty Officer, Chief of the Day for the Bethesda Medical Center, who chose six men who would carry the casket. They went to the entrance to the morgue, where the black ambulance pulled up. Six men in suits accompanied the body. One of the men identified himself as Secret Service. Dennis David supervised the men chosen to carry the shipping casket. David was not present when the shipping casket was opened, but he knew four people who were, Floyd Reibe (medical photographer), Jerrol Custer (X-Ray Technician), James Jenkins (laboratory technician), and Paul O'Conner (laboratory technician). All four of them saw the President's body, and all four stated that when they opened the casket, the body was in a body-bag. The President was totally nude and had a towel wrapped around his head.[73]

After leaving the morgue, David noticed two things. The second ambulance arrived around 6:55 with Mrs. Kennedy and the persons in the ambulance with her at the front entrance of the morgue. He also noticed from the second floor at the rotunda of the Naval Medical Center that a helicopter landed at the helicopter pad. There were several uniformed servicemen with boxes, perhaps of equipment. This might have been the escort for the body that had been talked about.[74]

The next night, David and his wife were watching television. They saw the President's casket coming off of Air Force One. Dennis commented, 'There's something screwy here. That's not the casket we got the body in."[75]

At 7:17, the ornamental casket was delivered to the morgue. Shortly thereafter, the body was taken from the morgue, placed in the casket, and the casket with President Kennedy's body was taken back to the grey hearse that brought the casket to the morgue. The object now was to have the Honor Guard "find" the grey ambulance, perhaps by driving slowly around the Bethesda Medical Center until the honor guard was able to find it, so that the body and casket could re-enter the morgue, accompanied by the Honor Guard.

Eventually, the Honor Guard was able to "find" the grey ambulance that previously held the empty coffin, but now had the same coffin with President Kennedy's body and delivered it to the Bethesda morgue, supposedly maintaining the "chain of custody." Perhaps at the time they thought their entry was the first casket delivery, rather than the third. The chain of custody appears to have been broken more than once. We are not absolutely sure where President Kennedy was from the time he left Parkland Hospital until he went into the Bethesda morgue at 6:35 p.m.

According to Doug Horne, either between 7:30 and 8:00, or when the Honor Guard Joint Service Casket Team began bringing the casket into the morgue at 8:00 p.m., the casket was dropped, breaking off a handle, and leaving scratches and dents on two corners of the casket. One of the team members was replaced by Brigadier General Godfrey McHugh; McHugh fell going up an incline.[76]

What Happened at the Pre-Autopsy?

Presumably, Dr. James Humes and Dr. J. Thornton Boswell were told that national security matters required removing any evidence of a shot from the front. Also, presumably, they understood that a court-martial might accompany their non-compliance. In any event, Dr. Humes did surgery about the forehead, removing an intact bullet that did not exit the head, lodged near the right ear.[77]

Only a small audience witnessed the pre-autopsy. The pre-autopsy began shortly after 6:35. p.m. and concluded shortly after 7:17 p.m. When the empty ceremonial casket arrived at 7:17, the president's body was placed into it and the casket was re-entered into the grey ambulance. The grey ambulance had to then be found by the Joint Service Honor Guard. That rendezvous was accomplished, and the Honor Guard would be allowed to save the appearance of maintaining the chain of evidence. The third entry was accomplished at 8:00 P.M. A new audience was there to see the autopsy; as far as most were concerned, they were the only audience to the autopsy. When the coffin was opened again, Dr. Humes exclaimed, "It is apparent that in addition to the tracheotomy, there has been surgery to the head area, namely, in the top of the skull."[78]

This drama was apparently some sort of effort to feign surprise about the surgery. For a person like Tom Robinson, a mortician for Gawler's Funeral Home, who witnessed the earlier surgery by Dr. Humes, it must have been something like, is this a joke? The very man exclaiming about surgery about the head was the guy who *did* the surgery in the head. Perhaps the military brass understood what was going on, but it would seem many of them were aghast at Dr. Humes for pointing out that the surgery occurred. Shortly after the autopsy had begun, Dr. Humes called Dr. Pierre Finck to help with the autopsy. The "best" qualification of the three physicians involved was that they were all officers in the armed services. They would have to follow the orders of men who had no background in the practice of pathology, but who did outrank the three physicians, who had at least some background.

Had the autopsy been performed in Dallas, at least the President would be attended to by competent civilians, who could most easily get around interference by military brass. Likely, if the military brass barked out orders, they would be removed from the room. The President would have had a competent autopsy. But at Bethesda, these three pathologists had only a modicum of actual experience, compared to the Dallas physicians, particularly in regard to gunshot deaths.

After Dr. Finck arrived, he seemed to take charge, at least among the pathologists. In the audience, Rear Admiral George Burkley and apparently General Curtis LeMay continued to bellow out orders; particularly, what procedures to avoid, including not tracing bullets in the President's body.[79]

Tom Robinson and Ed Reed

Both Tom Robinson and Ed Reed were somehow allowed to view portions of the autopsy that might have been "too much." Ed Reed testified at his AARB deposition that he witnessed Dr. Humes make an incision across the forehead near the hairline and employ a surgical saw to the cranium. Ed Reed and Jerrol Custer were then abruptly ordered to leave the morgue; they came back later to do X-Rays.[80]

Tom Robinson also reported that Dr. Humes used a saw to enlarge the area that was blown out in the rear portion of the head. Robinson presumed this was to allow the brain to be taken out of the larger hole. Inexplicably, Robinson was allowed to remain for the remainder of the autopsy and would help prepare the President's body for a possible open-casket viewing.[81]

Photographs, X-Rays, and the Autopsy Film

Photographers at the autopsy included John Stringer, a civilian navy medical photographer (the photographer of record for the autopsy) and his assistant, Floyd A. Riebe, navy corpsman 2nd class (E-5) and navy chief petty officer Robert Knudsen (E-7), a social photographer who had been a favorite of President Kennedy. Stringer and Riebe had been present and taking photographs for most of the autopsy. They were kept out of the autopsy room whenever X-Rays were being done. They were unaware that Knudsen came in later and took photographs of the latter part of the autopsy and also took additional photographs during and after the morticians worked on President Kennedy. At least 18 autopsy pictures are no longer available; these pictures include an entry wound in the occipital bone; views of the lung, which was bruised; photographs of probes in the body; pictures of the brain, after removal; a puncture wound above the right eye; pictures of the blow out in the back of the head, and several body views and "scene" photographs in the morgue.[82]

The X-Rays were taken by Jerrol F. Custer (E-4) and student, Edward F. Reed (E-4), under the direction of Commander John H. Ebersole, M.D. There is a discrepancy among the three as to who took and who developed the X-Rays. Two of the five skull X-Rays are missing. Additionally, a case for a forged X-Ray was made by David Mantik, Ph.D., M.D.[83] When Dr. Ebersole was asked by the House Subcommittee on Assassinations (HSCA) on March 11, 1978 by Dr. Michael Baden: "Do you on examination of these films have an opinion as to where the gunshot wound of entrance was in the head radiologically?" Dr. Ebersole's reply was, "In my opinion it would have come from the side [on] the basis of these films."[84]

Michael Baden and Robert Blakely had Dr. Ebersole's testimony sequestered for 50 years. The JFK Records Act forced the release of these documents.[85] Also, see Horne[86] for the significant testimony on the X-Rays.

Dennis David, who was the leader of the naval personnel who brought President Kennedy's body into the morgue at 6:35 p.m., was also a good friend of Lieutenant Commander William Pitzer. Pitzer was stationed at the Bethesda Naval Hospital where he was in charge of all audio-visual services. David said that 3-or-4 days after the assassination, Pitzer showed David photographic images in relation to the assassination. The 6-or-7 color slides and 4-or-5 black and white prints were all pre-incision images of President Kennedy. Additionally, Pitzer showed David a portion of a 16mm film of the autopsy. The portion David saw was pre-incision. The film was taken either from the gallery or well back in the room. The film has not resurfaced.

Pitzer never spoke to David again about the JFK autopsy; Pitzer and several other persons having anything to do with the autopsy were required to sign non-disclosure agreements. Pitzer is said to have committed suicide; the incident occurred October 29, 1966. The circumstances of the "suicide" are highly suggesting of homicide. There were two entry wounds in the forehead. David said the he and others tried to find out if someone had murdered Pitzer. The person they thought murdered Pitzer had been identified, and in 2002 that person was a physician living in Idaho. At the time of the alleged murder, the named person was in the Army.[87]

The End of the Autopsy, the Beginning of the Work of the Morticians, and the Social Photographer

Around midnight E.S.T., the formal autopsy concluded, and the work of the morticians began. Their objective was to make the President presentable for an open-casket scenario, suitable for viewing by the general public. In doing this, it was necessary to do significant reconstruction, particularly in regard to the head; the blowout to the rear of the skull was reconstructed to give the appearance that almost nothing happened. It was this reconstruction that was photographed by Robert Knudsen, E-7, the social photographer. While the morticians and Knudsen were wishing to do their best work, they did not recognize that the conspirators would use the picture of the intact rear portion of the head to falsely show that there was no blowout in the back of the head, thereby allowing the conclusion that all of the shots were from the rear and presumably fired by "the lone assassin on the sixth floor."

The morticians finished about 4 a.m., ending, for all concerned, a very long day. Unfortunately, it also was the day of the American coup d'état.[88]

Endnotes

1 Brown, M.D. (1997). *Texas in the Morning: The Love Story of Madeleine Brown and President Lyndon Baines Johnson*. Baltimore: Conservatory Press, p. 166.

2 Loc. cit.

3 Loc. cit.

4 Epstein, E.J. (1966). *Inquest: The Warren Commission and the Establishment of Truth*. New York: Viking Press, p. 138.

5 President's Committee on the Assassination of President Kennedy. (1964; 1993 reprint). The Warren Commission Report. Woodbury, NY: Platinum Press, p. 15.

6 Brown, M.D. p. 167.

7 Loc. cit.

8 Loc. cit.

9 Loc. cit. This rage by Johnson may have stemmed from President Kennedy's refusal to move Governor Connally to the limousine with Johnson and move Senator Yarborough to President Kennedy' s limousine. Some might interpret this proposed change would be to get Governor Connally out of the line of fire.

10 United Press International (UPI) and *Heritage Magazine* (HM), (1964). *Four Days: The Historical Record of the Death of President Kennedy*. Denver: The Rocky Mountain News, p. 9.

11 Ibid., p.11.

12 Retrieved from Prouty.org/nixon.html on July 20, 2017.

13 Palamara, V.M. (1993). "The Third Alternative – Survivor's Guilt: The Secret Service and the JFK Murder." Pittsburgh PA: Author. I received my copy directly from the author. More recently, it has been made available on the internet.

14 Ibid., p. 17.

15 Ibid., p. 18.

16 Ibid., p. 20.

17 Curry, J. (1969). *JFK Assassination File*. Dallas: Author, p. 21.

18 Shaw, J. G., Hansen, J., & Crenshaw, C. (1992). *Conspiracy of Silence*. New York: Penguin, pp. 53-54.

19 Vaughan, T.W. (1993). "Presidential Motorcade Schematic Listing: November 23, 1963, Dallas." Jackson MI: Author. This presentation for the most part lists persons by car and position in the car.

20 UPI International, p. 13; the positing of the up to 10 shots was made by Robert Groden: Groden, R.J. (1993). *The Killing of a President: The Complete Photographic Record of the JFK Assassination and the Cover-Up*. New York: Penguin, pp. 20-40.

21 On August 13, 1962, this writer saw President Kennedy at a high school football stadium in Pueblo, Colorado. I was frankly amazed by the amount of security afforded President Kennedy on that day. Not only were their scores of state patrolmen, deputies and local police motorcyclists surrounding President Kennedy, there were state trooper sharpshooters scattered about the stadium. As I went to choose a seat, I noticed my brother Gerald, a new state trooper, was standing, holding a rifle. I walked up to him and said, "Hi Gerald.' He ignored me. That weekend, I asked Gerald about the snub. Gerald's reply was, "My job was to protect the President, not to talk to my brother." Williams, J.D. (2009). "How "Typical" was the Protection for President Kennedy in Dallas?" *The Dealey Plaza Echo*, 13, 1, 1-4.

22 McBride, J. (2013). *Into the Nightmare: My Search for the Killers of President John F. Kennedy and Officer J.D. Tippit*. Berkley CA: Hightower Press, pp. 385-393.

23 Williams, J.D. & Conway, D. (2001). "The Don Reynolds Testimony and LBJ." *Kennedy Assassination Chronicles*. 7, 1, 19-28.

24 Tague, J.T. (2003). *Truth Withheld: A Survivor's Story*. Dallas: Excel Digital Press, pp. 12-13.

25 *Dallas Morning News*. 11/22/1963.

26 Epstein (1966). p. 106.

27 Ibid., p. 107.

28 Ibid., pp. 107-108.

29 Golz, E. (1978). "Was Oswald in the Window? Interview of Carol Arnold Johnson." *Dallas Morning News*, 12/19/1978.

30 Douglass, J.W. (2008). *JFK and the Unspeakable: Why He Died & Why it Matters*. Maryknoll NY: Orbis, p. 285; Armstrong, J. (2003). *Harvey & Lee: How the CIA Framed Oswald*. Arlington TX: Quasar Ltd., p. 819.

31 Ernst, B.W. (2013). *The Girl on the Stairs*. Gretna, LA: Pelican, p. 268. Williams, J.D. (2014). "The Girl on Stairs-Was Oswald Even at the Sixth Floor at the Time of the Assassination?" *JFK/Deep Politics Quarterly*-e, 1, 2, 3-16.

32 WCE 343.

33 2 H 261.

34 2 H 293.

35 7 H 439.

36 Baker, R. (2009). *Family of Secrets: The Bush Dynasty, the Powerful Forces that Put it in the White House, and What Their Influence Means to America*. New York: Bloomsbury Press, pp. 44-66.

37 McBride, pp. 268-282.

38 Ibid., pp. 285-289.

39 Ibid., p. 229.

40 Ibid., p. 509

41 Hosty, J.P. (1996). *Assignment: Oswald*. New York: Arcade, p. 62.

42 Myers, D.K. (1998). *With Malice: Lee Harvey Oswald and the Murder of Officer J.D. Tippit*. Milford MI: Oak Cliff Press, p. 86.

43 McBride, p. 202.

44 CE 2003 p. 292.

45 Newseum with Frost, C. & Bennett, S. (2003). *President Kennedy has been Shot*. Naperville, IL: Sourcebooks, pp. 43-67, p. 85.

46 WCR 57.

47 Crenshaw, C.A., Shaw, J.G., Aguilar, G. & Wecht, C. (2001). *Trauma Room One: The JFK Medical Cover-up Exposed*. New York: Paraview Press, p. 89.

48 Loc. cit.

49 Loc. cit.

50 Loc. cit.

51 Loc. cit.

52 Loc. cit.

53 Loc. cit.

54 Ibid., pp. 89-90.

55 Ibid., p. 90.

56 Marrs, J. (1989). *Crossfire: The Plot that Killed Kennedy*. New York: Carroll & Graff, pp. 42-44.

57 Personal telephonic communication with Walt Brown, Ph.D., 7/30/2017.

58 Wood, I.D. "November, 1963: A Chronology," in Fetzer, J.H. (2000). *Murder in Dealey Plaza*. Chicago: Catfeet Press, pp. 98-99.

59 Ibid., p. 104-105.

60 Apparently the choice of the lack of the use of notes or tape recordings was deliberate; if they did not exist, the defense counsel would be unable to receive them.

61 Wood, p. 102.

62 Ibid., p.108.

63 Ibid., p. 110.

64 Ibid., p. 115.

65 Ibid., p. 103, Baker, J.V. (2010) *Me & Lee: How I Came to Know, Love and Lose Lee Harvey Oswald*. Walterville, OR: Trine Day, p. 529.

66 Typescript of the Parkland Dr. Perry & Dr. Clark Press Conference November 22, 1963. Available at mcadams.posc.muedu/press.htm.

67 Livingston, R.B. "Statement of 18 November 1993." In Fetzer, J.H. (1998). *Assassination Science: Experts Speak out on the Death of JFK. Chicago*: Catfeet Press, pp. 161-166.

68 Horne, D.P. (2009). *Inside the Assassination Records Review Board: The U.S. Government's Final Attempt to Reconcile the Conflicting Medical Evidence in the Assassination of JFK.* Lexington KY: Author, pp. 482-483.

69 Ibid., pp. 482-484.

70 Ibid., p.484.

71 Loc. cit.

72 Ibid., pp. 481-482.

73 Williams, J.D. & Severson, G, (2001). "Interview of Dennis David in Dallas, November 18, 2001." Available at johndelanewilliams.blogspot.com/2010/12/interview-with-dennis-david-regarding.html

74 Ibid.

75 Ibid.

76 Horne, p. 678.

77 Ibid., p. 708.

78 Ibid., pp. 686-688.

79 Ibid., pp. 1050-1057.

80 Ibid., p. 628.

81 Ibid., pp. 629-630.

82 Ibid., pp. 255-388.

83 Mantik, D.W. (1998). "The JFK Assassination: Cause for Doubt." In Fetzer, J.H. (1998), pp. 93-139.

84 Horne, p. 407.

85 Ibid., p. 408.

86 Ibid., pp. 389-478.

87 Williams & Severson.

88 Russell, D. (2008). *On the Trail of the JFK Assassins: A Groundbreaking Look at America's Most Infamous Conspiracy*. New York: Skyhorse Publishing, pp. 278-298. This chapter is a telephonic interview of Douglas P. Horne by Dick Russell.

Chapter Fifteen

DALLAS NOVEMBER 23-25

November 23, 1963, 12:01 A.M. Evidence regarding Oswald and the assassination of President Kennedy in Dallas was turned over to Vincent Drain of the FBI to be hand-carried to the FBI in Washington D.C. for processing.[1]

Shortly after midnight, the police did a second search of Oswald's belongings in the Paine's garage. Supposedly found there, were two prints and one negative of the backyard photographs, i.e., Oswald in his backyard wearing a pistol in a holster and holding a rifle and some Communist pamphlets/magazines. Most of the evidence found against Oswald failed the chain-of-custody test.[2] In this regard, when Gary Severson and I were interviewing Madeleine Brown, she made a statement that I've never heard reported before:

> MB: See, through the years, I've met with Marina. Tell me what you want to know.
>
> You [Marina] couldn't speak English in those years. And she told [MB] that the police came out and picked up the rifle the next day *after* the shooting. I [MB] said, 'Are you sure?' She said, 'Yeah.[3]

That was truly astonishing. If the police picked up the rifle the day after the shooting, but did not report it as such, the implications would be enormous. The whole scenario at the School Book Depository would have to be changed. Also, the involvement of the Dallas Police Force would have to be seriously considered.

Around midnight, Lee Oswald was brought to the press in the basement assembly room at the Dallas Police Station. Henry Wade, Dallas District Attorney, mentioned that Oswald was a member of the "Free Cuba Committee." Jack Ruby, who was in the group of members of the press, shouted, "Henry, that's the Fair Play for Cuba Committee."[4] That Ruby knew the correct name of the Fair Play for Cuba Committee speaks volumes in itself. This would tend to belie the belief that Oswald and Ruby were unacquainted.

Press badges were lying on a table for anyone to pick up. There was no control on who might go to a press conference.[5]

Oswald was taken to a maximum-security cell in the Dallas Jail at 12:20 A.M.[6] At 1:30 A.M., Oswald was awoken, taken to a judge and formally charged with the murder of President Kennedy. The judge told Oswald that he could contact a lawyer of his choice. Oswald said that he'd been trying to contact John Abt all day. He told the judge that if Abt was not available, he would prefer a lawyer from the Dallas American Civil Liberties Union. He had tried calling Abt. He asked for legal representation at the press conference. Earlier, the Dallas American Civil Liberties Union had contacted the Dallas police to protect Oswald's rights, but they were told that Oswald had declined their offer.[7] It would seem that the Dallas police wanted to question Oswald without legal representation while he was in their custody.

Oswald (or Someone) Talked

John Elrod was arrested at 2:45 P.M. on November 22, 1963. Over the next few days, he had conversations with either his cellmate or someone in the next cell. The person that Elrod thought was Oswald was asked to identify another inmate who had a smashed face. The person with the smashed face was Laurence Reginald Miller, who had been arrested with Donnell Darius Whittier, by the FBI in relation to weapons that were stolen from the Texas National Guard Armory, near Dallas. Whittier and Miller tried to drive off and were pursued by the FBI and apprehended when Whittier crashed against a telephone pole. Both were initially taken to the Parkland Hospital. Miller was treated and taken to the Dallas jail. The police suspected that Miller might be known by Elrod's cellmate, which proved to be the case. The Oswald-like person said to Elrod that he had been at a motel with four other men, who received money. One of these men received $5000. One of the men was Jack Ruby. Noel Twyman[8] reasoned that the Oswald-like person was most likely James Thomas Mason, who did have a striking resemblance to Oswald. Mason had been involved with gun-running, and later had a gun store in Dallas until he lost his license. Twyman reasoned that the cellmate of Elrod was much more forthcoming in his conversations than Oswald typically was. Also, Mason had a history of gun-running, whereas Oswald did not.[9]

Jack Ruby in the Early Morning of November 23, 1963

After the press conference, Ruby seemed somewhat buoyed, and started handing out his calling cards, "Jack Ruby Your Host at the Carousel," to out-of-town reporters and invited them to come by for drinks and a show after his club re-opened. When veteran New York newsman Ike Pappas had trouble getting District Attorney Wade on the telephone, Ruby went and got Wade to speak to Pappas. When KLIF sent Russ Knight, a disc jockey known as "The Weird Beard," to interview Wade, Ruby arranged for that. Ruby then went to KLIF with sandwiches and celery tonic. On the 2 A.M. news, Knight gave Ruby a plug for helping him with Wade. Ruby headed toward the *Dallas Times Herald*, but saw one of his strippers, Kay Helen Coleman (working name "Kathy Kay") with a Dallas policeman, Harry Olsen, in a parking lot. He stopped and talked to them for an hour and then went to the *Dallas Times Herald*, where he announced that the Carousel Club would be closed in an ad with black borders.

Ruby wanted to show his roommate George Senator a sign put up by the John Birch Society ("Impeach Earl Warren"); at 5 A.M. Ruby called Larry Crafard, a recently hired Carousel employee who was sleeping at the club, to get a Polaroid camera, so a picture of the Impeach Earl Warren sign could be photographed. Ruby really had no idea who Earl Warren was. At 6 A.M., Ruby finally went to his apartment to go to bed.[10]

The Afternoon and Evening at the Dallas Police Station

Around 1 P.M., Police Chief Jesse Curry was considering a 4 P.M. transfer of Oswald to the County Jail, which was very close to the site of the assassination. An inspection of the area showed that it was crowded by persons paying their respects to the fallen president. The traffic was very heavy, close to a slow crawl. It was decided that a 4 P.M. transfer was too risky.

Later a night transfer was also considered too risky. Chief Curry settled on a 10 A.M. transfer, and the press was alerted, though some in the press corps thought the transfer would occur in the dead of night.[11]

During much of Saturday afternoon and evening, both Jack Ruby and Lee Oswald were at the Dallas Police Station; Ruby was roaming the halls, gleaning information, and further ingratiating himself with the police with more sandwiches. Oswald spent his time being interrogated or in his cell. Chief Curry was convinced that they would be unable to get a confession from Oswald, either for the murder of President Kennedy, or for the murder of Officer Tippit.[12]

At 8:15 P.M., Chief Curry made his plans official: "Oswald would not be transferred at night, but if a reporter were to come to the police station at 10 A.M. the next morning, there would be ample time to observe anything you care to observe." Threats against Oswald's life continued to be reported.[13]

Sunday November 24, 1963

George Senator awoke around 8:30 or 9:00 A.M. and noticed Jack Ruby was still asleep. Senator recalled that Ruby received a telephone call at 10:19 A.M. from Karen Bennett Carlin, a stripper whose stage name was Little Lynn. Payday at the Carousel was Sunday, but the club would not be open and she needed some money to pay rent and buy groceries. Ruby indicated that he would send $25 by Western Union; he was going downtown anyway.[14]

How did Ruby get into the Dallas Police Station?

According to Seth Kantor, Ruby was waiting for a call from the Dallas Police Department at the time Karen Carlin called, and he was in a hurry to get off the phone. Shortly after Ruby got off the phone with Carlin, a call was placed to his unlisted number. Ruby was told where to enter the station. The transfer van was already en route. Ruby got his snub-nosed pistol and put it in his pocket where it wouldn't show. In the event that Ruby was stopped by the police, he wanted to have an alibi for the gun. He got together $2400, mostly in $10, $20 and $100 bills, to say that the money was to be paid toward excise taxes he owed to the IRS, justifying the carrying of the gun; Ruby did not have a carry permit. This guise was to make the shooting a spur-of-the-moment decision. Ruby dressed up with a black tie, black shoes and a charcoal brown suit, all the better to blend in with the many newsmen that would be at the police station.[15]

Around 11:10 A.M., several additional officers began congregating in the basement of the police station. Between 11:10 and 11:15 A.M., the van was in place on the Commerce side ramp. The transfer plan seemed to be constantly changing. Two vans were being used, one as a decoy, and one for the transfer. Originally, the larger van was going to be the one holding Oswald. That was changed because the driver was not even known, but also, the larger van lacked maneuverability, which was a concern because of the traffic near the county courthouse. The smaller van was then chosen, and the larger van would become the decoy. The new plan had Oswald walking through a human corridor of detectives to the waiting transfer van. When Oswald got in the smaller van, the van would then follow the larger decoy van to the County Building.[16]

Ruby went to the Western Union Building, and sent $25 to Karin Carlin. The wired money was time-stamped as 11:17 A.M. Ruby promptly walked to the Main Street ramp, which was guarded by Roy. E.

Vaughn. Ruby did not go down the ramp. but went 55 feet further to the double door Main Street entrance to the police station's first floor. Then he could have easily gone down the same stairway that many reporters had used without being questioned by the police. His arrival would have then triggered the go-ahead signal for Oswald to be brought down. Ruby chose an innovative way to get into the basement. Coming off the elevator were Dave Timmons and John Tankersly, two cameramen from WBAP, Channel 5 TV, who were struggling with a large camera on tripod legs; Ruby jumped in and help push the camera; a policeman also helped stabilize the camera; then Ruby joined the crowd. According to Seth Kantor, the logical person to have forwarded the word that everything was ready was Lieutenant Woodrow Wiggins, the officer in charge of the basement office. Ruby was then in the basement awaiting the arrival of Lee Harvey Oswald. This description obviously involves a conspiracy against Oswald in the police department.[17]

An updated version of the transfer came shortly before Oswald's arrival. At 11:20, Lieutenant Rio Sam Pierce drove a black car up the Main Street ramp, accompanied by two sergeants; the black car was then to be the decoy car. Detective Brown drove a green car from the garage area to the Commerce Street ramp. Detective Charles Dhority drove an unmarked white car behind the green car. Dhority tried to move the white car forward to be able to allow Oswald to enter it, but there were too many people blocking the way. Not enough people knew about the change in plans to effect this new plan, and the white car couldn't be put in position to receive Oswald.[18]

When they brought the elevator holding Oswald down to the basement, as Captain J. Will Fritz, stepped out, he asked Lieutenant Woodrow Wiggins, "Are you ready?" Wiggins indicated that everything was ready. Unfortunately, everything was NOT ready.[19]

The policemen in the human shield were unfortunately joined by the reporters. James Leavelle, handcuffed to Oswald's right wrist, asked Jay Cutchshaw of the Juvenile Bureau's Criminal Investigation Division if things were alright, Cutchshaw replied that they were. His answer was probably in relation to what he and other policemen thought to be the plan, in relation to the armored vehicle, not the white unmarked car, which could not get in position to receive Oswald. Chief Curry was on the phone upstairs on a call from Dallas Mayor, Earle Cabell. Captain Fritz followed Lieutenant Richard Swain. Oswald came out next, handcuffed to Leavelle, and standing next to Detective L.C. Graves.[20]

The Murder of Oswald

Billy H. Combest, a detective from the vice section, saw Ruby lunge past Detective Blackie Harrison toward Oswald. A single shot from point-blank range was made into Oswald's stomach area.[21]

After the shot, Ruby was taken down by six detectives. Ruby said, "You know me. I'm Jack Ruby."[22]

A First-Aid Attendant working at the Dallas Police Department, Frederick A. Beiberdorf, heard the shot, rushed to Oswald and began rubbing his sternum, after failing to detect a pulse. When the ambulance arrived, Beiberdorf climbed into the ambulance and continued to rub Oswald's sternum and also used an oxygen cup resuscitator. (The latter can be fatal with gunshot wounds.). As they approached the hospital, Oswald attempted to dislodge the resuscitator.[23]

At the hospital, the doctors did all that could be done to save Oswald's life. While this was being done Lyndon Johnson, now President, asked that the physicians attending Oswald should try to get a confession out of the moribund patient.[24]

Why Did Jack Ruby Kill Lee Harvey Oswald?

Ruby had given the excuse that he wished to spare the President's widow the ordeal of testifying at Oswald's trial; an alternative explanation was the avenging of the death of President Kennedy, whom Ruby loved and revered. Yet another reason was that by killing Oswald, he might become a hero.[25] All of these reasons were specious.

Ruby's actual reason was given in a three-hour interview with Earl Warren (albeit without the specific impetus).

> "MR. RUBY: I tell you gentlemen, my whole life is in jeopardy. My sisters as to their lives.
>
> MR. WARREN: Yes?
>
> MR. RUBY: Naturally, I'm a forgone conclusion. My sisters, Eva, Eileen, and Mary. I lost my sisters. My brothers, Sam, Earl, Hyman, and myself, naturally – my in-laws, Harold Kaminsky, Marge Ruby, the wife of Earl, and Phyllis, the wife of Sam Ruby, they are in jeopardy of the loss of their lives. Yes they have, just because they are blood related to myself – does that sound serious enough to you, Chief Justice Warren?"[26]

That is, if Ruby didn't kill Oswald, not only would he be killed, also every one of his blood-relatives would also be killed. It was an offer, that he, as a member of the mafia, "could not refuse."

This offer was communicated to him by John Roselli from Santos Trafficante.[27]

The Burial of Lee Harvey Oswald

Oswald was buried the day after his death. As it happened, his burial occurred the same day as the burial of President Kennedy at Arlington Cemetery. It is hard to imagine a larger contrast between the two. Oswald was buried at Rose Hill Cemetery in Arlington, Texas under the name William Bobo, the name of an itinerant cowboy who had recently died; this was done in order to avoid vandalism to the grave site. Indeed, the original gravestone was stolen. Present at the funeral were Marina and her two daughters, Oswald's mother Marguerite, his brother Robert, and dozens of reporters and photographers. Seven of the reporters served as pallbearers.[28]

Endnotes

1 Wood, I.D. "22 November 1963." In Fetzer, J.H. (Ed) (2000). *Murder in Dealey Plaza: What We Know Now that We Didn't Know Then about the Death of JFK*. Chicago; Catfeet Press, p. 116.

2 Loc. cit.

3 Williams, J.D. and Severson, G. (2001). Interview with Madeline Brown at the JFK Lancer Conference, November 17-18, 2001, Dallas. Available at johndelanewilliams.blogspot.com.

4 Wood, p.116.

5 Loc. cit.

6 Loc. cit.

7 Ibid., p. 117.

8 Twyman, N. (1997). *Bloody Treason: The Assassination of John F. Kennedy*. Rancho Santa Fe CA : Laurel, pp. 585-589. See also, La Fontaine, R. and La Fontaine, M. Oswald Talked: The New Evidence in the JFK Assassination. Gretna LA: Pelican Publishing Co.

9 Twyman, pp. 585-589.

10 Kantor, S. (1978). *The Ruby Cover-Up*. New York: Zebra Books, Kensington Publishing Corp., pp. 102-111.

11 Ibid., pp. 111-119.

12 Loc. cit.

13 Ibid., p. 120.

14 Ibid., p.123, p. 131.

15 Ibid., pp. 231-234.

16 Ibid., p. 138.

17 Ibid., pp. 139-144.

18 Ibid., p. 147.

19 Ibid., pp. 147-148.

20 Ibid., pp. 147-149.

21 Ibid., p. 149.

22 Loc. cit.

23 Armstrong, J.A. (2003). *Harvey & Lee: How the CIA Framed Oswald*. Arlington TX: Quasar, p. 945.

24 Loc. cit.

25 Meagher, S. (1967). *Accessories After the Fact: The Warren Commission, The Authorities & the Report*. New York: Vintage, p. 392.

26 Testimony of Mr. Jack Ruby. (1964).Taken by Earl Warren & Gerald R. Ford, June 7, 1964 at the Dallas County Jail. accessed at mcadams.posc.mu.edu/russ/testimony/ruby_j1.htm, 8/13/2017.

27 Buick, R. C. (2019). *Tiger in the Rain: History will be Written by the Hunter*. Xlibrus, p. 396.

28 Groden, R.J. (1995). *The Search for Lee Harvey Oswald*. New York: Penguin, pp. 206-207.

Chapter Sixteen

DEVELOPMENTS WITH THE AUTOPSY

The Autopsy Reports

Three separate autopsy reports were prepared by the pathologists; the FBI wrote their own preliminary report based on what they heard and observed from what the three military pathologists said and did. This report is referred to as the lens One report. The two FBI men, James Sibert and Francis O'Neil, left the autopsy when they thought it was completed, around midnight. Their report includes two hits to the president, a shot to the back of the skull, which exited out the top of the skull, and a shallow, non-transiting back wound. The bullet from this second shot was presumed to have fallen out of President Kennedy's body during cardiac massage in Parkland Hospital. This set of conclusions was abandoned after Sibert and O'Neil left the autopsy. Shortly after the two FBI agents left, a conversation took place between Dr. Humes and Dr. Perry (Parkland Hospital) about the wound in President Kennedy's throat. This necessitated adding a third shot that hit President Kennedy, which then constituted lens Two, the first written draft reviewed by Dr. Humes, Dr. J. Thornton Boswell, and Captain R.O. Canada USN. The original notes that Dr. Humes made were said to have been destroyed in the fireplace.[1]

Lens Three

A third shot was added to lens One, a shot which purportedly entered high in the neck or low in the skull, exiting through the throat. In turn this lens was abandoned when it became known that one bullet missed the limousine and caused an injury to James Tague. A strong inference was made, that since three shells were found on the sixth floor, and one shot missed the limousine entirely, no more than two shots could have hit President Kennedy. This gave rise to the Third lens. The two shots then became, having a fragment causing a throat wound as it exited the body, plus the non-exiting back wound. This, in turn, became the second autopsy report, which was completed on November 24, 1963, and signed by the three participating pathologists. This record was retained by the Kennedy family and is not the version of the autopsy that was placed in the archives (CE387).[2]

Lens Four

Lens Three had to be rejected when the Zapruder film was reviewed; the Zapruder film showed that JFK was visibly reacting to the head shot (as in lens One and lens Two) and a shot that entered the upper back and transited through the throat (the previously non-transiting back wound).[3]

Douglas Horne surmised that "…the evolving autopsy findings serve as evidence not of true events of what happened in Dealey Plaza, but of what those in charge of the coverup *wanted us to believe* about the assassination – namely, *that all of the shots were fired from above and behind the limousine and from the same location.*"[4]

Two Brains

Doug Horne developed the rationale for establishing the fact that two different brains were involved with the JFK autopsy. Two separate examinations were conducted, the first on Monday, November 25. The second examination was on the substitute brain, one that was almost intact with very little loss of mass. At the first examination, Dr. Humes, Dr. Boswell, a corpsman, and John Stringer, the naval photographer were present. The second examination took place between Friday, November 29, and Tuesday, December 2. The second examination included Dr. Humes, Dr. Boswell, Dr. Finck, and an unnamed naval photographer, other than John Stringer.[5]

The first examination was apparently a normal examination for gunshot wounds, including sectioning the brain. Stringer took only superior (top) views of the intact brain. He shot serial sections of the brain. Stringer used unnumbered portrait pan film in duplex holders to create black and white negatives; unique notches were in each corner of each piece of film. Stringer used Ektachrome E3 film to create color positive transparencies. In the official collection of films of the brain, *none* of Stringer's photographs of President Kennedy's brain exist. Different film was used in the second examination, basal (bottom side up) views were photographed, and no sectioning was shown. The official photographs feature an almost intact brain, which was reported to weigh 1500 grams; a normal male intact brain weighs near 1500 grams. With at least one-third of President Kennedy's brain missing, this strongly suggests that a substitute brain was used. At the second examination, Dr. Finck suggested having a neuropathologist examine the brain; Dr. Humes refused.[6]

It was Douglas Horne's sense that the recording of the weight of President Kennedy's brain as exactly 1500 grams was a "red herring." This value may have been a plea, 'This weight is unlikely under the circumstances. 'My indicating the weight as exactly 1500 grams was a signal that there is something wrong here.'" Of course, Dr. Humes could never have said this. He was in a Hobson's choice of either violating his ethical code or violating the direct order of a high-ranking officer, which could have ruined his military career and perhaps put a roadblock to his medical career.

Humes made his choice, but that didn't mean that he was happy with it. At the end of his testimony to the Assassination Records Review Board (taken in 1997, some 34 years after the assassination), Dr. Humes was walking with three AARB personnel, Jeremy Gunn, David Maxwell and Doug Horne. Dr. Humes remarked, "I sure hope you guys can figure this out."[7] Perhaps Dr. Humes was hoping that they might discover a cover-up in the medical evidence. Were the pictures taken by John Stringer of the actual brain of President Kennedy to surface, the cover-up with the medical evidence would likely be exposed. Once Dr. Humes and Dr. Boswell agreed to falsify the record, they were vulnerable to being squeezed.

What Finally Happened to John F. Kennedy's brain?

The brain of John F. Kennedy was supposedly turned over to Admiral Burkley to be interred with his body on November 25, 1963. (This is highly suggestive that the second brain examination was not that of JFK.) Apparently, the re-internment of President Kennedy's brain with his body did not actually occur at that time. The staffers at the National Archives were aware that President Kennedy's brain was missing. In tracing the brain, it was in the possession of Admiral Burkley until it was transferred for storage at the Secret Service Locker in the Executive Office Building. Then on April 22, 1965, Robert Kennedy directed Admiral Burkley to transfer the brain and other materials to Evelyn Lincoln, JFK's former secretary, who then had an office in the National Archives. Three days later, Burke Marshall, acting as the Executor of John F. Kennedy's estate, released control of the materials to Robert Kennedy. Then Robert Kennedy had the materials sent to Evelyn Lincoln. When the materials were received by Mrs. Lincoln, an inventory showed that nothing was missing.[8]

One month later, Robert Kennedy called Mrs. Lincoln, informing her that his personal secretary, Angela Novello and Presidential Archivist Herman Kahn would be coming over to pick up the materials and take them to an undisclosed location. According to Mrs. Lincoln, Robert Kennedy's personal assistant and driver, Master Sergeant Joseph Giordano took the trunk containing the materials. Giordano claimed that he didn't move it and suggested George Dalton, another employee of Robert Kennedy, might know. On November 2, 1965 Public Law 89-318 was passed. As it affected the materials in the trunk, they were seen as stating that the JFK autopsy materials were evidence and belonged to the U.S. Government. The Attorney General at the time, Ramsey Clark, was initially unable to secure the materials. An agreement was reached on October 29, 1966 with Robert Kennedy. The trunk was returned to the archives. The National Archives counsel, Harry Van Cleve, noted that JFK's brain and other gross material were missing. Van Cleve noted, "We were borrowing trouble in exploring it any further."[9]

President Kennedy's body was re-interred, presumably with the brain, between 6 P.M.-midnight, March 14, 1967. In attendance were Senator Ted Kennedy, Senator Robert Kennedy, Richard Cardinal Cushing, and Defense Secretary Robert McNamara.[10]

When Mrs. Lincoln was asked in 1992, where President Kennedy's brain was, her reply was, "It's where it belongs."[11]

Endnotes

1 Horne, D.P. (2009). *Inside the Assassination Records Review Board: The U.S. Government's Final Attempt to Reconcile the Conflicting Medical Evidence in the Assassination of JFK.* Lexington KY: Author, pp. 845-847.

2 Ibid., p. 487.

3 Ibid., pp. 845-878.

4 Ibid., p. 879.

5 Ibid., p. 777.

6 Ibid., p. 797.

7 Ibid., p. 834.

8 Russo, G. (1998). *Live by the Sword: The Secret War Against Castro and the Death of JFK.* Baltimore: Bancroft Press, pp, 387-388.

9 Ibid., pp. 388-389.

10 Ibid., the four pages preceding p. 305.

11 Ibid., p. 390.

Chapter Seventeen

THE ZAPRUDER FILM AND OTHER FILMS AND PHOTOS

The Zapruder Film, 26 seconds of footage, is undoubtedly the best-known film or picture related to the JFK assassination. It is either the most famous, or infamous filmstrip from that horrendous day. It has its own history, and part of that history was its availability. For persons born after 1960, its availability would seem incongruous. Obviously, it was filmed November 22, 1963. It was bought and kept under the tight control of the Time-Life organization. They did make still-pictures of several frames and publish them in the then extant *Life* magazine, but then, silence reigned. The first individual to wrest any control from them was District Attorney James Garrison, who was prosecuting Clay Shaw in New Orleans for his alleged role in the death of President Kennedy. Garrison subpoenaed Time-Life for the film and was allowed to receive one copy which was several generations from the original, to be used in the trial. Jim Garrison and Mark Lane were having dinner one night while the trial was going on in 1969. They returned to Garrison's office, where Jim stood up and said, 'Mark, the Zapruder film is in there." He then added, "When you leave, just lock it up."[1]

The next morning, the film was back in Garrison's desk, and Mark Lane had 100 copies. The trial ended in the acquittal of Clay Shaw. The 100 copies were then distributed to persons involved in researching the JFK assassination.

One of these researchers, Robert Groden, agreed to show it on television. Appearing with Groden was comedian and civil rights leader Dick Gregory: they discussed both the importance of the film and people's right to see it. Geraldo Rivera was host of *Good Night America,* a television program during the 1970's (1974-1977), where the Zapruder film was shown for the first time on television, March 6, 1975.[2] There were threats of lawsuits against this use. It apparently kept others from trying to show the film on TV. Perhaps some of the researchers made further copies, and several younger researchers started showing the Zapruder film on university campuses. It was on one such occasion that I saw the Zapruder film for the first time, in March 1980. This distance from November 1963 speaks volumes about the success (to that point) of the suppression of the film. It also addresses the revolution in accessing media that was soon to come.

In the 1980's, video players (VP) and video cassette recorders (VCR) became common place. There were a few videos that came out by the time I purchased a VCR, in 1988. Perhaps one of the best renditions came out (on VHS) in 1993, by Robert Groden, *JFK: Case for Conspiracy.*[3] There are several aspects that make this video important (it is also available on DVD); the video was produced and enhanced by Robert Groden. On this version of the Zapruder film, Groden used a technique that he invented, Groden-scoping, which allowed stabilization of the film, removing the movement caused by the photographer, and smoothing out the picture.

This film is extraordinary, in that it incorporates several films shot at Dealey Plaza, beyond the Zapruder film, including Mark Bell (who filmed the motorcade prior to the assassination and the grassy knoll afterward); Orville Nix (on the side opposite Zapruder, producing the second most important film); Elsie Dorman, who filmed from the fourth floor of the Texas School Book Depository; and Dave Wiegman, NBC cameraman, who was filming from a press car a few car-lengths behind the JFK limousine. Also a film was recorded by Marie Muchmore, from NW Main & Houston; a film made by 13 year old Tina Tower was made from Elm & Houston; and a film by Charles Bronson, who was on the same side of the street as Orville Nix, are included in Groden's film. Other films covered in the Groden film include those by William Couch, WFAA-TV, Dallas; Tom Alyea, who filmed inside the Texas School Book Depository after the assassination; Robert Hughes; Ernest Charles Montesana; John Martin; and Jack Daniels.

And there were more films made along the motorcade route. At least three more were done in Dealey Plaza, by Patty Paschall, James Darnell, and one discovered in 2007, by George Jeffries. At least one more was recorded by Beverly Oliver, but she had the film and her camera confiscated by the FBI the same day as the assassination, at her apartment. Neither were returned to her.

One thing that the films that came into the hands of the U.S. government have in common were changes were made at the same or similar critical points: in particular, coinciding with the failure to make an acceptable turn by Presidential limousine driver William Greer, and the actual stop of the limousine at the time of the fatal shot—films that should show these missteps by Greer seem to have uniformly had the offending footage "cleaned."[4]

How about the Zapruder Film– Has It been Altered? If so, how Much, and Why?

First, three excellent references should be noted. An introduction to the Zapruder film was written by David R. Wrone.[5] Wrone gave an examination of the film, together with its history, and some analysis of individual frames. Wrone takes the position that the Zapruder film is not likely to be significantly altered. Yet in his frame-by-frame analysis, he is strongly supportive of multiple shooters. In the frame-by-frame publication of the Zapruder film in Volume XVIII (CE 885) of the 26 volumes of evidence accompanying the Warren Report, not all of the available pertinent frames are included. Frames 207-211 were destroyed, and frame 212 was badly damaged. I am not aware of any important event occurring in this time frame. In that many observers saw a complete stop of the Presidential limousine just prior to the fatal shot at frame 313, it could be argued that several frames were missing from there. The other missing frames are 335-343. These "lost frames" became available when Harold Weisberg sought them with a Freedom of Information request, and described the conundrum in his book, *Photographic Whitewash*.[6]

In particular Wrone focused on frames 337 and 338, about a second-and-a-half after the fatal head shot at frame 313. If the film is viewed at normal speed, the scenes go by quite quickly; by viewing the frames sequentially and individually, and by using slow motion, it can be seen that the President has been propelled violently backward, then falling over to his left toward Mrs. Kennedy. In that 1/9 of a second, the president's head, neck, shirt, and suit coat are shown in sharp detail. No hair is out of place on the back of his head, nor is there any evidence of an entry wound in the back of the head, which by itself discounts that a shooter from the sixth-floor was the single shooter. The transiting bullet had to be the entrance wound in the back of the head; lacking that entrance wound, the Warren Commission's Report is in error.[7]

The second reference of note is the book edited by James Fetzer, *The Great Zapruder Film Hoax: Deceit and Deception in the Death of JFK*.[8] Jack White[9] brings up several photographic issues, many of which relate not only to the Zapruder film but take into account others filming in Dealey Plaza. Several witnesses claimed to see a bullet hole in the front window of the limousine, an event denied by the Warren Commission. A photograph by James Altgens clearly establishes that the windshield had been pierced by a bullet.[10]

Beverly Oliver was shown in the Zapruder film with blonde hair covered, a black band across the top in a black dress and a white belt. Still photographs by Wilma Bond and others showed her to be wearing a long tan raincoat and a headscarf. Oliver was also an acquaintance of Jack Ruby.[11]

The badgeman, discerned to be such from a picture made by Mary Moorman with her Polaroid camera, received considerable notice (by everyone but the Warren Commission), partly because it was taken at the same moment President Kennedy was hit, apparently, by a person with a rifle behind the picket fence; that person appeared to have a badge on his uniform.[12]

Life magazine was trying to lay out the Dealey Plaza landscape with Dallas surveyors Chester Breneman and James West, to plot what each of the frames corresponded to in relation to Dealey Plaza. They were working from 11" X 14" enlargements of the Zapruder film. Four of the enlargements showed blobs coming out of the back of President Kennedy's head. These four frames are no longer in the Zapruder film (at least, with the blobs coming out of the back of President Kennedy's head).[13]

Several of the studies that have been reported would be termed "qualitative" in nature, though several of them also have quantitative aspects. James Fetzer and Scott Lederer[14] use four different versions of the Zapruder film for comparisons. That there are multiple versions of the Zapruder film is prima facie evidence that some tampering had been done, or there wouldn't be more than one version. John Costella[15] acknowledges that Jack White[16] was perhaps the person with the best intuitive sense about the film and where problems may lie.

Costella has also written programs to stabilize visuals of natural movement of a person holding a camera. David Healey[17] explained how the Zapruder film might have been altered (though he doesn't claim it was). As one example of a quantitative analysis, David Mantik[18] shows how a blur analysis can yield information. One interesting finding, in comparing the Zapruder film to the Muchmore film, iss that the Muchmore film is much smoother throughout the film than Zapruder's.

Was the Zapruder Film Altered? Doug Horne's View

Doug Horne, in an almost 200-page chapter, considered the issues of possible alteration.[19] Some of the areas that Horne addressed included:

1. Around frames 132 & 133, the slowing to a crawl of the Presidential limousine as it began the 120 degree turn onto Elm Street; Horne suggested that William Greer was driving poorly, almost running the limousine up onto the North curb near the TSBD's front door. Given what transpired seconds later, having what

amounted to an incompetent driver would be unacceptable on the film (particularly from the viewpoint of the Secret Service).[20]

2. Numerous eyewitness observers reported the limousine stopped briefly near the fatal shot (frame 313); the extant film showed no stopping.[21]

3. In the fatal shot (frame 313), many witnesses noted debris moving back from the limousine, consistent with a shot from the front. Motorcycle escort Bobby W. Hargis, who was the escort to the left rear of the limousine, closest to the left rear wheel stated, "...I felt blood hit me in the face, and the Presidential car stopped immediately after that and stayed stopped for about half a second, then took off at a high rate of speed."[22]

4. There are inconsistencies between the film developed in Dallas and shown to an audience in Dallas on November 22, 1963 and the copies made, independently in Rochester New York on November 23, 1963 and November 24, 1963. The second of these, performed on November 24, 1963 was undoubtedly a forgery, since the original version was cut in Dallas on November 22, 1963; Zapruder wanted to show the film in order to sell it to the highest bidder. The film processed in Rochester on Saturday night November 23, 1963 was a cut 8mm film. The film processed on Sunday, November 24 was a 16mm uncut film! Somehow they were able to send an uncut film, but it was definitely not the original. [23]

5. Cartha DeLoach of the FBI and Dan Rather of CBS News both saw President Kennedy's head move violently forward from their viewing of the Zapruder film on the weekend in Dallas. While this movement was evidence of a shot from behind, the scene also showed evidence of a shot from in front, a scenario consistent with a cross fire, and hence, not due to a lone assassin.[24]

6. The head wound seen in the right front skull in most scenes after 313, and particularly in frames 336 & 337, is inconsistent with the head wound seen in Parkland Hospital.[25]

7. There are undeniable differences between the Zapruder film and other Dealey Plaza films. In Zapruder's film Jean Hill and Mary Moorman are standing in the grass and wearing white shoes, and a slide taken by Charles Bronson shows both women standing in the street and wearing black shoes.[26]

It is likely that the Zapruder film alterations were made at the "Hawkeye Plant," a CIA facility within the Kodak plant in Rochester, New York, probably no later than Monday, November 25, 1963. Two separate, independent groups worked on successive nights on different versions of the Zapruder film. The two crews were entirely separate from each other, and presumably, unaware of the other crew. In Horne's view, the second crew, working from what they thought was the original film were working from a copy of the Zapruder film prior to the original being slit; the original was slit in Dallas, and several persons saw the original film; Zapruder was trying to market the film to the highest bidder. The how can be read in Horne's Chapter 14.[27] Horne refers to the work of David Healey[28] as to how the alterations could be accomplished.

What happened to the original film that Zapruder had in his camera? One might surmise that intelligent conspirators would have destroyed this evidence to prevent it eventually being found out. Dick Russell[29] reported that Paul Rothermel, Jr., a high level aide to oilman H.L. Hunt, took a large amount of money (around $100,000) to get the original film. He insists he got one of the original copies for Hunt. Horne speculated that Hunt may even have purchased the original.[30]

A Hollywood Connection

When Horne finished his Chapter on the Zapruder film, he got in touch with Sydney Wilkinson, an accomplished professional in film and video post-production in Hollywood. Wilkinson purchased the best available copy (a dupe negative) of the Zapruder film from the National Archives. She, along with several colleagues, looked at the film in terms of authenticity. The film was determined to be a fake – and in some ways – a poor fake.[31]

Undoubtedly, those who held the extant Zapruder film knew that, even with the changes, someone would eventually determine the fakery. The presumably best means of continued concealment was to keep close control over the film. The efforts of Jim Garrison to finally get a copy out of the hands of Time-Life was a godsend to the critical research community, and more importantly to the American people. While in Garrison's control reportedly 100 bootleg copies of the film were made. It is not clear to me which version of the Zapruder film Garrison made available.

Endnotes

1 Lane, M. (2012). *Last Word: My Indictment of the CIA in the Murder of JFK.* New York: Skyhorse Publishing, p. 18. Mark Lane is also the author of arguably, the book that got critical research on the JFK assassination: Lane, M. (1966). *Rush to Judgement: A Critical Review of the Warren Commission's Inquiry into the Murders of President John F. Kennedy. Officer J.D. Tippit and Lee Harvey Oswald.* New York: Holt, Rinehart & Winston.

2 Groden, R. (1993). *JFK Assassination Files: JFK; Case for Conspiracy*. This film is available at e-bay and Amazon.com, among others.

3 The appearance by Groden and Dick Gregory is available for viewing at U-Tube on the Internet.

4 *The Many Historical JFK Assassination Films – Analysis, Notes, and Review of the Historical Films*. (February 6, 2013). Accessed on U-Tube 8/21/2017.

5 Wrone, D.R. (2003). *The Zapruder Film: Reframing JFK's Assassination*. Lawrence KS: The University of Kansas Press.

6 Weisberg, H. (1967, 1976). *Photographic Whitewash: Suppressed Kennedy Assassination Pictures*. Frederick MD: Author.

7 Wrone, pp. 184-185.

8 Fetzer, J. H. (Ed.) (2003). *The Great Zapruder Film Hoax: Deceit and Deception in the Death of JFK*. Peru IL: Catfeet Press.

9 White, J. "Mysteries of the JFK Assassination: The Photographic Evidence from A to Z." In Fetzer, (Ed.) (2003). pp. 45-112.

10 Ibid., p. 49.

11 Ibid., p. 51.

12 Ibid., pp. 52-54.

13 Ibid., p. 59.

14 Fetzer, J.H. & Lederer, S.A. (2003). "Which Film is the Zapruder film?" In Fetzer (2003). pp. 29-44.

15 Costella, J.P. (2003). "A Scientst's Verdict: The Film is a Fabrication." In Fetzer (2003). pp.145-221.

16 See footnote 9, White.

17 Healey, D. (2003). "Technical Aspects of Film Alteration." In Fetzer (2003). pp. 113-144.

18 Mantik, D.W. (2003). "The Dealey Plaza Home Movies: The Reel Story or the Real Story?" In Fetzer, pp. 291-308. In comparing qualitative and quantitative analyses in relation the JFK assassination, I wrote a chapter on this very topic: Williams, J.D. (2001). "The qualitative- quantitative continuum: Research on the JFK Assassination." In Hathaway, R. (Ed.)*Annals of the Joint Meeting of the Association for the Advancement of Educational Research and the National Academy of Educational Research 1998-1999*.Lanham MD: University Press of America, pp. 317-328.

19 Horne, D.P. (2009). Chapter 14. "The Zapruder Film Mystery." In Horne, D.P. (2009). *Inside the Assassination Records Review Board: The U.S. Government's Final Attempt to Reconcile the Conflicting Evidence in the Assassination of JFK*. Lexington KY: Author, 1185-1377.

20 Horne, *Inside the Record Review Board*, pp. 1297-1299

21 Ibid., pp. 1299-1301.

22 Ibid., p. 1299.

23 Ibid., p. 1276.

24 Ibid., p. 1294.

25 Ibid., p. 1303.

26 Ibid., pp. 1318-1319.

27 Ibid., p. 1317.

28 Healey.

29 Russell, D. (1992).*The Man Who Knew Too Much*. (Original Edition). New York: Carroll & Graf, p. 584.

30 Horne, *Inside the Record Review Board*, p.1342.

31 Ibid., p. 1361.

Chapter Eighteen

WASHINGTON, NOVEMBER 23, 1963 TO JANUARY 23, 1964

On Saturday, November 23, 10:01 A.M. President Johnson spoke with FBI Director, J. Edgar Hoover on the telephone. Hoover first informed Johnson that Oswald had been charged with the murder of the President. Hoover indicated that evidence they had at that time was not strong.

President Johnson asked if anything more had been established regarding the visit by Oswald to the Soviet Embassy in Mexico City in September.

> HOOVER: No, that's one angle that is very confusing, for this reason – we have up here the tape and the photograph of the man who was at the Soviet embassy, using Oswald's name. That picture and the tape do not correspond to this man's (Lee Harvey Oswald) voice, nor to his appearance. In other words, it appears that there is a second person who was at the Soviet Embassy down there. We do have a copy of a letter which was written by Oswald to the Soviet Embassy here in Washington, inquiring as well as complaining about the harassment of his wife and the questioning of his wife by the FBI. Now, of course, that letter information – we process all mail that goes to the Soviet Embassy. It's a very secret operation. No mail is delivered to the embassy without being examined and opened by us, so we know what they receive – The case as it stands now, isn't strong enough to get a conviction.... Now if we can identify this man who was at the ... Soviet Embassy in Mexico City... This man Oswald has denied everything. He doesn't know anything about anything, but the gun thing, of course, is a definite thing.[1]

There are several interesting points in this discourse. There is the revelation that Oswald was being impersonated in Mexico City in September 1963. This has been verified by J. Edgar Hoover, the FBI Director, and communicated to the new President. Also, there is the assessment that the case to be made against Oswald is very weak, and unlikely to obtain a conviction. None of this was communicated to the general public. In fact, much of this information was withheld for years.

Also on November 23, 1963, President Johnson held a conversation with Senator George Smathers (D-Florida). Smathers was thinking about trying to get around Senator Harry Byrd, Chairman of the Senate Finance Committee, who was holding up the budget; Smathers was sure they had the votes to do this.[2]

President Johnson responded, "No, no, I can't do that. This would destroy the [Democratic] party, and destroy the election, and destroy everything. We've got to carry on. We can't abandon this man's [President Kennedy's] program, he is a national hero and there is these people [who] want his program passed and we've got to keep this Kennedy aura with us through this election."[3]

In a sense, this Lyndon Johnson was very different from the Lyndon Johnson just 36 hours earlier. He somehow became deferential to the fallen president. In a sense, Lyndon Johnson had become "Presidential."

Whitney Young and Civil Rights

Given what Whitney Young, National Director, Urban League, knew about Lyndon Johnson's activity in the Senate, there was little to expect in a civil rights legislative agenda from the new President Johnson. In 1957, he weakened what was only a modest civil rights bill, which was the first such bill in 82 years. Yet President Johnson was on the phone with him (Sunday, November 24), asking for his advice in regard to a new proposal on civil rights.[4] On the following day, President Johnson spoke to Martin Luther King, telling Rev. King that they would be trying to get a new civil rights bill through Congress.[5]

The Beginnings of What Would Become the Warren Commission

When the suggestion was made that a national commission be formed to investigate the Assassination of President John F. Kennedy, President Johnson thought that the already-begun FBI investigation and an inquiry by the state of Texas was sufficient regarding the assassination. One of those persons who was touting some federal investigation was Joseph Alsop, a columnist for the *Washington Post,* who wrote a column to that effect and spoke to President Johnson on the phone regarding this idea (Monday, November 25, 1963) trying to help persuade the president to move toward a federal investigation beyond that done by the FBI.[6]

National Security Action Memorandum No. 273

NSAM 273 was written to be a replacement of NSAM 263. Since President Kennedy had kept NSAM 263 secret, and presumably, would have kept it a secret until at least the election of 1964, a hue and cry at the time of the issuance of NSAM 273 (November 26, 1963) would have been limited. The original draft was written in Honolulu just prior to President Kennedy's assassination, probably on November 21, 1963; a result of the Honolulu Conference. Recall that NSAM 263 called for bringing home 1000 servicemen before the end of 1963 and bring home all military personnel by 1965. The replacement was written to appear to be an update to the NSAM 263, which of course, only a few persons were aware of. NSAM 273 was sent to The Secretary of State, The Secretary of Defense, The Director of Central Intelligence, The Administrator for the Agency for International Development, and The United States Information Agency. This was of course authorized by President Johnson.[7]

> NSAM 273 began: 1. "It remains the central object of the United States in South Vietnam to assist the people and Government of that country to win their contest against the externally directed and supported Communist conspiracy. The test of all U.S. decisions and actions in this area should be the effectiveness of their contribution to this purpose."[8]
>
> 2. "The objectives of the United States with respect to withdrawal of U.S. military personnel remain as stated in the White House statement of October 2, 1963."[9]

In regard to the first goal of withdrawal, that is the removal of 1,000 military personnel by the end of 1963, the actuality was a paper reduction; some personnel were rotated back to the United States in December; the size of the troop strength more than recuperated in the next two months.[10]

The remaining eight points address specific areas of concern (the Mekong Delta, Laos, and Cambodia) that collectively increase United States involvement in Vietnam, rendering a complete pullout from Vietnam in any near future only a diminishing and remote possibility. [11]

The comparison of the two documents can come down to a simple contrast. In NSAM 263, the argument was made that the war was Vietnam's war not ours. It was their war to win or lose. Before all of our troops are withdrawn, the Government of Vietnam's army should be trained to take on the efforts themselves, and this goal could be accomplished by the end of 1965.

NSAM273 would lead to the United States being more involved in directing the war, and hence, presumably in the war for the duration, meaning an unlimited commitment of American troops to Vietnam. Future NSAMs by President Johnson would solidify this position.[12]

Lyndon Johnson Before a Joint Session of Congress, 11/27/63

Having neither heard nor read President Johnson's speech to the joint session of Congress prior to writing this section (alas, I found Johnson to be on the boring side), and only intuiting that he probably had done so, I was frankly shocked by the rhetorical genius in the speech. I immediately surmised that Theodore Sorensen had a major part in the construction of the speech; also involved was a speechwriter who'd worked with Johnson before, Horace Busby.[13] Reading it now for the first time, it is clear that this was a great speech, likely the best ever delivered by Lyndon Johnson. Excerpts follow:

> The greatest leader of our time has been struck down by the foulest deed of our time. Today, John Fitzgerald Kennedy lives on in the immortal words and works that he left behind. He lives on in the mind and memories of mankind. He lives on in the minds of his countrymen.
>
> No words are sad enough to express our sense of loss. No words are strong enough to express our determination to continue the forward thrust of America that he began.
>
> The dream of conquering the vastness of space – the dream of partnership across the Atlantic – and across the Pacific as well – the dream of a Peace Corps in less developed nations – the dream of education for all of our children – the dream of jobs for all who seek them and need them – the dream of care for our elderly – the dream of all-out attacks on mental illness – and above all, the dream of equal rights for all Americans, whatever their race and color – these and other American dreams have been vitalized by his drive and his dedication.
>
> ...
>
> An assassin's bullet has thrust upon me the awesome burden of the Presidency. I am here today to say I need your help; I cannot bear this burden alone. I need the help of all Americans and all America. This nation has experienced a profound shock, and in this critical moment, it is our duty, yours and mine, as the Government of the United States to do away with uncertainty and doubt and delay, and to show that we are capable of decisive action; that from the brutal loss of our leader we will derive not weakness, but strength; we can and will act and act now.
>
> ...
>
> On the 20th of January in 1961, John F. Kennedy told his countrymen that our national work would not be finished in the first thousand days, nor in the life of this administration, nor even perhaps in our lifetime on this planet. But, he said, "Let us begin."

Today, in this moment of new resolve, I would say to all my fellow Americans, let us continue.

This is our challenge – not to hesitate, not to pause, not to turn about and linger over this evil moment, but to continue on our course so that we may fulfill the destiny that history has set for us. Our most immediate tasks are here on this Hill.

First no memorial oration or eulogy could more eloquently honor President Kennedy's memory than the earliest possible passage of the civil rights bill for which he fought for so long. We have talked long enough in this country about equal rights. We have talked for one hundred years or more. It is time now to write the next chapter and write it into the books of law.

I urge you again as I did in 1957, and again in 1960, to enact a civil rights law so that we can move forward to eliminate from this Nation every trace of discrimination and oppression that is based on race or color. There could be no greater source of strength to this Nation both at home and abroad.

And second, no act of ours could more fittingly continue the work of President Kennedy than the early passage for which he fought all this long year. This is a bill designed to increase our national income and Federal revenue, and to provide insurance against recession. That bill, if passed without delay, means more security for those now working, more jobs now for those without them, and more incentive for our economy.

In short, there is no time for delay. It is time for action – strong forward-looking action on the pending education bills to help bring the light of learning to every home and hamlet in America – strong, forward-looking action on youth employment opportunities; strong, forward-looking action on the pending foreign aids bill, making clear that we are not forfeiting our responsibilities to this hemisphere or to the world, without erasing Executive flexibility in our conduct of foreign affairs – and strong, prompt and forward-looking action on the remaining appropriation bills.

I profoundly hope that the tragedy and the torment of these terrible days will bind us together in new fellowship, making us one people in our hour of sorrow. So, let us highly resolve that John Fitzgerald Kennedy did not live – or die – in vain. And on this Thanksgiving eve, as we gather together to ask the Lord's blessing, and give Him our thanks, let us unite in these familiar and cherished words:

America, America,
God shed His grace on thee,
And crowned thy good
With brotherhood
From sea to shining sea.[14]

Without question, this was the finest speech ever delivered by Lyndon Johnson. Much of the speech apparently was oriented to enacting much of the agenda of President Kennedy. What was missing was the extraction of the United States from the mire of Vietnam; the termination of our commitment to ending U.S. participation in the war in Vietnam was secreted in NSAM 263, which would not see the light of day until the 1990's. The pressing for the civil rights bill would have a long-term outcome – the formerly solid South in the Democrat column, partially through the political acumen of Richard Nixon in courting southern votes in the 1968 & 1972 elections, would unleash the so-called "Southern Strategy,"[15] moving a still "Solid South" into the Republican column.

This speech was all the more remarkable, given Johnson's animus toward the Kennedys; for example, as he displayed on the early morning of November 22, 1963, "*After tomorrow those goddamn Kennedy's will never embarrass me again – that's no threat – that's a promise.*"[16]

What would explain Johnson's pushing forward many of Kennedy's agenda issues? It would appear that Johnson subsumed his ideas beneath President Kennedy's issues. Or was it just shrewd politics? It could very well be a combination of these factors, but likely would include that many of Kennedy's issues were aligned with Johnson's own; this apparently was particularly so in regard to civil rights. Using Kennedy's martyrdom and Johnson's knack for getting legislation through, Johnson was "striking while the iron was hot." In the coming months, success would come on many of the issues.

There was, of course, one area where Johnson and Kennedy were of very different minds – Vietnam. The problem was, with the non-release of NSAM 263, very few outside President Kennedy's inner circle were aware that his intention was to remove us from Vietnam by the end of 1965. It was fairly straightforward for Johnson to change the trajectory from training the Vietnamese people and government to conduct their own war – which turned out to be an open-ended commitment. Working to fulfill the agenda of the fallen president was by-and-large generally accepted as appropriate, helping the new President to receive general acceptance and insure his winning the nomination and ultimately the next presidential election. In retrospect, it seemed to be a winning plan. As Johnson would find out, there would be the beginning of the "Southern Strategy" in the 1964 presidential election.

Johnson's Warming to a National Commission to Investigate the Assassination

As of Monday morning, November 25, 1963, Johnson was satisfied that an FBI investigation, which would result in a written report from the Bureau, plus a Texas State investigation conducted by the Texas Attorney General, was sufficient; this was conveyed to Joseph Alsop, a Columnist for the *Washington Post* in a telephone conversation that morning.[17] While LBJ was satisfied with the FBI Investigation and a State of Texas Court of Inquiry on Monday (November 25) By Thursday (November 28, Thanksgiving), he not only had moved to a Presidential Commission, he had already selected the members; he had to convince the final two members the following day – Supreme Court Chief Justice Earl Warren, and Senator Richard Russell from Georgia. Russell in particular did not want to be on the Commission; President Johnson did not inform him that Chief Justice Warren had agreed to be Chairman. In particular, Senator Russell did not want to serve with Earl Warren. When the Commission was announced on Friday, November 29, Russell had not yet agreed to be on the Commission; after he finally assented, Johnson let him know that Earl Warren was also on the Commission. With a great deal of reluctance, Senator Russell stayed on.

Johnson's Stream-of-Consciousness Rant to Katharine Graham

On Monday, December 2, 1963, President Johnson called Katherine Graham, President of the Washington Post Company, and publisher of the *Washington Post* newspaper. In a long and rambling rant, President Johnson lamented that Congress had taken a Thanksgiving recess, and he was concerned that Congress was not working, and thus not doing anything about the needs of the nation, as seen by Johnson. It was as if Johnson couldn't remember being both in the House, and then in the Senate.[18] Apparently, in his mind, Congress was an equal branch of government when he was in Congress, but now that he was the President, the Executive branch should be *more* equal.[19] Congress was acting very similarly to when Johnson was the Majority Leader of the Senate, when he called the shots. In his mind, it would appear that he should be able to have even more control of Congress now that he was President.

Governor Connally

On December 5, 1963, Governor John Connally was released from Parkland Hospital. When shot in the motorcade, his left arm was shattered.[20]

Later, the Warren Commission determined that a bullet hit President Kennedy, then deflected, making at least a 90 degree turn, and then hit Governor Connally in the arm. The bullet that did all this damage to both President Kennedy and to Governor Connally was, famously in pristine condition after boring through the two men – the "magic bullet."[21]

President Johnson's Concern About the Bobby Baker Scandal

In a December 6, 1963, a telephone conversation took place with Senator B. Everett Jordan, Chair of the Senate Rules Committee. In this conversation, President Johnson revealed his continuing concern regarding the testimony of Donald Reynolds. The Senate Rules Committee had met on the day of the assassination and was considering the testimony of Donald Reynolds regarding an insurance policy that was purchased for Lyndon Johnson back in 1957, which involved kickbacks to Johnson.[22] Jordan intended to keep the issue from exploding.[23]

The FBI Report on the Assassination

On December 9, 1963, the FBI released their version of the events that took place in Dallas.

Their report was completed 18 days after the assassination. It was 400 pages long in 5 volumes, which makes it sound weightier than it was. The essence of the report was that three shots were fired, two hitting President Kennedy, and one hitting Governor Connally. There were some limited details about the life of Lee Harvey Oswald, but the 400 pages could easily have been fit into a 60-page document.[24] It was Hoover's belief that this document should have been the focus of the Warren Commission. If the Commission was privy to this notion, one would expect a lot of laughter from the seven commissioners. There was very little substance beyond their conclusion. For the FBI Report to be accurate, there would have to have been at least four shots, because of the shot that missed and caused a facial injury to James Tague.[25] This is not to suggest that the Warren Commission had a more accurate conclusion than the FBI version of events. As it was, there were problems beyond scarcity of details in the FBI version. Hoover knew that not much of a case could be built against Oswald,[26] but this lack of evidence did not deter him from labeling Oswald as the shooter.

A simple analysis of the FBI Report is that, whether or not it is more accurate than the forthcoming Warren Commission Report, the FBI Report is too thin on facts to be seen as having any finality. Their view of the actual shooting was not nearly as driven to arrive at a pre-chosen conclusion, and that its simplicity might be somewhat more accurate. The discovery of the shot that caused an injury to James Tague would never be addressed in any revised FBI Report. The FBI did not change their conclusion that two shots hit President Kennedy, and a separate shot hit Governor Connally.

State of the Union Message, January 8, 1964

President Johnson's presentation[27] of January 8, 1964 was similar in content to the eloquent presentation of November 27, 1963 but lacking in the eloquent structure in the earlier speech, likely due to Ted Sorensen's decision to leave the Johnson administration. The newer speech had considerably more detail that might be pleasing to the assembled members of Congress. Johnson's continued push for a new civil rights bill would undoubtedly have been less well-received by many of the nominal Democrats from the South. One point that would have been pleasing to most was the anticipated dropping of the national debt from $10 billion to 4.5 billion. To fact check this statement, Johnson was saying that instead of increasing the national debt in 1964 by $10 billion, he was increasing the national debt by 4.5 billion. In retrospect, the actual figure for increase in the National debt in 1963 was $6 billion, as it was in 1964, another debt of $6 billion. In other words, the savings Johnson was railing about failed to materialize.[28]

Johnson's opening salvo was,

> Let this session of Congress be known as the session that did more for civil rights than the last hundred sessions combined; as the session which enacted the most far-reaching tax cut of our time; as the session that declared all-out war on human poverty and unemployment in these United States; as the session that finally recognized the health needs of all of our older citizens; as the session that reformed our tangled transportation and transit policies; as the session that achieved the most effective, efficient foreign aid program ever; and as the session which helped to build more homes, more schools, more libraries and more hospitals than any single session of Congress in the history of our Republic.[29]
>
> ...
>
> Let us carry forward the plans and programs of John Fitzgerald Kennedy – not because of our sorrow or sympathy, but because they are right.
>
> ...

Unfortunately, many Americans live on the outskirts of hope – some because of their poverty, and some because of their color, and all too many because of both. Our task is to replace their despair with opportunity.

...

The administration today, here and now, declares unconditional war on poverty in America. I urge this Congress and all Americans to join me in this effort.

...

Our chief weapons are a more pinpointed attack will be better schools, and better health, and better homes, and better training, and better job opportunities to help more Americans, especially young Americans, escape from squalor and misery and unemployment rolls where other citizens help to carry them.

...

We must create a National Service Corps to help the economically handicapped of our own country as the Peace Corps now help those abroad.

...

All members of the public should have equal access to facilities open to the public. All members of the public should be equally eligible for Federal benefits that are financed by the public. All members of the public should have an equal chance to vote for public officials and to send their children to good public schools and to contribute their talents to the public good.

Today, Americans of all races stand side by side in Berlin and in Viet Nam. They died side by side in Korea. Surely than can work and eat and travel side by side in their own country.

...

In establishing preferences, a nation that was built by immigrants from all lands can ask those who now seek admission; What can you do for our country? But we should not be asking: 'In what country were you born?'

...

John Kennedy was a victim of hate, but he was also a builder in faith – faith in our fellow Americans, whatever their creed or color or their station in life, in the future of man, whatever his divisions and differences.

Johnson presumably knew that much of his presentation would not be well received by Southern members of Congress who were reticent to see segregation under siege. This might become an issue with the coming Presidential election in November. This presentation addressed the nuts & bolts of President Johnson's agenda. Introduced was the concept of the National Service Corps, a domestic Peace Corps. (This program is now called AmeriCorps.)[30]

The 24th Amendment to the Constitution – Removal of the Poll Tax

The 24th Amendment was ratified on January 23, 1964.

The amendment is:

> Section 1. The right of citizens of the United States to vote in any primary or other election for President or Vice President, for electors for President or Vice-President or for Senator or Representative in Congress, shall not be denied or abridged by the United States or any State by reason of failure to pay any poll tax or other tax.
>
> Section 2. The Congress shall have power to enforce this article by appropriate legislation.[31]

Poll taxes originated in the South after Reconstruction following the civil war, as a means to marginalize voting by Blacks, without violating the constitution. The poll taxes not only stopped many Blacks from voting, it also stopped poorer Whites from the voting process. By the 1960's, most of the states with poll taxes were the former Confederate states. Curiously, Wyoming also introduced poll taxes.[32] In the passing of the 24th Amendment, 38 states had to ratify it; only two states that were in the confederacy ratified the amendment. Tennessee was the 21st state to ratify, and Florida was the 27th state. A Supreme Court decision in 1966 removed poll taxes from all elections.[33]

Endnotes

1 Beschloss, M.R. (1997). *Taking Charge: The Johnson White House Tapes, 1963-1964*. New York: Simon & Schuster, pp. 22-23.

2 Ibid., p. 25.

3 Loc. cit.

4 Ibid., pp. 28-30.

5 Ibid., pp. 37-38.

6 Ibid., pp. 32-35.

7 National Security Action Memorandum No. 273. [NSAM 273] Foreign Relations of the United States, 1961-63, Volume IV, Vietnam, August-December, 1963. retrieved at history/state/gov/historicaldocuments/frus1961-63v4/d331, retrieved 8/30/2017.

8 Loc. cit.

9 Loc. cit.

10 Ellsberg, D. (1972). *The Pentagon Papers: The Defense Department History of United States Decision Making in Vietnam*. Boston: Beacon Press, Vol. 2, p. 303.

11 NSAM 273.

12 Prouty, L.F. (2011). *JFK: The CIA, Vietnam, and the Plot to Assassinate John F. Kennedy*. New York: Skyhorse Publishing, pp. 102-117.

13 Barrett, A. "Lyndon B. Johnson," "Let Us Continue" (27 November 1963). archive.vod.umb.edu/citizen/lbj1963int.htm retrieved 9/5/2017.

14 Loc. cit.

15 Murphy, J.R. & Gulliver, H.S. (1971). *The Southern Strategy*. New York: Charles Schribner's Sons.

16 Brown, M.D. (1997). *Texas in the Morning: The Love Story of Madeleine Brown and President Lyndon Baines Johnson*. Baltimore: The Conservatory Press, p. 166.

17 Beschloss, pp. 32-35.

18 Ibid., pp. 66-68.

19 As in George Orwell's *Animal Farm* (Orwell, G. (1945). *Animal Farm: A Fairy Story*. London: Secher & Warberg)

20 Beschloss, p. 91.

21 Lane, M. (1966). *Rush to Judgment: A Critique of the Warren Commission's Inquiry into the Murders of President John F. Kennedy, Officer J.D. Tippit and Lee Harvey Oswald*. New York: Holt, Rinehart & Winston, pp. 69-80.

22 Williams, J.D. & Conway, D. (2001). "The Don Reynolds Testimony and LBJ." *Assassination Chronicles*, 7,1, 19-28.

23 Beschloss, pp. 92-94.

24 The document given to the Warren Commission by the FBI can be seen at maryferrell.org.

25 Tague, J.T. (2003). *Truth Withheld: A Survivor's Story*. Dallas, TX: Excel Digital Press, Inc.

26 Beschloss, p.23.

27 Annual Message to the Congress and the State of the Union, President Lyndon B. Johnson, presidency.ucsb. edu/ws/?pid=26787, retrieved on 9/15/2017.

28 Amadeo, K. (2017) U.S. Debt by President: By Dollar and Percent, thebalance.com/us_debt_by-president_by_dollar_and_percent_3306296 retrieved 9/15/2017.

29 Annual Message to Congress and State of the Union, 1/8/1964.

30 Ibid.

31 *The World Almanac 2017* (2016).New York: World Almanac Books, pp. 513-514.

32 I was living in Wyoming in 1962 and went to vote; to my surprise, there was a $6 poll tax. I had never heard of a poll tax before. The 24th Amendment removed the poll tax in Wyoming.

33 Twenty-fourth Amendment to the Unites States Constitution. wikipedia.org/wiki/twenty-fourth_amendment_to_the_United-States_Constituition, retrieved 9/17/2017.

Chapter Nineteen

ADVOCACY RESEARCH: REVISITING THE WARREN COMMISION

In "typical" court proceedings, an advocacy research/presentation of the facts is envisioned. The prosecutor presents the evidence that the prosecutor thinks is the best case for convicting the defendant. In a perfect world (which we DO NOT live in), exculpatory evidence which suggests that some doubt exists as to whether the defendant is guilty, would at least be made available to the defense. The advocate for the defense is charged with defending his/her client, testing the evidence brought by the prosecution, and presenting countering evidence that can show, at least, that a reasonable doubt exists. The forgoing does not come anywhere close to the activities of the Warren Commission.

Hypothetically, the Commission and the staff were to examine all of the information (presumably facts), and without prejudice, render a report that fairly addressed the assassination of President John F. Kennedy. Prejudice can be simply being stated as prejudging. In fact, the Warren Commission was from the moment of its conception, prejudiced. The first meeting of The President's Commission on the Assassination of President John F. Kennedy (the actual title of the Commission that has come to be known as The Warren Commission) took place on January 27, 1964. The entire transcript of that meeting was published with annotations and comments by Harold Weisberg,[1] courtesy of the Freedom of Information Act. Howard Willens, a staff member who came from Bobby Kennedy's Justice Department, wrote a memorandum for the record on the day following the meeting: "... (W)hat the commission was up to from the first, [was] the search for means of foisting off a preconceived conclusion, the deliberate hiding of what actually happened when JFK was killed."[2] Willens early-on made the case that the Warren Commission was in fact prejudging the work before them.

The Relation of Bayesian Statistical Analysis to Prosecutorial Advocacy

A lesser known (but not less important) statistical approach, is Bayesian analysis, after the British statistician Thomas Bayes. A Bayesian analysis[3] differs from a standard approach by allowing an individual's (or group's) beliefs about an event to enter to into the decision process. A natural analog is a horse race. In projecting the winner of a race, the odds of a horse winning are not based on an objective analysis of performance data (though persons may use objective information in assessing their subjective choices). The "odds" reported are pari-mutuel odds, that is, the "average" of people's subjective choices when they place their bets for the race. Of course, many times a favorite does not win the race. The race is the objective outcome, which need not correspond to the bettor's choice. Bayesian analysis also allows for testing past events that have an unknown aspect. In particular, solving a murder case involves an outcome (the murder) with an "unknown" cause. In a murder case there may be several suspects. In the particular case of the JFK assassination, we might have the following suspects: (1) Lee Harvey Oswald, acting alone, (2) Lee Harvey Oswald, as part of a conspiracy, (3) members of the Dallas Police, (4) the CIA, (5) the FBI, (6) Texas oilmen, (7) Cubans supporting Castro, (8) anti-Castro Cubans, (9) the Mafia, and (10) the Russians. This is by no means a complete list, and some might want combinations, such as the CIA and the FBI. What others might have preferred would have been for the Warren Commission to investigate each of the listed entities.

The persons chosen by the Warren Commission to weigh the evidence for a preliminary report were for the most part young lawyers, whose training was to be an advocate for a position. And pointedly, no person was given the role of being an advocate for Oswald (Mark Lane volunteered for this role, but was not accepted by the Commission).

It would appear that only the first two options were considered by the Commission, and hence, considered only by the young lawyers they hired to sift the collected data. Most of the evidence was in fact collected by the FBI; any veering away from objectivity would taint whatever data was collected. The prior beliefs of certain principals could easily taint the data collection process. Further, if Oswald were considered to be in a conspiracy, the cleanness of the outcome could be politically problematic. Hence, for some participants, the prior probability of Oswald's having acted alone likely would have been very near certainty (i.e. a probability of near to 1). Some of the staff members entertained the second option (i.e., Oswald was the shooter, but also involved in a conspiracy). For most of the persons involved (the Commission, the Commission's staff, and the FBI), the expectancy was that the shooter was most likely Oswald. It would seem that the belief Oswald was the shooter was a given for most of the persons involved with the investigation. The lack of an advocate for Oswald left little doubt as to who would be blamed. The goal of the group seemed to be to find the facts that supported "convicting" Oswald, and in some way, show that all exculpatory information suggesting Oswald wasn't the shooter, was somehow in error. Simply, the overall goal of the Warren Commission was to come to the conclusion that Oswald and no other person was responsible for the assassination of President Kennedy, and to come to that conclusion prior to the Presidential election in November 1964.

The Handling of "Data" – the Case of Victoria Adams

Victoria Adams was an employee at the Texas Schoolbook Depository (TSBD), who was, along with three other women, watching the Presidential motorcade from a fourth-floor window on November 22, 1963. Directly after the last shot, she and another employee, Sandra Styles, went down the stairs to the first floor. They neither saw nor heard anyone on the stairs. The only person they encountered was a large black man, also an employee at the TSBD, whom they saw on their way out of the building. A third employee, Dorothy Ann Garner, immediately situated herself in a chair by the stairs and the freight elevator, where she would notice anyone going up or down the stairs or elevator. At no time did she see Lee Oswald. It was several minutes before anyone passed her on the stairs. They included Roy Truly, TSBD Building Superintendent, and policemen going up the stairs to investigate. Collectively, the four women's observations would preclude Oswald being on the 6th floor at the time of the assassination. The fourth woman was Elsie Dorman.[4] Among the four women, only Vicky Adams was interviewed by the Warren Commission, and had that interview made public. Dorothy Ann Garner stated that she too was interviewed by the Warren Commission, though no record has yet been found. Perhaps after interviewing her, a decision was made *not* to do a deposition. Each of the four women had been interviewed by the FBI (CE 1381). Victoria Adams' deposition follows:

FD-302 (Rev. 3-3-59) FEDERAL BUREAU OF INVESTIGATION

Date 11/24/63

1

VICKIE ADAMS, 3651 Fontana Street, Dallas, Texas furnished the following information:

She is employed as office service representative by the Scott Foresman and Company, with offices located on the fourth floor of the Texas School Book Depository Company, Dallas.

On November 22, 1963, she was on duty at her place of employment and at about 12:20 PM on that date she went to the second window from the left of the building on the fourth floor and opened same in order to watch out of this window to observe the passing of the motorcade, bearing President KENNEDY and group. She took her lunch with her at this time and stationed herself there with a fellow employee, SANDRA STYLES, 2102 Grauwyler Street, Dallas. They observed the motorcade as it approached and began passing in front of her window and at about 12:30 PM, as the car containing President KENNEDY, Governor CONNALLY and his wife, was passing, she heard three loud reports which she first thought to be fire crackers of a crank and she believed the sound came from toward the right of the building, rather than from the left and above as it must have been according to subsequent information disseminated by the news services. After the third shot, she observed the car containing President KENNEDY to speed up and rush away. She had not been able to fully observe the President at the exact moment he was shot, inasmuch as her view was partially obstructed. She and her friend then ran immediately to the back of the building to where the stairs were located and ran down the stairs. No one else was observed on the stairs at this time, and she is sure that this would be the only means of escape from the building from the sixth floor. She and her friends ran out of the building, turned to the left and ran across the railroad tracks in the direction where they observed other people running, inasmuch as they felt that an attempt had been made on the life of the President, and they wanted to find out more about this situation. They had not gone far until they were stopped by a police officer who instructed them to return to the building. Consequently, they returned to the building and re-entered it.

on 11/24/63 at Dallas, Texas File # DL 89-43

by Special Agents EDMOND C. HARDIN & PAUL L. SCOTT /ss Date dictated 11/24/63

39

This document contains neither recommendations nor conclusions of the FBI. It is the property of the FBI and is loaned to your agency; it and its contents are not to be distributed outside your agency.

Only Victoria Adams was interviewed and deposed by the Warren Commission among the four women. Vickie Adams' later interview (on April 24, 1964) with the Warren Commission was conducted by David Belin, a member of the Warren Commission staff investigator team. In Vicki Adams' testimony, a curious sentence was added; that she had encountered Bill Shelley and Billy Lovelady on the first floor. It strongly appears Belin (or someone else within the Warren Commission staff) added this statement after Vickie Adams had seen the typescript of her testimony. Vickie was astonished by the change, which she only became aware of years later. The change, of course, would have allowed Oswald time to come down the stairs, in that Lovelady did not enter the building until five minutes after the shooting. It becomes clear that the evidence was being changed by the Commission staff to save the appearance that Oswald could have been the shooter. By not interviewing (and producing a record) of any of the other three women, and changing the testimony of Miss Adams, Belin was introducing a lie.[5] Had a lawyer such as Mark Lane been able to rebut the information inserted by Belin, the Warren Commission might well have had a different outcome, apparently something not desired by the "powers that be." In her interview with Belin, a curious sentence appeared to have been added, different from Miss Adams statement, that she encountered Bill Shelley and Billy Lovelady on the first floor after she came down the stairs, directly after the assassination. Her seeing Shelley and Lovelady actually occurred several minutes later, after she re-entered the building.

A pertinent part of the interview follows:

> Mr. BELIN: When you got to the bottom of the first floor, did you see anyone there as you entered the first floor from the doorway?
>
> Miss ADAMS: Yes, sir.
>
> Mr. BELIN: Who did you see?
>
> Miss ADAMS: Mr. Bill Shelley and Billy Lovelady.
>
> Mr. BELIN: Where did you see them on the first floor?
>
> Miss ADAMS: Well this is the stairs, and this is the Houston Street dock that I went out. They were approximately in this position here, so I don't know how you would describe that.
>
> Mr. BELIN: You are looking now at a first-floor plan, or diagram of the Texas School Book Depository, and you have pointed to a position where you encountered Billy Lovelady and Mr. Shelley?
>
> Miss ADAMS: That's correct.
>
> Mr. BELIN: It would be slightly east of the front of the east elevator, and probably as far south as the length of the elevator, is that correct?
>
> Miss ADAMS: Yes, sir.
>
> Mr. BELIN: I have here a document called Commission's Exhibit No. 496, which includes a diagram of the first floor, and there is a

> No.7 and there is a circle on it, and I have pointed to a place marked No. 7 on the diagram, is that correct?
>
> Miss ADAMS: That is approximate.[6]

Though no one questioned this testimony at the time of the publication of the 26 volumes of Appendices to the Warren Report, on its face there appear to be inconsistencies in the interview. There are six couplets of dialog between Mr. Belin and Miss Adams. The last couplet, where Belin introduces CE No. 496, would seem to precede the other couplets. But there is also an issue in the last couplet: how would Belin know where Victoria Adams encountered Mr. Shelley and Billy Lovelady wherein he would have pinpointed the location on the first floor where Shelley and Lovelady were positioned had already been circled? Would it not have been more appropriate for Belin to ask Miss Adams to circle that place herself? The fourth couplet has Miss Adams looking at the first-floor plan. It would surely seem this would have occurred after the last couplet. In retrospect, the unmistakable interpretation is that someone has significantly edited the testimony of Victoria Adams.

She only saw the published transcript of her testimony years after it was published in Volume VI of the 26 volumes of Appendices. Victoria Adams vehemently denied that the published transcript was accurate;when Adams was presented a copy of the published version of her testimony by Barry Ernest in 2002, it was the first time she ever saw it. She had previously only seen a typescript after the interview, at which time she made several corrections. Multiple changes were made in her deposition. The person she spoke to on the first floor was a large black man who was near the door as she exited.

She never spoke to either Shelley or Lovelady, nor apparently did she even see them together.[7] She did not see either person on her way out directly after the assassination. In Shelley and Lovelady's depositions, Shelley said he saw Victoria Adams on the fourth floor (Adams' work station) somewhat after the assassination. Lovelady wasn't even sure he saw Victoria Adams. Neither Shelley nor Lovelady reported any conversation with her.[8]

It strongly appears Belin (or someone else within the Warren Commission staff) added changes after Vickie Adams had seen the typescript of her statement. The changes of course, would have allowed Oswald time to come down the stairs, in that Shelley and Lovelady did not enter the building until five minutes after the shooting. It becomes clear that the evidence was being changed by the Commission staff to save the appearance that Oswald could have been the shooter. .

It can be seen that the testimony of Victoria Adams and her three co-workers would minimally place in doubt the conclusions of the Warren Commission and cast David Belin (or some un-named staff member) as a person willing to bolster the case against Oswald and remove evidence that was exculpatory to Oswald. Had her actual testimony, unaltered by Belin (or someone else in the commission staff), been included in the testimonies in the 26 volumes of Appendices to the Warren Commission Report, the United States may have had a very different history since 1963; that history might have been much more truthful.

Oswald's Income

Before looking at the FBI's and CIA's involvement in the Warren Commission's workings, it is instructive to look at Oswald's income in the two months preceding the assassination.

Warren Commission staff lawyer Richard Mosk and IRS supervisor Phillip Barson filed a report to the Warren Commission on Oswald's income and expenses for September 25, 1963, the day he left New Orleans for Mexico, until the assassination, slightly less than a two month period. "His [Oswald's] income, including salary and unemployment insurance, totaled $3665.89, while his expenses, including the cost of the Mexico trip, totaled $3,497.79. It was a difference of $168, and that money was apparently accounted for, since Oswald left the $170 in cash for Marina in a drawer in the bedroom dresser."[9]

That statement is astonishing. Oswald's only official employment was at the TSBD, from October 16, 1963 until November 22, 1963, five weeks and three days. At a wage of $1.25 per hour, Oswald would have earned around $280 at the TSBD during his employment there. As to unemployment insurance, Oswald cashed his last unemployment check from the State of Texas on October 15, 1963, in the amount of $6.[10] Clearly, Lee had other sources of income. A likely source was the CIA-financed research project in New Orleans headed by Dr. Alton Ochsner: "...Lee Oswald secretly worked as a team member on Ochsner's bio-weapon project,... Oswald met with Ochsner personally, and that it was actually Lee Oswald who requested that Dr. Ochsner set up his media coverage to help position him as a pro-Cuban activist, so that he could get into Cuba more easily and deliver their bio-weapon to sympathetic doctors, who would use it to kill Castro."[11] The CIA, through the New Orleans research project, would likely have funded not only his employment through the clandestine project, most likely they funded his trip to Mexico as well. The FBI likely also paid Oswald money during this period for some of his activities performed for the FBI.

The FBI and the Warren Commission

Prior to the first executive session of the Warren Commission, January 27, 1964, the FBI had issued a 400-page, five volume report on the assassination of President Kennedy on December 9, 1963.[12] They stated that Oswald was the assassin without accomplices. Three shots were fired, two hit President Kennedy and a third shot hit Governor Connally. Initially, the staff of the Warren Commission used this scenario as the description of the assassination. When it was discovered that one of the shots missed the limousine entirely, the magic bullet hypothesis was adopted, wherein a single bullet hit first President Kennedy, and then struck Governor Connally. Connally insisted that he was hit by a separate shot. The FBI did not revise their analysis to correspond to the magic bullet scenario. The FBI was assigned the task of collecting information from potential witnesses, including witnesses regarding Oswald's background. Presumably, they generally did a more honest job than David Belin. Which is not to say that the FBI reported in a completely fair manner. A woman, Alma Cole, wrote a letter to President Johnson on December 11, 1963, regarding Oswald having been present in Stanley, North Dakota for several weeks in the summer of 1953; Oswald was said to have spent quite a bit of time with her son. The FBI did several interviews in Stanley. Many Stanley residents were questioned as to whether the Oswalds resided there [Of course not; they were transients!] Many of the persons interviewed would have been adults at the time Oswald was reported to have been visiting there. Not surprisingly, most responded that they didn't recall anyone by the name of Oswald living there. Some of the persons interviewed who were close to Oswald's age did recall Oswald.[13] Still, what the FBI did report was accurate even if incomplete, although their choice of wording in their questions was sometimes typically misleading.

The FBI and Oswald

Lee Rankin, the general counsel for the Warren Commission, effectively stated, regarding the rumor that Lee Harvey Oswald was a paid informant for the FBI, "We have a dirty rumor...and it must be wiped out."[14] It is clear that investigating this "rumor "was not even a consideration. From Rankin's view, and perhaps many of the Commission members' views, it was simply untrue (From a Bayesian point of view, for the Commission and its staff lawyers, the probability that Oswald was a paid informant was zero, there was no chance that it could be true, therefore they need not investigate it.) In simple terms this is the definition of prejudging. Were Oswald a paid informant (for which there is ample evidence), it would be most likely that the number of persons knowing this would be limited to his FBI handler and perhaps the handler's supervisor. All other personnel in the FBI could honestly claim that they were unaware of Oswald's being a paid informant. Oswald's relationship with Guy Banister, a former FBI agent who had strong feelings against persons that he saw as "subversive," nevertheless was cordial to Oswald, even as LHO stored his "Fair Play for Cuba" pamphlets near Guy Banister's office in New Orleans. When Delphine Roberts, Banister's secretary, inquired about Oswald handing out pro-Castro literature, Banister replied, "Don't worry about him.... He's with us. He's associated with this office."[15] On August 9, 1963, Lee was arrested along with three Cubans who confronted him for passing out the leaflets in favor of Castro and Cuba. The next day, from jail, Oswald called the New Orleans FBI office. Special Agent (SA) John Quigley took the call, and then went to the police station. The FBI would almost never have gone to a jail to interview someone who was there for disturbing the peace. When Quigley left the jail, he went back to the office and asked FBI employee William Walter to see if the FBI had a file on Oswald. A file was located, which had an "informant" classification.[16] William Walter was the employee present when the New Orleans office of the FBI received a telegram, Sunday morning, November 17, 1963 from Dallas (and presumably from information supplied to the Dallas FBI from Oswald), regarding a planned assassination attempt against President Kennedy in Dallas, either on November 22 or 23.[17]

We also know that the FBI was questioning a man, Junior Moore, in Mobile, Alabama on November 21, 1963 regarding whether he was aware of a person named Lee Harvey Oswald in Mobile; Oswald had spoken at Spring Hill College in Mobile in July of that year.[18] The FBI might have been searching in Mobile because of Mobile's proximity to New Orleans, and the telegram sent to the FBI in New Orleans the previous Sunday.

The CIA and the Warren Commission

The CIA had one of its former Directors on the Commission, Allen W. Dulles. When asked at the first official session how the CIA handled its informants, Dulles explained that if Oswald would have been an informant to the CIA, he would expect the CIA to deny it, and he would expect the FBI to deny Oswald was an informant to the FBI. In fact, an agent of the CIA might choose to lie under oath in circumstances that were deemed necessary.[19] The Commission then understood that the US clandestine agencies were not likely to reveal information that they chose not to produce. These "alleys" would simply be blind alleys to the Commission. Basically, the CIA was given a "pass" regarding the Commission's investigation. This would be another example that the government has a very difficult time trying to honestly investigate itself. It would fall to independent researchers to try to fill this void. John Newman is one such independent researcher who has written a seminal book on Oswald and the CIA. Newman laments the amount of government misconduct in lying to governmental investigative bodies and in effect, the obstruction of justice, in particular by the CIA.[20]

The Staff of the Warren Commission

Phillip Shenon has written a very interesting book about the Warren Commission.[21] He begins with his belief in their conclusions, and then writes a book that exposes a large number of the foibles of the Commission and its staff. As indicated earlier is this writing, such behavior is the essence of a true believer;[22] they are unswayed by any evidence that they are wrong. In Bayesian terms, there is a probability of 1 (i.e., certainty) that Oswald was the shooter, and a high probability there was no conspiracy, from a true believer's viewpoint. Today, belief in the magic bullet theory seems concentrated in the mainstream press (often controlled by right-wing owners). In this regard, Upton Sinclair's comment in the book he wrote about losing the 1934 California gubernatorial election seems appropriate: "It is difficult to get a man to understand something when his salary depends on him not understanding."[23]

The staff of the Warren Commission were mainly young lawyers, some newly graduated from law school and others not too advanced in their careers. Their individual mindsets might sometimes be at cross-purposes with the Commissioners. One of the young, but somewhat experienced staff members (he worked as a prosecutor and had significant contact with the FBI) was Burt Griffin, 31, who came to the Commission with the expectancy that a conspiracy would be found. Eventually, Griffin's estimation of the FBI was that if a conspiracy had even a smattering of sophistication, it would elude the FBI. He felt that several of the younger staff members were "downright excited" in the possibility that the Commission would find a conspiracy. Griffin's assignment was writing a biography of Jack Ruby.[24]

J. Lee Rankin was the general counsel and the liaison to both the Commission, and initially, to the FBI. Because of past workings with the FBI, Rankin thought a cordial relationship could be established with Director Hoover. Hoover dispelled him of this foolish notion early in their first meeting. To Hoover, the FBI had already done the study of the assassination; all the Commission had to do was to accept his December 9, 1963 final report. This view set Hoover at loggerheads with the Commission and particularly with Rankin. Rankin began to understand that the FBI was to be the Commission's main investigative arm, which would not likely produce evidence to the Commission in disagreement with the FBI's already finished report. Rankin would be the final editor of the Commission's report at the staff level. The Commission, of course, was the final arbiter.

The major writer of the staff report was David Slawson. Slawson, who graduated from Harvard Law School, chose to begin his law career in Denver as a protégé of Byron "Whizzer" White, a well-known All-American football star at the University of Colorado, two-time All-Pro halfback in the NFL, and later, a Supreme Court justice appointed by President Kennedy. Slawson remained at the Denver law firm, Davis, Graham & Stubbs, after White's departure to the Supreme Court. Slawson would be on the team investigating a foreign conspiracy. Slawson determined that two persons whom it would be important to interview in this regard were Sylvia Duran, who in 1963 was a secretary in the Cuban Embassy in Mexico City, and Sylvia Odio, a former Cuban living in Dallas. Earl Warren refused to allow an interview with Duran (supposedly because "We don't talk to Communists. You cannot trust a dedicated Communist to tell the truth, so what's the point?").[25] As to interviewing Sylvia Odio, that task would fall to Wesley James Liebeler, who managed to create a fiasco out of it.

Slawson would find many impediments in attempting to find a foreign conspiracy. Slawson found out long after the Warren Commission had ended, that James Angleton of the CIA filtered the reports that went from the CIA to the Warren Commission. Further, Angleton swept down to Mexico City and removed all of Win Scott's (Mexico City CIA station chief) files and memoirs upon Scott's death in 1971. The files revealed just how much information was withheld from the Warren Commission.[26] Other later revelations were like bombshells – the CIA Mafia Castro plots, the revelation that Hoover suspected an Oswald impersonator, and that a file was kept by the FBI on Oswald, beginning in 1959. Slawson was calling for a new investigation of the JFK assassination. When Slawson's views were reported in the New York Times, he was called by James Angleton, then recently fired from the CIA. Angleton made it clear that he was monitoring negative information about the CIA in the media.[27]

Wesley James Liebeler was easily the most "different" of the staff members. A native North Dakotan, Liebeler was a graduate of the University of Chicago Law School. Unlike his liberal colleagues, Liebeler was strongly politically conservative (announcing his support for Barry Goldwater), but socially, considerably more of a libertine. Though married, he announced that he would be chasing skirts in D.C. and bragged about his "successes." He didn't mind violating rules. He would take classified reports with him on weekends, flying to his home in Maine. He would read them on the plane in full view of other passengers, one of whom reported him. Liebeler was given the assignment of interviewing Sylvia Odio in Dallas. Liebeler interviewed Odio in the offices of the United States Attorney. When her testimony was completed, Liebeler asked Odio out to dinner. They ate at the Sheraton hotel in downtown Dallas, where Liebeler was staying. A third person joined them, supposedly a lawyer for Marina Oswald. Liebeler told the other man, "If we do find that this is a conspiracy, you know that we are under orders from Chief Justice Warren to cover this thing up."[28] Liebeler invited Odio to his hotel room, supposedly to view some assassination pictures. There, he attempted to seduce her. Liebeler wrote a report on Oswald's motivation in the assassination as his part of the Warren Report. The Commission completely rejected his writing.

Arlen Specter and the Single Bullet Theory

Specter was allowed to choose the area that he would investigate. He chose to focus on the last hours of President Kennedy's life, and the murder itself. Specter was to be the junior partner of Francis Adams, the former Commissioner of Police in New York City, who later became a very successful lawyer with his own firm in New York City. When the two men met, they agreed that the investigation should be quite quick, given that Oswald was so obviously guilty. As time dragged on, Adams absented himself from the Commission, leaving Specter on his own in the investigation. Specter got his idea for the single bullet theory partly out of necessity. One of the shots missed the limousine entirely, hitting the curb in front of the limousine, and cement from the curb injured James T. Tague.[29] Something on the order of the single bullet theory would be necessary, though such a scenario was, according to some accounts, already being considered by Specter.

Important parts of the evidentiary base were, however, not made available to the Warren Commission staff. Warren was opposed to having the autopsy photographs made available to the Warren Commission, apparently so that the photographs of the autopsy would not be made public; the photographs were apparently in the possession of Bobby Kennedy. The autopsy photographs were also not available to Commander James Humes M.D. for his review before his testimony to the Warren Commission. Instead, a navy sketch artist, who also did not have access to the autopsy photographs but only Humes' faulty memory of the wounds and his verbal description of them, sketched the wounds. Also, to be taken into account was the decision to have Humes, almost totally lacking in autopsy experience with gunshot homicides, as the lead pathologist in the autopsy; you'd think the President of the United States would have deserved better. Perhaps Humes inexperience made him more malleable to the military brass in attendance at the autopsy. Wouldn't it have been better to have had a non-military pathologist who had considerable experience with gunshot homicide autopsies who could have ignored the brass in the audience, and cleared them out if they continued to put themselves into the proceedings? Surely, a more experienced pathologist would not have burned his notes written at the autopsy. An experienced pathologist would have insisted on probing the trajectory of the bullets in the president's body. And the misindentification of the wound in the president's throat could have been avoided by talking to Dr. Perry at Parkland Hospital in Dallas. Perhaps one of the first mistakes made with the autopsy was to hold it in a military hospital with unqualified military physicians doing the autopsy.

As a research effort, the Warren Commission was an utter failure. The process was strictly advocacy research, but without an advocate for the other side. An advocacy approach without representation of the other side can have only one outcome, an unfairness so egregious that truth is the first casualty.

Endnotes

1 Wiesberg, H. & Lesar, J. (1974). *Whitewash II: JFK Assassination Transcript*. Frederick, MD: Authors. The Commission decided to stop having transcripts made of meetings as of June 23. After that, only summaries were provided.

2 Willens, H.P. in Weisberg & Lesar, p. 25.

3 Phillips, L.D. (1974). *Bayesian Analysis for Social Scientists*. New York: Thomas Crowell.

4 Elsie Dorman was filming the motorcade at the window. Directly after the three women left the window area Dorman stayed at the window for a while.

5 Ernest, B. (2013). *The Girl on the Stairs*. Gretna, LA: Pelican.

6 Excerpt from Victoria Adams testimony, VI, 386-393; also found in Ernest, pp. 284-294.

7 Ernest: also see Williams, J.D. (2014). "The Girl on the Stairs-Was Oswald even on the Sixth Floor at the Time of the Assassination?" *JFK-E/ Deep Politics Quarterly*, 1,2. 3-16.

8 The relevant parts of the depositions of Billy Nolan Lovelady and William H. Shelley are given in Ernest, pp. 295-297.

9 Shenon, P. (2013). *A Cruel and Shocking Act: The Secret History of the Kennedy Assassination*. New York: Henry Holt & Co., p. 452. Income at the level that Oswald was receiving during those two months could have supported a much higher lifestyle for him and his family. [Indeed, Oswald was paid well over three times as much as this writer during that same time period, while teaching mathematics and statistics at a junior college.] Perhaps Oswald was expected to appear to be almost penniless by his handlers.

10 Armstrong, J. (2003). *Harvey & Lee: How the CIA Framed Oswald*. Arlington, TX: Quasar, p. 725.

11 Haslam, E. (2007). *Dr. Mary's Monkey: How the Unsolved Murder of a Doctor, a Secret Laboratory in New Orleans and Cancer-Causing Monkey Viruses are Linked to Lee Harvey Oswald, the JFK Assassination and Emerging Global Epidemics*. Walterville, OR: Trine Day, p. 337.

12 Investigation of Assassination of President John F. Kennedy (FBI Report 12/9/1963) Commission Document #1. See Mary Ferrell.org.

13 Williams, J.D. & Severson, G. (2000). "Oswald in North Dakota? Part I." *The Fourth Decade: A Journal of Research on the John F. Kennedy Assassination*. 7,2, 21-26.

14 Wiesberg & Lesar, p. 26.

15 Marrs, J. (1989). *Crossfire: The Plot that Killed Kennedy*. New York: Carroll & Graf, pp. 235-237.

16 Armstrong, p. 566.

17 Williams, J.D. (2004). "Was the FBI Searching for Oswald the Day Before the Assassination?" *Dealey Plaza Echo*, 8, 2, 46-52.

18 Ibid.

19 Wiesberg & Lesar, p. 52.

20 Newman, J. (1995). *Oswald and the CIA*. New York: Carroll & Graf.

21 Shenon.

22 Hoffer, E. (1951). *The True Believer: Thoughts on the Nature of Mass Movements*. New York: Harper & Row.

23 Sinclair, U. (1934, 1994). *I, Candidate for Governor, and How I Got Licked*. Berkeley: U of California Press.

24 Shenon, p. 124.

25 Ibid., p. 311.

26 Ibid., p. 546.

27 Ibid., pp. 537-538.

28 Ibid., p. 417.

29 Tague, J.T. (2003). *Truth Withheld: Why We will never Know the Truth about the JFK Assassination*. Dallas: Excel Digital Press. An unnamed member of the staff lawyers for the Warren Commission claimed the single bullet theory was his idea, not Specter's. p. 161.

Chapter Twenty

1964: THE BEGINNING OF THE WORST OF TIMES

January, 1964

Two concerns that surfaced were the Bobby Baker scenario, which involved the Senate Rules Committee, which was meeting on November 22, 1963 at about the same time the President Kennedy was assassinated; and the tax bill, which Johnson was trying to get through Congress. Also of concern was the imminent departure of Ted Sorensen, the speechwriter who had been so effective for President Kennedy.

The Secret Service notified President Johnson that several members were seeking transfers from the White House detail. President Johnson was furious about a memo reporting that his Secret Service agents disliked working for him and asked to be transferred out. On the evening of January 6, 1964. Johnson was taking his ire out on Rufus Youngblood, who had shielded Johnson on the day of the assassination. Johnson told Youngblood that he told James Rowley, Chief of Secret Service, to get the men together and take anyone's resignation who was interested, including Rowley himself. In his rant, he gave the same option to Youngblood, suggesting that the FBI could do a better job of protecting the President. Youngblood refused a transfer assignment.[1]

As to the tax bill, it was President Kennedy's thought that tax rates could be drastically cut by eliminating some of the multitudinous tax loopholes. The tax bill put forward by President Johnson did the tax cuts without significantly touching any loopholes.[2] President Johnson was perturbed by Senator Everett Dirksen, who was additionally trying to remove about $450 million in excise taxes through an amendment that Dirksen had gotten added to the bill from the Senate Finance Committee. Later in the month the Committee removed Dirksen's amendment by a vote of 9-8.[3]

The loss of Ted Sorensen from President Johnson's speechwriter crew was a severe blow, not just because Sorensen was a gifted writer, but President Johnson also understood him to give sage advice. Sorensen resigned as of February 29, 1964. Sorensen was to become the President of the Motion

Picture Association of America, which had its embassy in Washington, D.C. President Johnson extracted from Sorensen the promise to come running to Johnson's side within 30 minutes if the situation called for it.[4]

The Resumption of the Hearings of the Senate Rules Committee

The Senate Rules Committee resumed its hearings on January 9, 1964. Donald Reynolds was apprehensive. Now, he would be testifying, to some degree, about the President of the United States. Though the three Republican members of the committee still thought that their sessions might be a stumbling block for Lyndon Johnson, the other six members were Democrats. The focus at the hearing on January 9 was Bobby Baker, Johnson's former Senate aide. Baker had already resigned his job in the Senate in October 1963. One particular issue was Bobby Baker's extra source of income, where he ran a call-girl service for elite clients. One client of interest was John F. Kennedy, who purportedly enjoyed the services of Ellen Rometsch, who was reportedly well appreciated by her other clients. President Kennedy knew little about Ms. Rometsch; unknown to JFK was that she was born in East Germany and had held memberships in more than one communist youth group. She was married and divorced in Germany, and was married to her second husband, a sergeant in the West German Air Force, who was assigned to the German Embassy in Washington, D.C. Perhaps the main thing for JFK was that she was very attractive, with a strong resemblance to Elisabeth Taylor. She also was known to be a professional prostitute, who took the money and kept silent.

During the time that JFK was seeing Ellen Rometsch, the Profumo scandal broke out in London, prompting John Profumo to resign his position of Secretary of War in the British government on June 5, 1963. Profumo had a short relationship with 19-year-old Christine Keeler in 1961. The scandal would ultimately lead towards Harold MacMillan's resignation from Prime Minister in October 1963; MacMillan's Conservative Party would lose the 1964 election to the Labour Party.[5] Robert Kennedy, wishing to avoid a Profumo-type scandal for his brother, had Ellen Rometsch expelled from the United States, and returned to Germany.[6] The fear that existed in January 1964 was that the revealing of the scandal could not only profoundly affect the 1964 election, it might also be a deterrent to any future political life for Bobby Kennedy.[7]

Donald Reynolds was an insurance salesman whom Bobby Baker introduced to Senator Lyndon Baines Johnson, who had recently (in 1955) experienced a heart attack. Reynolds provided a policy to Johnson with the proviso of an extra $5,000 of hazardous premium, due to Johnson's heart attack. Baker would get about 55% for the first two years of insurance which would be about $5,000 a year to Reynolds. Bobby Baker then asked for kickbacks, a TV stereo set for both Baker and Johnson ($585 each) and advertising at Lady Bird's TV station in Austin, Texas at a cost of $1208 (Reynolds didn't have the slightest need to advertise in Texas; Reynolds was able to sell the advertising time to a company that sold pots & pans, for $160).[8]

To get such paybacks by a government employee was illegal. Johnson's view that he actually got the TV stereo set came from Bobby Baker, though the invoice Johnson received listed Don Reynolds as the payer. The sale at the TV station in Austin was simply a purchase of television time. While in one sense, this indiscretion was "small potatoes," it was an indication that Johnson had skirted the law. Presumably, from a Republican point of view, the indiscretions of both would bode well in the 1964 election for the Republican party.

Reynolds testified to the Senate Rules and Administration Committee on November 22, 1963. These hearings (including earlier testimony by Robert Baker) have been characterized by Burkett Van Kirk, Republican (minority) counsel, as leading to the loss of the Vice-Presidency by Johnson. Van Kirk stated, "There is no doubt in my mind that Reynold's testimony would have gotten Johnson out of the Vice-Presidency."[9]

Evelyn Lincoln held a discussion with President Kennedy on November 19, 1963. In this discussion, President Kennedy said, "At this time, I am thinking about Terry Sanford of North Carolina, but it will not be Lyndon."[10]

Bobby Kennedy was said to be working secretly with Van Kirk for weeks, through intermediaries, to accumulate evidence of payola against Johnson and Bobby Baker, Johnson's former aide.[11]

No report was made of this committee meeting, as the committee had not made any conclusions regarding the evidence presented. It could be surmised that the elevation of Lyndon Johnson to President might have rendered moot in the discussions of that day.

On January 17, another hearing of the Senate Rules Committee took place; no further hearings in this matter would be held until December 1, 1964. In substance, the January 17 session seemed to be a rehash of the previous meeting; however, President Johnson was moved to have a press conference where the issues would be addressed in a statement, and then allow questions from the press corps. Ted Sorensen was of the opinion that Johnson would be best served by reading a statement but by plan, take no questions, since

Johnson had too few discussions with his writers to be prepared for a question-and-answer period (the discussion between Johnson and Sorensen took place January 23, 1964).[12] Also on January 23, 1964, in a conversation with Senator Abraham Ribbicoff, Johnson stated, "I've had 56 days in this job, and they've been the most miserable fifty-six days I've ever had."[13]

On January 24, Johnson held the press conference with questions from the press, against the advice of Ted Sorensen. The outcome of the press conference was the disaster predicted by Sorensen. As Johnson gave his explanation of events, questions came about as in a flood. Each answer seemed to incite the press. Tom Wicker of the *New York Times*, stated in a page one story the next day that Johnson left the room before the newsmen could question him.[14]

February, 1964

Johnson was all about politics: twisting arms was his particular forte. Johnson had decided that he wanted Sargent Shriver to be the leader of the new program in the War on Poverty. He spoke to Shriver on the early afternoon of February 1, 1964. Shriver had led the Peace Corps to a stellar start; Shriver preferred to remain with that program. Johnson informed Shriver that he wanted to announce Shriver as the head of the new War on Poverty at his press conference later that afternoon. No amount of pleading from Shiver could dissuade Johnson from appointing Shriver.[15]

Only minutes later, President Johnson was informed that John Connally was greatly displeased that Johnson had come to a truce and would support Senator Ralph Yarborough for reelection. Part of Connally's displeasure was brought on by Yarborough's brother Don, who was challenging Connally for the Democratic nomination as Governor of Texas. This was adding insult to injury; John Connally disliked both Ralph Yarborough's liberal orientation, and apparently, Yarborough as a person. Lyndon Johnson decided the way to ameliorate this situation was to get Representative Jim Wright to give up his seat in the House of Representatives and run for the Democratic nomination for Senator against Ralph Yarborough. Wright was not particularly oriented to give up his safe seat in order to challenge Yarborough. Johnson, assuming he would be elected President in November, said that in the event that he didn't beat Yarborough, he would be given a good job after he left the House. At the last minute, Wright chose not to challenge Yarborough, and keep his House seat. Unaware of all of this maneuvering, Ralph Yarborough thought that President Johnson had cleared the way for Yarborough to run unopposed for the Senate nomination, and he thanked

Johnson profusely for his "help." Johnson, of course, accepted the praise and promises of loyalty from Yarborough.[16]

Don Reynolds

The Don Reynolds situation seemed to linger. The newest issue to arise was the information that Reynolds had his own reputation problems. It seemed that as a military attaché in the U.S. Embassy in Germany, Reynolds had traded passports for sex with some young girls. Jack Anderson, then a nationally known columnist, asked permission to report about the derogatory information on Reynolds. The consensus inside the administration was that, it was improper for the administration to give permission. In fact, the Johnson administration saw nothing good coming from that revelation.[17]

Ted Sorensen

Ted Sorensen was expecting to become the President of the Motion Picture Association of America; however, the negotiations kept extending. Sorensen declined the Motion Picture Association of America position, deciding instead to join a New York City law firm.[18]

The House Vote on the Civil Rights Bill

The House of Representatives voted 290 to 110 to pass Johnson's civil rights bill.[19] By that evening, instead of being elated, his wife Lady Bird noted that Johnson was much upset and disturbed.[20] Apparently two issues were confronting him. The difficulty of getting the civil rights bill through the senate was obvious; the opponents could filibuster the bill, and Johnson knew the political skills of Senator Russell, a bill opponent, might be insurmountable. Additionally, Johnson had heard that an attempt to have Bobby Kennedy run a write-in campaign for Vice-President. Johnson feared that more persons might use their votes for Bobby Kennedy, which could be embarrassing to President Johnson.[21]

The Tax Reduction Act of 1964

Originally proposed by President Kennedy in 1963, President Johnson pressed for a new program. In its final form passed by the Senate on February 26, 1964 and signed into law by President Johnson the same day, the law reduced taxation by roughly 20%. The highest tax rate for individuals earning $100,000 or more or couples earning $180,000 or more, dropped from 91% to 70%. Corporate rates dropped from 52% to 48%. A standard deduction was inaugurated at $300, with $100 exemption for each dependent.[22] The goals of the act were to raise personal incomes, increase consumption and increase capital investments. It had the added effect of decreasing unemployment. Unemployment dropped from 5.2% in 1964 to 4.5% in 1965 to 3.8% in 1966.[23]

March, 1964

Johnson had been musing about Vietnam and how that conflict might play in the upcoming Presidential election. Johnson thought that his opponent in the 1964 election would be Richard Nixon. In a state poll in North Dakota, for Republicans, Johnson had 30% and Nixon had 58%. Among Democrats, Johnson had 95% and Nixon had none. Johnson was pleased with this result.[24] Johnson continued his harangue regarding the Bobby Kennedy write-in campaign for Vice President.[25]

On March 21, 1964, President Johnson and his wife invited the McNamara's, Senator Fulbright and his wife, and Walter Lippmann and his wife to a dinner party at the White House. Lady Bird recorded in her diary her concerns about the conversations during the dinner party, "The talk was of Vietnam and it's pretty terrifying to hear McNamara speak of how dedicated the opposition soldiers are over there. They apparently have an intensive training in ideals that is lacking on our side. One little odd manifestation is in a determination...for cleanliness that causes them as part of their military training to just be forced to brush their teeth every day, and they wear their tooth brush in their pocket! I suppose it's a sort of status symbol of 'We belong to the up and coming.' "[26]

April, 1964

A CIA backed military coup toppled leftist President, Joao Goulart on April 3 in Brazil. The rationale given was that Goulart was removed because of their fear that Goulart might be toppled by a Communist movement.[27] General Humberto Castelo Branco was later installed as President.[28]

Johnson, who entered no primaries in 1964, did not intend to campaign for any of the primaries as President. He wanted to be seen as being beyond partisan politics, a President for all, so to speak. However, he was quite willing to support "favorite sons" who pledged themselves to Johnson, in many of the primaries.[29] Polls showed that Johnson had historic highs, with an overall approval rating of 77%.[30]

The civil rights bill had been sent to the Senate, March 9. Considerable Southern state opposition existed. Several amendments had been offered. One called for a jury trial to address when the civil rights law was being violated. Johnson saw this amendment as a deal breaker. He reasoned that, generally speaking, all-white juries would not convict white violators of the civil rights law. The new cloture law, which required at least 67 Senators voting to end discussion and vote on the then current bill, had not yet been used. Thus, the Civil Rights Bill was on the floor through April (and then May) because they did not want to "precipitously" call for cloture – and not have the votes to get cloture to end the debate.[31]

The Bobby Kennedy for Vice-President Dilemma

As an outcome of the write-in votes for Bobby Kennedy in New Hampshire, there was a continued effort to get Robert Kennedy be drafted to become Lyndon Johnson's running mate. There were at least two persons who opposed a Johnson-Kennedy ticket—Lyndon Johnson and Bobby Kennedy.[32]

Johnson had little use for Robert Kennedy – Robert had seemed to be the force behind trying to get Johnson removed from the ticket in 1964 with President Kennedy. There were a variety of reasons for Bobby's distaste for Lyndon Johnson, perhaps including the possibility that Johnson was in some way related to his brother's assassination. But it appears Bobby Kennedy wanted Johnson to feel the need to offer the Vice-Presidency to Bobby, if only for the pleasure Bobby might have in turning Johnson down once the offer was made. The two men had a strong dislike for each other.

On the other hand, Johnson originally thought he might need Bobby Kennedy as his running mate to ensure his victory in the election. Several polls were taken, with (and without) different running mates. By June, Barry Goldwater was securely in front of the Republican contenders. Johnson had a comfortable lead over Goldwater, with very little difference as to who Johnson's running mate was. Still Johnson was taking no chances on a drafting of Robert Kennedy to be his Vice-President. Johnson had the planned tribute to the fallen President Kennedy moved to occur after the vote for the nomination of the Vice-President.

As to Robert Kennedy, he had decided that he would prefer to run for the Senate from the state of New York. The dilemma was solved for both men.[33]

The Civil Rights Bill

Once the Civil Rights Bill crossed over to the Senate, Johnson knew that it would be difficult to get it through "The Gentlemen's Club." Arcane rules were sometimes difficult to get around. The filibuster had been an effective way to delay or even defeat legislation. Only recently had the Senate introduced a procedure called "cloture," which allowed a 2/3 majority to close discussion and move to a vote. But the procedure had not yet been used. With 100 members in the Senate, 67 votes were necessary to invoke cloture. President Johnson wanted to use the procedure only after lengthy discussions took place AND he had to have at least 67 votes to win the cloture vote. But as time went on President Johnson was becoming impatient; it had been almost 60 days since the bill moved over from the house.[34]

Senator Hubert Humphrey was shepherding the Civil Rights Bill through the Senate. When Humphrey was sure of the passage of the bill, on June 12, 1964, the cloture vote was taken: the final vote was 71-29 in favor of cloture.[35]

Knowing that the success of the cloture vote was tantamount to the approval of the Civil Rights Bill, President Johnson was brooding over the situation. At last, he emotionally realized that the South would have its culture fundamentally changed. In response to Bill Moyers, who asked the President why he was so glum, Johnson replied, "Because, Bill, I think we just delivered the South to the Republican Party for a long time to come."[36] The signing party was set for July 2, 1964.

The Gulf of Tonkin Resolution

Johnson's approach to Vietnam from the start of his presidency was to give Vietnam a low level of priority. Specifically, he wished to avoid it as an election issue. True, he did sign off on NSAM 273, replacing President Kennedy's NSAM 263, which would have us withdrawing all personnel by the end of 1965; still Johnson was conflicted by what to do about Vietnam. As late as June, 1964, Johnson's preference was to put the issue of Vietnam on hold until after the election.[37] Johnson asked his friend and confidant, Senator Richard Russell, to address the Senate and ask for a withdrawal from South Vietnam. This would take some of the heat off Johnson, with the likelihood that Senator Barry Goldwater would get the Republican nomination for President; Goldwater was a hawk on defense and suggested that generals could make some of the decisions previously made only by a President. Though Johnson was not currently contemplating withdrawal from Vietnam, he reasoned that Senator Russell's statement would help him with the South. However, Russell chose not to make such a plea before the Senate. As Johnson continued to revisit the Vietnam situation, he revised his thinking with the knowledge that we had treaty obligations with South Vietnam.[38]

By late July, Johnson's stand was to bolster the South Vietnamese, but avoid extending the conflict; in his view, taking Goldwater out of the equation regarding the election. Johnson also had secret operations, known as 34-A, increased. On the night of July 30-31, one such operation took place against two North Vietnamese islands in the Gulf of Tonkin. The following day, the USS *Maddox* began a patrol in the same area. On August 2, it was reported that three North Vietnamese torpedo boats attacked the *Maddox*.[39] There was no damage to the *Maddox*; one of the torpedo boats was "dead in the water," and the other two retreated. A second report was made of an attack on the *Maddox* based primarily on sonar soundings.[40] However this so-called second attack was termed "ambiguous." That is, it was not clear that this attack had occurred. Nevertheless, the "second attack" was the basis for a retaliation. The retaliation was debated in Washington. Cooler heads were asking for stronger proof that the second attack did occur. President Johnson was not one of the cooler heads. He seemed determined to proceed with the retaliation.[41] According to Robert McNamara, Secretary of Defense, an estimated 25 North Vietnamese patrol boats were destroyed or damaged, and 90% of the petroleum in that area had been destroyed. This area held 10% of North Vietnam's petroleum capacity.[42]

It could be surmised that President Johnson's step to the right in supporting South Vietnam's war effort was to undercut Goldwater in his quest to win the presidency. Johnson called Goldwater and discussed the issue of military involvement in Vietnam. Goldwater assured Johnson that he approved of the actions.[43]

The Gulf of Tonkin Resolution passed the House with no "No' votes. Only Adam Clayton Powell, a pacifist, voted "present." In the Senate, 88 voted for the bill and two Senators voted "no," Wayne Morse of Oregon and Ernest Gruening of Alaska.[44]

The actions taken in the Gulf of Tonkin, and the Resolution itself, likely were seen as achievements by Lyndon Johnson. His earlier concerns about Vietnam being an unwinnable war represented a more honest assessment of reality. But the reality Johnson was presently most interested in was the political war for President. In the political war, Lyndon Johnson adroitly out-maneuvered Barry Goldwater. But it could also be said that he out-maneuvered himself. His earlier thinking that Vietnam was a quagmire with no good outcomes was the better reasoning. What changed was his desire to win the Presidency and win it big. His full term would be his time to "repent at leisure."

August 1964

August 1964 had several newsworthy events beyond the Gulf of Tonkin and the resulting Resolution in congress. On Tuesday August 4, the bodies of Michael Schwerner, Andrew Goodman and James Cheyney were found six miles from where they were last seen alive, near Philadelphia, Mississippi. The civil rights workers had been missing since June 21, 1964.[45]

The poverty bill passed the House on August 8; the Senate passed the House version on the same day. The title of the bill was The Economic Opportunity Act of 1964, with several different threads. It was signed into law by President Johnson on August 20. Included in the bill were Job Corps, Neighborhood Youth Corps, Work Study for lower income college students, Urban and Rural Community Action, Adult Basic Education, Voluntary Assistance to Needy Children, Loans to Rural Families, Assistance to Migrant Agricultural Employees, Employment and Investment Incentives to Small Businesses, Work Experience, for those unable to care for themselves, and Volunteers in Service to America (VISTA). This legislation was part of President Johnson's Great Society program.[46]

The Democratic National Convention was another event that took up much of Lyndon Johnson's time and thoughts. The Mississippi delegation was a huge issue to him. First, he asked John Steinbeck, author of several novels, including *The Grapes of Wrath*,[47] to help him with his acceptance speech for the Democratic nomination for President; Lady Bird had been a classmate of Steinbeck's wife at the University of Texas.[48] Steinbeck agreed and came to the White House to help.[49]

An issue had come up among the delegates from Mississippi. An all-white group of delegates was chosen in the "usual manner," i.e., white-only voters. They were challenged by a Freedom Caucus who elected black delegates. How would the Democratic Party solve this issue? Both groups were coming to the Convention. Johnson started to consider the options, and they seemed like losers to him; in somewhat of a depressive moment, Johnson relayed to his friend and neighbor A.W. Moursund, that he was inclined to withdraw his name as a Presidential candidate and retire to Texas.[50] This may well have been a ploy to get the party to "draft" him to run. However, a compromise was agreed to, with the Black Mississippi delegates being seated also, and getting two at-large votes.[51] As was expected, LBJ was nominated on the first ballot; Hubert Humphrey was chosen as his running mate.

The Vietnam situation was again becoming fragile. The Gulf of Tonkin action seemed to embolden the South Vietnamese leaders, who wanted the Americans to shoulder an even bigger part of the burden.[52] It appears that the Gulf of Tonkin, with its ramifications, was President Johnson's Waterloo.

Landslide Lyndon

"Landslide Lyndon" was not a nickname given to Lyndon Johnson for having won any election by a landslide, rather the term was a pejorative moniker following the runoff election for the Democratic nomination for US Senator from Texas in August 1948. In July of 1948, Texas held the Democratic primary. Former Governor Coke Stevenson, led Lyndon Johnson by 71,000 votes; Stevenson narrowly missed winning the nomination in the primary, but he failed to get over 50% of the votes, as several other candidates were on the ballot. A runoff election between Johnson and Stevenson was scheduled for August 28. It was a do or die situation for Johnson; both he and Edward Clark, a well-known lawyer in Austin, Texas had taken out loans that would be impossible to pay off were he not elected. Johnson began a frantic campaign. As was usual in Texas politics in those years, both Johnson and Stevenson paid off certain influential persons in certain Texas counties. At the end of the run-off election, Stevenson appeared to have won a narrow victory, winning by 854 votes. As more votes came in (and more votes were cast by those willing to take Ed Clark's money), Johnson was still 114 votes short. Clark sent a lawyer from his firm, Don Thomas, to Alice, Texas. His job was to secure 200 more votes for Johnson. Because, Clark was Lyndon Johnson's lawyer, and Thomas was from Clark's firm, this highly illegal buying of votes could not be charged to Johnson, who was not made privy to the shenanigans being done by the lawyers. It was in Alice that 202 votes were added to the total, 200 for Johnson, and 2 for Stevenson. Those votes were from Box 13 in Jim Wells County. Johnson would be declared the winner by 87 votes.[53] The 202 new ballots were cast in alphabetical order, all in the same handwriting.[54] It was the contention of J. Evetts Haley[55] that, of the 202 new votes, only one was for Stevenson. More importantly, many of the new votes were from voters whose last known residence was the cemetery.[56] Thus, " Landslide Lyndon" was hung on LBJ.

What was the effect on Lyndon Johnson from this election? One might surmise that the emotional turmoil was severe. He *almost* saw his future go down the drain. He was unlikely to forget the difficulty of going through this. By all rights, his future would have gone down the drain, were it not for the full-scale cheating that occurred on his behalf, because of the debt that had been acquired. Winning the nomination, probably by illegal means, may have left him with insecurity that haunted him through his life.

Johnson did not wish to engage in the 1964 primary for the nomination for becoming the Democratic nominee. Johnson was more attuned to winning the nomination at the convention. That was not to be, nor have the conventions with their back-room dealings been the deciding point in either party since then. During the 1964 primaries, Johnson did not personally participate, yet he was able to get the nomination on the first ballot.

He delayed participation in the 1964 election until September. And the mudslinging began. It was a question of how much each side knew about the opposition. Certain areas were too touchy for either to address, such as Bobby Baker. Johnson's exposure was obvious; Goldwater had reportedly promised Bobby Baker a pardon for dirt on Johnson, if Goldwater won the election.[57] Then, of course, there was Johnson's relationship to Billie Sol Estes. Then there were Johnson's dalliances with several different women, which purportedly resulted in children being born while Johnson was married to Lady Bird.[58] On the other side, Barry Goldwater apparently had two psychological breakdowns, referred to as "nervous exhaustion;" Goldwater's wife Peggy had written an article published in the May 1964 issue of *Good Housekeeping*. They were trying to get ahead of any reports regarding Goldwater's mental condition.[59] Also, there were rumors of Goldwater having liaisons with prostitutes and a paternity suit against Goldwater by a Houston woman.[60]

Perhaps the major reason many of the scurrilous scandals weren't used is that both of them would have been at risk of exposure. In any event Johnson would have plenty of information that was in the public domain. There was the statement by Goldwater that he favored giving the supreme Allied Commander in Europe, General Lyman Lemnitzer, authority to fire nuclear weapons without first asking the White House.[61] Goldwater had opposed the Partial Nuclear Test Ban Treaty passed under President Kennedy in 1963.[62] And in Goldwater's acceptance speech at the Republican National Convention, he stated, "I would remind you that extremism in the defense of liberty is no vice."[63] An area that Lyndon Johnson feared would become a campaign issue was the arrest of his aide Walter Jenkins on October 7, on a morals charge in a men's restroom; he was found in a compromising situation with another man.[64] This situation would cost Jenkins his career, it did not seem to have an effect on the outcome of the election. During the course of the campaign, it became clear that the passing of the bill on civil rights would cost Johnson several states in the South. On a day-to-day basis,

Johnson would vacillate on his sense of the upcoming election. It was Johnson's desire to carry all 50 states. With several Southern states evading his grasp, he knew objectively that he likely would experience a significant win; subjectively, he couldn't arrive at the same place; in his darker moments, Johnson seemed to lapse into a degree of fear and depression.

In the election, Johnson carried 44 states and in fact won in a landslide. Five of the six states that Goldwater won were part of the former Confederacy. Johnson was not even on the ballot in Alabama; there the Democrat candidate was, "Unpledged Democratic Electors"; Goldwater won with over 69% in Alabama. Mississippi gave Goldwater his largest percentage victory; Johnson received only 14.4% of the vote. Goldwater also won his home state of Arizona, but by less than 1%. In the overall results Johnson received 61.1% of the vote.[65]

There seemed to be no celebration for the newly elected president. He continued to focus on the issue of Walter Jenkins, of Donald Reynolds, and the various issues with governing the United States. Vietnam would not go away; Just how bad was the loss of the South in the election? Would this loss be long-term?

The Senate Rules Committee Again met with Donald Reynolds

One additional meeting with the Senate Rules Committee and Donald Reynolds took place on December 1, 1964; it would be the last such meeting. By December, the die was cast; the more extensive war in Vietnam had become a reality, and Lyndon Johnson had won the 1964 presidential election in a landslide of historic proportions. Johnson's vulnerability had seemingly passed. The Committee had adjourned their work in July. Information from Reynolds to Senator John Williams (R-Delaware) would lead to a resumption of the hearings.[66]

The hearing was preceded by Don Reynolds' written statement (August 18, 1964) about the disposition of funds received from Matt McCloskey for the bond to build the D.C. Stadium. McCloskey was also the Treasurer of the National Democratic Party at the time (1960). McCloskey was subsequently appointed as Ambassador to Ireland by President Kennedy. As Reynolds would point out in his December 1 testimony, the reason he wrote on August 18, 1964 to Senator John Williams of Delaware, "Was to let Senator Williams know after I obtained a check which I had mentioned previously, sir, of an overpayment that I wanted to at least get something in writing to the best of my knowledge at the moment, what was there, in case something might happen to me unfortunately on the route, that he would have on record, sir."[67]

The cost of the bond was $73,631.28, of which Reynolds would get $10,031.28. He would pay Bobby Baker $4,000 and William McLeod, a lawyer, $1500. However, the invoice to Mr. McCloskey, as instructed by Bobby Baker, was for $109,209.60. The difference, $35,578.32, would be cut up, according to Bobby Baker's instructions, into three $5000 amounts (a total of $15,000), to be paid in $100 bills to Baker to put money into Johnson's election funds. This process allowed McCloskey to skirt the election laws that limited contributions to $5,000 per person, and also allowed McCloskey to use the contribution as a business deduction. Bobby Baker would get an additional $10,000 in cash and Reynolds would get $10,578.32 for being the bagman. Reynolds said that he hadn't mentioned the arrangement regarding the disbursing of this money earlier because he didn't have the documentation of the check at that time, Senator Williams was able to acquire copies of the front and back of the check. Reynolds was then willing to testify about the interactions.

The hearings held on December 1, 1964, showed animosity toward Reynolds. An example can be seen in the interchange between Senator Carl Curtis and General Counsel McClendon:

> Senator Curtis: I think we would proceed further if we attempted to get information rather than attempting to impeach the witness, but you are harassing him.
>
> Mr. McClendon: I am trying to ascertain the truth, and whatever it takes to ascertain the truth.
>
> Senator Curtis: No, sir. A great deal of effort has been put forth to discredit this witness; it is quite evident to anybody watching.[68]

Indeed, there was animosity between committee members on the basis of party. The Democrats were in control 6-3; the members often voted on party lines. Republican senators continued to point out that General Counsel L.P. McClendon harassed Don Reynolds. Toward the end of the session impugning remarks were made to Senator Williams, who had persuaded Donald Reynolds to testify before the committee. This led Senator Curtis to make the following remark:

> Senator Curtis: Mr. Chairman, I have sat here all day and heard the General counsel sandbag the witness, and now a Senator is on trial, and he is not even a member of this committee and not charged with investigating, and you are.[69]

On December 1, 1964 Don Reynolds testified about his testimony of November 22, 1963 before the Rules and Administration Committee. This testimony has been said to perhaps have set the stage for removing Lyndon Johnson from the Vice-Presidency. It was also thought that the meeting was interrupted by news of the assassination.[70] In Donald Reynold's testimony on December 1, 1964, General Counsel McClendon moved the discussion back to November 22, 1963:

> Mr. McClendon: You were interviewed in this building the very day that President Kennedy was shot, were you not?
>
> Mr. Reynolds: And I was questioned in the same manner as you are doing, now, Sir.
>
> Mr. McClendon: You mean by that you were asked to tell the truth?
>
> Mr. Reynolds: No, Sir.
>
> Mr. McClendon: And you wouldn't tell it?
>
> Mr. Reynolds: With the hostile intent manner, sir.
>
> Mr. McClendon: All right: because you were examined in a hostile atmosphere, that justified you in not telling the truth?
>
> Mr. Reynolds: No, sir, but may I give you a statement?
>
> Mr. McClendon: No, I don't want any statements.
>
> Mr. Reynolds: I know you don't.
>
> Mr. McClendon: I am trying to get at the facts. You were interviewed practically the whole day of November 22, weren't you?
>
> Mr. Reynolds: No, sir.
>
> Mr. McClendon: Well, how long?
>
> Mr. Reynolds: Until about 1 O'clock, about 10 to 1.
>
> Mr. McClendon: By Mr. Drennan?
>
> Mr. Reynolds: I don't remember who it was.
>
> Mr. McClendon: It was nobody who is with the staff now, was it?
>
> Mr. Reynolds: I don't know, sir.
>
> Mr. McClendon: And you know that he made a written report of the Interview?
>
> Mr. Reynolds: No, I didn't.
>
> Mr. McClendon: And your counsel was present?
>
> Mr. Reynolds: But I did not know about a written report.[71]

From Reynolds' testimony, he was questioned until 1 P.M. Eastern Standard time, which would have been 12 noon in Dallas. Clearly, the testimony was *not* interrupted by news of the shooting of President Kennedy; the shooting occurred half an hour later, at 12:30 P.M. Dallas time. Also, it can be seen that Reynolds was questioned more as a hostile witness. Given that the Rules and Administration Committee was composed of 6 Democrats and 3 Republicans, and Johnson had served as the Majority Leader of the Senate until he became Vice-President, the committee was not likely to take action against LBJ, unless there were compelling reasons to do so. But most of Reynolds contact regarding Lyndon Johnson was through Bobby Baker. Reynolds had little direct contact with Johnson that would have been of use to an investigation. Baker did not speak to Lyndon Johnson after his resignation, until 1972; Baker visited the former President at his ranch in Texas, when Johnson was a dying man.[72]

Perhaps Johnson had underestimated the lengths to which his party's Senate committee members might go to protect "one of their own." What is important, as it might relate to Johnson's possible involvement in a conspiracy, was his state of mind and his subjective evaluation of the likelihood of his removal from office or replacement on the national ticket in 1964.

In 1964, seemingly several things went right for the new President; his agenda and finishing the unrealized agenda of the assassinated President Kennedy, were enacted by Congress. Hopefully those changes, particularly in civil rights, would become permanent. Programs made to implement the "Great Society" had been enacted as well. Two troubling areas remained. The passage of the civil rights law might have delivered the South to the Republican party for decades to come. Perhaps even more important was the directionality of the war in Vietnam. At the juncture of 1964, the enormity of that war was simply not envisioned. The war was turned over by the French in the mid-fifties to then-President Eisenhower. President Kennedy had set up an exit plan in in the secret NSAM 263; upon assuming the presidency, Johnson's NSAM 273 negated that exit plan.

Endnotes

1 Beschloss, M.R. (1997). *Taking Charge: The Johnson White House Tapes, 1963-1964.* New York: Simon & Schuster, pp. 149-150.

2 Lowndes, C.L.B. (1964). "The Revenue Act of 1964: A Critical Analysis." *Duke Law Journal,* pp. 667-705.

3 Beschloss, (1997), p. 178.

4 Ibid., p. 108.

5 Profumo Affair, en.wikipedia.org/wiki/Profumo_ affair, retrieved 11/5/2017.

6 Hersh, S.M. (1997). *The Dark Side of Camelot*. Boston: Little, Brown & Co., pp. 389-411.

7 Loc. cit.

8 Williams, J.D. & Conway, D. (2001). "The Don Reynolds Testimony and LBJ." *Kennedy Assassination Chronicles*, 7,1, 19-28.

9 Hersch, p. 447.

10 Lincoln, E. (1968). *Between Kennedy and Johnson*. New York: Holt Rinehart & Winston; Hougan, J. (1984). *Secret Agenda*. New York: Random House; Scott, P.D. (1993). *Deep Politics and the Death of JFK*. Berkley: The University of California Press.

11 Hersch, pp. 446-447.

12 Beschloss (1997), p. 176.

13 Ibid., p. 178. Actually, Johnson had been in the office of President for sixty-two days.

14 Beschloss, (1997) p. 179.

15 Ibid., pp. 202-205, pp. 208-213.

16 Ibid., pp. 205-207, pp. 215-218.

17 Ibid., pp. 191-192, p. 215, pp. 232-235.

18 Ibid., pp. 221-222.

19 Dallek, R. (1998). *Flawed Giant: Lyndon Johnson and His Times 1961-1973*. New York: Oxford University Press, p. 116.

20 Beschloss, (1997), p. 236. This information came from Lady Bird's diary entry for February 10, 1964.

21 Dallek, pp. 216-221.

22 Revenue Act of 1964, wikipedia.org/wiki/Revenue_Act_of_1964, retrieved 11/10/2017.

23 Dolan, C., Frendreis, J., & Tatalovich, R. (2008). *The Presidency and Economic Policy*. Lanham, MD: Rowman & Littlefield, pp. 172-176.

24 Beschloss, (1997), p. 271.

25 Ibid., pp. 271-273.

26 Ibid., p. 294.

27 Ibid., p. 306.

28 Ibid., p. 318.

29 Ibid., p. 309.

30 Loc. cit.

31 Ibid., pp. 333-335.

32 Dallek, pp. 135-139.

33 Ibid., pp. 135-143.

34 Beschloss (1997), pp. 341-344.

35 Dallek, pp. 119-120.

36 Ibid., p.120.

37 Ibid., p. 143.

38 Ibid., p. 145.

39 Ibid., p.147.

40 Loc. cit.

41 Dallek, pp. 151-153.

42 Beschloss, (1997), p. 504.

43 Loc. cit.

44 Ibid., p. 508.

45 Ibid., pp. 501-502.

46 en.wikipedia.org/wiki/Economic_Opportunity_Act_of_1964 retrieved 11/28/2017.

47 Steinbeck, J. (1939). *Grapes of Wrath*. New York: Viking Press.

48 Beschloss, (1997), p. 522.

49 Ibid., p.522n.

50 Ibid., p. 533.

51 Ibid., p.534.

52 Ibid., p.546.

53 McClelland, B. (2003). *Blood, Money, and Power: How L.B.J. Killed J.F.K.* New York Hanover House, pp. 87-92.

54 Ibid., p.92.

55 Haley, J. E. (1964). *A Texan Looks at Lyndon: A Study in Illegitimate Power.* Canyon, Texas: Palo Duro Press, pp. 21-54.

56 Ibid.

57 Beschloss, M. (2001). *Reaching for Glory: Lyndon Johnson' Secret White House Tapes 1964-1965.* New York: Simon & Schuster, p. 83.

58 One such person was Madeleine Duncan Brown, (Brown, M. D. (1997). *Texas in the Morning: The Love Story of Madeleine Brown and President Lyndon Baines Johnson.* Baltimore: The Conservatory Press.) who bore Johnson a son in 1950. Brown & Johnson had an ongoing affair throughout his senatorial years. Brown also asserted that Johnson had recruited a beautiful young Texan to be a secretary to him during his Vice-Presidency, who became pregnant; she was married off to one of Johnson's aides. See Williams, J.D. & Severson, G. {November 17-18, 2001; transcript 2002). Interview of Madeleine Duncan Brown Concerning JFK Assassination Information in Dallas. In johndelanewilliams.blogspot.com.

59 See Beschloss, (2001), p. 39n.

60 Ibid., p. 87.

61 Ibid., p. 30.

62 Loc. cit.

63 Wilkinson, W. On the saying that "Extremism in Defense of Liberty is no Vice." Niskanencenter.org/blog/on-the saying-that-extremism-in-defense-of-liberty-is-no-vice. Retrieved 12/22/2017.

64 Beschloss, (2001), pp. 54-90.

65 Results of the 1964 election can be found in detail in the World Almanac publications, from 1965-1972; with summary data since that date. See also, White, T.H. (1965). Making of the President 1964. New York: Atheneum Publishers.

66 Williams, J.D. & Conway, D.

67 Hearings Before the Committee on Rules and Administration of the United States Senate (1964). Construction of the D.C. Stadium, and Matters Related Thereto. Part 1. Testimony of Don B. Reynolds, December 1, 1964. Washington: U.S. Government Printing Office, p. 147.

68 Ibid., p. 150.

69 Ibid., p. 223.

70 Ibid., p. 192.

71 Loc. cit.

72 Baker, B. and King, L.L. (1980). *Wheeling and Dealing: Confessions of a Capitol Hill Operator.* New York: W.H. Norton & Co., p. 182.

Chapter Twenty-One

JOHNSON'S FULL TERM 1965-1969

Johnson's intent appears to have been to go about getting his "Great Society" agenda passed and implemented. The one black cloud that could stand in the way was the activity in South Vietnam that was looking much more like a war everyday. Though one can only interpret what seems to be guiding another person, it did appear that Lyndon Johnson desperately wanted to be a "good" president. It seems his idea and example of a good president was the extraordinary President, Franklin Delano Roosevelt. Roosevelt was President when Johnson entered the House of Representatives. Though a young representative from a Southern state, one could surmise that the liberal nature of Roosevelt's presidency, perhaps because of the needs of the times, appealed to the young Lyndon Johnson. But Johnson probably also noted that Roosevelt, who came from wealth, decided instead to make his presidency about the needs of the common person, rather than represent the gentry.

Johnson had embraced the civil rights bill of his predecessor President John F. Kennedy. Johnson's drive in pursuing the Civil Rights Bill may have been more his own beliefs about injustice, particularly to those who came from a legacy of slavery. It can be conjectured that Johnson truly believed in the passing of the civil rights bill and appeared to subsume himself as "getting President Kennedy's agenda passed" as a political way of getting the bill passed. As we move to the aspects of the Great Society, Johnson was seemingly following the New Deal of President Roosevelt more than the agenda of John F. Kennedy. President Johnson was seemingly running a three-ring circus with the different aspects of the Great Society being addressed simultaneously in Congress.

The Great Society

It is daunting to consider the full scope of Johnson's agenda. The major components were civil rights, the War on Poverty, Education, Health, Welfare, the arts and cultural institutions, transportation, consumer protection, the environment, housing, rural development and labor.[1]

The Civil Rights Act of 1964 forbade job discrimination and segregation of public accommodations. The Voting Rights Act of 1965 suspended the use of "literacy" or other voter qualification tests that effectively kept African-Americans off of voter registration lists.[2] The Act also provided for federal lawsuits to end discriminatory poll taxes.[3]

The War on Poverty was intended to eliminate hunger, illiteracy and unemployment with the Economic Opportunity Act of 1964. Federal funds were provided for special educational programs in impoverished areas. Some of the programs begun were Job Corps, Volunteers in Service to America (VISTA, a domestic Peace Corps) Upward Bound, which assisted financially disadvantaged high school students to enter college, legal services for the poor and the Food Stamp Act of 1964. Also, the Community Action Program which promised to help the poor become self-sufficient. Project Head Start was a program designed to give children from poorer family's educational experiences to help them be ready for formal schooling. Social Security was improved to move some recipients out of poverty.[4]

The Elementary and Secondary Education Act of 1965 provided significant federal aid to public schools that enrolled a high concentration of children from low-income families. The Higher Education Facilities Act of 1963, signed into law a month after President Johnson assumed office, greatly increased aid to colleges for libraries, several new graduate centers, new technical institutes and twenty-five to thirty new community colleges a year. The Higher Education Act of 1965, which increased money given to universities, established Teacher Corps to provide teachers to poverty-stricken areas and moved student aid to individuals. The National Defense Act was improved in 1964.[5] The Bilingual Education Act of 1968 aided school districts to address the needs of children with limited backgrounds in English.[6]

Medicare

The Social Security Act of 1965 authorized Medicare and provided funding for many of the medical costs for persons over 65 who were covered by social security. This action was bitterly fought by the medical establishment, who deemed this act, "socialized medicine." Later Medicare was extended to persons afflicted by certain (usually terminal) conditions and also to certain disabled citizens.

Medicaid

Beginning in 1966 welfare recipients received care through the new Medicaid program. This program is typically run by state administrators, though they are monitored through the federal Centers for Medicare and Medicaid Services.

Welfare

A variety of other changes or new programs, including the Food Stamp Act of 1964 and the Child Nutrition Act (1966) and the School Breakfast Program, incrementally helped the poor and indigent; but they were still poor.[7]

The Arts and Cultural Institutions

In September 1965, President Johnson signed into law the creation of the National Endowment for the Arts and the National Endowment for the Humanities as separate independent agencies. This was undertaken to bring funding for the arts and humanities more in line with programs that had previously been made available to the sciences.[8] The Public Broadcasting Act of 1967 led to the Corporation for Public Broadcasting, a private non-profit corporation. The public television and radio stations, now mainly funded by private donations, continue to the present.[9]

Transportation

President Johnson consolidated all transportation under a new office, The Secretary of Transportation, authorized by Congress on October 15, 1966. New programs included The Urban Transportation Act of 1964, which provided funds for large-scale urban public or private railroad projects; the High-Speed Ground Transportation Act of 1965 led to a high-speed rail connection between New York and Washington D.C.[10] Also included was the National Traffic and Motor Vehicle Act of 1966, a bill that followed the lead of Ralph Nader and his book, *Unsafe at any Speed.*[11]

Consumer Protection

The Cigarette Labeling Advertising Act of 1965 required packages to carry warning labels.[12] Also created were the National Highway Safety Administration, The Child Safety Act of 1966, the Flammable Fabric Act, and The Wholesome Meat Act, which required inspections that met federal standards. The Truth-in-Lending Act of 1968 required lenders and credit providers to provide information regarding the full cost of finance charges in both dollars and annual percentage rates. The Wholesome Poultry Products Act of 1968 required inspections that met federal guidelines. The Land Sale Disclosure Act of 1968 provided safeguards against fraudulent and deceptive practices in land sales. The Radiation Safety Act of 1968 provided standards and protocols for recalls of electronic devices.[13]

The Environment

The number of Acts in the environmental protection arena was astonishing: the Water Quality Act of 1965; the Clean Air Act of 1963; the Wilderness Act of 1964; the Endangered Species Act of 1966; the National Trails System Act of 1968; the Wild and Scenic Rivers Act of 1968; the Land and Water Conservation Fund Act of 1965; the Solid Waste Disposal Act of 1965; the Motor Vehicle Air Pollution Act of 1965; the National Historic Preservation Act 1966; the Aircraft Noise Abatement Act of 1968; and, the National Environmental Policy Act of 1969.[14]

Housing

The Housing and Urban Development Act of 1965 included such things as rent subsidies for low-income families, housing rehabilitation grants to enable low-income families in urban renewal areas to improve their homes rather than relocate to another community. The Demonstration Cities Act of 1966 addressed housing renovation, urban services, neighborhood facilities, and job creation.[15]

Rural Development

Under the Economic Opportunity Act of 1964, special programs were used to address rural poverty. The office for Economic Opportunity was allowed to be a lender for rural families to permanently increase their ability to have higher earning capacities. Job Corps enrolled school dropouts. This included the Youth Conservation Corps to clean up and conserve National Forests. The Community Action Programs was used for job training, housing, health and welfare assistance.[16]

Having lived through the Johnson era as an adult, I was then (and until recently) not knowledgeable of the successes that were achieved in his administration, though many of the programs have been discontinued under subsequent Republican administrations. Much of the "Great Society" addressed the need of the most vulnerable of our citizens, not unlike the "New Deal" from President Franklin Roosevelt's tenure. Roosevelt had taken under his wing the young member of the House of Representatives, Lyndon Johnson; apparently Johnson was impressed by Roosevelt's contributions. Still, the scope of Johnson's achievements was not seemingly predictable from his time in the Senate and his time as Vice-President.

The Vietnam War

The war in Vietnam can be looked at in several ways. One way is a contemporaneous point of view, that is, those who were experiencing it in that time frame, together with the world-view of that time. A second is to look at it from a distance in time, that is to say, with a lot of hindsight. First, we'll use hindsight. There were four groups to consider: The South Vietnamese government, the Viet-Cong, the North Vietnamese, and the U.S. forces, which included the U.S. military, with substantial involvement of the CIA. The South Vietnamese government was led by Diem, who was born in North Vietnam and was a Catholic. Diem urged North Vietnamese, with concern for their future because of their religion, to emigrate to South Vietnam; about one million did in fact emigrate to the South, of whom 60% were Catholic.

Among those who had a religious affiliation, most of the South Vietnamese were Buddhist. Those in power in the government were Catholics, who mostly had come from North Vietnam. The Viet-Cong tended to be rural and/or poorer from what had become known as South Vietnam, for those who made such a distinction. Most likely, they saw themselves as Vietnamese. Prior to this, at the Geneva Conference, separate governments were established for North and South Vietnam, with the proviso that an election would take place in 1956 to reunite the two areas. In 1954, Diem was asked to be the prime minister in South Vietnam. The South was badly torn into factions, and Diem moved to consolidate powers.

In 1955, an election was held to establish the leader of the South. Diem ran against the man who appointed him Prime Minister, Bao Dai. The election was badly rigged. In Saigon alone, Diem received around 300,000 more votes than there were voters in Saigon. Diem was elected in October 1955 with 98.2% of the vote. Diem had gained backing from the United States. Perhaps Diem realized that there was little likelihood that the voters would prefer remaining split into two separate countries, particularly if a fair vote would be enforced. No election was held in 1956 to reunite the two sections of Vietnam, apparently with the hegemony of the United States.[17]

The U.S. was effectively abrogating the Geneva agreement. If the U.S. accepted the continuation of a separate South Vietnam, then the U.S. is responsible, along with South Vietnam, for ignoring the Geneva Conference. "You broke it, you bought it."

What is the view that became the rationale for ignoring the ubiquitous 1956 election? In a phrase, the "domino theory"; that is, as one country falls to communism, the countries next to the fallen state are likely to follow.

Whatever the truth or falsehood of the "domino theory," the theory was widely held to be true, at least in government circles in the United States.[18]

The original hegemony of disregarding the Geneva agreement of 1954 occurred under the Eisenhower administration. The belief in the "domino theory" did not fade with the election of John F. Kennedy. Though Kennedy wrote NSAM 263, it was not made public during his lifetime. It is not clear that the actual content of this Memorandum was ever fully communicated to President Johnson.

President Johnson agonized over the direction of the war in Vietnam, particularly in the months of May, June and July, 1965. Among other concerns, Johnson thought his "Great Society" was likely to be imperiled by the war, due to the greatly increasing demands for more men and more money. President Johnson reasoned that the war in Vietnam would amount to the end of his presidency.[19] Johnson disliked American mothers having a son killed or maimed in a faraway place. The issue that seemed to carry the day for him was that the United States government had signed a treaty with the government of South Vietnam.[20] In a book published in 2018, Daniel Ellsberg, who brought the Pentagon Papers to the American public through the *New York Times* during the Nixon administration, regrets that he did not reveal the files he had in his safe in 1965, at the time of the vote to greatly increase the American military effort in Vietnam.[21] Had Ellsberg released the files he held at that time, perhaps President Johnson would have embraced the information as a means to insure the continuation of the Great Society, or, perhaps not. That hypothetical situation, unfortunately, went untested. The war would drudge along, sucking up the lives of young Americans, and many more Vietnamese.

The Tone of the Johnson Full Term

The passing of the Great Society legislation was the linchpin of Lyndon Johnson's full term. But the expansion of the "military action in Vietnam" overshadowed his legislative successes; the heating up of the war was the issue that fairly defined his Presidential legacy. The following table shows the number of American war deaths in Vietnam.

American Deaths During the Vietnam Era[22]

1956-59	4
1960	5
1961	16
1962	53
1963	122

1964	216
1965	1,928
1966	6,350
1967	11,363
1968	16,899
1969	11,780
1970	6,173
1971	2,414
1972	759
1973	68
1974	1
1975	62
1976-86	0
1987	1
1988-89	0
1990	1
1991-99	0
2000-06	5
TOTAL	58,220

It can be seen in terms of American deaths that the war claimed many more lives from 1965 to 1972, maximizing in 1968 (by any measure a focal year in American History).

Perhaps because of the war, the years of Johnson's full term became increasingly tumultuous. Events both abroad and at home became a quagmire for the bewildered president. Continuing dissent about the war and several riots that had causes beyond Vietnam dogged the President. A slogan that rang through these years was, "Hey, Hey LBJ – How many boys did you kill today!"

France Withdraws from NATO

France formally withdrew from NATO on June 21, 1966. One could suspect that they did not want to be drawn into any further Vietnam action. President de Gaulle reportedly was concerned about the loss of sovereignty for France. France remained outside the NATO alliance until 2009.[23]

The Attack on the USS *Liberty*

Though long kept a secret, perhaps President Johnson's most heinous act as President was the destruction of the USS *Liberty*. On the fourth day of the six-day war, June 8, 1967, Israel attacked the USS *Liberty*, which was in international waters near Israel and Egypt. Before the war supposedly began, Israel had eliminated the airplanes of the Egyptian military (which included at least 30 Soviet airplanes). In a sense, the six-day war was practically over on the "first day." The planning of this war was a joint effort of the United States and Israel. The United States (or rather, Lyndon Johnson) wanted to enter the war to eliminate President Nasser of Egypt. To accomplish this, the Israelis were supposed to sink a designated American ship and assign the blame to Egypt, setting the stage for American entry into the war. This scenario considered the possibility that the Soviet Union may enter the fray, thereby precipitating World War III. In such a case, Johnson and the military presumably intended to use a first strike of nuclear weapons against the Soviets were they to signal their entry into the war. The designated vessel, chosen perhaps because of its name, was the USS *Liberty*.[24]

Two weeks prior to the Six Day war, the USS *Liberty*, docked in the Ivory Coast, was ordered to proceed to the Mediterranean Sea off the coast of Egypt at full speed (18 knots). At 8 A.M. Washington time on June 8, 1967, three Israeli Mirage jets (with their insignias painted out) began strafing the USS *Liberty* with 30mm cannons, rockets and napalm. The pilots of the jets would have seen the huge American flag, and before the shooting started, persons on the USS Liberty waved to the pilots, who waved back.

The next phase of the attack was the firing of torpedoes at the *Liberty* by three Israeli gunboats. The *Liberty* out-maneuvered four torpedoes, but the fifth left a 22- by 39-foot hole on the starboard side, which should have sunk the *Liberty*, but did not. Gunboats then circled the USS *Liberty*. Several sailors were ordered to abandon the ship into lifeboats, which were also attacked by the gunboats. Because the *Liberty* had not yet sunk, it would mean that survivors would be able to testify that they were attacked by the Israeli military, not Egyptian, delaying the entry of the U.S. into the war. Twice, rescue of persons on the *Liberty* was denied by persons in Washington (most likely Lyndon Baines Johnson, along with Secretary of Defense Robert McNamara). In fact, McNamara ordered planes that had been sent to rescue USS *Liberty* survivors to abort their mission and return to their base. President Johnson reportedly made the comment, that he didn't give a damn if the ship sank, he would not embarrass his allies.[25]

It is inconceivable that McNamara's instruction was not given to him by the Commander-in-Chief (Johnson). Presumably, the hope was that the ship and its crew would all perish. The ship made it to Crete where they were told to continue to Malta; perhaps it might sink on its way there. The ship made it to Malta on June 14, 1967. Of the original 294 crew members aboard, 34 had been killed in the attack, and at least 172 more were wounded. Fortunately, because the USS *Liberty* got to Malta after the end of the six-day war, the U.S. was precluded from entering the war. The sailors aboard the USS *Liberty* were the heroes of this incident. A total news blackout was imposed. The crew members were warned, "*You are never, repeat never, to discuss this with anyone, not even your wives. If you do, you will be court-martialed and end your lives in prison, or worse.*"[26]

The megalomania of the Commander-in-Chief is clearly evident. Several books and many websites have been created by survivors of the incident, in defiance of the warning they received in Malta. Doing a Google search of "USS *Liberty*" brings literally hundreds of sites. And perhaps to no one's surprise, there is a controversy not unlike the Warren Report. Those trying to "save appearances"[27] for President Johnson, the American military, the American government, the Israeli military and the Israeli government, maintain the lie that the attack was a simple mistake of misidentification by the Israeli military.

A book that appears to be an even presentation of the available information regarding the USS *Liberty* was written by Robert Allen.[28] Whatever the intentions of the United States were, the large presence of Soviet ships (at least 70) led to the U.S. speaking on the hot-line to Russia at the time of the Six Day War, and both sides were apprised of the other's concerns; a nuclear war with the Soviets was very likely off the table. Both the Soviets and LBJ would have liked the removal of Nasser. The Soviets were ready to unleash their military if Israel did not pull back from their offensive against Syria; the U.S. was also opposed to the Israeli invasion into Syria. The American planes that were called back from aiding the USS *Liberty* were prepared to attack whomever was attacking the USS *Liberty*. The attack by Israel was deemed to be deliberate, and they (e.g. Moshe Dayan) knew that the ship was American. The Israelis also knew the ship was a spy ship, collecting information from both the Egyptians and the Israelis. In the Israeli view, they could not be sure whether the Americans were sharing information with the Soviets or Egyptians, justifying the attack, at least to them.[29]

The Detroit Riot in July, 1967

In any given year, riots have broken out in the United States. In 1967, 159 riots occurred. The Detroit riot, July 23 to July 29, was one of the most significant. Many of the rioters (but not all) were Black. There were 43 dead civilians. The number of police, state police, National Guard and the 103rd Airborne was 17,000.[30] One policeman was killed. An eye-witness stated that one man had come out to surrender, "But it seemed as though an officer went to hit the other man. When he tried to retaliate, they began scuffling and both men (the policeman and one suspect) appeared to grab for the shotgun."[31] Danny Royster and officer Jerome Olshove, were struggling for the gun when it went off, killing Officer Olshove. Both suspects were subsequently charged with first-degree murder.[32]

1968-The USS *Pueblo*

The year 1968 was a momentous year in American history. The first major incident was the North Koreans capture of the USS *Pueblo*. This event, with the North Koreans holding the ship, the captain and crew in hostage where the crew members were beaten and abused, was the first peacetime surrender of a United States military vessel. The USS *Pueblo* had been within the 12-mile limit for several days before it was intercepted. The intercept took place on January 22, 1968. The embargo on the men and the ship would continue for 335 days. The USS *Pueblo* was indeed a spy ship, equipped to accomplish its mission. The detention of the ship and men was an embarrassment to both President Johnson and the navy brass. The military wanted Commander Lloyd Bucher punished for having surrendered his ship. The surrender took place after a demand was made, "Heave to, or I will open fire."[33]

The view of Michael Lerner[34] was that American foreign policy failed to consider that smaller Communist countries had a need for their own sovereignty, apart from whether they fell under the influence of either Russia or China. Like the domino theory, the U.S. seemed to use simplistic thinking regarding smaller Communist entities.

The Tet Offensive

On the Vietnamese Lunar New Year, Tet, the Tet Offensive began (January 30, 1968). This began while the U.S. was still on the heels of the North Korean capture of the USS *Pueblo*. The Tet offensive was a massive multi-region effort to take much of South Vietnam. More than 8000 North Vietnamese troops and Viet-Cong attacked 36 provincial capitals, one-third of the district centers and five of the six major cities in the South. The North Vietnamese temporarily took control of much of South Vietnam. At the end of two weeks, most of the lost territory had been taken back. Intense fighting went on for months after the attack. President Johnson and the military had disappointed the American populace. Apparently, the administration and military advisors had painted a rosy picture that came under suspicion with the Tet offensive. President Johnson would reconsider the strategy in Vietnam.[35]

The New Hampshire Primary

The New Hampshire Primary was held March 12, 1968. President Johnson was on the ballot, though he did not campaign there. One person opposed President Johnson in this primary, Senator Eugene McCarthy of Minnesota. McCarthy was not well known, but he represented an alternative to President Johnson. Johnson "won" the primary, 49% to 42%. McCarthy saw this as a win, and he was encouraged to continue in the primaries.

The My Lai Massacre

Hundreds of unarmed Vietnamese were murdered by U.S. forces, led by 2nd Lieutenant William Calley on March 16, 1968. Calley was the only participant convicted in subsequent trials. He served 3½ years of house arrest until he was pardoned by President Nixon in 1974. Details about the atrocity were not known to the public for about a year after the occurrence of the massacre.

Robert Kennedy Enters the Presidential Race

Robert Kennedy, brother of John F. Kennedy, entered the Democratic race for the nomination to President. He would have been seen as a formidable opponent for President Johnson.

Johnson Announces His decision to not Seek Re-election

On March 31, 1968, in a prime-time televised address, President Johnson announced his decision to not seek re-election. Johnson stated "There is division in the American house now. There is divisiveness among us all tonight. And holding the trust that is mine, as President of all the people, I cannot disregard the peril to the progress of the American people and the hope and prospect of peace for all people…I do not believe that I should devote an hour or a day of my time in any personal partisan causes.… Accordingly, I shall not seek, and I will not accept, the nomination of my party for another term as your President."[36]

While in a military sense, the U.S.-South Vietnamese coalition won the Tet offensive, the reporting of this part of the War took its toll on American public support of the war. The military had requested an additional 206,000 troops for Vietnam. Clark Clifford, Johnson's new Secretary of Defense, advised against this escalation, recommending only 20,000 new troops. President Johnson decided against the military's request, and announced a partial bombing halt against North Vietnam, during his address on March 31, 1968.[37]

The Murder of Martin Luther King

The Reverend Martin Luther King, Jr., a winner of the Nobel Peace Prize, was assassinated on a balcony of the Lorraine Motel in Memphis, Tennessee on April 4, 1968. The person accused of this crime was James Earle Ray. Ray later pled guilty to the assassination. Many riots spontaneously took place across the U.S. At a meeting held in Indianapolis, Robert Kennedy addressed a crowd of mostly black persons, and sadly announced the assassination of Martin Luther King. In his six-minute speech, Robert Kennedy spoke to the assembled persons from the heart, giving what has been called, "The Greatest Speech."[38]

Despite James Earle Ray having pled guilty, there appeared to be reasons to suspect that there was a great deal more to be learned about the assassination of Martin Luther King.[39]

The California Democratic Primary

The California primary occurred on the first Tuesday in June, coinciding with the South Dakota primary. The previous week had a primary in Oregon and a state convention in North Dakota.[40] In a hotly contested California primary, Kennedy won over Eugene McCarthy 46% to 42%. After the California primary, the delegate total stood at Humphrey, 561, Robert Kennedy 393, and Eugene McCarthy, 258. Humphrey had not participated in the primaries but got his delegates either at state conventions or from favorite-son candidates.

Clearly, the much more important issue was the assassination of Robert Kennedy on June 5, 1968, shortly after his victory speech at the Ambassador Hotel in Los Angeles. As Robert Kennedy and his wife were walking through the kitchen pantry on the way to a press conference, a young man fired 8 shots from his .22 caliber gun. He was apprehended immediately. His name was Sirhan Sirhan. Robert Kennedy was laying on the floor, obviously in considerable distress. Curiously, there was a bow tie near his hand; it was not his own. Kennedy was rushed to the hospital where emergency surgery was performed. Robert Kennedy died from his injuries 26 hours later.

The coroner for Los Angeles Thomas Noguchi M.D., performed the autopsy after he called Cyril Wecht M.D., J.D., a well-known coroner in Alleghany County Pennsylvania. At the time of the call Robert Kennedy was still alive, but with little hope. Noguchi wanted to avoid the pitfalls that surrounded the autopsy of Robert's brother, President John F. Kennedy. He also would have liked to have Dr. Wecht in attendance at the autopsy. Dr. Wecht was torn by the request, which he would very much liked to have fulfilled. However, Wecht's wife had just given birth to their daughter, and he felt that he needed to be home when his wife and daughter were released from the hospital. Wecht was able to give advice to Noguchi. First and foremost, the autopsy was, by law, required to be held in California; as was the case when President Kennedy was assassinated; his autopsy by law should have taken place in Texas. The body of President Kennedy, as we know, was forcibly removed to the naval hospital in Bethesda, Maryland, where all of the physicians were in the armed forces: the autopsy was effectively under the direction of non-pathologist military brass. Wecht was concerned that the government would insist on performing the autopsy in the D.C. area.

Wecht suggested to Noguchi that he get Pierre Salinger, JFK's Press Secretary to serve as a go-between for Noguchi. Wecht also suggested that Noguchi call the Armed Forces Institute of Pathology (AFIP) and have two or three of their pathologists attend the autopsy; Dr. Pierre Finck was the head of AFIP and having Finck present would be a plus. Having Finck and other AFIT pathologists attend would likely be viewed positively by the government. Wecht also suggested that the physicians who operated on Robert Kennedy at the Good Samaritan Hospital in Los Angeles be in attendance. Two days later, Wecht flew to Los Angeles to review Dr. Noguchi's information from the autopsy he performed and other forensic information. Together Dr. Noguchi and Dr. Wecht would craft the formal report of the autopsy.[41]

The findings were that Robert Kennedy was hit by three shots, all from behind. The fatal shot was fired at point blank range, no more than an inch-and-one-half from Kennedy's head, near his right ear. In that Sirhan was in front of Robert Kennedy, and never closer than three feet, it would seem highly improbable that the fatal shot that hit Kennedy was fired by Sirhan.[42]

One person who was next to Kennedy, Thane Eugene Cesar, drew his pistol; he claimed he did not fire it. It was Thane Cesar's bowtie that was found next to the fallen Kennedy. The Los Angeles Police Department did not expend much effort investigating Cesar. Cesar was known to have a pistol; he claimed having sold the pistol *before* June 5, 1968. It was later determined that Cesar sold his handgun to Jim Yoder on September 6, 1968. Cesar had shown the handgun to Yoder at their place of employment, Lockheed. Yoder retired shortly after buying the gun and moved to Arkansas. His gun was stolen from him there.[43]

Sirhan had a lawyer appointed by the court, Grant Cooper. Cooper chose to use a diminished-capacity defense, disregarding the exculpatory forensic evidence. The jury did not accept the diminished-capacity defense, and the evidence showing that Sirhan had not shot Robert Kennedy was never presented to the jury. Sirhan was sentenced to death. The death sentence was removed by the Supreme Court in 1972, when they outlawed all death penalties.[44]

The Democratic National Convention

Lyndon Johnson still harbored the idea of being drafted for the nomination of the Democratic Party. He also thought he might attend the Convention in Chicago. Three days before the convention began, there were anti-war protesters in the streets; Johnson worried about his own safety in attending the convention. On August 27th, one day before the convention began, he let his supporters know that he would not accept a draft.[45]

The Democratic National Convention in Chicago was like no other. Prior to the convention persons protesting the war in Vietnam filled the streets of Chicago. Clashes with police were frequent. My own most vivid memory of the convention was a woman motorist who was stopped by the police and apparently beaten by them. Inside the convention, the anti-Vietnam war delegates, led by candidate Eugene McCarthy, were calling for an end to the war. McCarthy, who had won six primaries, and forced Johnson out of the race in New Hampshire, would lose the nomination to Hubert Humphrey, who didn't participate in the primaries. At the convention, Humphrey came forward with the plan to begin bringing troops home from Vietnam in 1969.This greatly angered President Johnson, who was rethinking supporting Humphrey. The selection process of delegates favored Humphrey. Humphrey won the nomination, but for a party that was at odds with itself. A splintered party rarely wins an election; 1968 would not change that outcome.[46]

The 1968 Election

Johnson wanted to give the appearance of being above the political fray in the election. It could be argued that Johnson was upset by Humphrey's distancing himself from Johnson's policies, and preferred Nixon. An indication of this was a report that Greek military dictators had funneled more than a half-million dollars into the Nixon campaign. Were this information to be made public, it could well have been very favorable to Hubert Humphrey. Johnson chose to not have this information disclosed.[47]

The election had three candidates with electoral votes (The third, George Wallace, Alabama governor, was running on the American Independent Party). Nixon with 31.8 million popular votes and 301 electoral votes, won the election. Humphrey had 31.3 million popular votes and 191 electoral votes. Wallace had 9.9 million popular votes and 46 electoral votes. Nixon won the election with under 44% of the popular vote, beating Humphrey by less than one percent.

The End of the Johnson Presidency

Lyndon Johnson did not wish to go "softly into the night." He wanted to ensure his legacy for "The Great Society." In the second half of 1968, he was like a whirling dervish on behalf of domestic advance. Johnson had much unfinished business that he wanted Congress to act upon. He sought natural gas pipeline safety, the 18-year-old vote, ending discrimination in hiring, more effective urban transit, and a ten-fold increase in funds for low- and middle- income housing. He wanted programs for family planning, and additional funding for Black economic progress. He anticipated 50 major bills that Congress should address.[48]

Within a month of asking for the new bills, passing were acts to eliminate barriers for handicapped persons, protection from flammable, toxic, and corrosive gasses, the establishment of the National Eye Institute, and the enactment of the Health Manpower Act, to help various medical and nursing schools train healthcare professionals. Before the election, he signed bills beginning food stamps, and aiding agricultural interests with the Food and Agricultural Act. Educational bills included help for higher and vocational education and extending veteran's benefits.[49]

In a controversial move, Johnson attempted to appoint Associate Justice Abraham Fortas to replace Chief Justice Earl Warren. Though the Judiciary Committee approved Fortas by a vote of 11-6, the full Senate went into a filibuster; a cloture vote failed. In the following year, under the threat of impeachment, Fortas resigned.[50]

President Johnson was trying to have secret negotiations with the North and South Vietnamese in Paris. Johnson looked to end the bombing in North Vietnam, providing the North Vietnam government make an appropriate de-escalation. It would appear that the North Vietnamese would welcome a cessation of bombing but were willing to wait out the Americans and eventually defeat the government in Saigon. The Saigon government wanted to retain American support, both monetarily and the American troops. This attempt to make a bargain in Vietnam became known to Richard Nixon and he worried that a settlement in Vietnam prior to the election would bury his own attempt to win the Presidency. For this, Nixon decided to have contact made with the Saigon government. Prior to the election, President Johnson became aware of Nixon interfering with the Paris Peace talks; the talks were being deliberately delayed until the day after the Humphrey-Nixon election. Johnson was also aware of an illegal $500,000 contribution to the Nixon campaign by the military dictatorship in Greece. This illegal contribution was said to have caused President Johnson to become livid. With what little time was left, Johnson made a few appearances supporting Vice President Humphrey.[51]

One situation, that occurred shortly before Lyndon Johnson's death (January 22, 1973) was President Nixon was trying to short-circuit a Senate investigation, by asking Johnson to ask the Democratic Senators not to go ahead with the investigation, to avoid Nixon releasing information about Johnson, who, according to Nixon, had Nixon's and Spiro Agnew's phones bugged during the 1972 election campaign. Nixon was told by Johnson that the FBI did not approve a wiretap; Johnson got only a list of telephone numbers contacting Nixon or Agnew. Nixon was also told that information regarding Nixon's interfering in the Peace talks with North and South Vietnam could be released, as well as the $500,000 illegally received by Nixon for the 1972 election from the Greek military Junta. Were this information released, the impeachment-resignation process could have been greatly hastened.[52]

What, Can be Said About the Lyndon Johnson Presidency?

For those with a solid belief in the supremacy of capitalism, there would be little to say about Lyndon Johnson's Presidency. His insistence in looking out for minorities and poor whites would have likely soured market-based persons. For those with a humanitarian view, some of Johnson's War on Poverty and Great Society successes likely were applauded. But the other war, the war in Vietnam, overshadowed his attempt to help the "common man"; indeed, the war diminished the success of his agenda for the common good. The war was itself a divider of persons on the Homefront. And surely the deaths that occurred on his watch in Vietnam would be a strong negative to his presidency. Over 58,000 young Americans lost their lives, many more were wounded, and the Veterans of this war were not treated as heroes. But there are also the darker parts of his legacy. By knowing prior to the assassination of President Kennedy that an attempt would be made on his life and not at least reporting this threat to proper authorities, places a black cloud on his ascending to the presidency. The cover-up of the Warren Commission was at the behest of Lyndon Johnson on the timeline he set forth in naming the Commission. Were the details about the sabotage of the USS *Liberty* known at the time of its occurrence, this could have had the effect of torpedoing his presidency.

Endnotes

1 en.Wikipedia.org/wiki/Great-Society retrieved 1/13/2018.

2 An ironic "joke" told prior to the passing of the Voters Rights Act concerned a well-dressed and well educated Black man who was attempting to register to vote in the deep South. Upon entering the registration office, he was told that a literacy test would be required. He held a PhD in a scientific field, and a J.D. in law. He was asked to explain the meaning of the first and second amendments to the Constitution (right to free speech and religion; the right to bear arms). He of course explained the first two amendments with surgical accuracy. He was then told that the next question dealt with integration. The question he was asked was to find the area between the line/curve y=x+4 and the X-axis, with the limits of 2 & 4. He had a puzzled look on his face and then smiled. He replied, "That question almost threw me, but because of your hint that it involved integration, I remembered my calculus and the answer is 14 units. Did you want me to explain? The examiner moved on to the next question without any expression at all. The examiner gave him two paragraphs written in a foreign language. The Black men noticed that it was in French, a language he had studied for his PhD language examinations. He gave the examiner both a literal and meaning based translation. The examiner remained expressionless and handed the Black man a newspaper that appeared to be in either Chinese or Japanese. He was asked, "Can you read this?" The Black man looked at it for a minute or so and responded, "I can't read it exactly, but I think can tell you what it means." The examiner, became animated, and asked, "What does it mean?" The well-dressed Black man said," It means this Black man is not going to be allowed to vote in this election."

3 en.wikipedia.org/wiki/Great Society.

4 Loc. cit.

5 I finished my undergraduate work on a National Defense Education loan; this program originated under the Eisenhower administration in 1959.

6 en.Wikipedia.org/wiki/Great Society.

7 Ibid. While there were some improvements for the poor, many were still living on the margin. I do remember a cartoon, with an older man and woman shopping for food. The man was wistfully looking at a can of Alpo dog food (a slightly more expensive dog food), with his wife saying, "Put that back George. You know we can't afford to eat that. Get something cheaper."

8 Ibid. On many an occasion the spending, particularly in the Arts, has come under fire from critics. One such expenditure that I'm aware of occurred in the 1980's. A person had been given a grant to create artistic pyrotechnics. One such exhibit was planned at the University of North Dakota (where I was a faculty member). Many employees were encouraged to attend this artistic event in early April (meaning it was pretty cold outside). The event was attended by a crowd of perhaps 200 (cold) people, lasted no more than 30 seconds, and the artist received $20,000 for his efforts. I said to an employee standing next to me, that the 30 second performance was approximately equal to my yearly salary. The other employee said in response, "That's because you make a lot more than I do."

9 Ibid.

10 Ibid.

11 Nader, R. (1965). *Unsafe at any Speed: The Designed in Dangers of the American Automobile*. New York: Grossman Publishers.

12 It is interesting how a person addressed earlier in this book also played a very different role that affected the new standards that came through Johnson's Great Society Program. Alton Ochsner, M.D. was the person in charge of the program that ran the CIA project that intended to assassinate Castro through the use of fast acting cancers, was also one of the first physicians to blame cigarettes as being a main cause of lung cancer.

13 en. Wikipedia.org/wiki/Great Society, retrieved 1/16/2018.

14 Ibid.

15 Ibid.

16 Ibid.

17 en.Wikipedia.org/wiki/Ngo_Dinh_Diem, retrieved 1/17/2018

18 en.Wikipedia.org/wiki/DominoTheory, retrieved 1/17/2018.

19 Beschloss, M. (2001). *Reaching for Glory: Lyndon Johnson's Secret White House Tapes, 1964-1965*. New York: Simon & Schuster, p. 178.

20 Ibid., pp. 378-417.

21 Ellsberg, D. (2018). *The Doomsday Machine: Confessions of a Nuclear War Planner*. New Yok: Bloomsbury Publishing.

22 archives.gov/research/military/Vietnam-war/casualty-statistics, retrieved 2/15/2018.

23 csis.org/analysis/nato-and-France, retrieved 2/16/2018.

24 Nelson (2014), pp. 375-408.

25 Bamford, J. (2001). *Body of Secrets*. New York: Doubleday, p. 226.

26 Nelson (2014). p. 390.

27 Barfield, O. (1965). *Saving the Appearances: A Study in Idolatry*. New York: Harcourt Brace & Jovanovich,

28 Allen, R.J. (2012). *Beyond Treason*. Create Space. (Available through Amazon.com.) This undoubtedly is one of the better presentations of the USS Liberty and its abandonment by President Johnson.

29 Allen, (2012), pp. 393-342. Another excellent source is Hounan, P. & Simpson, J. (2003). *Operation Cyanide: Why the Bombing of the USS Liberty Nearly Caused World War III*. Chatham Kent, UK: Mackays of Chatham. A pro-Israeli view that emphasizes that the attack on the USS *Liberty* was simply a misidentification is Cristol, A.J. (2002). *The Liberty Incident: The 1967 Israeli Attack on the Navy Spy Ship*. Dulles, VA: Brassey's Inc. (Books International).

30 Sugrue, T.J. "Introduction: John Hershey and the Tragedy of Race." In Hershey, J. (1968, 1996) *The Algiers Motel Incident*, Baltimore: The Johns Hopkins University Press, p. ix.

31 Hershey, p. 129.

32 Loc. cit. A motion picture about one aspect of the riot, Detroit, was directed by Katherine Bigelow. This 2017 release closely follows the book by John Hershey.

33 Lerner, M.B. (2002). *The Pueblo Incident: A Spy Ship and the Failure of American Foreign Policy*. Manhattan, KS: The University of Kansas Press, pp. 1-3.

34 Lerner.

35 Dallek, R. (1998). *Flawed Giant: Lyndon Johnson and his Times 1961-1973*. New York: Oxford University Press, pp. 502-513.

36 Ibid., p. 529.

37 Ibid., pp. 529-532.

38 The Greatest Speech Ever.youtube.com/watch?v=GokzCff8Zbs. Retrieved 2/23/2018.

39 Pepper, W.F. (1995). *Orders to Kill: The Truth Behind the Murder of Martin Luther King*. New York: Carroll & Graf Publishers.

40 I attended the North Dakota Democratic Convention, supporting Senator Eugene McCarthy of Minnesota. I remember an event that made absolutely no sense at the time. Both Hubert Humphrey and Eugene McCarthy were in attendance and their names were placed in nomination. Robert Kennedy's name was also placed in nomination, but he was not present; he was campaigning in the South Dakota, Oregon and California primaries. Then, among a group of older persons dressed in Red, White, and Blue outfits, a person stood up and placed Lyndon Johnson's name in nomination. Then the entire crowd of older persons in Red, White, and Blue, got up and danced around the convention floor for what seemed to be at least half an hour. As this went on, I marveled at them – Did they not remember that Lyndon Johnson stated less than two months previously that he would neither pursue nor accept his party's nomination for President? I now marvel at my

naivete. In retrospect I can see the path to the nomination that was being done for Johnson despite Johnson's earlier denial of seeking re-election. If Robert Kennedy won California and perhaps South Dakota or Oregon, the delegate count would be spread among McCarthy and Kennedy, with Humphrey having secured several delegates in non-primary states, and of course Johnson already had several delegates of his own (Johnson won New Hampshire and presumably the Texas delegates would support a Johnson candidacy). If a first or second ballot failed to secure a nominee, the convention could have drafted Johnson for a second term. This scenario was exploded with the assassination of Bobby Kennedy following his win in California.

41 Wecht, C. (1994) *Cause of Death*. New York: Penguin, pp. 79-90.

42 Ibid.

43 Turner, W. & Christian, J. (1993,1978). *The Assassination of Robert F. Kennedy: The Conspiracy and Cover-up*. New York: Thunder Mouths Press, pp. 165-168.

44 Wecht.

45 Dallek, pp. 569-579.

46 Ibid.

47 Ibid., pp. 577-578.

48 Dalleck, p. 551.

49 Ibid., p. 552.

50 Ibid., pp. 563-564; biography.com/people/abe-fortas, retrieved 3/3/2018.

51 Dallek, pp. 579-590.

52 Ibid., pp. 618-619.

LIFE

EXCLUSIVE

OSWALD

ARMED FOR MURDER

In full and extraordinary detail, the life of the assassin

AS JACK RUBY GOES TO TRIAL

Cast of Characters; How the Law Applies

Chapter Twenty-two

WHY IS OSWALD STILL CONSIDERED THE ASSASSIN?

Initially, Lee Harvey Oswald was labeled as the assassin of John F. Kennedy, first by Henry Wade, the Dallas District Attorney, but also by the media, J. Edgar Hoover and the FBI, along with the Presidential Commission handpicked by Lyndon Johnson. Later, several well-known authors (well paid for their efforts) wrote books that continued to uphold the Warren Commission's findings, including Gerald Posner[1] and Vincent Bugliosi.[2] For the most part, the mainstream media still considers Oswald to be the assassin.

A Post-Assassination Conspiracy – The Warren Commission

John F. Kennedy's replacement, Lyndon Baines Johnson, immediately after taking office, appointed a Commission to investigate the murder of John Fitzgerald Kennedy.

As is well known, that commission eventually delivered to President Johnson what apparently was his desired document, in time for the 1964 election. But what sort of investigation was it? Fortunately, we have several documents and writings that help address that question. We, of course, have the Commission document itself, with its 26 volumes of Appendices.[3] We also have, through the Freedom of Information Act, a transcription of the January 27, 1964 meeting of the President's Committee on the Assassination of John F. Kennedy (more commonly referred to as "The Warren Commission").[4] This first meeting of the Warren Commission is telling in regard to the direction of the "investigation." Harold Willens, a staff member for the Warren Commission, who came to the Commission from Bobby Kennedy's Justice Department, wrote a note following this first meeting, "(W)hat the Commission was up to from the first (was) the search for a means of foisting off a preconceived conclusion, the deliberate hiding of what happened when JFK was killed."[5]

It is argued in Williams[6] that the Warren Commission was, in fact, operating in the arena of advocacy research, and from the prosecutorial viewpoint, arguing for Oswald's guilt as a lone assassin. That is, the evidence that pointed toward Oswald's guilt was, in the long run, the only evidence they wished to entertain. Most of the investigation was actually conducted by the FBI. The Commission's staff would choose which evidence to pursue and which evidence to file away. Investigations and interviews were conducted by the Commission's staff. As can be detected, at least one staff member was entering deliberately falsified information. Also, the Warren Commission chose to not allow an advocate for the defense of Oswald to participate. Marguerite Oswald (Oswald's mother) asked attorney Mark Lane to represent her son's interests before the Warren Commission. The Commission denied Lane an opportunity to act as Oswald's defense counsel.[7]

One Commission staff member, Wesley Liebeler, took issue with the nature of the report being written, which he viewed as a "brief for the prosecution" against Oswald. Liebeler[8] chose to turn over most of his internal files to Edward Jay Epstein, who would eventually write *Inquest.*[9] In a remarkable book on the Warren Commission, Shenon[10] accepted Oswald as the lone assassin, but then proceeded to dissect the work of the Commission, pointing out many points of unethical conduct, the shutting out of the staff from exculpatory information regarding Oswald, and the "rush to judgment." It should be remembered that the investigation was proposed by Lyndon Johnson, who picked the seven commissioners, wanted (and got) the investigation completed in advance of the November 1964 presidential election. Is it any wonder that none of the Commission's interests included any investigation of Johnson himself? It would not be until 1998 when Walt Brown held a press conference in Dallas that would announce that Mac Wallace, a convicted murderer (who was sentenced to a five-year unsupervised probation by a Texas court; Wallace was also LBJ's hit man), was the person whose fingerprint was found on the sixth floor of the Texas Schoolbook Depository (TSBD) directly after the assassination.[11] Shenon bemoaned the unanswered questions about the assassination, and the failure of entities such as the CIA to share information; indeed, James Jesus Angleton swooped down to Mexico City in 1971 upon the death of the CIA station Chief Win Scott, collecting everything he could find regarding Scott's tenure in Mexico City (which included the time of Oswald's 1963 visit).[12]

Victoria Adams and her Three Co-Workers: Proof that Oswald wasn't on the Sixth Floor at the Time of the Assassination

Victoria Elizabeth Adams was an employee of the Scott Foresman Co. in the TSBD, who along with three other women watched the Presidential motorcade from a fourth-floor window on November 22, 1963. Directly after the last shot, she and another employee, Sandra Styles, went down the stairs to the first floor. They neither saw nor heard anyone on the stairs. The only person they encountered on their way out of the building was a large black man, who was also employed at the TSBD. A third employee, Dorothy Ann Garner, had situated herself in a chair between the stairs and the elevator, where she would have noticed anyone going up or down the stairs and the elevator. It was several minutes before anyone passed her on either. Those persons who did pass by her were policemen going up the stairs to investigate. Collectively, the observations of these three witnesses would preclude Oswald from being on the 6th floor at the time of the assassination. Among the four women, only Vicky Adams was interviewed by the Warren Commission, though each had been interviewed by the FBI.[13]

The interview of Victoria Adams is found in Chapter 19 of this volume. It is argued there that the sequence of the interview has been re-arranged, Also, the questions asked appear to have sometimes been rewritten. Had an unaltered version of Victoria Adams' testimony been published in the reports accompanying the Warren Report, it would have been seized upon as exculpatory evidence for Lee Harvey Oswald.[14]

Highly Unusual Reports on Oswald Prior to November 22, 1963.

a) Adele Edisen and her Encounter with Dr. Jose Rivera.

Here, two different accounts are reviewed that suggest Oswald was known reasonably well to persons employed by the United States government that render those within the government who claim Oswald was not on the government's radar to be guilty of falsehoods. The first is regarding Adele Edisen, who was re-entering the workforce by applying for a post-doctoral fellowship from the National Institute of Neurological Diseases and Blindness (NINDB) at Tulane University in New Orleans School of Medicine, working in neurophysiology; she was awarded a two-year fellowship. She attended a meeting in Atlantic City, NJ in April, 1963, where she met Dr. Jose Rivera, who was in charge of grants at the NINDB, a subdivision of the National Institutes of Health (NIH). They made arrangements to meet in Washington a few days later. Rivera, who had made reservations for dinner for the two of them, began talking about his travels with his work. Rivera said, "When you go to Dallas, you should go to the Carousel Club because it is a very nice night club." Rivera then said, "Do you know Lee Oswald?" Edisen replied she did not. Rivera told

Edisen that Oswald had lived in the Soviet Union, was married to a Russian woman, and had a child. They were living in Dallas and were moving to New Orleans. "You should get to know them, because they are a lovely couple." From what was said, Edisen inferred that Oswald was a scientist and a friend of Rivera's.[15]

Later, as they were driving by the White House, Rivera, out of the blue, asked, "I wonder what Jackie will do when her husband dies?" When Edisen exclaimed, "What?," Rivera came back, "Oh. Oh, I meant the baby, she might lose the baby." Shortly thereafter, Rivera said, "Write down this name: Lee Harvey Oswald. Tell him to kill the chief." When Rivera realized that Edisen had written down precisely what he had said, he exclaimed," No, no, don't write that down. You'll remember it when you get to New Orleans. We are just playing a little joke on him."

Rivera then began to explain where "it" would happen. He explained there would be men on the fifth floor. Only after the assassination did Edisen understand that the assassination was referred to as "it." Rivera also stated, "Oswald was not what he seems. We're going to send him over to the library to read about great assassinations in history. After it's over, he'll call Abt[16] to defend him. Again, after it's over, someone will kill him. After it happens, his best friend will commit suicide. He'll jump out of a window because of his grief." Then Rivera continued: "When does the Shriner's Circus come to New Orleans? Oh, I remember, in November. It will happen after the Shriner's Circus comes to New Orleans." Then, "After it's over, the men will be out of the country."

Rivera dictated a number for Oswald, 899-4244. On her return to New Orleans, Edisen called the number and asked for Oswald. The man who answered said that there was no one there by that name. Thinking she might have misdialed, she called a week later, getting the same man. She again asked for Oswald. He said, "Oh, they've just arrived. Would you like to speak to his wife?" Edisen said yes, and a Slavic sounding woman said, "Hello." Edisen asked if she or her husband knew a Colonel Rivera. Marina Oswald didn't know but indicated Edisen could call back when her husband was home. The next time Edisen called, the man (landlord) got Oswald on the phone. Edisen asked Oswald if he knew of Colonel Rivera, who worked in Washington with the NIH. Oswald replied, "No, I don't." Edisen replied, "That's strange, because he apparently knows you and your wife." Edisen then asked for the location of the phone, and Oswald gave the address at 4909 Magazine Street, which Edisen recalled was in a run-down part of town, a strange place for a scientist to live.

When Edisen called the Secret Service in New Orleans after the assassination, she was asked to come down to the FBI office. As she entered the room, she was told that Oswald had just been shot. She immediately remembered that Rivera had told her that, "After it's over, someone will kill him. They will say his best friend killed him." A liaison FBI officer joined the two of them. After Edisen gave her information, the FBI officer asked if he could have the note with Oswald's phone number on it. Edisen complied with his request.[17] It is clear that Dr. Rivera had considerable detailed information known only to those planning the assassination.

It should be noted that researcher Bill Kelly interviewed Edisen extensively in 1999, after which he revealed that "Edisen also believes that Rivera surreptitiously gave her some drugs – a Mickey Finn, possibly an LSD psychotic [inducing] drug, and she believes he was testing some sort of drug on her and was involved in some sort of experiment or secret operation."[18]

b) The Search for Lee Harvey Oswald in Mobile, AL on November 21, 1963.

A telegram was sent from Dallas to the New Orleans FBI on November 17, 1963, probably sent by an FBI agent for Oswald to J. Edgar Hoover, which warned of an assassination attempt on the life of President Kennedy in Dallas, on November 22 or 23, 1963. This telegram was likely the rationale for FBI agent James Ambrose, stationed in Mobile Alabama, to seek out Naif Michael Moore, Jr. (Junior Moore), proprietor of Jimmy's Billiards in Mobile, and a known gambler; being called upon by law enforcement as a potential source of information for persons such as Moore, who made their livings outside the then current laws. Moore had been brought in and questioned numerous times previously.[19] Moore voluntarily walked the four blocks to the Mobile FBI office where he was questioned about Lee Harvey Oswald on the afternoon of November 21, 1963, a time the FBI would maintain that they had at most minimal information on Oswald. This interview with Moore showed that such disclaimers by the FBI having no interest in Oswald was an outright lie. Further, when Moore tried to contact Ambrose in January, 1964, Moore was stonewalled about Ambrose's then current location.

As time went on, various things would be addressed in the media that would rekindle Moore's interest in the meaning of his experience. In 1975, Moore saw a Dan Rather television program, titled," The American Assassins." A segment of this program involved William Walter, the FBI agent in New Orleans who handled the teletype on November 17, 1963, about a probable assassination attempt on JFK in Dallas. Moore would eventually get together with Walter. First, he tried again to tell the civil authorities about his 1963 experience in Mobile. At this time (1975), Moore was living in Blythville, Arkansas. Moore told his story to George Ford, Sheriff of Mississippi County (which contains Blythville). Ford turned the information over to Ed Cunningham, an FBI agent in Jonesboro, Arkansas. Cunningham passed the information onto his superiors, who, in turn, asked Cunningham to get a statement from Moore. Eventually, an 8-page report was made, which included Moore's story and a denial by former FBI agent James Ambrose that an interview of Moore regarding Lee Harvey Oswald ever took place.[20] After moving back to Mobile, Moore then told his story to a reporter, Cathy Donelson from the *Mobile Press Register*. Donelson also contacted both Ambrose and Cunningham, who both denied talking to Moore about Lee Harvey Oswald. A few years later, the FBI report was released showing that such conversations had indeed taken place. Donelson's article[21] was published February 23, 1992. A few days later Donelson was fired.[22]

Moore contacted William Walter, the former FBI agent who received the November 17, 1963 teletype at the New Orleans FBI station with the JFK assassination warning for Dallas. They got together and a videotape was filmed by Ruby Moore, Junior Moore's wife. Moore and Walter told their respective stories, with a discussion between them about their respective roles.[23]

This is just another example of the lack of truthfulness in the Federal bureaucracy when it comes to the JFK assassination.

The Telegram Sent to the New Orleans FBI

A telegram was received by William Walter and his wife Josey on Sunday morning, November 17, 1963, at the FBI office in New Orleans. They made a copy of that telegram. The telegram is reproduced on the next page.

"According to William Walter, the security clerk on duty at the time of Oswald's request, Quigley asked Walter to check the security indices to determine if there was an existing file on Oswald. Walter did indeed find a file on Oswald, which he recalled carried an informant classification. He also recalled that Special Agent Warren deBrueys' name was on the jacket of that file. Amazingly, Walter would testify that he had also seen a Telex shortly before the assassination, warning that a "militant revolutionary group may attempt to assassinate President Kennedy on his proposed trip to Dallas." Since no other FBI employee could (or would) corroborate Walter's revelations, the HSCA chose to disregard his testimony. But the HSCA could not provide any motive for Walter's supposed subterfuge. He had no ax to grind with the FBI, he left the Bu-

URGENT 1:45 AM EST 11-17-63 HLF 1PAGE

TO ALL SACS

FROM DIRECTOR

THREAT TO ASSISINATE PRESIDENT KENNEDY IN DALLAS TEXAS
NOVEMBER TWENTYTWO DASH TWENTYTHREE NINETEEN SIXTYTHREE.
MISC INFORMATION CONCERNING.

INFO HAS BEEN RECEIVED BY THE BUREAU
BUREAU HAS ~~XXXXXXXXXXXXXXXXXXXXXX~~ DETERMINED THAT A MILITANT
REVOLUTIONARY GROUP MAY ATTEMPT TO ASSINATED PRESIDENT
KENNEDY ON HIS PROPOSED TRIP TO DALLAS TEXAS ~~XXXXXXXXXX~~
~~XXXXXXXX~~ NOVEMBER TWENTYTWO DASH TWENTYTHREE NINETEEN
SICTYTHREE.
ALL RECEIVING OFFICE SHOULS IMMIDIATELY CONTACT ALL CIS;
PCIS LOGICAL RACIAL AND HATE GROPUP INFORMANTS AND DETERMINE IF
ANY BASIS FOR THREAT. BHRGEU SHOULS BE KEPT ADVISED OF ALL
DEVELOPEMENTS BY TELETYPE .
SUBMIT FD THREE ZERO TWOS AND LHM
OTHER HOFFICE HAVE BEEN ADVISED
END AND ACK PLS
MO....
DL.....
NO.....
KT TI TU CLR..@

reau on good terms, and started a career in banking. He also did not seek notoriety or financial gain and believed the Warren Commission's conclusions. Walter summed up nicely for the HSCA his thoughts about his colleagues' silence, "I had gotten the [gut] feeling from everybody I talked to that 'we know it is true, but we are not going to talk about it.'" From Walter's Executive Session testimony to the HSCA, March 23, 1978, HSCA document #014029."[24]

Oswald as a Covert Operator

We don't have many extensive firsthand accounts about Oswald, but we have at least two such accounts. The first was written by Ernst Titovets,[25] regarding his interactions with Oswald in the Soviet Union, covering 1960-1962. The second is by Judyth Baker,[26] covering April 1963 to November 1963. Together, they render the interpretation of Oswald described in the Warren Report as highly untenable. What we can do is piece together Oswald's life circumstances for the critical period after Oswald's repatriation to the United States.

What was Oswald doing, or, more to the point, what did Oswald think he was doing? It seems a reasonable hypothesis that Oswald desired to be a spy. This probably did not go unnoticed by government agencies likely to have come in contact with him.[27] It is conceivable that Oswald was, in his view, getting a chance to live out this dream. His Russian episode has been interpreted as probably acting as a spy for some U.S. agency or agencies. Otherwise, after attempting to renounce his American citizenship in Moscow and living in the Soviet Union for 32 months (October, 1959 to June, 1962), his repatriation on his return, with a Russian wife and their Russian born daughter, without any apparent repercussions, seems inexplicable.[28]

Though the CIA is unlikely to ever confirm that Oswald was a false defector, E. Howard Hunt confided to his son that Oswald was one of the false-defectors in the CIA false-defector program.[29]

Apparently, the American agencies may have seen that, for a small investment, they might be able to use him in some future operation. Oswald's employment by the Jaggars-Chiles-Stovall Company (referred to by the Warren Commission as "a graphic arts company") could well have had a clandestine direction for Oswald; Jaggars-Chiles-Stovall did secret photographic work for the U.S. government. Oswald's employment there started (October 11, 1962) just days before the Cuban missile crisis.[30]

To re-iterate, perhaps both the CIA and the FBI may have had some relationship with Oswald. It seems that this became intensified (more likely with the CIA) when he returned to New Orleans in April 1963. Oswald was hired by the William B. Reily Coffee Company, though much of his actual time was spent as a courier for a clandestine research project headed by Alton Ochsner, M.D., presumably funded by the CIA. The project involved developing a fast-acting cancer which might successfully be used on Fidel Castro.[31] As a courier, Oswald received biological tissues from David Ferrie and took them to either Mary Sherman, M.D. or to Alton Ochsner, M.D. or to the Communicable Disease Laboratory at the US

Public Health Service. Oswald also was scheduled to take the developed cancerous materials to Mexico City to a drop where the cancerous material would then be taken to Cuba by another person.[32]

As indicated in Chapter 19, Oswald was determined to have an income of $3665.59 for the slightly less than two month period preceding his death. His expenses accounted for all but $168, close to the amount ($170) in his wallet, left in Marina's bedroom dresser[33] Other than $6 from Texas unemployment insurance.[34] and the $280 he would have earned employed at the Texas Schoolbook Depository, the bulk of his income would likely have been from the CIA sponsored bio-weapon program, developing materials to be used eliminating Fidel Castro.[35]

Was Oswald involved in a Conspiracy or Conspiracies to Assassinate JFK?

This is an interesting question. Insofar as Oswald is concerned, there are four different kinds of conspiracies he could have been involved with. The first is an actual conspiracy, where all participants were working together to effect the assassination of President Kennedy. The second is that Oswald was the only participant in the conspiracy actively pursuing JFK's assassination, with the other participants being informants to some other entity. The third possibility is that Oswald had infiltrated a group planning the assassination, and fourth, unbeknownst to the participants, *all* were persons who were seeing themselves as infiltrators to an actual assassination group, when in fact none of them were actually participating in any plan to assassinate the president.

The first scenario, that all participants were involved in an actual conspiracy, seems unlikely. If this were the case, they presumably were all being paid by the same entities. What Oswald would bring to such a group, other than as a patsy, seems questionable. The second scenario, while a possibility, seems ludicrous. Given that Oswald was in the lunchroom at the time of the assassination, or at least *not* on the sixth floor of the TSBD, this scenario can be discarded. The third scenario, that Oswald infiltrated a group planning the assassination probably seemed plausible to Oswald. It seems this is how he perceived the situation. Still, the last possibility seems the most attractive possibility. The actual planners of the assassination may have prepared each of the participants as potential patsies, while the actual assassination teams were going about planning the assassination. This scenario had to be discarded, at least by the Warren Commission, as the result the new president had in mind was a lone assassin. Finding a conspiracy was too messy. The so-called conspirators (the potential patsies) may be allowed to actually tell the truth, which could extend the Warren Commission's "deliberations" beyond the time of the November 1964 election; Johnson wanted the assassination removed as an issue prior to the November election. In fact, letting truth be known could have ended Johnson's presidency. Besides, to many in government, Oswald was conveniently dead. Any prior relationship between Lee Harvey Oswald and his assassin, Jack Ruby, could be denied.

Sorting out the Conspiracy Scenarios- A meeting of "Conspirators" in late August, 1963

We know from the work of Dick Russell[36] that, according to Richard Case Nagell, a meeting involving Oswald took place in an undisclosed location, but which might have been Houston. The date of the meeting was between August 23 and August 27, 1963. In attendance were Richard Case Nagell, Lee Harvey Oswald, "Angel," and a fourth unidentified person. Nagell claimed to have surreptitiously recorded the meeting;[37] Russell had never found the recording. Nagell was serving as a double agent, somewhat to his surprise. Nagell signed a contract in 1962, stating that he was employed by the CIA.[38] But it appeared that his orders were coming from the Soviet KGB. The Soviets were aware that there might be plots against President Kennedy; they wanted Nagell to "eliminate" Oswald because they feared that, were Kennedy to be assassinated, Oswald would be blamed and, by inference, because of Oswald's having lived in the USSR, Soviet Russia may be seen as directing his actions. Were Oswald dead, it would be much harder to blame the Soviets.[39]

Nagell was in a quandary over what to do. Nagell had gone to New Orleans in mid-September trying to convince Oswald to abandon his efforts, particularly of going to Mexico later that month. Then Nagell returned to Texas. He was in El Paso on the night of September 19, 1963, when he decided on his course of action. He did not wish to commit murder (on Oswald) particularly as it was being dictated to him by Soviet Russia. Nagell felt he had been "given over" to the KGB by the CIA, and he thus felt abandoned by the CIA. On the morning of September 20, 1963, he mailed three letters. One, containing $500 and an airline ticket to Mexico City, was sent to Oswald in New Orleans.

A letter was also sent to Desmond Fitzgerald, CIA, and a "nastier' note to another person in the CIA.[40] A question to be asked here – if Nagell was to eliminate Oswald if Oswald wouldn't change his plans, why then did Nagell personally pay Oswald's expenses and pay for the ticket to Mexico

City? One explanation is, this change of mind for Nagell occurred when he visited Oswald in New Orleans. Likely, Nagell figured out that Oswald was also involved in another CIA project (the project involving developing fast acting cancers to be used on Fidel Castro), and in a manner somewhat similar to Nagell, was also a double agent (CIA & FBI) and also trying to prevent Kennedy's assassination.

To this end, when Nagell showed up at the Consulate General's Office in Barcelona on March 10, 1969 to discuss his circumstances with Consul Richard C. Brown, Brown reported, "He [Nagell] said that the reason he was arrested in the first place [in El Paso] was he had worked with Lee Harvey Oswald in an assignment with a U.S. intelligence agency."[41] That would also mean that the August meeting was bogus. It would seem likely that all participants were playing a role for their separate handlers. Another possibility of course, is that if some entity wanted a patsy for the assassination: any one of the participants could have been used.

Nagell's plan was to have him enter a bank, carefully shoot into the ceiling so that no one was injured, and then walk out and wait to be arrested. Strangely, he thought his actions would result in a misdemeanor. Instead, Nagell was convicted of a felony, and he was imprisoned until 1968.[42]

Why Oswald?

Oswald was a convenient, designated scapegoat. By focusing on Oswald, the machinations and manipulations in the background would go undiscovered perhaps indefinitely, for those involved in framing him. Perhaps one of the few blanket statements that could be made about the JFK assassination is that Oswald was not the shooter. But at this point, pinpointing the actual shooters eludes us, perhaps forever. A likely scenario is that the shooter or shooters were themselves fairly quickly eliminated. Perhaps even those who eliminated them were eliminated themselves. What that suggests is that those planning the murder of President Kennedy hoped the truth would be skirted "long enough." Surely, long enough so that the principals would avoid exposure during their lifetimes.

The Maintaining of False Beliefs

One of the false beliefs which was disproven centuries ago, but still maintains adherents, is the concept of a flat earth. Even though disproven, there was concern that explorers like Columbus might fall off the edge of the earth. There still exists today a Flat Earth Society; their website is: http://flatearthsociety.org. There are still those who maintain, probably for religious reasons, that the earth is less than 11,000 years old; geology can't be right. Geology has made some mistakes, but suggesting the earth is much older than 11,000 years is not one of them. One of their mistakes, which was still being taught when I was an undergraduate student, is that there was no such thing as continental drift, a theory proposed in the early 1900's, and dismissed as impossible by the geologists of the day. In the middle 1960's, continental drift, under the new name "plate tectonics," replaced the concept of stationary continents.[43]

The idea that the earth was the center of the universe held sway even after the writings of Copernicus were published (shortly before and shortly after his death) in 1543. Galileo took up Copernicus' theory, and added his understanding of gravity. Still, Galileo was placed under house arrest for his final eight years, dying in 1642. By 1758 the Catholic Church lifted the ban on his books supporting Copernican theory.[44] And on November 4, 1992, Pope John Paul II announced that the denunciation of Galileo was a tragic error.[45] It took 358 years for an apology to be delivered.

How Does This Apply to Oswald?

It is clear that there can often be a long interval before appropriate corrections get made regarding tragic inaccuracies that have previously been accepted as true. In Oswald's situation, a political dimension impinges on accurate reporting. In most of the other cited cases, either a political or religious/political dimension was also present. Changing the verdict at the official level could be perceived by current stakeholders as endangering their position. Such a circumstance would lead to foot dragging or other delaying tactics. One such delaying tactic, if the preponderance of opinion were to accept that Oswald was not the shooter, would be to implicate Oswald in some other way, e.g., reposition Oswald as being involved in a conspiracy.

So, When Will Oswald be Exonerated?

Will it take as long as Galileo? That was 358 years. Perhaps an issue is that "solving" the assassination would be embarrassing to various parts of the government, and to influential families whose patriarchs participated in some way. Were we to know how parts of our government participated either in the assassination or the cover-up, it would be likely that many of us would demand change.

That change, would likely be considered dangerous to the status quo, which seems always to have its defenders. I would guess that the process for exonerating Oswald will remain slow. A difficulty for some is that, not only is Oswald a poor candidate for being the assassin, there presently doesn't seem to be a good replacement. Likely, the JFK assassination will move to the unsolved list, and that would not sit well with many. But finding the actual killer is not our present direction, though highly sought. Getting the person wrongly accused exonerated, however, is. It will take as long as it takes.

Endnotes

1 Posner, G. (1993). *Case Closed*. New York: Random House. For those that posit a possible shot from the Dal-Tex Building, Posner inadvertently shows the constructed ballistic evidence would include the Dal-Tex Building as being in the cones of possible origin of the shots. Posner eliminated this possibility by simply removing the Dal-Tex building from the drawings, thus leaving a "gaping" hole in his evidence. See Posner's Appendix A.

2 Bugliosi, V. (2007). *Reclaiming History: The Assassination of President John F. Kennedy*. New York: Norton.

3 Report of the President's Commission on the Assassination of President John F. Kennedy and the 26 Volumes of Hearings and Exhibits. (1964). Washington, D.C.: U.S. Government Printing Office. Incredibly, no index accompanied this voluminous work. Fortunately, an excellent index was eventually completed by Walt Brown: Brown, W. (1995). *Referenced Index Guide to the Warren Commission*. Wilmington, DE: Delmax.

4 Weisberg, H. & Lesar, J. (1974). *Whitewash IV: JFK Assassination Transcript*. Frederick, MD: Weisberg.

5 Willens, H.P. (1974). In Weisberg & Lesser, p. 25.

6 Williams, J.D. (2016). "Advocacy Research: Revisiting the Warren Commission." *Dealey Plaza Echo*, 1, 19, 14-19.

7 Lane, M. (1966). *Rush to Judgment*. New York: Holt, Rinehart & Winston, p. 9.

8 Shenon, P. (2013). *A Cruel and Shocking Act: The Secret History of the Kennedy Assassination*. New York: Henry Holt. p. 500.

9 Epstein, E.J. (1966). *Inquest: The Warren Commission and the Establishment of Truth*. New York: Viking Press.

10 Shenon.

11 Brown, W. (1998). "TSBD Evidence Places LBJ 'Hitman' in Sniper's Nest." Extra Edition of *JFK Deep Politics/Deep Politics Quarterly*, 3,3. A. Nathan Darby made a six-point match of Mac Wallace's fingerprint to the previously unidentified fingerprint found in the sniper's nest at the TSBD. Later, a 34-point match confirmed Wallace's presence on the sixth floor of the Depository, reported in Brown, W. (2001). "Malcolm Wallace Fingerprint: 'It's Him!!'" *JFK/ Deep Politics Quarterly*, 7,1,4-6. Among the critics of identifying Wallace from the fingerprint were Glen Sample and Mark Collom, who earlier wrote *The Men on the Sixth Floor* (1997). Garden Grove, CA: Sample Graphics. Sample & Collom had hypothesized that Wallace was present on the sixth floor of the Texas Schoolbook Depository at the time of the assassination. It seemed strange that they would question a finding that gave evidence that their earlier assertion was likely true.

12 Shenon, pp. 532-534.

13 CE 381.

14 Ernest, B. (2013). *The Girl on the Stairs*. Gretna, LA: Pelican. See also Williams, J.D. (2014). "The Girl on the Stairs-Was Oswald Even on the Sixth Floor at the Time of the Assassination?" *JFK-E/ Deep Politics Quarterly*, 1, 2, 3-16.

15 Turner, K.S. (1999)." From April to November and back Again." *The Third Decade*, 8, 1, 2-5. K.S. Turner was a pseudonym for Adele Edisen. She had also reported her experiences on the then extant website, JFK Research. H.P. Albarelli conducted several interviews with Edisen for his book, which also includes CIA clandestine use of hypnosis. Albarelli, H.P. (2013). *A Secret Order: Investigating the High Strangeness and Synchronicity of the JFK Assassination*. Waterville, OR: Trine Day, pp. 127-162.

16 John J. Abt was an attorney in New York City to whom Oswald attempted to place a collect call, but the call was refused; Abt was out of town at the time. Benson, M. (1993). *Who's Who in the JFK Assassination*. New York: Carol Publishing Group, p. 4.

17 Turner (1999), Albarelli (2013).

18 Woody Woodland Interview of Bill Kelly on "Between the Lines" live radio program on WSMN A.M. 1590, Nashua, NH December 29, 1999. See jfkcountercoup2.blogspot.com/2012/10/bill-kelley-interview-1999.html

19 Moore, N.M, & Darring, W. (1992). *Crossroader: Memoirs of a Professional Gambler*. Mobile: Regency Press.

20 FBI File no. 62-109060-741; AARB record no. 124-10056-10063.

21 Donelson, C. (1992). "Did the FBI ask Him about Oswald the Day before Kennedy Was Killed?" *Mobile Press Register*, February 23, p. 1A+.

22 A copy of that telegram can also be found in Williams, J.D. (2006). "Was the FBI searching for Oswald in Mobile on November 21, 1963?" *Dealey Plaza Echo*, 8, 2, 46-52.

23 Ruby Moore videotaped the meeting between Moore and Walter. Junior Moore sent me a copy of the videotape.

24 www://ctka.net/Let JusticeBeDone/notes.htm The copy of the telegram was provided by Judyth Baker.

25 Titovets, E. (2010). *Oswald Russian Episode*. Minsk, Belarus: Mon Litera Publishing House.

26 Baker, J.V. (2010). *Me & Lee: How I came to Know, Love and Lose Lee Harvey Oswald.* Walterville, OR: Trine Day.

27 Ibid., pp. 133-134.

28 Ibid., pp. 132-133.

29 Hunt, S.J. (2015). From Cuba to Watergate, Murder and the Deathbed Confession - My Parents. Presented at JFK Assassination Conference 2015, Dallas, Texas, November 22. Also see Hunt, S.J. (2012). *Bond of Secrecy: My Life with CIA Spy and Watergate Conspirator*. Walterville, OR: Trine Day.

30 Benson, M. (2002). *Encyclopedia of the JFK Assassination*. New York: Checkmark Books, p. 179.

31 Baker, pp.165-187.

32 Ibid., p. 482, p. 486, pp. 491-496.

33 Shenon, p. 452.

34 Armstrong, J. (2003). *Harvey & Lee: How the CIA Framed Oswald.* Arlington, TX: Quasar, p. 725.

35 Haslam, E. (2007). *Dr. Mary's Monkey: How the Unsolved Murder of a Doctor, a Secret Laboratory in New Orleans and Cancer-Causing Monkey Viruses are Linked to Lee Harvey Oswald, the JFK Assassination and Emerging Global Epidemics*. Walterville, OR: Trine Day p. 337.

36 Russell, D. (1992, 2003). *The Man Who Knew Too Much*. New York: Carroll & Graf. The page numbers in the references relate to the 2003 edition.

37 Russell (2003), p. 275.

38 Ibid., p. 283.

39 Loc. cit., p. 283

40 Ibid., p. 290.

41 Ibid., p. 437.

42 Ibid., pp. 1-3.

43 Henderson, B. (2014). *The Next Tsunami: Living on a Restless Coast*. Corvallis, OR: Oregon State University Press.

44 biography.com/people/Galileo

45 lavistachurchofchrist.org/LVarticles/LearningFromTheVaticansReversalOnGalileo.html

Chapter Twenty-Three

WHO IS RESPONSIBLE?

In addressing responsibility for the assassination of President Kennedy, a rehash of the several possible shooters is not the way to assign responsibility. In the previous Chapter we addressed the implausibility of Lee Harvey Oswald as the shooter; his involvement seemed to be more in trying to prevent the assassination. In that regard, he was unsuccessful.

In regard to the shooter(s), the likelihood is that whoever they were, they received the same treatment as Lee Harvey Oswald; that is, after the assassination, they were quickly dispatched, but without public notice. One such situation was described by Michael Milan.[1]

As a young man (Milan was born in 1924) Milan had been a boxer; Meyer Lansky bankrolled Milan's first professional fight. Lansky would serve as a mentor to Milan in the underworld of crime. He was a member of the Office of Strategic Services in 1944, serving in the European theatre. After his discharge, he became a trusted associate (like Meyer Lansky) of "The Families," perhaps better known as the Mafia. He was recruited by Frank Costello to be a strong man, helping to enforce the Luciano family's dealings. Costello was running the Luciano family while Luciano was in Sicily; Costello had become the "boss of bosses" in The Families.[2]

In 1947, Milan was recruited by J. Edgar Hoover of the FBI to be a member of Hoover's "Squad." These persons were known for their "enforcement" abilities, including being professional hitmen. Most had previous engagements with the law. They would do "jobs" that Hoover deemed necessary that were to "make things right," but illegal, often involving killing someone that in Hoover's view should be eliminated.[3]

By 1963, Michael Milan continued to do jobs for both the FBI and The Family, run by Frank Costello. Business for Milan from both the FBI and the Family had slowed down; it'd been over a year since his last hit. By this time Milan had become a car salesman in the New York City area, and was becoming used to the straight life, planning for when he might own his own car business. He was also promoting professional boxing matches, locally. On November 22nd, 1963, after 3:30 E.S.T. in New York, he heard that President Kennedy had been shot in Dallas. It was decided to close the business down for the weekend at the car dealership, with a sign, "Closed For The Afternoon in Respect for President Kennedy."[4]

Milan knew he should go to his other "office." Milan had an office at the precinct station on West 30th in New York City, where since 1962 Milan held the rank of Sergeant Detective in the NYC criminal intelligence unit. Milan had the ID and the shield to go along with his office, but this was set up apparently through the FBI. He had all the appearances of being a detective sergeant, but it was more a courtesy appointment. He would stop on many days to see if there were any phone calls for him to respond to. On this day, he was told, that his phone had been ringing constantly. The calls had been from Washington, D.C. There was a number on the desk for him to call. When Milan placed the call, he was patched directly to "Pencil" at Quantico. He was told he would need a handgun and a silencer. He would find tickets in an envelope with his name on it at the American Airlines counter at La Guardia Airport. His instructions were to call the Dallas Yellow Cab Company and ask that Gerald Brinkman be his driver. Milan would have a briefcase, which would be waiting for him at the luggage counter at the Dallas Airport, with his name on it; his destination was Dallas, and he would arrive early the next morning. After the business was completed at the Faracee's Disposal Company, he was to take the next flight to D.C.[5]

At 7 A.M., Milan met Brinkman, and they proceeded toward Faracee's Disposal Company. Brinkman was wary of what this ride might bring. Faracee's was at a deserted area near Fort Worth; there was no one around. Milan had told Brinkman that he was buying the place. Brinkman responded, "There's nobody here." Milan said, "I own the place and I'm here."

Brinkman turned to Milan and asked why was Milan going to kill him? Milan wanted to know more about the hit on President Kennedy. Brinkman denied any knowledge of the assassination, until Milan started to rough him up. Finally, Brinkman started to talk. Milan asked him, "Someone you never met before tells you someone you don't know wants you to shoot the president, and you expect me to believe that?" Brinkman replied, "That's not the way it was. I never met the man before I was introduced to him by this broad at the Carousel Club. And I didn't shoot nobody."[6]

Brinkman continued, "There was me and two other guys. We weren't even after the President. We were supposed to shoot the governor, but things happened too fast. They were gone before anybody could do anything."[7]

When asked who put out the contract, Brinkman answered, "I didn't know the guy. This gal over at the Carousel set us up. She knew I needed the dough and she got the OK from her boss."[8]

Her boss was, of course, Jack Ruby.[9]

Then, Milan told Brinkman to open the trunk. After this, Milan completed his assigned task, putting the body in the trunk, followed by the gun. Milan drove the cab to the edge of the junkyard where there was a giant magnet suspended by a crane by an autobody compression machine. Then, Milan went to the shack and found the keys to the car that he would drive to the airport, and catch the next plane to D.C.[10]

When Milan got to D.C., J. Edgar Hoover was waiting in the V.I.P. lounge. Hoover told Milan, "You already know too much... I'll just say: Johnson. No doubt. We stand away. You get it?" Hoover followed this with, "Take a long vacation. Very long."[11]

A point to be noted is that Milan wore several hats: FBI, Mafia, and New York Police Department, in addition to his car salesman hat. So also do many of the other actors in the assassination; to say that the CIA or the FBI or the Mafia, or some other organization was uniquely responsible for the assassination is simplistic and in error.

Chicago, Tampa, and Dallas: Three Cities, Three Patsies

Chapter 12 relates the details of three planned assassination attempts in November 1963: November 2 (Chicago), November 18 (Tampa) and November 22 (Dallas). This information was not publicly known until years later. The men had interesting similarities. Their public images were that they were loners, former servicemen, and had some degree of dissatisfaction with the social milieu. In reality, Oswald was more gregarious than his loner stereotype. Oswald's time in Russia[12] or in New Orleans[13] showed that he had a more normal social life than has been generally reported. With three different possible patsies, there clearly had to be coordination at some level to keep each of the potential patsies ready for use. Also, three different sets of shooters may even had to be available for their use as well.

Lee Harvey Oswald

The previous chapters go into detail about Oswald and his involvement in various clandestine activities. While Oswald was used as the patsy in Dallas, his efforts were more in the area of trying to avoid the assassination of President Kennedy. We know that at the time of the assassination Oswald was not on the sixth floor of the Texas Schoolbook Depository.

Lyndon Johnson

In some ways, Lyndon Johnson remains an enigma. He was personally involved in the assassination in at least two ways. First was the involvement of Johnson prior to the assassination. We know that from the Murchison party early November 22, 1963. From what he told his former mistress, Madeleine Brown, that he wouldn't have to put up with the Kennedy's anymore, it appeared that Johnson had perhaps just found out that the hit was on for later on November 22. (then, only hours away). The details he seemed to be aware of was that the shooting would occur in the motorcade, perhaps in Dealey Plaza. Johnson was unable to get President Kennedy to change the seating in the motorcade, moving John Connally from the President's limousine to the Vice-President's limousine, and moving Senator Yarborough from Johnson's limousine to President Kennedy's limousine. If the hit was on, one of Lyndon Johnson's best friends would be in the line of fire. Perhaps it speaks more of Lyndon Johnson's psychological make-up; Johnson's starting to duck as his limousine was turning to go through Dealey Plaza spoke more to concern that he too might be a target of an assassin's bullet. In retrospect, we know that no bullets landed in Johnson's limousine.

Lyndon Johnson's major aspect in the assassination conspiracy was in the cover-up. His major role here was appointing the Warren Commission. The new President appointed the seven members of the Commission that he wanted on the Commission. Chapter 19 addresses the methodology of the commission, which was to arrive at the "right" outcome in plenty of time prior to the November Presidential election. The direction of the Warren Commission was made apparent by the publication of the transcript of the first meeting of the President's Commission on the Assassination.[14]

In a generic sense, persons who were "LBJ men" may well have been closer to the center of assassination planning than was Johnson. This would include Ed Clark and Cliff Carter. Ed Clark was Lyndon Johnson's personal attorney and the head of his law firm. Clark, in 1948 had been Johnson's attorney for several years; in 1948, his team of lawyers created the Box 13 fiasco[15] which was instrumental in gaining Johnson the Democratic nomination for Senator over Coke Stevenson. After the assassination, Clark went about collecting two million dollars from the oil industry for "services rendered"- the elimination of President Kennedy.[16] Barr McClellan became aware of a huge trove of materials stored away from all inquiring eyes by Ed Clark relating to the activities of Lyndon Johnson. They were stored in the top floor of the building where Ed Clark's law firm was housed in Austin. To get to the penthouse a person would have to go through two locked doors. The Johnson materials were in an area with another barrier and lock. At that time, only Ed Clark had the key to this area.[17]

The sense of Cliff Carter being a "mastermind" in the assassination comes from Billie Sol Estes. Carter was the man in Washington who was coordinating activities around Johnson. Johnson's main job in Washington was to make sure President Kennedy got to Texas. Carter contacted (according to Estes) several top Mafia kingpins to arrange for possible shooters.[18]

The larger enigma regarding Lyndon Johnson was the change that took place shortly after the assassination. During his Vice-Presidency he took the position that the Kennedy administration should go slow on any number of issues relating to race, equality or other progressive ideas. Only hours before the assassination, Johnson was (apparently in anticipation of Kennedy's demise) boastful about never having to put up with the Kennedy's after tomorrow. Johnson's first legislative moves were to get Kennedy's programs passed in Congress as a memorial to Kennedy; in retrospect, Johnson saw these programs as programs that passed under Kennedy's name.

As time passed, as Johnson rolled out his "Great Society" programs, he was going beyond proposing social programs that Kennedy had endorsed. One difference was Johnson's going along with an expansion of the War in Vietnam, rather than contracting it (President Kennedy's plan for reducing, and by the end of 1965, eliminating, our involvement in Vietnam, was not known to the public). The rolling out of social programs continued through his presidency.

Perhaps the largest nemesis for Johnson was the war in Vietnam. It seemed to be the quicksand of his presidency. Then, there was the disaster of the USS *Liberty*. While this was kept a secret for many years (It is still secret; those who lived through it have given it considerable publicity, however). Perhaps Robert Dallek's characterization is reasonably accurate; Johnson was a "Flawed Giant."[19]

The CIA

In discussing the CIA in particular, persons involved likely have another entity with which they were involved. The CIA was involved with the finding and grooming of patsies. The CIA, after the Bay of Pigs, were involved with training Cuban exiles who were willing to go back for another invasion in Cuba. Several such training centers were in existence; one was near New Orleans. This training center was raided by the FBI in July, 1963. Bradley Ayers has written about his hand at a camp headquartered at buildings at the University of Miami. This effort was known as Zenith Technical Enterprises. It was known also as a part of JM/WAVE. Ayers was a Captain in the Army as a Ranger special operations officer; for the Zenith assignment, Ayers was on loan to the CIA. This assignment effectively ended with the assassination of President Kennedy.[20]

An important part of the CIA's effort against Cuba were the various plots for assassination of Fidel Castro. There were several different plots involving the efforts of the Mafia, often with a plan to poison Castro.[21] Another CIA operation that is highlighted in this book is the efforts to get a cancer agent that would relatively quickly kill Castro. This operation was run by Dr. Alton Ochsner in New Orleans. Judyth Baker was a cancer researcher in this operation, and Lee Harvey Oswald was a courier between researchers with specimens. It was also his job to take the cancer product to Mexico City and deliver it to a Cuban medical person who would take it back to Cuba to have it inoculated into Fidel Castro. Because of a hurricane in Cuba, the Cuban medical person did not show up.[22]

The FBI

The involvement of the FBI was generally limited to the top-level personnel, particularly J. Edgar Hoover. Hoover was a conduit of information to Lyndon Johnson; Hoover called for at least one killing of a shooter in the assassination. The FBI agents were the mainstay of investigation for the Warren Commission. In this role, the FBI agents apparently did not vary significantly from their usual investigative procedures. Through the Freedom of Information Act and the Assassination Records Review Board, many of their reports have been made available to the public. Hoover was said to have enmity toward President Kennedy, because the President did not wish to allow Hoover to continue as the Director of the FBI after he reached the age of mandatory retirement at 70 on January 1, 1965.[23] Hoover had an FBI report of the assassination prepared in early December, 1963. In the report, three shots were described, two hitting President Kennedy, and one hitting Governor Connally. No missed shots were described. When the Warren Commission came up with the "magic bullet theory," requiring one shot to have hit both President Kennedy and Governor Connally, to make up for the shot that missed the Presidential limousine entirely and hit the curbing in front of the limousine, causing an injury to James Tague.[24] Hoover chose not to alter the original FBI report after the Warren Commission invented the "magic bullet theory."

The Mafia

The Mafia, or their preferred name, "The Families" had several grievances against President Kennedy. Their view was that for the help provided JFK in the 1960 election, both monetarily and for delivering Illinois in the Kennedy column through, among other things, "graveyard voting" , that is, the casting of votes by persons who have already died. For their efforts, they found JFK appointing his brother Robert Kennedy as Attorney General, who in turn pursued "The Families," and in particular James Hoffa, President of the Teamsters Union. For others, the distress with the Kennedy's was more personal. Carlos Marcello, the Don in New Orleans, had been deported; others faced deportation. Those involved in gambling and prostitution in Cuba lost significant income, and American playboys lost their Caribbean playground.

The Mafia began a series of plots to assassinate Fidel Castro. They were working in tandem with the CIA in this regard. But it is much more likely that the Mafia were in a secondary position to other entities. The Mafia most likely played a role in recommending potential shooters for at least the three known sites of possible assassinations (Chicago, Tampa, and Dallas). It is likely the Mafia served a role in eliminating persons who could have caused the cover-up to unravel. As secondary actors, it is likely that the Mafia was paid at least some of their expenses (if not significantly more) for their actions.

One of their more interesting payoffs came from Jimmy Hoffa, who had pleaded with Santo Trafficante, the Don in Tampa to "get rid of President Kennedy." Trafficante decided to take advantage of Hoffa after the assassination. By getting the word to Hoffa that now that he got what he wanted, it was time for the payoff. Hoffa arranged for a "loan" of $4.6 million dollars from the Teamsters, to build a hospital in Hialeah, Florida.[25] Trafficante apparently also bilked the CIA for unperformed services related to the "get Castro" project.[26]

The Secret Service

The Secret Service's involvement in the assassination was mainly in security stripping.[27] This included many of them being in less than their best physical and mental condition due to their late-night drinking into the morning of November 22, 1963. Other security stripping was the relative lack of security available for the Dallas trip. Apparently, someone reduced the number of motorcycle police, none of whom were abreast of the limousine. At the time of the shooting only one Secret Service agent, Clint Hill, actually got to the limousine; a second agent attempted to get to the Presidential limousine but was ordered back to the Secret Service automobile.

As the limousine was parked at Parkland hospital Secret Service agents began cleaning up the blood, thus beginning the destruction of evidence. Back at the White House garage, the evidence was further tampered with by the Secret Service as they continued trying to clean out the limousine, which was then flown to Dearborn Michigan, where the windshield was replaced, the old one destroyed and the interior of the automobile redone. The only persons with the authority to have these changes made were President Lyndon Johnson and Chief of the Secret Service James Rowley.[28]

The Secret Service was instrumental in removing President Kennedy's body at gunpoint from Parkland Hospital in Dallas. This removal was illegal; by law, murders in Texas required a Texas autopsy. At the autopsy, Admiral Burkley, who was also President Kennedy's personal physician, would have had an interest in the pathologists' work at the autopsy. He may have had an objective to *not* divulge information regarding President Kennedy being afflicted by Addison's disease.

The Military

When President Eisenhower was leaving office, he warned against "the military-industrial complex." He had initially intended to warn of "the military-*congressional*-industrial complex" but was talked out of this appellation.[29] By continuing the cold war, the military machine was being fed, requiring more expansion of military goods and fattening the bottom line of military suppliers. Congress would have to approve these expenditures. To ensure that the largess kept on coming, campaign contributions would need to be made to an increasing number of congressmen. Will Rogers said it best, "America has the best politicians money can buy."[30]

What would be the reason(s) the military wished to be relieved of President Kennedy? First, there was the Bay of Pigs fiasco. Given the failure of the Cuban exiles to begin a counter-revolution against Fidel Castro (and relieve the US of having a Communistic nation only 90 miles away), President Kennedy refused to send in massive air support to overthrow Castro (never mind that the CIA had lied to Kennedy about the effectiveness of the exiles in gaining support on the island of Cuba). At the time of the Cuban missile crisis, Kennedy refused to allow the military to go in and overturn Castro's regime.[31] Then, on June 10, 1963, in his Peace Speech at American University in Washington, DC, Kennedy stated that he intended to work toward Peace with the Soviet Union, and he intended to enter into a test ban treaty with them. Finally, President Kennedy issued NSAM 263 in which he intended to bring home 1000 troops by the end of 1963 and withdraw all American troops by the end of 1965.

Also to be taken into consideration was the calculation by military planners that there would be a window of opportunity, from Spring 1962, right through the Autumn of 1963, in which the United States could launch a first strike against the Soviet Union, survive the collateral damage, and "win" the Cold War."[32] Never mind that the carnage in innocent persons killed in such a scenario would have been in, all probability, the worst ever experienced. November 22, 1963 was near the end of Autumn, and still within the window of opportunity for launching a first-strike against the Soviet Union.

What we do know of military involvement in particular is the autopsy of President Kennedy. The military brass present made a shambles of the autopsy. After the news of President Kennedy's assassination became known to General LeMay, who immediately began plans to get to the autopsy in Bethesda. A plane was flown from Andrews Air Base to Wairton. A message was also sent by Secretary of the Air Force Eugene M. Zuckert to LeMay for him to meet Zuckert at Andrews Air Base, to be there for the arrival of President Kennedy's body. LeMay chose to disobey his Superior, clearly to facilitate his own arrival at the Bethesda Hospital where the autopsy was to be performed. During the autopsy, one or more high military brass shouted out to the pathologists conducting the autopsy as to what they could or couldn't do. The autopsy did not include tracing the routes of the bullets that hit Kennedy during the assassination. The pictures and x-ray's have several issues of either removal, or attempts to change the nature of the pictures. Some of the pictures appear to be contradictory- some pictures exist that show the back of President Kennedy's head to be intact (these might have come from the work done by morticians as they reconstructed his head, in case of an open casket viewing), there are other pictures showing the blowout of the back of President Kennedy's head.

The Oil Cartel

One concern of the oilmen was the idea that President Kennedy was thinking of reducing the oil depletion allowance from 27.5% to

17.5%. The oil cartel, which had both H.L. Hunt and Clint Murchison in their fold, would have been unlikely to be in the group of individuals who called the shots on President Kennedy, but they surely were in a position to take part in financing them. Wars have a collateral outcome of needing war materials that are supplied by well-paid war-related industries, several of which happened to be in Texas. "Of LBJ, the Texans demanded a war. The Texas defense industry was mammoth." Madeleine [Brown] remembers Lyndon saying, 'Goddam. I'll give him the war.'"[33]

The Military-Congressional-Industrial Complex

As pointed out earlier in this chapter, Walt Brown indicated that President Eisenhower initially intended to warn against the military-congressional-industrial complex, though he was talked into not including the political aspect in his warning.[34] Discussed herein are members of each of those entities. Baker & Schwartz point out that, "The beneficiaries of the illegal system that came into power with JFK's death selected and groomed their heirs, keeping the government in the hands of an oligarchy that cannot allow the truth to be exposed, lest they lose control."[35]

The Warren Commission

When approached about heading the President's Commission on the Assassination of John F. Kennedy, Supreme Court Chief Justice Earl Warren at first declined, due to potential conflict of interest concerns, were a case from the assassination to reach the Supreme Court. Also, Warren was being asked to take a job in the Executive Branch of the government, which would conflict with his position in the Supreme Court. Warren did not wish to be part of a process that might lead to a "rush to judgment."[36] President Johnson brought up the suggestion that Cuban or Soviet involvement in the assassination would provoke an international crisis. Johnson feared "that it might even catapult us into a nuclear war if it got a head start."[37] This appeal appeared to work. The Warren Commission had a strong expectancy: to come up with a report that would avoid a conspiracy, any international implications, and be finished sufficiently before the next presidential election. The initial meeting of the Commission (January 27, 1964) was characterized by Howard Willens as searching for a means of foisting off a preconceived conclusion, hiding what actually happened in Dallas.

There were two aspects to the investigation that had already begun by the FBI. They would interview witnesses, or persons who potentially had relevant information. While the investigation process of the FBI could be criticized, to their credit they did not substantially alter that process for this particular investigation. Their skepticism would show up in evaluating the collected information. On the other hand, the staff of the Warren Commission conducted a much smaller number of interviews, usually by the lawyers on their staff. The handling of these interviews could tend to re-orient the testimony to meet the needs of a prosecutorial approach vis a vis 1964. Evidence veering away from the preconceived conclusion was often ignored, and in the case of at least one witness, substantially altered to keep alive the assumption that Lee Harvey Oswald was on the sixth floor of the Texas Schoolbook Depository at the time of the assassination. Were Oswald not on the sixth floor, the whole case would be altered. Some of the exculpatory evidence was published in the accompanying 26 volumes to the Warren Report, and more was made available due to the Assassination Records Review Board in the 1990's.

The Commission chose not to have a lawyer represent the interests of Lee Harvey Oswald. Oswald's mother contacted Mark Lane (who would later author *Rush to Judgment.*)[38] Lane in turn contacted the Warren Commission and offered to represent Oswald's interest pro bono. His offer was turned down.

And the dreams of President Kennedy, of world peace, of a world not at the will of a Pentagon and the corporate military industrialists lining their pockets with an unending banquet at the military trough; a world safe from annihilation from the sky, or poisoning from radiation, and a world where co-operation, not competition, would be the preferred mode of political life.

The dreams of President Kennedy died in Dealey Plaza. "(T)here had to be a command and control structure to guarantee that nothing would occur or be discovered that could seriously jeopardize the facade of an execution that had been performed not by a military-industrial-intelligence combine, but rather by a lone malcontent against which there is no protection."[39]

Endnotes

1 Michael Milan is a pseudonym of an otherwise unnamed person. Milan was a hitman for both the Mafia and J. Edgar Hoover's FBI. Milan, M. (1989). *The Squad: The US Government's Secret Alliance with Organized Crime*. New York: Shapolsky Publishers.

2 Ibid., pp. 1-37.

3 Ibid., pp.38-49.

4 Ibid., pp. 216-221.

5 Ibid., pp. 221-224. The name Gerald Brinkman was likely a pseudonym.

6 Ibid., p. 232.

7 Loc. cit.

8 Loc. cit.

9 Loc. cit.

10 Ibid., pp. 233-234.

11 Ibid., p. 234.

12 Titovets, E. (2010). *Oswald Russian Episode*. Minsk, Belarus: MonLitera Publishing Company.

13 Baker, J.V. (2010). *Me & Lee: How I Came to Know, Love, and Lose Lee Harvey Oswald*. Walterville, OR: Trine Day.

14 Weisberg, H. (1974). *Whitewash IV: JFK Assassination Transcript*. Frederick, MD.: Author.

15 McClellan, B. (2003). *Blood. Money and Power: How L.B.J. Killed J.F.K.* New York: Hannover House, pp. 9, 12, 81. Also see Williams, J.D. (2004). "What McClellan Does not Tell Us." *JFK/Deep Politics Quarterly*, 9, 3, 19-29.

16 Ibid., pp. 231-235, p. 242.

17 Ibid., pp. 223-225.

18 Estes, B.S. (2005}. *Billie Sol Estes: A Texas Legend*. Granbury, TX: BS Productions.

19 Dallek, R. (1998). *Flawed Giant: Lyndon Johnson and his Times 1961-1973*. New York: Oxford University Press.

20 Ayers, B.E. (1976). *The War that Never Was: An Insider's Account of CIA Covert Operations Against Cuba*. New York: Bobbs-Merrill; Ayers, B.E. (2006). *The Zenith Secret: A CIA Insider Exposes the Secret War Against Cuba and the Plot that Killed the Kennedy Brothers*. Brooklyn: Vox Pop.

21 Ragano, F. & Raab, S. (1994). *Mob Lawyer*. New York: Scribner's, pp: 209-210, pp. 323-326, p. 341, p. 356, p. 357.

22 Baker, Ibid.; Haslam, E.T. (1995). *Mary, Ferrie & the Monkey Virus: The Story of an Underground Medical Laboratory*. Albuquerque: Wordsworth Communications; Haslam, E.T. (2007). *Dr. Mary's Monkey: How the Unsolved Murder of a Doctor, a Secret Laboratory in New Orleans and Cancer Causing Viruses are Linked to Lee Harvey Oswald, the JFK Assassination and Emerging Global Epidemics*. Walterville, OR: Trine Day.

23 North, M. (1991). *Act of Treason: The Role of J. Edgar Hoover in the Assassination of President Kennedy*. New York: Carroll & Graf, p. 121.

24 Tague, J.T. (2003). *Truth Withheld: A Survivor's Story*. Dallas: Excel Digital Press.

25 Ragano & Raab, pp. 160-161.

26 Ibid., p. 149, p. 340; Demaris, O. (1981, 2010). *The Last Mafioso: The Treacherous World of Jimmy ("the weasel") Fratianno*. The Bronx: Ishi Press.

27 Palamara, V. (1993). *The Third Alternative* – "Survivor's Guilt" The Secret Service and the JFK Murder." Pittsburgh, PA: Author.

28 Weldon, D. (2000). "The Kennedy Limousine: Dallas 1963," in Fetzer, J.H. (2000). *Murder in Dealey Plaza: What We Know Now that We Didn't Know Then About the Death of JFK*. Chicago: Catfeet Press, pp. 129-158.

29 Brown, W. (2014,2015). *The Kennedy Execution: Six Seconds that kept the Military-Industrial Complex Alive*. Hillsdale, NJ: Author.

30 willrogerstoday.com/will-rogers-quotes//quotes.cfm?qID=4. Retrieved 3/18/2018.

31 Several years later we found out that (a) the captain of the Soviet submarine stopped by the American blockade had nuclear weapons on his ship and the authority to use them; he decided to not proceed unless given a specific order from Moscow, (b) the missiles in Cuba were prepared for launch. Starting a nuclear war could have caused untold millions of lost lives.

32 Brown W., (2014, 2015), p. 211.

33 Brown, M. and Kritzberg, C. (1997). *Dallas Did It!* Dallas: Authors, p.52.

34 Brown, W. (2014, 2015).

35 Baker, J.V. & Schwartz, E. (2017). *Kennedy & Oswald: The Big Picture*. Walterville, OR:Trine Day, p. 140.

36 Brown, W. (1996). *The Warren Omission: A Micro-Study of the Methods and Failures of the Warren Commission*. Wilmington, DE: Delmax, p. 39.

37 Dallek, pp. 51-52.

38 Lane, M. (1966). *Rush to Judgment*. New York: Holt, Rinehart & Winston.

39 Brown, W. (2014, 2015), p. 271.

Chapter Twenty-Four

THE CONTINUING COVER-UP

While Lyndon Johnson was the "author" of the original cover-up of the JFK assassination, the continuing cover-up, particularly after his death in 1973, was carried on by those who still had something to lose. True, Lady Bird Johnson and Jack Valenti successfully stopped the distribution of Episode 9 of *The Men Who Killed Kennedy,* which was shown on the History Channel. This episode addressed Johnson's involvement in the conspiracy. But the cover-up continues to the present.

Of course, the first, and most massive cover-up of the JFK Assassination was the Warren Commission Report at the behest of Lyndon Johnson. The report of this Commission held the status as the official report of the United States government. Some still hold this report as being the final word on the JFK assassination.

The Manchurian Candidate Who Couldn't Shoot Straight

Robert Kennedy had begun collecting evidence that could be used in a new inquiry about his brother's assassination; the necessary major step was to seek the presidency where he could control a new investigation. Bobby's announcement of seeking the Democratic nomination closely coincided with Lyndon Johnson's announcement that he would neither seek nor accept the nomination of his party for another term as President.

Effectively, the contenders for the Democratic nomination were Senator Eugene McCarthy, Vice-President Hubert Humphrey, and Senator Robert Kennedy. Senator McCarthy had been the major factor in Johnson's choice not to run again, given McCarthy's surprising showing in the New Hampshire primary, gaining 42% of the primary votes to President Johnson's 49%. Hubert Humphrey was seeking support outside the primaries. Senator Kennedy was making a determined effort to run in the remaining primaries as well as seek delegates in non-primary states. The focal point was the California primary. Winning the California primary was Kennedy's best chance at the Democratic nomination. Stopping Robert Kennedy was seen as imperative to avoid a reopening of the JFK assassination.

Robert Kennedy won the winner-take-all California Democratic Presidential primary. After delivering his victory speech with "Let's go to Chicago, and win!," Senator Kennedy began walking toward the pantry, and shots rang out. Senator Kennedy, surrounded by bodyguards, was hit by at least three shots. The young Sirhan Sirhan was pounced on by the bodyguards. Sirhan was shooting up as Senator Kennedy was walking on a stage above the area where Sirhan was standing. Sirhan was immediately taken into custody by the Los Angeles police. Senator Kennedy never regained consciousness and succumbed to his wounds.

The coroner responsible for doing an autopsy on Senator Robert Kennedy was Tom Noguchi, M.D. Dr. Noguchi was well aware of the foibles of the botched autopsy of President Kennedy. As is described in Chapter 21, Dr. Noguchi was able to avoid the issues that plagued the autopsy of President Kennedy for Robert Kennedy.[1] The failure of Sirhan Sirhan's court appointed attorney to address the forensic evidence, which showed that Sirhan was not the shooter of the fatal shot, and strongly suggest that the actual assassin should be sought, the outcome of the trial could have been different, particularly in forcing the seeking of the actual assassin. Sirhan was originally sentenced to the death penalty, which turned into a life sentence due to a 1972 Supreme Court decision eliminating the death penalty.[2]

The Inheritance and the JFK Assassination

After the assassination of President Kennedy, his personal secretary, Mrs. Evelyn Lincoln, moved her office to the National Archives, where she was entrusted with various documents and artifacts from the time that JFK was elected to the Senate until his assassination. Through the years, Mrs. Lincoln gifted or sold various specimens from the Kennedy collection. She became friendly with a young man named Robert White, who had the ambition to build a museum to John F. Kennedy.

Upon her death in 1994, Robert White was willed a significant portion of the remaining items under Mrs. Lincoln's trust.[3] White had begun his effort to planning for his future museum. In that process he had begun selling some of the pieces to Christopher Fulton, a young successful builder who lived in Vancouver, British Columbia. Fulton held both American and Canadian citizenship. Unknown to Fulton, White did not hold actual ownership of the items sold to Fulton (probably unknown to White as well).

JFK's Gold Cartier Watch

One of the items purchased by Christopher Fulton from the inheritance of Robert White was a gold Cartier watch. Fulton knew that the watch was given to John Kennedy by his wife Jaqueline as an anniversary gift when he was a Senator. Fulton was otherwise unaware of the watch's history. After Senator Kennedy wore the watch during his 1960 Presidential campaign, the watch was put away by Jaqueline; John Kennedy secured another watch that he preferred. Prior to going to Dallas, the Secret Service supposedly were doing a routine radiation check for metallic materials worn by President Kennedy; presumably they would be returned to him after he returned to Washington. One could posit that this action by the Secret Service was another aspect of security-stripping related to the Dallas trip.[4] When President Kennedy turned to look at his watch on the trip, she noticed he did not have one; His wife retrieved his gold Cartier watch from her effects and handed the watch to him in Dallas.[5]

This information became known to Fulton in an encounter with person associated with the Canadian Security Intelligence Service. Fulton also learned that the watch was the one worn by JFK on the day of the assassination and the watch had been sought by the CIA and the Mafia for 33 years.[6]

Still unclear to both White and Fulton was that, because the watch was worn by President Kennedy at the time of the assassination, it was covered by the act of 1965 that included assassination materials. By that act, assassination materials related to President Kennedy were deemed to be owned by the United States government and were not subject to any other disposal. It can be conjectured that Johnson feared Bobby Kennedy was amassing evidence against him – the act would require these materials to be turned over to the government. Thus, the Kennedy's were apparently acting on the belief that the act did not pertain, or should not pertain, to them.

Most of the assassination-day materials were turned over to the FBI laboratory for analysis; but not the gold Cartier watch. Fulton began investigating the chain of custody for the watch. It was originally removed from President Kennedy's wrist and taken by nurse Diana Bowron in Trauma Room One of Parkland Hospital; she turned it over to O.P. Wright, head of security at Parkland Hospital. Wright turned it over to Roger Warner, Secret Service agent, who turned the watch over to Robert Bouck (SS) who turned it over to Clint Hill (SS), who then gave the watch back to Jacqueline Kennedy. From there, it came into the possession of Evelyn Lincoln.[7]

Fulton's Conversations with Robert Bouck

Having the gold Cartier watch became the ticket of admission to intriguing conversations with Robert Bouck, a venerable long term former Secret Service employee. Bouck retired from the secret service in 1969 after 30 years of service. Fulton's conversations with Robert Bouck began in August, 1997. Bouck was forthcoming on many issues of interest to Fulton regarding the Kennedy presidency and details following the assassination. It became clear to Fulton that Bouck had presumed Fulton to be an agent for John F. Kennedy, Jr. Fulton chose not to attempt to dispel Bouck of this misunderstanding. Among the revelations made to Fulton were several points that either confirm suspicions or may be new information.

The taking of President Kennedy's metallic materials was done by a Secret Service Agent. The securing of the metallic objects removed the possibility that they might serve as some degree of protection on November 22, 1963. Robert Bouck told Fulton about the re-interment of President Kennedy with considerable assassination materials that Robert Kennedy had collected to be placed in his brother's coffin – and to be brought out when Robert Kennedy had become president. The re-interment took place in March 1967.

Earlier, Bobby had become so upset with Johnson, that he held the Cartier watch for Johnson to see, and demanded to know why Johnson had killed his brother. Johnson then (1965) had congress pass a bill requiring that all evidence in the assassination of President Kennedy had to be turned over to the federal government to be secured and classified. Bobby decided that he would not give up evidence; Jackie also gave Bobby evidence to put in the coffin of President Kennedy.

Jackie was asked by Bobby Kennedy to get back the pink suit she wore during the assassination. She was refused by the government. No one was supposed to get to look at these clothes until 2103, and they would never be subject to public display or research.

In the assassination, President Kennedy was hit by a frangible bullet filled with mercury. The bullet entered his right temple and exploded inside the President's head. The mercury would have disbursed in fragments in his head, strewing his blood, brain and skull fragments all over Jackie, the back of the limousine, and the windshield of the car behind them. The Cartier watch was less than 5 inches away from the explosion. Both the watch and Jackie's pink outfit would likely yield evidence that would be inconsistent with the Warren Report.

Bouck mentioned that the Cartier watch had been tested. Fine striations had been caused by the shockwave of the bullet. Mercury and other particles had been embedded in the crystal, as well as inside the watch. The mercury was consistent with top grade U.S. munitions.[8]

Fulton Makes the FBI's 10 Most Wanted List

Fulton made the FBI's Most Wanted List, with the admonition that he was armed and dangerous, This action was preceded by his selling the Cartier watch, garnering him $604,000. It was bought at auction, in all likelihood by John F. Kennedy, Jr. The two had discussed the issue privately and agreed on a public sale through auction. The actual charges against Fulton included structuring to avoid tax reporting requirements – this could be charged to any individual who moves over $10,000, even internally among their own bank accounts. This may have been in relation to his sale of the Cartier watch. Also, a second charge was bank fraud, stemming from his obtaining credit cards with statement of income/assets higher than his actual assets. A third charge was using the credit cards which stemmed from the fraudulent statements.

Fulton was picked up and held in a Canadian detention center until extradition to the United States could be addressed. Were he only a Canadian citizen, it would have been difficult to extradite him. But Fulton was a dual Canadian/American citizen. Given that fighting extradition would only delay the process, Fulton waived his rights, and was flown from Vancouver, BC to Seattle, Washington.

In the custody of the United States federal government, he became accustomed to con-air and Diesel Therapy. Con-air was the airplanes used by the American government to transport persons in custody. Diesel Therapy was the inane process of continuous touch-and-goes, where the airplane would come to an airport, touch down and immediately take off again, from early morning until darkness. Finally, they would land, take the plane-load of persons in custody to another detention center, stay there till 4 A.M., and repeat, day in and day out. This went on for about a month. Apparently, this was done to break the spirit of the detainees. Some might call this cruel and unusual punishment. The detainees were not convicted, and many had not even been charged.[9]

Further Detention and the Legal Proceedings

Fulton was finally placed in the Charles County Detention Center in La Plata, Maryland. From here at some point, he would be interrogated, though he never knew when. The interrogations were done to insure that he would not have a lawyer with him. When Fulton was finally interrogated, he took the position that he simply wouldn't talk to his tormentors. During the last interrogation (March 31, 1999), the interrogator, asked Fulton "Mr. Fulton, are you aware of law 89-318 enacted November 2, 1965?" Fulton answered, "No," the interrogator continued, "The provisions of this law make it clear that all Kennedy materials directly related to President Kennedy's assassination are evidence, rightfully belonging to the U.S. government. A federal order was issued that all such materials be turned over to the government within one year of the law's enactment. Thus you are guilty of harboring assassination evidence, and the government considers you to be an accessory after the fact in the murder of President Kennedy." Fulton thought to himself, "How clever-If you don't turn over evidence that proves there was a conspiracy ... to the very people who are protecting that conspiracy, you will be the one accused of aiding and abetting."[10]

During the time he was originally put into custody, two persons seemed to be present, an agent of the IRS and one from of the FBI. The FBI agent seemed to have some empathy for Fulton. Just prior to the court hearing, he told Fulton to do exactly as he said: Take this note and hand it to the judge *before* the decision is made. Don't let anyone stop you.

Fulton followed this order, to the dismay of the prosecution. The judge read the note, and then got up and walked out. While not knowing the contents of the note, Fulton felt that it might have some positive value to him. He would later find that it read: "Working under executive order of Ronald Reagan, President of the United States."[11]

The Sentence

The prosecutor, formally recommended a sentence of 25 years. A federal judge pronounced a sentence of 102 months, counting time served. Fulton had less than eight years to go. His life would continue on hold. He was first incarcerated at Loretto Prison in Lorretto, PA.[12]

The Ensuing Incarceration

During Fulton's stay at Loretto, a minimum-security prison, his life was riddled with personal losses. Both his grandparents had died. He was informed by his in-laws that his wife had left him. Also, on July 16, 1999, John F. Kennedy, Jr., his wife and sister-in-law were killed in an airplane crash into the ocean near Long Island.

Loretto was a breeze in comparison to his earlier incarceration experiences. After several months he was transferred to the Lewisburg, PA Prison and Camp.

At several camps both before and after his formal conviction, Fulton met inmates who could enlighten him about his circumstances as he became aware of theirs. At Lewisburg, he met a former policeman who had tape recorded Arabic speaking persons at the barber shop he frequented. He had the tape translated; they were going through flight training and mentioned the towers. The former policeman was arrested by the FBI for helping illegal immigrants get jobs. Shortly after his arrest, the twin towers went down on 9/11/2001.[13]

The Continuing Cover-up

The inescapable conclusion is that there is still something that desperately needs to be kept hidden from the public regarding the assassination of President John F. Kennedy. But to keep these things hidden, more crimes and the miscarriage of justice continue to be committed by government actors. It would be difficult to list all of the changes that have occurred in American society related to the continuing cover-up. Even picking the ugliest would be daunting. But one change that should seem to cause disbelief is the the military sending their surplus military equipment to local police departments and sheriff's offices. The outcome of this is that now local police have armored vehicles, tanks and military-level heavy weaponry at their disposal. The use of these materials would give every appearance of a war zone. While this gesture might be good for the continued production of war materials, keeping the military-industrial complex in high gear production, such a policy is inconsistent with a democratic free society.

Endnotes

1 Wecht, C. (1993, 1994). *The Cause of Death: The Shocking True Stories Behind the Headlines-a Forensic Expert Speaks out on JFK, RFK, Elvis, Chappaquiddick, and other Controversial Cases.* New York: Penguin Books, pp. 78-80.

2 Ibid., pp. 85-90.

3 Roth, J. M. (2006). "Reclaiming Pieces of Camelot: How NARA and the JFK Library Recovered Missing Documents and Artifacts." *Prologue Magazine*, 38, 2. Retrieved from archives/publications/Prologue/2006/summer/Camelot.html, 12/1/2018.

4 See Palamara, V.M. (2013). *Survivors Guilt: The Secret Service and the Failure to Protect President Kennedy*. Walterville, OR: Trine Day. According to Palamara, many aspects of the Secret Service's behavior and decision making was commensurate to specifically stripping security for the Dallas trip.

5 Fulton, C, & Fulton, M. (2018). *The Inheritance: Poisoned Fruit of JFK's Assassination*. Walterville, OR: Trine Day.

6 Ibid., pp. 15-18.

7 Ibid., pp. 27-30.

8 Ibid., pp. 96-130.

9 Ibid., pp. 189-230.

10 Ibid., p. 285.

11 Ibid., pp. 283-284, 286-287.

12 There was a change in judges. Judge Harris had sent to Judge Chadawick pertinent information from the earlier hearings, including the information that Fulton was working under the orders of former President Ronald Reagan.

13 The book describing Christopher Fulton's struggles, *The Inheritance* is both informative and, frankly, an exciting read.

Index

A

B

Q

R

S

T

U

V

W

Y

Z

Dr. Mary's Monkey

How the Unsolved Murder of a Doctor, a Secret Laboratory in New Orleans and Cancer-Causing Monkey Viruses are Linked to Lee Harvey Oswald, the JFK Assassination and Emerging Global Epidemics

BY EDWARD T. HASLAM, FOREWORD BY JIM MARRS

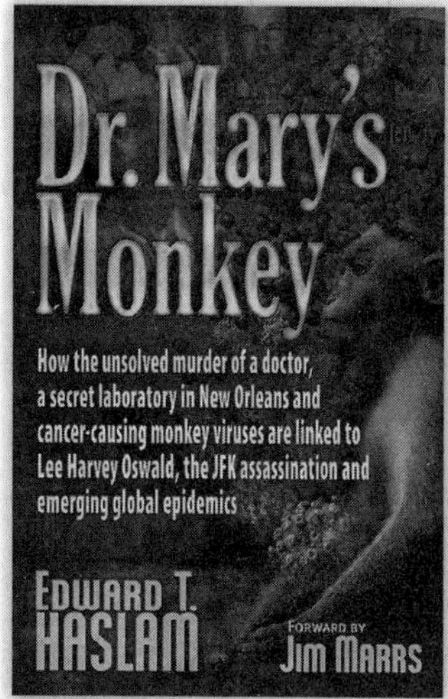

Evidence of top-secret medical experiments and cover-ups of clinical blunders
The 1964 murder of a nationally known cancer researcher sets the stage for this gripping exposé of medical professionals enmeshed in covert government operations over the course of three decades. Following a trail of police records, FBI files, cancer statistics, and medical journals, thisscontaminated polio vaccine, the genesis of the AIDS virus, and biological weapon research using infected monkeys.

Softcover: **$19.95** (ISBN: 9781634240307) • 432 pages • Size: 5 1/2 x 8 1/2
Hardcover: **$24.95** (ISBN: 9781937584597)

Me & Lee

How I Came to Know, Love and Lose Lee Harvey Oswald

BY JUDYTH VARY BAKER

FOREWORD BY EDWARD T. HASLAM

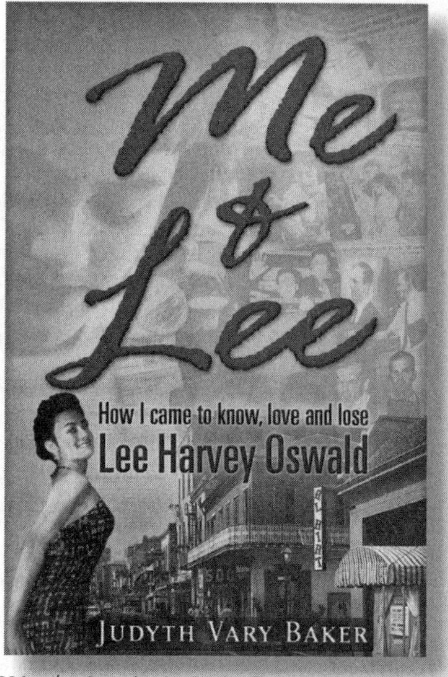

JUDYTH VARY WAS ONCE A PROMISING science student who dreamed of finding a cure for cancer; this exposé is her account of how she strayed from a path of mainstream scholarship at the University of Florida to a life of espionage in New Orleans with Lee Harvey Oswald. In her narrative she offers extensive documentation on how she came to be a cancer expert at such a young age, the personalities who urged her to relocate to New Orleans, and what lead to her involvement in the development of a biological weapon that Oswald was to smuggle into Cuba to eliminate Fidel Castro. Details on what she knew of Kennedy's impending assassination, her conversations with Oswald as late as two days before the killing, and her belief that Oswald was a deep-cover intelligence agent who was framed for an assassination he was actually trying to prevent, are also revealed.

JUDYTH VARY BAKER is a teacher, and artist. Edward T. Haslam is the author of *Dr. Mary's Monkey*.

Hardcover • $24.95 • Softrcover • $21.95 ISBN 9780979988677 / 978-1936296378 • 608 Pages

The Inheritance

Poisoned Fruit of JFK's Assassination

By Christopher and Michelle Fulton, introduction by Dick Russell

How one man's custody of Bobby Kennedy's hidden evidence changed our past and continues to shape our future

Christopher Fulton's journey began with the death of Evelyn Lincoln, late secretary to President John F. Kennedy. Through Lincoln, crucial evidence ended up in Christopher's hands—evidence that was going to be used to facilitate a new future for America. But the U.S. government's position was clear: that evidence had to be confiscated and classified, and the truth hidden away from the public. Christopher was sent to federal prison for years under a sealed warrant and indictment.

The Inheritance, Christopher's personal narrative, shares insider information from his encounters with the Russian Government, President Ronald Reagan, Donald Trump, the Clinton White House, the U.S. Justice Department, the Secret Service, and the Kennedy family themselves. It reveals the true intentions of Evelyn Lincoln and her secret promise to Robert Kennedy—and Christopher's secret promise to John F. Kennedy Jr.

The Inheritance explodes with history-changing information and answers the questions Americans are still asking, while pulling them through a gauntlet of some of the worst prisons this country has to offer. This book thrillingly exposes the reality of American power, and sheds light on the dark corners of current corruption within the executive branch and the justice and prison systems.

At the height of his success in commercial construction in Canada, Christopher Fulton was extradited and sent to U.S. federal prison for his possession of physical evidence in JFK's assassination. He currently resides in California. Michelle Fulton was born in Vancouver, Canada. She earned her Bachelor of Music Degree from the University of British Columbia. She resides in California with her husband, their two children, and their rescue dogs.

Softcover • **$24.95** • ISBN 9781634242172 • 528 Pages

See No Evil

The JFK Assassination and the U.S. Media

By Jim DeBrosse

An examination of new theories and media engagement with JFK's assassination.

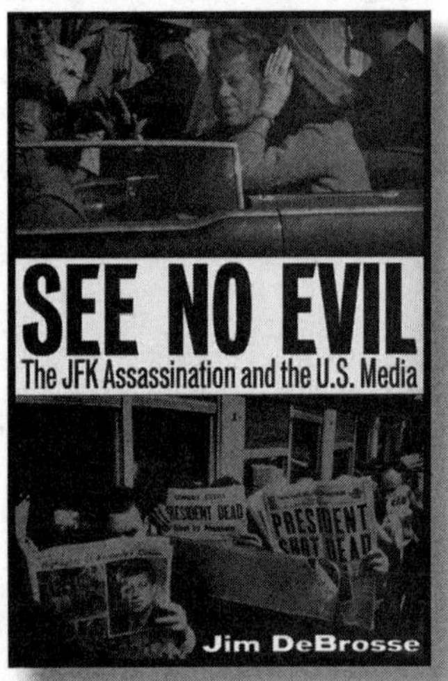

After more than fifty years of new evidence and new theories, the Warren Commission's claim that Lee Harvey Oswald acted alone and without clear motive in assassinating John F. Kennedy, has become a wheezing jalopy running on missing and broken parts and fueled with lies. And yet the U.S. media continue to support its findings as the only "factual" explanation for the murder of JFK.

Why does the media marginalize and even ridicule more plausible conspiracy theories when the majority of American people long ago wrote off the Warren Report as a cover-up? See No Evil analyzes the built-in biases of the U.S. corporate media, exposes its complicity in the whitewashing, and advocates for the broadest possible investigation into the key players who may have been responsible for the Crime of the Twentieth Century, including the CIA, Organized Crime, and Israel. This book is meant for readers who seek the truth no matter where it leads.

Jim DeBrosse, Ph.D, is an author and veteran journalist who has been named Ohio's Best Reporter (SPJ, 2001), Best Feature Writer (AP, 2004) and Best Columnist (SPJ, 2006; AP, 2007) and has won awards from the National Press Club, Education Writers Association and Military Reporters and Editors.

Softcover • **$19.95** • ISBN 9781634241625 • 192 Pages

Burying the Lead

THE MEDIA AND THE JFK ASSASSINATION

by Mal Hyman

An updated review of the case's facts and novel analysis of the way elite power works with the media during times of crisis

The Cold War ushered in a time of secrecy—and willing media cooperation to keep those secrets. But even after winning that war, the vault of secrets remains firmly locked, especially surrounding John F. Kennedy's murder. Even for those who fundamentally oppose the current presidential administration, notions of a national security state and "fake news" must be examined to maintain a functional democracy. This book explains the rapid decline in confidence in government that started after the assassination of JFK. The mainstream media failed to go beyond repeating the official story, and by 1991 they, along with academe and the government, had stopped investigating altogether.

It was filmmaker Oliver Stone whose film fueled public outrage and led to the JFK Act to declassify all of the remaining documents. Almost four million pages of documents were then released—that even Congress had not yet seen. The JFK Act stated that all files must be released by October 2017, yet thousands are still withheld on the grounds of national security. This volume examines the tight alliances that have allowed this cover-up for more than 50 years.

President Kennedy declared in October 1963 that "men who create power make an indispensable contribution to a nation's greatness, but the men who question power make a contribution just as indispensable, especially when they are disinterested, for they determine whether we use power or power uses us."

MAL JAY HYMAN has taught for 40 years in public schools, a medium security men's prison, and at Coker College as a professor of sociology. Mal has done human rights work in eight countries, monitored two foreign elections with the UN, and is a Democratic candidate for the US Congress SC 7th.

Softcover • **$24.95** • ISBN 9781634241878 • 571 Pages

At The Cold Shoulder of History

The Chilling Story of a 21-year old Navy Hospital Corpsman Who Stood at the Shoulder of JFK during the Bethesda Autopsy

by James Curtis Jenkins

with William Matson Law

At the Cold Shoulder of History gives an in-depth look at what happened in the aftermath of President John F. Kennedy's assassination. One of the only living participants in President Kennedy's autopsy now comes forward after almost 54 years of silence and speaks about what truly took place inside of the morgue at Bethesda Naval Hospital on the night of November 22, 1963. Jenkins gives a detailed account about the procedures performed on the President's remains. What he learned that night led him to believe there was a conspiracy in the murder of the 35th President of the United States and caused him to undertake his own personal journey into the labyrinth of the assassination.

JAMES CURTIS JENKINS was born in 1943. After enlisting in the United States Navy he won a place at the Medical Technology School that was part of Bethesda Naval Hospital, where John F. Kennedy's body was taken the day of his assassination. Along with fellow students, he was asked to assist in the autopsy of Kennedy

WILLIAM MATSON LAW has been researching the Kennedy assassination for over 25 years. Results of that research have appeared in more than 30 books, including Douglas Horne's magnum opus Inside the Assassination Records Review Board. Law is the author of In the Eye of History and is working on a book about the murder of Robert F. Kennedy with the working title: Shadows and Light. He lives with his family in Central Oregon.

Softcover • **$19.95** • ISBN 9781634242110 • 216 Pages

A Secret Order

Investigating the High Strangeness and Synchronicity in the JFK Assassination

by H. P. Albarelli, Jr.

Provocative new theories that uncover coincidences, connections, and unexplained details of the JFK assassination

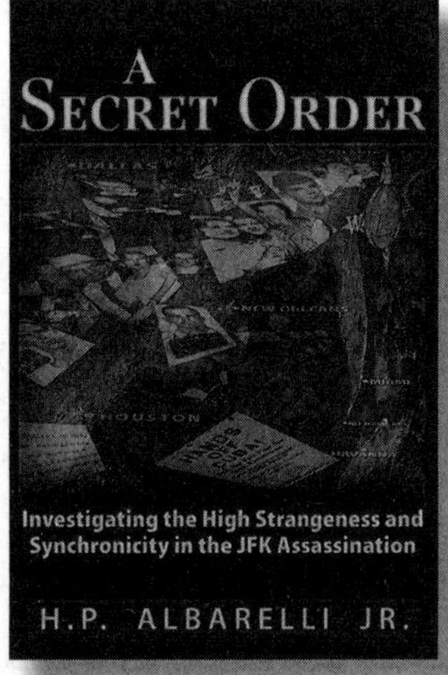

Reporting new and never-before-published information about the assassination of John F. Kennedy, this investigation dives straight into the deep end, and seeks to prove the CIA's involvement in one of the most controversial topics in American history. Featuring intelligence gathered from CIA agents who reported their involvement in the assassination, the case is broken wide open while covering unexplored ground. Gritty details about the assassination are interlaced throughout, while primary and secondary players to the murder are revealed in the in-depth analysis. Although a tremendous amount has been written in the nearly five decades since the assassination, there has never been, until now, a publication to explore the aspects of the case that seemed to defy explanation or logic.

H. P. Albarelli Jr. is an author and reporter whose previous works can be found in the Huffington Post, Pravda, and Counterpunch. His 10-year investigation into the death of biochemist Dr. Frank Olson was featured on A&E's Investigative Reports, and is the subject of his book, A Terrible Mistake. He lives in Indian Beach, Florida.

Softcover • **$24.95** • ISBN 9781936296552 • 469 Pages

Survivor's Guilt

The Secret Service and the Failure to Protect President Kennedy

by Vincent Michael Palamara

The actions and inactions of the Secret Service before, during, and after the Kennedy assassination

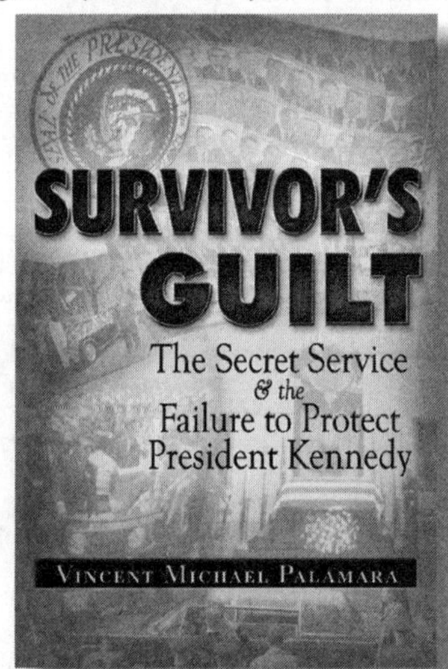

Painstakingly researched by an authority on the history of the Secret Service and based on primary, firsthand accounts from more than 80 former agents, White House aides, and family members, this is the definitive account of what went wrong with John F. Kennedy's security detail on the day he was assassinated.

The work provides a detailed look at how JFK could and should have been protected and debunks numerous fraudulent notions that persist about the day in question, including that JFK ordered agents off the rear of his limousine; demanded the removal of the bubble top that covered the vehicle; and was difficult to protect and somehow, directly or indirectly, made his own tragic death easier for an assassin or assassins. This book also thoroughly investigates the threats on the president's life before traveling to Texas; the presence of unauthorized Secret Service agents in Dealey Plaza, the site of the assassination; the failure of the Secret Service in monitoring and securing the surrounding buildings, overhangs, and rooftops; and the surprising conspiratorial beliefs of several former agents.

An important addition to the canon of works on JFK and his assassination, this study sheds light on the gross negligence and, in some cases, seeming culpability, of those sworn to protect the president.

Vincent Michael Palamara is an expert on the history of the Secret Service. He has appeared on the History Channel, C-SPAN, and numerous newspapers and journals, and his original research materials are stored in the National Archives. He lives in Pittsburgh, Pennsylvania.

Softcover • **$24.95** • ISBN 9781937584603 • 492 Pages

From an Office Building with a High-Powered Rifle

A report to the public from an FBI agent involved in the official JFK assassination investigation

by Don Adams

An insider's look at the mysteries behind the death of President Kennedy

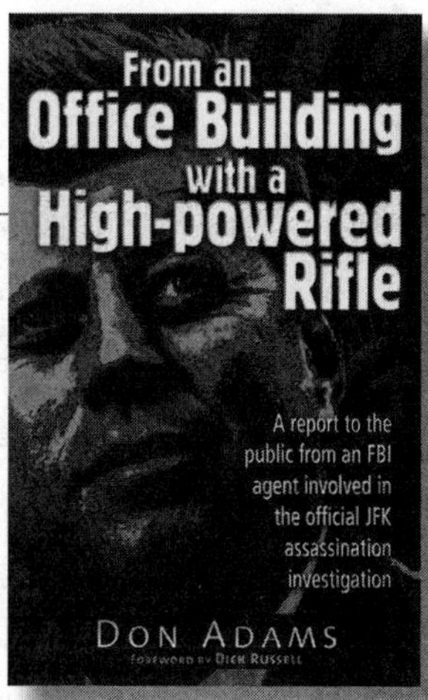

The personal and professional story of a former FBI agent, this is the journey Don Adams has taken over the past 50 years that has connected him to the assassination of the 35th president of the United States. On November 13, 1963, Adams was given a priority assignment to investigate Joseph Milteer, a man who had made threats to assassinate the president. Two weeks later John F. Kennedy was dead, and Agent Adams was instructed to locate and question Milteer. Adams, however, was only allowed to ask the suspect five specific questions before being told to release him. He was puzzled by the bizarre orders but thought nothing more of it until years later when he read a report that stated that not only had Joseph Milteer made threats against the president, but also that he claimed Kennedy would be killed from an office building with a high-powered rifle. Since that time, Adams has compiled evidence and research from every avenue available to him, including his experiences in Georgia and Dallas FBI offices, to produce this compelling investigation that may just raise more questions than answers.

Don Adams is a former FBI agent who participated in the investigation of the assassination of John F. Kennedy. He is the author of numerous articles on the subject and is considered a respected authority on the topic. He lives in Akron, Ohio.

Softcover • **$24.95** • ISBN 9781936296866 • 236 Pages

Betrayal

A JFK Honor Guard Speaks

by Hugh Clark

with William Matson Law

The amazing story that William Law has documented with his historical interviews helps us to understanding our true history. This compelling information shreds the official narrative.In 2015, Law and fellow researcher Phil Singer got together the medical corpsman, who had been present at Bethesda Naval Hospital for President Kennedy's autopsy with some of the official honor guard, who had delivered the president's coffin. What happened next was extraordinary. The medical corpsmen told the honor guards that they had actually received the president's body almost a half-hour before the honor guard got there. The honor guard couldn't believe this. They had met the president's plane at Andrews, taken possession of his casket and shadowed it all the way to Bethesda. The two sides almost broke into fisticuffs, accusing the other of untruths. Once it was sifted out, and both sides came to the understanding that each was telling their own truths of their experience that fateful day, the feelings of betrayal experienced by the honor guards was deep and profound.

Hugh Clark was a member of the honor guard that took President Kennedy's body to Arlington Cemetery for burial. He was an investigator for the United Nations. After Hugh left the service he became a New York City detective and held that position for 22 years.

William Matson Law has been researching the Kennedy assassination for over 25 years. Results of that research have appeared in more than 30 books, including Douglas Horne's magnum opus Inside the Assassination Records Review Board. Law is the author of In the Eye of History and is working on a book about the murder of Robert F. Kennedy with the working title: Shadows and Light. He lives with his family in Central Oregon.

Softcover • **$19.95** • ISBN 9781634240932 • 144 Pages

David Ferrie

Mafia Pilot, Participant in Anti-Castro Bioweapon Plot, Friend of Lee Harvey Oswald and Key to the JFK Assassination

by Judyth Vary Baker

One of the more eccentric characters linked to the JFK assassination

Of the all the people surrounding the assassination of President Kennedy, few are more mysterious and enigmatic than David William Ferrie of New Orleans. Author Judyth Vary Baker knew David Ferrie personally and worked with him in a covert project in New Orleans during the summer of 1963, and this book examines his strange and puzzling behavior both before and after the assassination. At the time of the assassination, Ferrie was a 45-year-old New Orleans resident who was acquainted with some of the most notorious names linked to the assassination: Lee Oswald, Clay Shaw, Guy Banister, Jack Ruby, and Carlos Marcello. He possessed assorted talents and eccentricities: he was at one time a senior pilot with Eastern Airlines until he was fired for homosexual activity on the job; he was also a hypnotist; a serious researcher of the origins of cancer; an amateur psychologist; and a victim of a strange disease, alopecia, which made all of his body void of hair. His odd lifestyle was embellished with an equally bizarre appearance featuring a red toupee and false eyebrows. This is the first book focused solely on David Ferrie and his alleged involvement in the conspiracy to assassinate President John F. Kennedy.

JUDYTH VARY BAKER is an artist, writer, and poet who first became known as a young prodigy in cancer research, then, later, for her assertion that while conducting cancer research in New Orleans in the summer of 1963, she had a love affair with Lee Harvey Oswald. She is the author of *Me & Lee: How I Came to Know, Love and Lose Lee Harvey Oswald*. She lives in Europe.

Softcover • **$24.95** • ISBN 9781937584542 • 528 Pages

LBJ and the Kennedy Killing

By Eyewitness

James T. Tague

This is unlike any other book about the assassination of President John F. Kennedy. The author, James Tague, was there and he was wounded by the debris from a missed shot on that fateful day. He stood up to our Government when the Warren Commission was about to ignore what really happened and spoke to the true facts. James Tague's testimony changed history and the "magic bullet" was born in an effort by the Warren Commission to wrongly explain all the wounds to President Kennedy and Governor Connally, and to try and convince the public that Lee Harvey Oswald was the "lone nut assassin." Tague, a long time Dallas area resident, initially believed the Warren Report, but time, diligent research and amazing revelations told to him by prominent Texans has given James Tague an inside look at what really happened. Be prepared to learn new facts, never before published, about one of our nation's darkest moments.

JAMES T. TAGUE spent 5 years in the Air Force, had a career in the automobile business rising to top management and is today recognized as a top researcher on the Kennedy assassination. It was an accident of timing that he was in Dealey Plaza that November day in 1963, receiving a minor injury.

Softcover • **$29.95** • ISBN 9781937584740 • 433 Pages

Kennedy & Oswald *–The Big Picture–*

by Judyth Vary Baker and Edward Schwartz

Unraveling the many strands of hidden history behind the assassination of President Kennedy is not an easy task. Co-authors Baker and Schwartz guide us toward the conclusion that ultimately, the motivation was total governmental control, a coup d'état, changing us from a democratic republic to a oligopoly – a corporatocracy. With help from new witnesses regarding the "Crime of the Century," we are led to the realization that the "War of Terror" and the Patriot Act were predesigned to undermine our US Constitution and our Bill of Rights. The very moment Kennedy died our own government turned against "We the People." Baker and Schwartz provide a compelling narrative showing Oswald's innocence and a condemnation of the conspirators who planned and carried out the assassination of our 35th president and our Republic.

Softcover • **$24.95** • ISBN 9781634240963 • 408 Pages

In the Eye of History

Disclosures in the JFK Assassination Medical Evidence

Second Edition

by William Matson Law

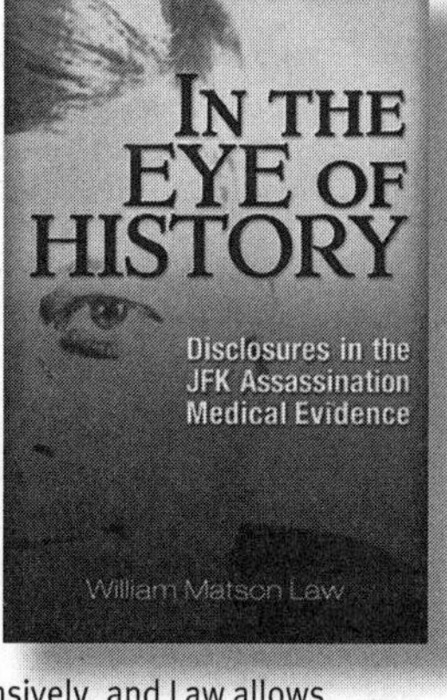

An oral history of the JFK autopsy

Anyone interested in the greatest mystery of the 20th century will benefit from the historic perspective of the attendees of President Kennedy's autopsy. For the first time in their own words these witnesses to history give firsthand accounts of what took place in the autopsy morgue at Bethesda, Maryland, on the night on November 22, 1963. Author William Matson Law set out on a personal quest to reach an understanding of the circumstances underpinning the assassination of John F. Kennedy. His investigation led him to the autopsy on the president's body at the National Naval Medical Center. In the Eye of History comprises conversations with eight individuals who agreed to talk: Dennis David, Paul O'Connor, James Jenkins, Jerrol Custer, Harold Rydberg, Saundra Spencer, and ex-FBI Special Agents James Sibert and Frances O'Neill. These eyewitnesses relate their stories comprehensively, and Law allows them to tell it as they remember it without attempting to fit any pro- or anticonspiracy agenda. The book also features a DVD featuring these firsthand interviews. Comes with DVD.

Softcover: **$29.95** (ISBN: 9781634240468) • 514 pages • Size: 6 x 9

JFK from Parkland to Bethesda

The Ultimate Kennedy Assassination Compendium

by Vincent Palamara

An all-in-one resource containing more than 15 years of research on the JFK assassination

A map through the jungle of statements, testimony, allegations, and theories relating to the assassination of John F. Kennedy, this compendium gives readers an all-in-one resource for facts from this intriguing slice of history. The book, which took more than 15 years to research and write, includes details on all of the most important aspects of the case, including old and new medical evidence from primary and secondary sources. JFK: From Parkland to Bethesda tackles the hard evidence of conspiracy and cover-up and presents a mass of sources and materials, making it an invaluable reference for anyone with interest in the President Kennedy and his assassination in 1963.

Softcover: **$19.95** (ISBN: 9781634240277) • 242 pages • Size: 6 x 9

The Polka Dot File on the Robert F. Kennedy Killing

Paris Peace Talks connection

by Fernando Faura

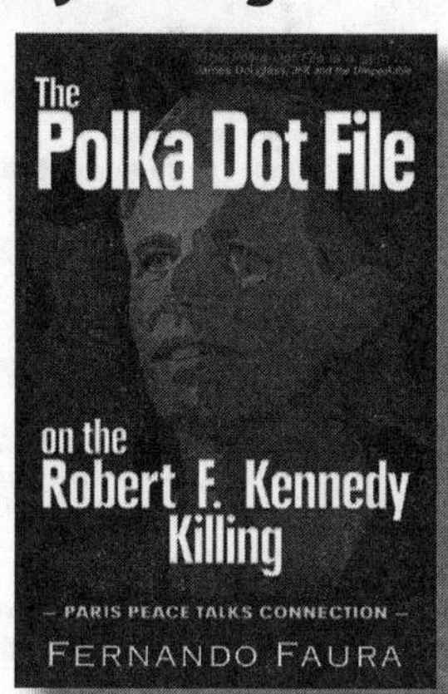

"The Polka Dot File is a gem in the field of RFK assassination research. Read it and learn."

—Jim Douglass, author, *JFK and the Unspeakable*

The Polka Dot File on the Robert F. Kennedy Killing describes the day-to-day chase for the mystery woman in the polka-dot dress. The book comments on but does not dwell on the police investigation, and reads like a detective thriller instead of an academic analysis of the investigation. It incorporates actual tapes made by an important witness, and introduces the testimony of witnesses not covered in other books and it is a new take on the assassination and the motives for it introduces a new theory for the reasons behind the assassination. Original and highly personal, it reaches a startling and different conclusion not exposed by other books.

Fernando Faura graduated cum laude with a degree in journalism from the California State University. In 1967 he joined *The Hollywood Citizens News*. Fernando has won awards from the Press Club, the National Newspaper Publishers Association, and was nominated for a Pulitzer Prize.

Softcover: **$24.95** (ISBN: 9781634240598) • 248 pages • Size: 6 x 9

Silent Coup

The Removal of a President

by Len Colodny & Robert Gettlin

25th Anniversay Edition – Includes Updates

Foreword by Roger Morris

This is the true story of betrayal at the nation's highest level. Unfolding with the suspenseful pace of a le Carre spy thriller, it reveals the personal motives and secret political goals that combined to cause the Watergate break-in and destroy Richard Nixon. Investigator Len Colodny and journalist Robert Gettlin relentlessly pursued the people who brought down the president. Their revelations shocked the world and forever changed our understanding of politics, of journalism, and of Washington behind closed doors. Dismantling decades of lies, *Silent Coup* tells the truth.

Len Colodny is a journalist. In 1992 he co-wrote with Robert Gettlin: *Silent Coup: The Removal Of Richard Nixon*. In the book the authors claim that John Dean ordered the Watergate break-in because he knew that a call-girl ring was operating out of the Democratic headquarters. The authors also argued that Alexander Haig was not Deep Throat but was a key source for Bob Woodward, who had briefed Haig at theWhite House in 1969 and 1970.

Softcover • **$24.95** • ISBN 9781634240536 • 520 Pages

Bond of Secrecy

My Life with CIA Spy and Watergate Conspirator E. Howard Hunt

by St. John Hunt

Foreword by Jesse Ventura

A father's last confession to his son about the CIA, Watergate, and the plot to assassinate President John F. Kennedy, this is the remarkable true story of St. John Hunt and his father E. Howard Hunt, the infamous Watergate burglar and CIA spymaster. In Howard Hunt's near-death confession to his son St. John, he revealed that key figures in the CIA were responsible for the plot to assassinate JFK in Dallas, and that Hunt himself was approached by the plotters, among whom included the CIA's David Atlee Phillips, Cord Meyer, Jr., and William Harvey, as well as future Watergate burglar Frank Sturgis. An incredible true story told from an inside, authoritative source, this is also a personal account of a uniquely dysfunctional American family caught up in two of the biggest political scandals of the 20th century.

Softcover • **$24.95** • ISBN 978-1936296835 • 192 Pages

Dorothy

The Murder of E. Howard Hunt's Wife – watergate's Darkest Secret

by St. John Hunt

Foreword by Roger Stone

Dorothy Hunt, "An Amoral and Dangerous Woman" tells the life story of ex-CIA agent Dorothy Hunt, who married Watergate mastermind and confessed contributor to the assassination of JFK. The book chronicles her rise in the intelligence field after World War II, as well as her experiences in Shanghai, Calcutta, Mexico, and Washington, DC. It reveals her war with President Nixon and asserts that she was killed by the CIA in the crash of Flight 553. Written by the only person who was privy to the behind-the-scenes details of the Hunt family during Watergate, this book sheds light on a dark secret of the scandal.

Softcover • **$24.95** • ISBN 978-1634240376 • 192 Pages

Saint John Hunt is an author, a musician, and the son of the infamous and legendary CIA covert operative and author, E. Howard Hunt. Saint John spent more than ten years searching for the truth about his father's involvement in JFK's death, resulting in his first book Bond of Secrecy. In his second book, Dorothy, he explored his mother's life as a CIA spy and her war with Nixon, which resulted in her murder. He lives in south Florida.